Collins

INTERNATIONAL PRIMARY MATHS

Workbook 5

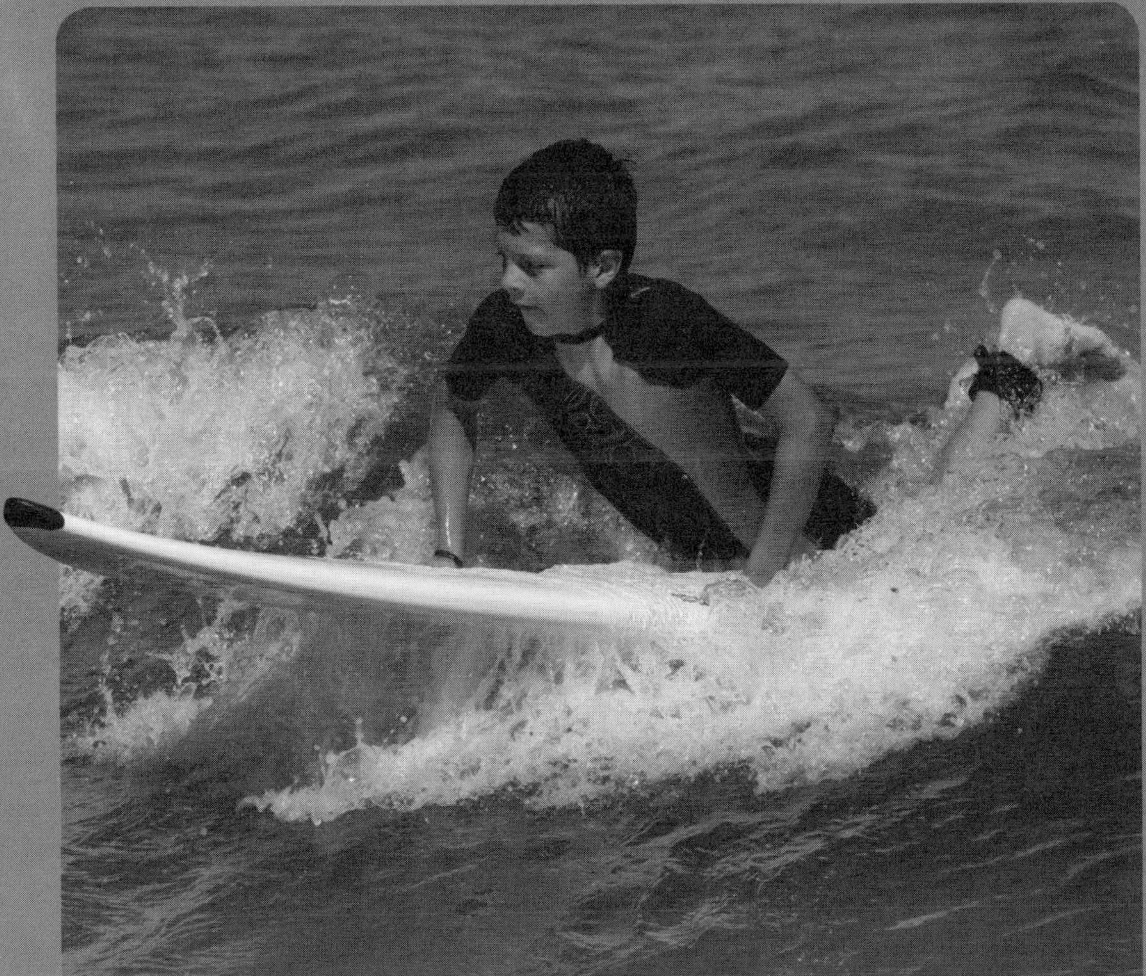

William Collins' dream of knowledge for all began with the publication of his first book in 1819. A self-educated mill worker, he not only enriched millions of lives, but also founded a flourishing publishing house. Today, staying true to this spirit, Collins books are packed with inspiration, innovation and practical expertise. They place you at the centre of a world of possibility and give you exactly what you need to explore it.

Collins. Freedom to teach.

An imprint of HarperCollins*Publishers*
The News Building
1 London Bridge Street
London
SE1 9GF

Browse the complete Collins catalogue at www.collins.co.uk

10 9 8 7 6 5 4 3 2 1

ISBN 978-0-00-816000-5

Paul Hodge asserts his moral rights to be identified as the author of this work.

British Library Cataloguing in Publication Data
A catalogue record for this publication is available from the British Library.

Publishing manager Fiona McGlade
Series editor Peter Clarke
Managing editor Caroline Green
Editor Kate Ellis
Project managed by Emily Hooton
Edited by Tanya Solomons
Proofread by Tracy Thomas
Cover design by Amparo Barrera
Cover artwork by sylv1rob1/Shutterstock
Internal design by Ken Vail Graphic Design
Typesetting by Ken Vail Graphic Design
Illustrations by Ken Vail Graphic Design, Advocate Art and Beehive Illustration
Production by Lauren Crisp

Printed and bound by Grafi ca Veneta S. P. A.

Contents

Lesson 1: Counting on and back (1)

• Count on and back in steps of equal size

Challenge 1 Count on or back in the steps given.

a Count on in steps of 2.

18, ___, ___, ___, 26, ___, ___, 32, ___, ___

b Count back in steps of 5.

125, ___, ___, ___, 105, ___, ___, 90, ___, ___

c Count on in steps of 3.

31, ___, ___, ___, 43, ___, ___, 52, ___, ___

d Count back in steps of 10.

290, ___, ___, ___, 250, ___, ___, 220, ___, ___

Challenge 2 Count on or back in the steps given.

a Count on in steps of 9.

46, ___, ___, ___, 82, ___, ___, 109, ___, ___

b Count back in steps of 7.

83, ___, ___, ___, 55, ___, ___, 34, ___, ___

c Count on in steps of 8.

13, ___, ___, ___, 45, ___, ___, 69, ___, ___

d Count back in steps of 4.

61, ___, ___, ___, 45, ___, ___, 33, ___, ___

e Count back in steps of 10.

210, ___, ___, ___, 170, ___, ___, 140, ___, ___

Challenge 3

Circle the number on the card if it is part of the sequence given.
Use the number line to help you.

a 17 Start at 56, count back in steps of 5.

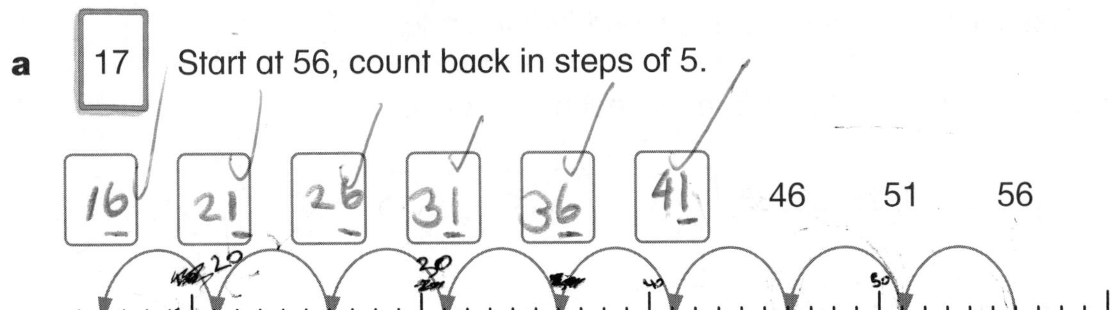

b 55 Start at 17, count forward in steps of 8.

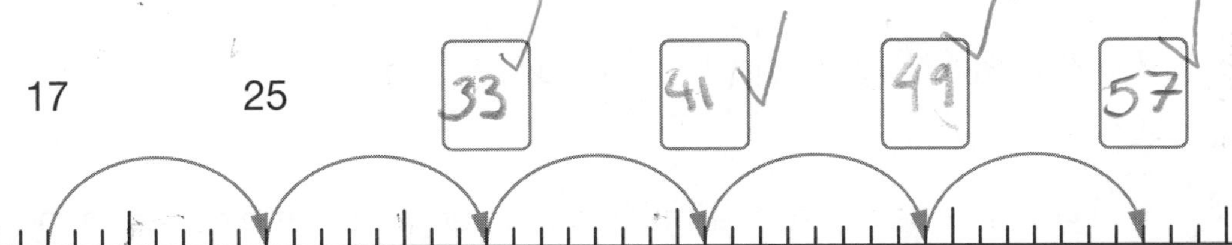

c 29 Start at 73, count back in steps of 11.

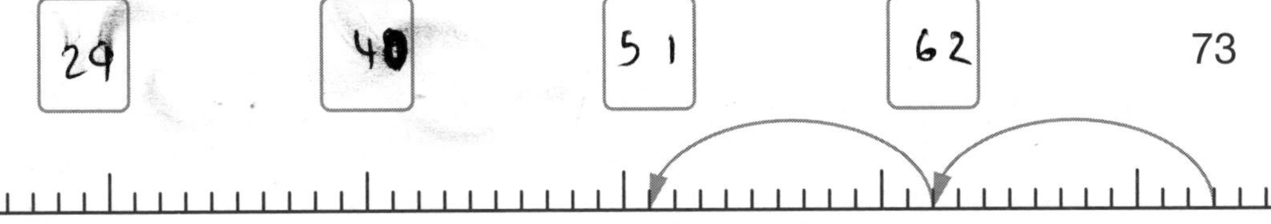

d 75 Start at 21, count forward in steps of 9.

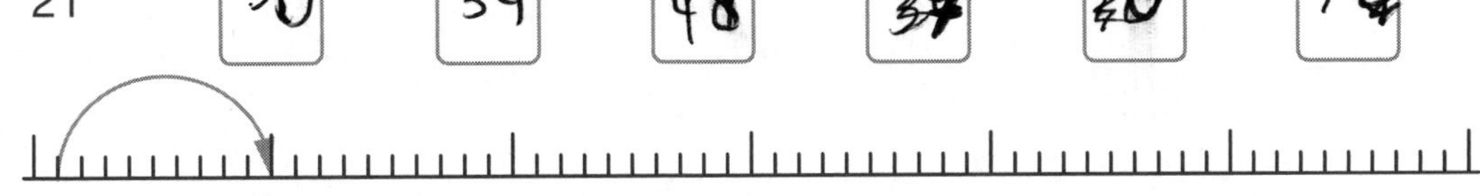

Number

Lesson 2: Number sequences

- Describe number sequences and find the rule

Write the next three terms in each sequence.

a 15, 20, 25, 30, 35, [40], [45], [50]

b 2, 5, 8, 11, 14, [17], [20], [23]

c 90, 80, 70, 60, 50, [40], [30], [20]

d 21, 19, 17, 15, 13, [11], [9], [7]

1 Write the next three terms in each sequence and describe the rule.

a 87, 79, 71, 63, 55, [47], [39], [31]

Rule: −8

b −29, −23, −17, −11, −5, [1], [7], [13]

Rule: +6

2 Fill in the missing terms in these sequences.

a					–35	–42	–49	–56
b				32	37	42	47	

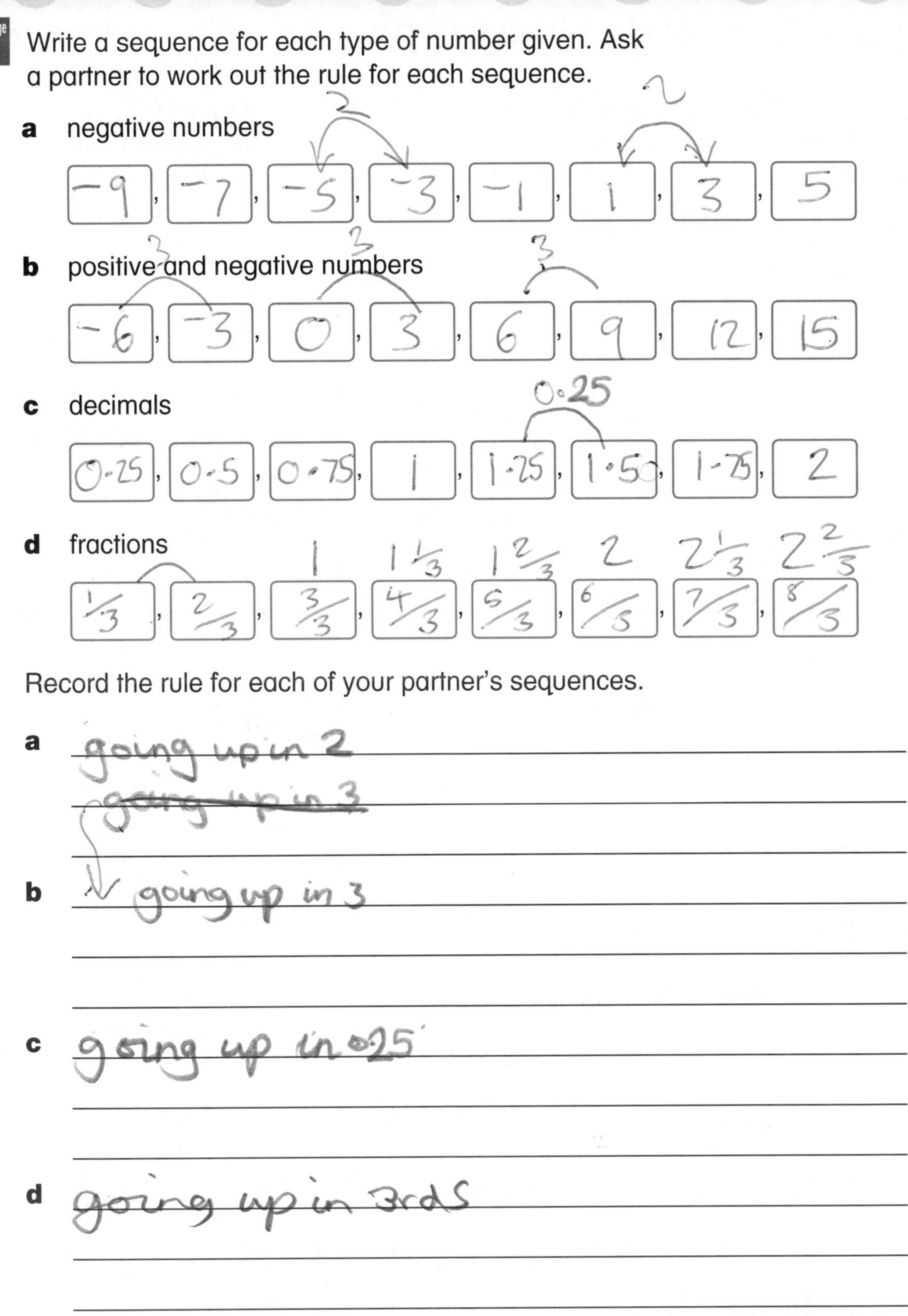

Challenge 3

Write a sequence for each type of number given. Ask a partner to work out the rule for each sequence.

a negative numbers

−9, −7, −5, −3, −1, 1, 3, 5

b positive and negative numbers

−6, −3, 0, 3, 6, 9, 12, 15

c decimals

0·25, 0·5, 0·75, 1, 1·25, 1·50, 1·75, 2

d fractions

$\frac{1}{3}$, $\frac{2}{3}$, $\frac{3}{3}$, $\frac{4}{3}$, $\frac{5}{3}$, $\frac{6}{3}$, $\frac{7}{3}$, $\frac{8}{3}$

Record the rule for each of your partner's sequences.

a going up in 2

~~going up in 3~~

b going up in 3

c going up in 0·25

d going up in 3rds

Number

Lesson 3: **Place value (1)**

- Know what each digit represents in a five- or six-digit number

You will need
- coloured pencils

Write the correct label in the box above each number. One has been done for you.

		thousands			
6	3	1	7	0	9

tens

hundred thousands

~~thousands~~

hundreds

units

ten thousands

Colour the digit in the hundreds place blue.

Colour the digit in the units place green.

Colour the digit in the ten thousands place yellow.

Colour the digit in the thousands place pink.

Colour the digit in the tens position red.

Colour the digit in the hundred thousands position grey.

1 Write the place value of each of the underlined digits.
The first one has been done for you.

a 23864 (underlined: 3) — 3000

b 40389 (underlined: 8)

c 98214 (underlined: 8)

d 77508 (underlined: 0)

e 417937 (underlined: 4)

f 118496 (underlined: 8)

2 Use each set of digits to make the largest and smallest number possible.

Digits	Largest number	Smallest number
4 7 2 1 8		
6 0 3 9 2		
7 1 0 5 8 3		
6 2 4 6 8 0		
3 2 8 8 3 9		

Write a number in each box to make the statements true.

a 45561 > ☐ > 44952 > ☐ > 44948

b 68327 < ☐ < 68423 < ☐ < 68425

c 30409 > ☐ > 30407 > ☐ < 29999

d 777777 > ☐ > 767777 > ☐ > 766777

e 303303 < ☐ < 302333 < ☐ < 333302

Lesson 4: **Place value (2)**

- Use place value to partition any number up to one million

Challenge 1

Fill in the missing numbers.

a 37 431 = 30 000 + ☐ + 400 + 30 + 1

b 58 089 = ☐ + 8000 + 80 + ☐

c 666 345 = 600 000 + ☐ + 6000 + ☐ + 40 + 5

d 409 999 = ☐ + 9000 + 900 + ☐ + 9

Challenge 2

1 Write each number in words. The first one has been done for you.

a 34 209 = Thirty-four thousand, two hundred and nine.

b 70 933 = ____________________

c 60 717 = ____________________

d 44 444 = ____________________

e 829 645 = ____________________

f 505 202 = ____________________

g 711 010 = ____________________

h 333 033 = ____________________

2 Each of these numbers has been split into its separate place values. Write the number in numerals and in words.

a 40 000 7000 200 30 5

______

b 80 000 3000 40 1

______

c 900 000 20 000 1000 600 20 3

______

d 500 000 4000 500 90 8

______

e 100 000 70 000 800 6

______

f 600 000 100 60 7

______

Challenge 3 Write the place value of the bold digit.

a 145**6**3 The 6 is worth 60 (6 tens)

b 2**8**957 ______

c **3**03 482 ______

d 478 **2**65 ______

e 7**1**1 232 ______

Number

Lesson 5: **Multiplying and dividing by 10 or 100**

- Multiply and divide whole numbers by 10 or 100

Challenge 1

Use the place value grid to multiply or divide by 10.

	TTh	Th	H	T	U
a 326 × 10 = 3260	3	2	6	0	
b 6270 × 10 = 62700					
c 2340 ÷ 10 = 234					
d 9080 ÷ 10 = 908					

Challenge 2

1 Use the place value grid to multiply or divide by 100.

	TTh	Th	H	T	U
a 4973 × 100 = 497300					
b 2829 × 100 = 282900					
c 8090 × 100 = 809000					
d 7900 ÷ 100 = 79					
e 3800 ÷ 100 = 38					
f 9900 ÷ 100 = 99					

2 Put each number through the multiplication and division function machine. What number comes out the other side?

Challenge 3 Work out the ticket prices.

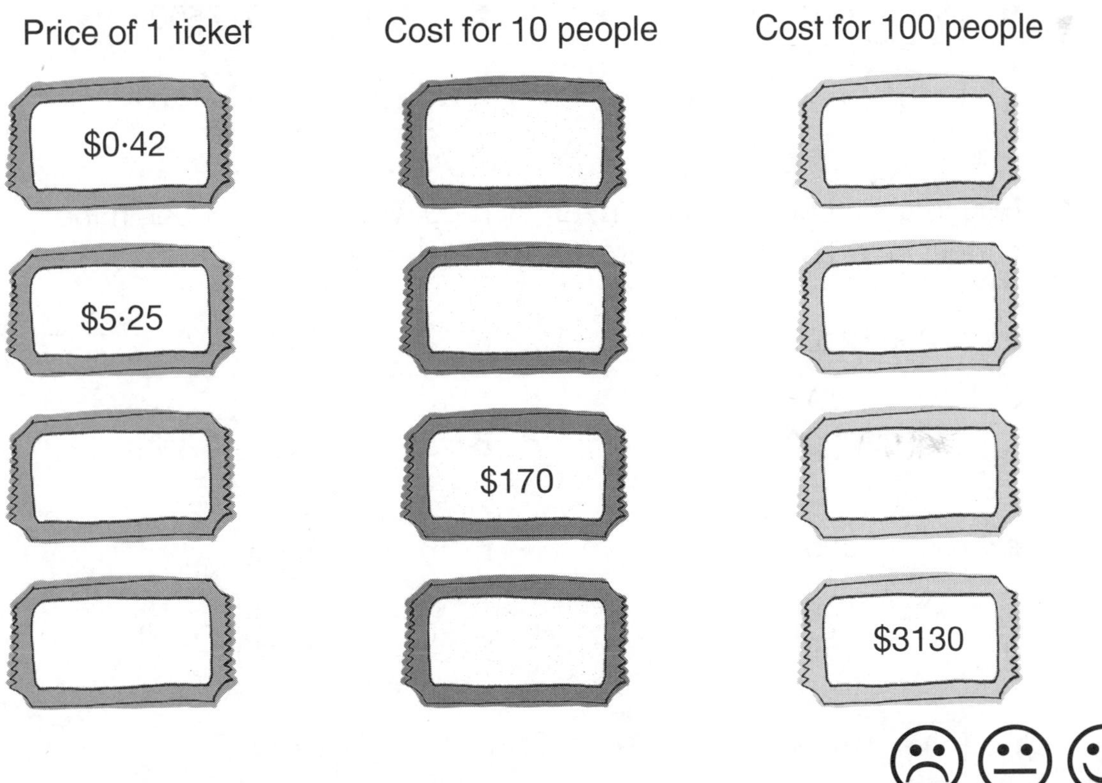

Number

Lesson 6: Rounding

- Round 4-digit numbers to the nearest 10, 100 or 1000

Challenge 1

Circle the multiple of 10 that the number rounds to.
The first one has been done for you.

a 3240 3249 3250 **b** 4550 4555 4560

c 1230 1234 1240 **d** 7810 7811 7820

e 6330 6336 6340 **f** 9980 9982 9990

Challenge 2

1 Circle the multiple of 100 that the number rounds to.
The first one has been done for you.

a 6200 6241 6300 **b** 1400 1487 1500

c 3000 3011 3100 **d** 2600 2650 2700

e 8000 8001 8100 **f** 7700 7755 7800

g 4100 4199 4200 **h** 5000 5030 5100

2 Round each number to the nearest 1000. Write the number in the correct box. The first one has been done for you.

a 2000 2107 ☐ **b** ☐ 4449 ☐

c ☐ 7200 ☐ **d** ☐ 9499 ☐

e ☐ 6051 ☐ **f** ☐ 5500 ☐

g ☐ 3699 ☐ **h** ☐ 8701 ☐

i ☐ 9551 ☐ **j** ☐ 6737 ☐

Challenge 3 Help these learners to find the secret numbers.

My number is the smallest possible number that can be rounded to the nearest 10 to become 650.

Maya

My number is the smallest possible number that can be rounded to the nearest 1000 to become 5000.

Sarah

Kyle

My number is the largest possible number that can be rounded to the nearest 100 to become 7900.

Puneet

If I round my number to the nearest 1000 it is 4000 and to the nearest 100 it is 4500. If you add 1 to the number and round it to the nearest 1000 it would be 5000.

Number

Lesson 7: **Comparing and ordering**

- Use the > and < signs to order and compare numbers up to a million

You will need
- dice, or 1–6 spinner

Compare the distances of pairs of flights.
Use > or < to show which is the greater distance.

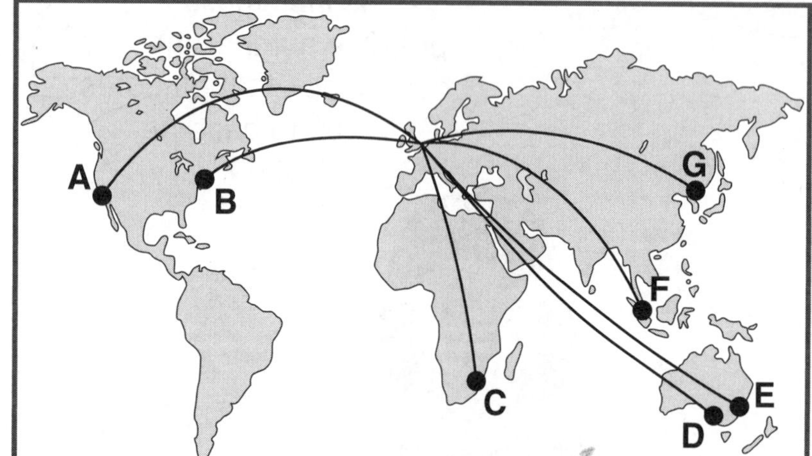

Route	Distance (km)
A	876
B	505
C	3420
D	874
E	7012
F	550
G	7019
H	3430

a Route A [>] Route D **b** Route F [>] Route B

c Route H [>] Route C **d** Route E [>] Route G

1 Each rocket has travelled a different distance (km). Write the distances of the rockets in order from smallest to greatest distance.

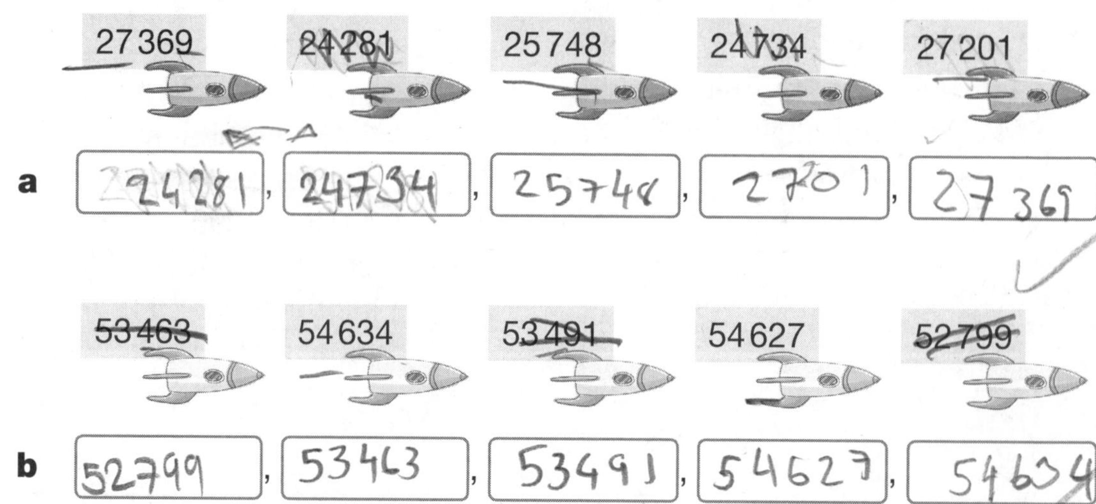

a 24281, 24734, 25748, 27201, 27369

b 52799, 53463, 53491, 54627, 54634

2 Order each set of numbers, from smallest to largest.

a 673 656, 323 567, 428 913, 789 452, 428 139

____

b 117 566, 107 656, 117 656, 102 522, 102 255

____

c 123 990, 124 099, 125 909, 124 909, 123 909

____

d 827 697, 872 770, 827 679, 872 707, 827 696

____

e 308 505, 305 080, 305 008, 308 550, 305 800

____

Challenge **3** Roll a dice to create eight 6-digit numbers. Write the numbers below.

Order the numbers from smallest to largest. Using a place value grid may help you compare the digits.

HTh	TTh	Th	H	T	U

Lesson 8: **Odds, evens and multiples (1)**

- Recognise odd and even numbers and multiples of 5, 10, 25, 50 and 100

You will need
- coloured pencils

Challenge 1

Circle the odd numbers blue. Circle the even numbers green. Circle multiples of 5 in red, circle multiples of 10 orange.

23 99

340

48

337

862

450 990

Challenge 2

1 Colour the circle blue if the answer is odd. Colour the circle green if the answer is even and red if it is a multiple of 5, 10 or 100.

243 + 349

552 + 638

957 – 478

782 – 356

779 + 436

836 – 463

2 Colour the circle blue if the answer is odd. Colour the circle green if the answer is even and red if it is a multiple of 5, 10 or 100.

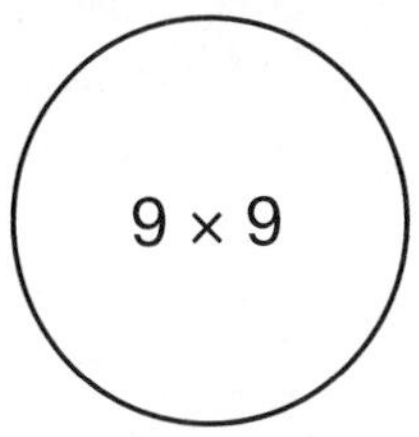

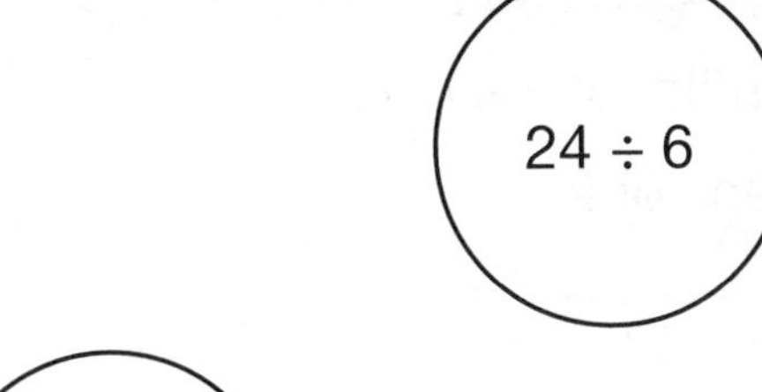

5 × 14

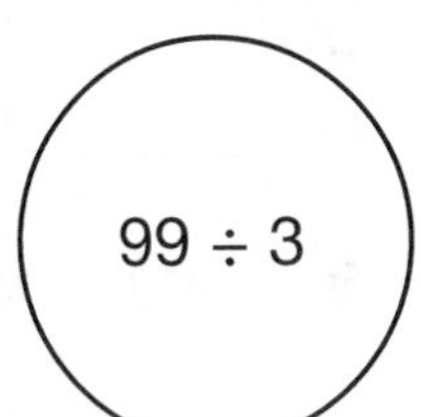

4 × 12

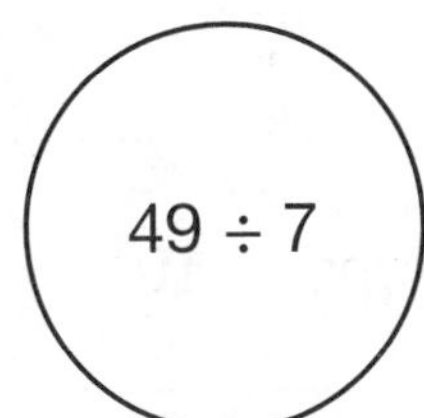

Challenge 3

How many three-digit numbers only have odd digits?
Use the boxes to make an ordered list, then find the answer.

Number

Lesson 1: **Whole numbers**

- Describe and continue number sequences, including negative numbers

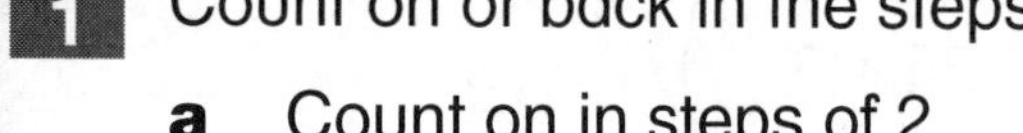

Challenge 1 Count on or back in the steps given.

a Count on in steps of 2.

–6, ____, ____, ____, 2, ____, ____, 8, ____

b Count back in steps of 5.

10, ____, ____, ____, –10, ____, ____, –25, ____

c Count on in steps of 10.

–60, ____, ____, ____, – 20, ____, ____, 10, ____

d Count back in steps of 10

20, ____, ____, ____, –20, ____, ____, –50, ____

Challenge 2 Count on or back in the steps given.

a Count back in steps of 6.

12, ____, ____, ____, –12, ____, ____, –30, ____

b Count on in steps of 0·1.

–0·9, ____, ____, ____, –0·5, ____, ____, –0·2, ____

c Count on in steps of 8.

–20, ____, ____, ____, 12, ____, ____, 36, ____

d Count back in steps of 7.

15, ____, ____, ____, –13, ____, ____, –34, ____

e Count on in steps of 3.

–14, ____, ____, ____, –2, ____, ____, 7, ____

f Count back in steps of 9.

12, ____, ____, ____, –24, ____, ____, –51, ____

Challenge 3 Fill in the missing numbers in each sequence.

a ____, –27, –33, –39, –45, ____, ____, ____

b ____, ____, 25, 17, 9, 1, ____, ____

c ____, ____, ____, –5, –2, 1, 4, ____

d ____, ____, ____, ____, 8, 13, 18, 23

Number

Lesson 2: **Positive and negative numbers**

- Order and compare negative and positive numbers on a number line and temperature scale

Draw lines to order the temperatures.
The first one has been done for you.

Temperatures around the world on Monday

Reykjavik –3°C

Cairo 18°C

London 7°C

Moscow –9°C

New York 4°C

Wellington 19°C

Cape Town 16°C

Oslo –4°C

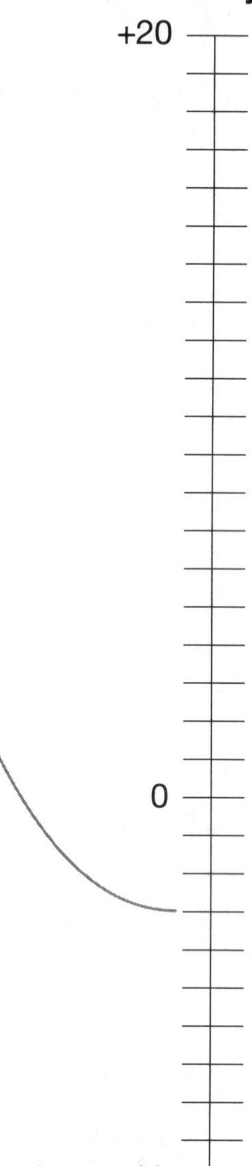

Which city was coldest? ____________________

Which city was warmest? ____________________

Student's Book page 10

Use the number line to put these numbers in order, from smallest to largest.

a 7, –3, –11, 8 ____________________

b –14, –17, 8, 1 ____________________

c 15, –10, 12, –4 ____________________

d 0, –19, –5, 13 ____________________

In golf, the player with the lowest score wins. Write the golfers' names on the scoreboard in the correct order.

Tiger Woods 1

Jason Day –1

Rory McIlroy 4

Bubba Watson 0

Louis Oosthuizen –3

Branden Grace –2

Sergio Garcia 2

Emiliano Grillo 7

Position	Name	Score

Number

Lesson 3: **Calculating temperature change**

- Work out differences between temperature readings on a thermometer

Challenge 1

Use the number line to work out the change in temperature. The first one has been done for you.

	morning	afternoon	temperature change
Day 1	5 °C	16 °C	rise of 11 degrees
Day 2	7 °C	21 °C	
Day 3	11 °C	2 °C	
Day 4	–1 °C	13 °C	
Day 5	3 °C	–4 °C	
Day 6	–3 °C	12 °C	
Day 7	–4 °C	11 °C	

20 19 18 17 16 15 14 13 12 10 9 8 7 6 5 4 3 2 1 0 –1 –2 –3 –4 –5 –6 –7 –8 –9 –10 –11 –12 –13 –14 –15 –16 –17 –18 –19 –20

Challenge 2

1 What is the difference between the temperature readings in each pair?

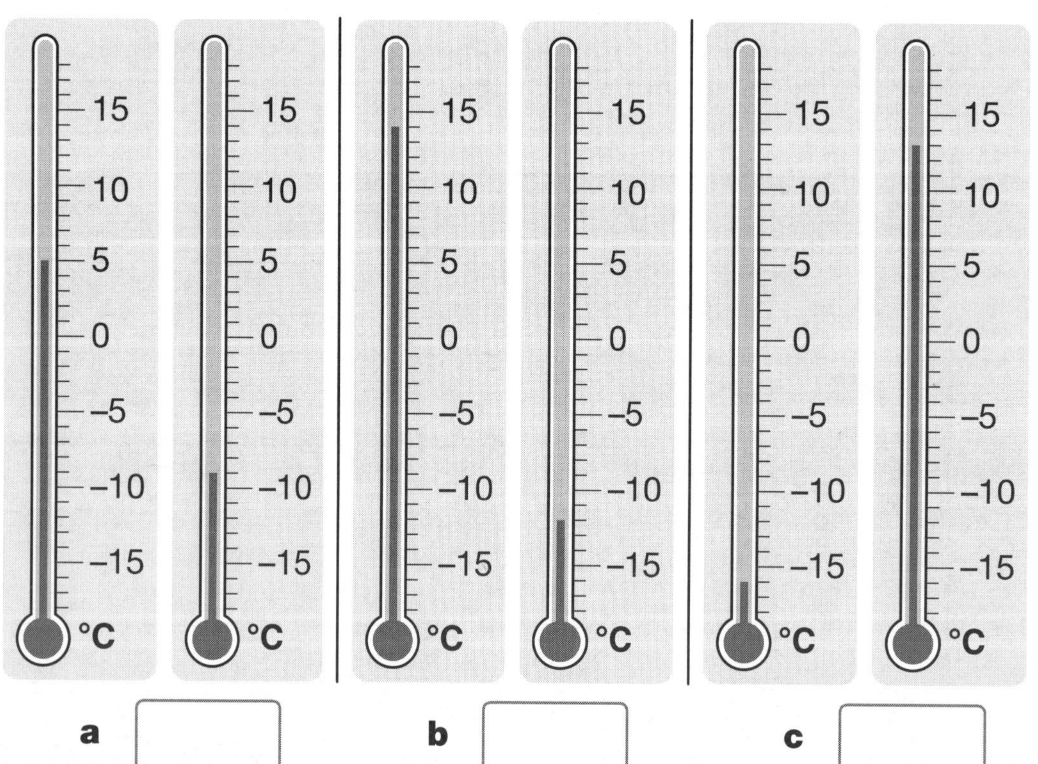

2 Complete this table.

	Day 1	Day 2	Day 3	Day 4	Day 5	Day 6	Day 7
morning	−5 °C	4 °C	−3 °C	−5 °C	2 °C	−5 °C	−3 °C
afternoon	7 °C	−5 °C	14 °C	15 °C	−7 °C	19 °C	−6 °C
temperature change							
	By how many degrees would the afternoon temperature need to rise to reach 30 °C?						

Challenge 3 Look at the graph and answer these questions.

a How many degrees did the temperature rise between midnight and 10:00 a.m.? ☐°

b What was the temperature change between 6:00 p.m. and 10:00 p.m.? ☐°

c How much would the temperature at 4:00 a.m. need to rise to be 22 °C? ☐°

d How much would the temperature at 8:00 p.m. need to fall to be −5 °C? ☐°

City temperature over 24 hours

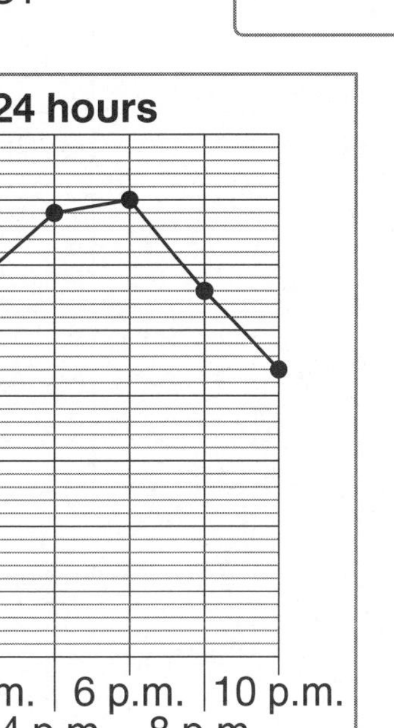
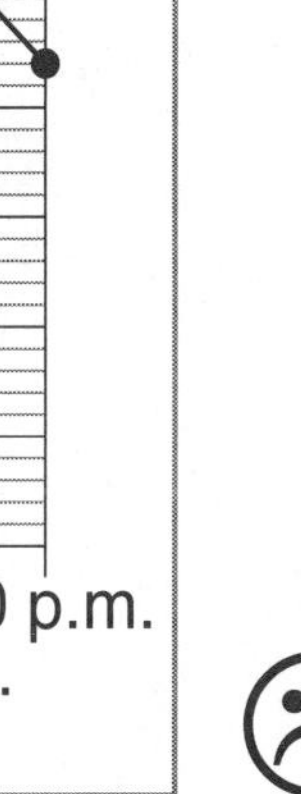

Number

Lesson 4: **Odds, evens and multiples (2)**

- Make general statements about sums, differences and multiples of odd and even numbers

You will need
- 15 cubes or counters

Write your predictions for each addition, subtraction or multiplication. Say whether each combination will result in an odd or even number.

Addition	Subtraction	Multiplication
even + even =	even – even =	even × even =
even + odd =	even – odd =	even × odd =
odd + even =	odd – even =	odd × even =
odd + odd =	odd – odd =	odd × odd =

1 Test the predictions you made in Challenge 1 by writing three examples of each combination.

a

Addition	Subtraction	Multiplication
even + even	even – even	even × even
even + odd	even – odd	even × odd
odd + even	odd – even	odd × even
odd + odd	odd – odd	odd × odd

b Were all of your predictions correct? ________________

c Do you think that odd and even numbers will always behave in this way? Explain your answer.

Challenge 3

Play a game with a partner. You will need 15 cubes or counters.

Rules:

- Take turns to take 1, 2 or 3 cubes at a time.
- Continue until no cubes remain.
- The winner is the player who finishes up with an odd number of cubes.
- Repeat several times.

Can you think of a strategy to win the game? Explain. ________________

Lesson 1: **Tenths**

- Write tenths in decimals and understand what each digit represents
- Count up and down in tenths

Challenge 1

The rectangles have been divided into 10 equal parts.
Write the fraction and decimal shown by the shaded part.

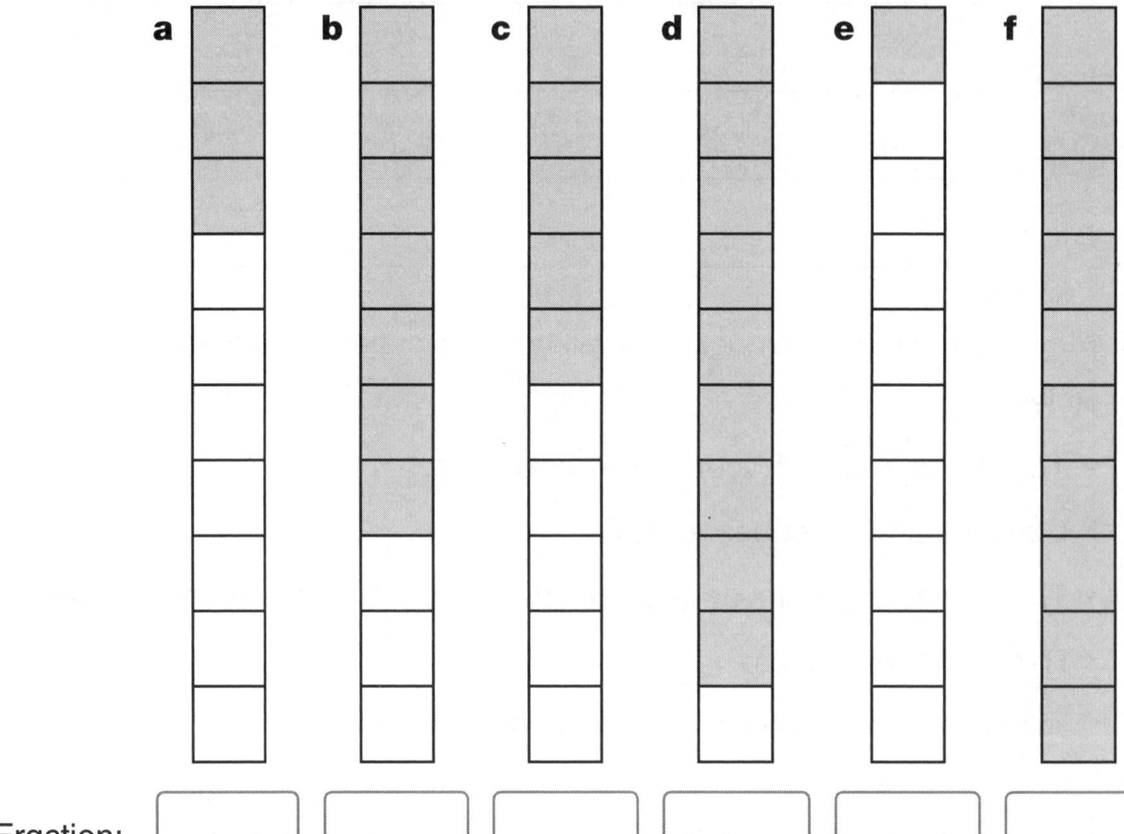

Fraction:

Decimal:

Challenge 2

1 Write the correct decimal on the number line.

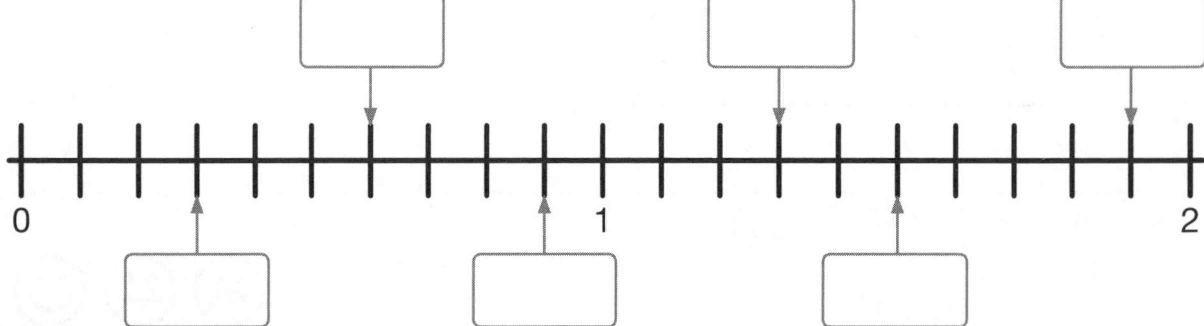

2 Write the decimal that is equivalent to each fraction.

a $\frac{3}{10}$ = ☐　　**b** $\frac{9}{10}$ = ☐

c $\frac{1}{10}$ = ☐　　**d** $\frac{6}{10}$ = ☐

e $\frac{4}{10}$ = ☐　　**f** $\frac{8}{10}$ = ☐

g $\frac{10}{10}$ = ☐　　**h** $\frac{7}{10}$ = ☐

3 Write the next two terms in each sequence.

a 0·1, 0·2, 0·3, ☐, ☐　　**b** 0·6, 0·7, 0·8, ☐, ☐

c 0·8, 0·7, 0·6, ☐, ☐　　**d** 0·5, 0·4, 0·3, ☐, ☐

e 1·2, 1·3, 1·4, ☐, ☐　　**f** 1·6, 1·7, 1·8, ☐, ☐

Challenge 3

Write each fraction as a decimal. In the second box write the tenth that comes after this number. The first one has been completed for you.

a $1\frac{7}{10}$ 1·7 (1·8)　　**b** $2\frac{2}{10}$ ☐ (☐)

c $4\frac{3}{10}$ ☐ (☐)　　**d** $3\frac{5}{10}$ ☐ (☐)

e $7\frac{6}{10}$ ☐ (☐)　　**f** $18\frac{8}{10}$ ☐ (☐)

g $10\frac{4}{10}$ ☐ (☐)　　**h** $20\frac{2}{10}$ ☐ (☐)

i $17\frac{2}{10}$ ☐ (☐)　　**j** $13\frac{4}{10}$ 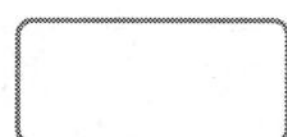 ()

Lesson 2: **Hundredths**

- Recognise that hundredths arise when dividing an object by 100
- Recognise and write decimal equivalents of any number of hundredths

Challenge 1

The squares have been divided into 100 equal parts. Write the fraction and decimal shown by the shaded part.

a

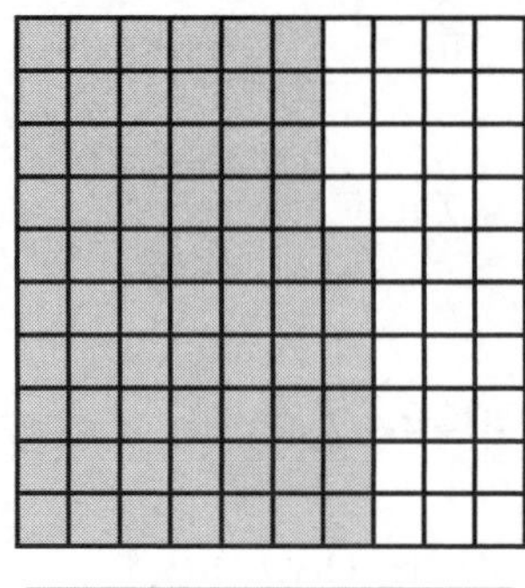

b

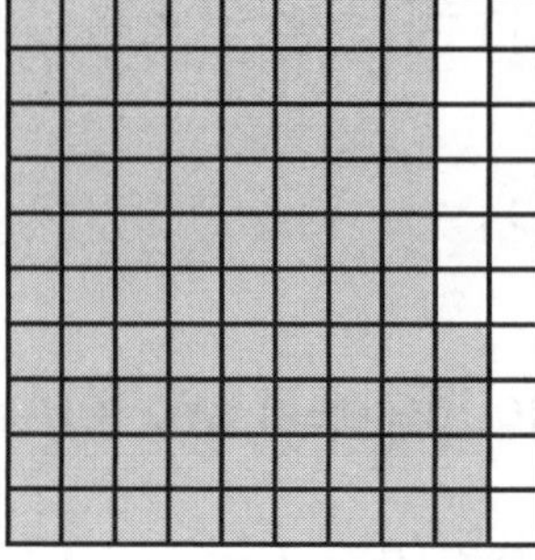

Fraction:

Decimal:

c

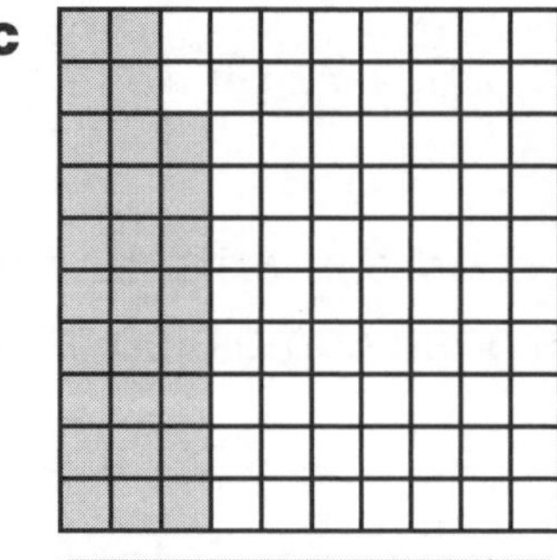

d

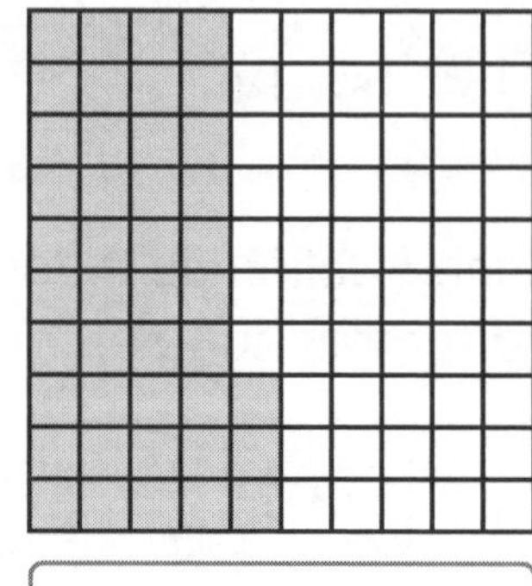

Fraction:

Decimal:

Challenge 2

1 Write the number the arrow points to in the box.

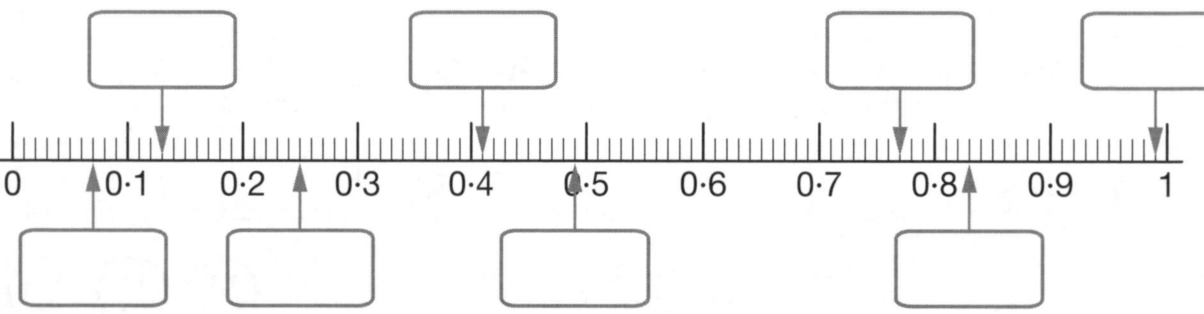

2 Write the decimal that is equivalent to each fraction.

a	$\frac{33}{100}$ = ☐	**b**	$\frac{47}{100}$ = ☐
c	$\frac{79}{100}$ = ☐	**d**	$\frac{11}{100}$ = ☐
e	$\frac{70}{100}$ = ☐	**f**	$\frac{1}{100}$ = ☐
g	$\frac{61}{100}$ = ☐	**h**	$\frac{50}{100}$ = ☐

3 Write the next two terms in each sequence.

a 0·23, 0·24, 0·25, ☐, ☐

b 0·66, 0·67, 0·68, ☐, ☐

c 0·87, 0·88, 0·89, ☐, ☐

d 0·43, 0·42, 0·41, ☐, ☐

e 1·97, 1·98, 1·99, ☐, ☐

f 0·05, 0·04, 0·03, ☐, ☐

Choose the decimal to make each statement true.
Write the letter in the box and reveal a secret phrase.

0·19 > ? > 0·13	0·46 < ? < 0·52	0·7 > ? > 0·6	0·89 < ? < 0·93	0·12 > ? > 0·1	0·61 < ? < 0·64	0·3 > ? > 0·2

0·35 < ? < 0·45	1·01 > ? > 0·99	1·4 < ? < 1·5	2·79 > ? > 2·77	4·99 < ? < 5·01

1	0·49	0·9	5	0·62	0·4
A	U	D	S	E	P

0·16	2·78	0·29	1·45	0·65	0·11
H	T	D	R	N	R

Lesson 3: **Multiplying by 10 or 100**

- Multiply any number by 10 or 100

You will need
- yellow and blue coloured pencils

Challenge 1 Put the numbers through the machines.

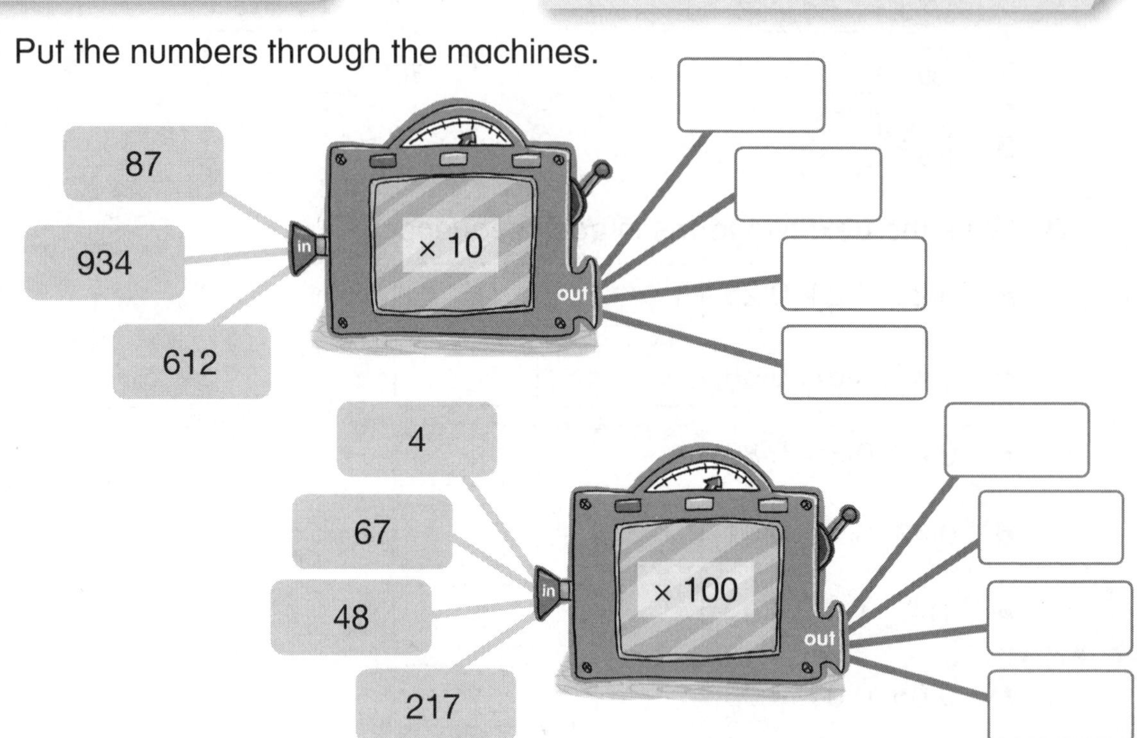

Challenge 2

1 The number to be multiplied is in bold. The product of the multiplication is below it. Colour yellow the squares containing numbers that have been multiplied by 10. Colour blue the squares containing numbers that have been multiplied by 100.

55 5500	**484** 48 400	**9** 90	**123** 12 300	**237** 2370
6 600	**5054** 505 400	**708** 7080	**99** 9900	**106** 10 600
22 220	**404** 40 400	**10 000** 1 000 000	**303** 3030	**1** 100
666 66 600	**1111** 111 100	**37** 3700	**4043** 40 430	**8089** 808 900

2 Complete the table by converting the amount in dollars to cents.

$	3	45	725	1150	1903	4004	7007
cents							

Challenge **3** Work out the cost of of each set of items.

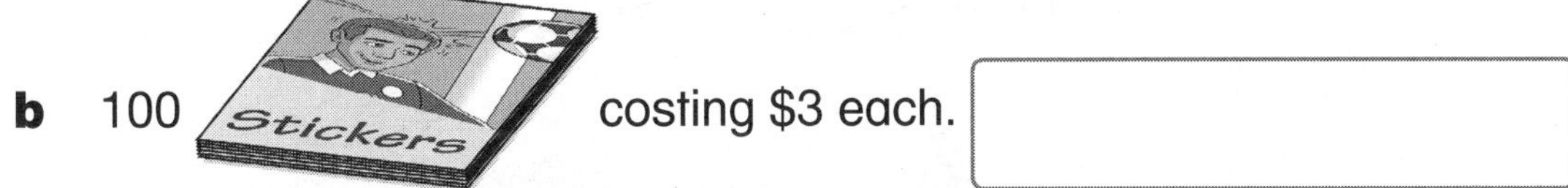

a 10 costing $2 each.

b 100 costing $3 each.

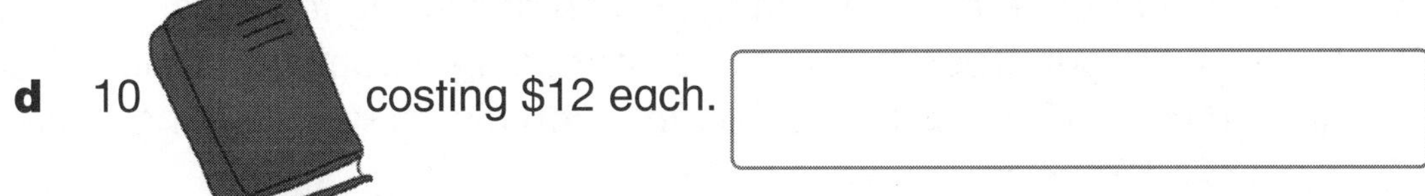

c 100 costing $5 each.

d 10 costing $12 each.

e 10 costing $250 each.

f 100 costing $999 each.

Lesson 4: **Dividing by 10 or 100**

- Divide any number by 10 or 100

You will need

- green and red coloured pencils

Challenge 1

Put the numbers through the machines.

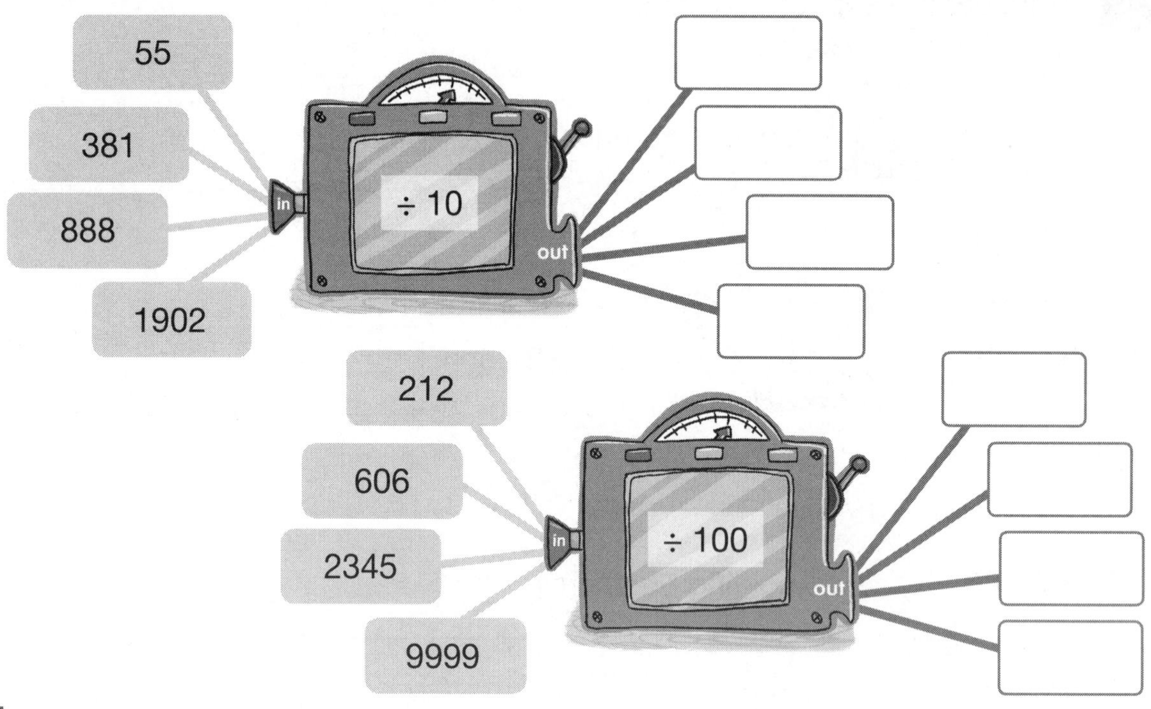

1 The number to be divided is in bold. The answer to the division is below it. Colour green the squares containing numbers that have been divided by 10. Colour red the squares containing numbers that have been divided by 100.

437 4·37	**11** 1.1	**51** 5·1	**2302** 23·02	**3330** 333
717 71.7	**77 777** 7777·7	**606** 6·06	**1010** 10·1	**3** 0·03
6006 600·6	**2** 0.2	**8100** 81	**5505** 550·5	**44** 4·4
99 009 990·09	**299** 29.9	**9191** 919·1	**7272** 727.2	**51 005** 510·05

2 Complete the table by converting the amount in cents to dollars

cents	4	70	58	204	3009	24 089	532 488
$							

Challenge 3 Work out the cost of each item.

a 10  costing $102·50 in total. Price for 1: 

b 100  costing $2725 in total. Price for 1:

c 10  costing $7889 in total. Price for 1:

d 100  costing $87 640 in total. Price for 1:

e 10  costing $87 345·50. Price for 1:

f 100  costing $9330. Price for 1:

Lesson 1: **Tenths and hundredths**

- Use decimal notation for tenths and hundredths
- Write decimals in expanded form

Write in words the place value of each underlined digit. The first one has been done for you.

a 0·26 six hundredths

b 1·47 ______________________

c 2·98 ______________________

d 6·06 ______________________

e 5·55 ______________________

f 3·31 ______________________

g 60·06 ______________________

h 814·37 ______________________

1 Write the decimals in expanded form.

a 0·67 = ☐ + ☐

b 0·33 = ☐ + ☐

c 0·51 = ☐ + ☐

d 4·89 = ☐ + ☐ + ☐

e 9·11 = ☐ + ☐ + ☐

f 6·06 = ☐ + ☐

g 5·55 = ☐ + ☐ + ☐

2 Write the decimals equivalent to these words. The first one has been done for you.

a 4 tenths and 3 hundredths = 0·43

b 7 tenths and 2 hundredths = ______

c 9 units, 6 tenths and 1 hundredth = ______

d 6 units and 6 hundredths = ______

e 2 tens, 4 units, 7 tenths and 8 hundredths = ______

f 6 tens, 9 units and 5 hundredths = ______

g 8 hundreds and 8 hundredths = ______

h 9 thousands, 1 hundred, 4 tens, 5 tenths and 2 hundredths = ______

i 6 thousands, 6 tenths and 6 hundredths = ______

Challenge **3** Find the total in each box.

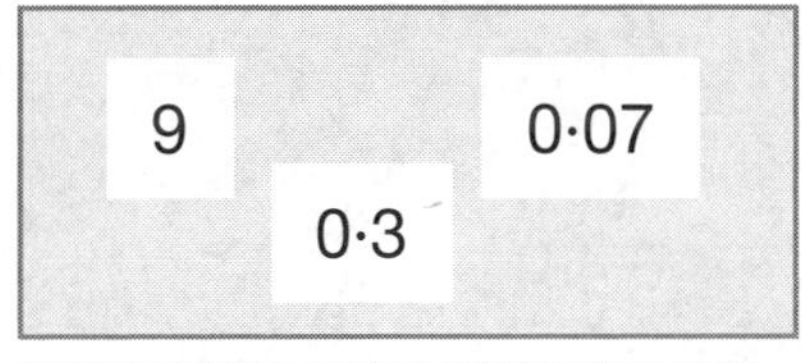

a ______

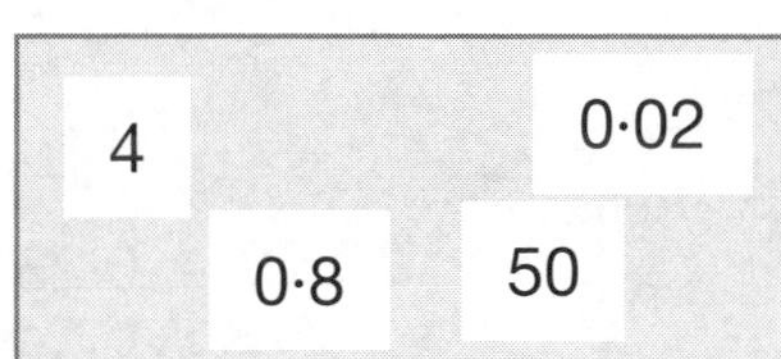

b ______

5 0·1 200 30 0·0

c ______

500 7 0·06 0·2 70

d ______

800 6 0·0 4000 40

e ______

90 0·9 0·9 900 9000 9

f ______

Number

Lesson 2: **Comparing decimals**

- Compare numbers with 1 or 2 decimal places

Follow the route of greater numbers to get to the treasure. Circle the larger number each time. The treasure is hidden behind one of the numbers at the bottom of the map. Write the number on the box.

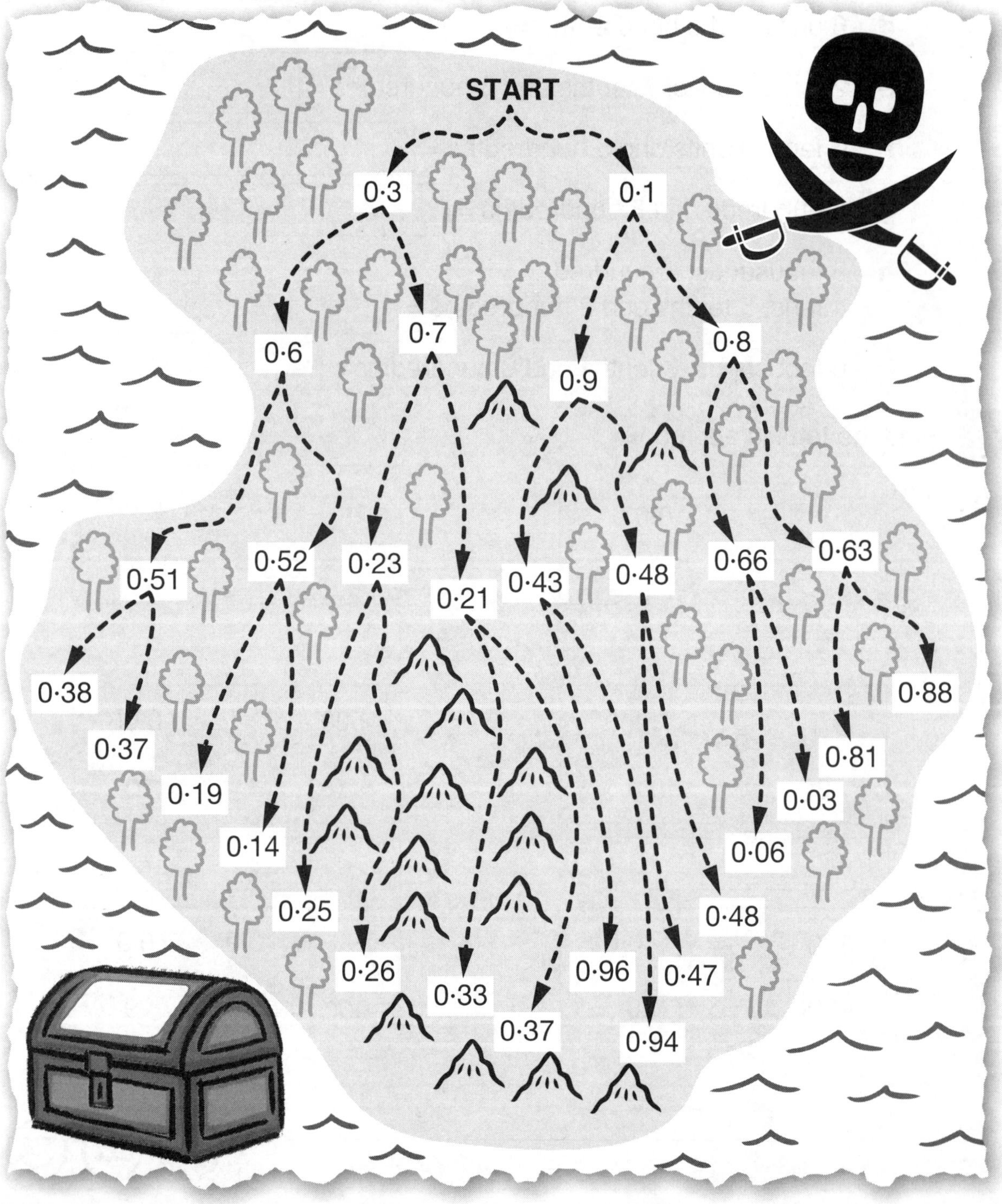

1 Write the correct symbol, < or >, to compare each pair of decimals.

a 0·4 ☐ 0·8

b 0·3 ☐ 0·1

c 1·7 ☐ 1·9

d 0·45 ☐ 0·42

e 0·66 ☐ 0·67

f 2·55 ☐ 2·54

g 5·05 ☐ 5·01

h 11·03 ☐ 11·3

i 91·49 ☐ 91·94

j 16·43 ☐ 16·5

2 Write the correct symbol, < or >, to compare each pair of measurements.

a 0·5 m ☐ 0·3 m

b 0·9 kg ☐ 0·8 kg

c 0·7 cm ☐ 0·4 cm

d 0·32 km ☐ 0·37 km

e 0·44 *l* ☐ 0·4 *l*

f 4·82 mm ☐ 4·83 mm

g 12·2 g ☐ 12 g

h 50·07 ml ☐ 50·01 ml

i 77·5 min ☐ 77·6 min

j 25·6 m ☐ 25·55 m

Complete the decimals to make each statement true.

a 2·4 < 2·☐

b 210·5☐ > 210·☐9

c 13·☐4 > 13·☐9

d 199·☐9 < 199·☐9

e 20·8☐ < 20·8☐

f 105·1☐ > 105·☐8

g 10·0☐ > 1☐·☐3

h 400·0☐ < 400·0☐

i 37·☐ < 37·☐5

j 354.☐6 < 354.5☐

Lesson 3: **Ordering decimals**

- Order numbers with 1 or 2 decimal places

Challenge 1 Use the number line to answer the questions.

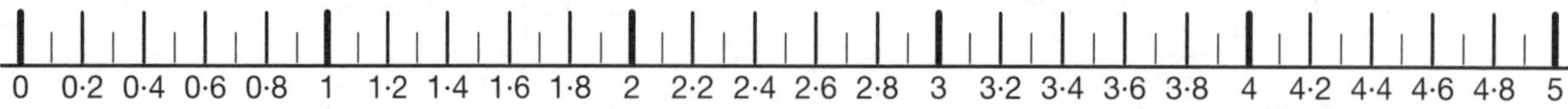

1 Order the sets of decimals.

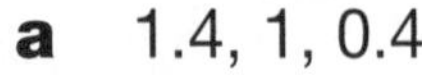

a 1.4, 1, 0.4

b 3.6, 2, 3.2

c 4.8, 4.2, 2.4

2 Which number is halfway between …

a 1·2 and 1·8?

b 3·5 and 4·1

c 0·1 and 0·9?

d 2·4 and 3·4?

Challenge 2 **1** Order each set of decimals, from smallest to largest.

a 4·25, 4·23, 4·12, 4·24, 4·17

b 7·32, 7·26, 7·34, 7·17, 7·25

c 2·94, 2·87, 2·91, 2·86, 2·99

d 9·58, 9·02, 9·51, 9·01, 9·56

2 Complete the statements.

a 23·46 > ☐ > 23·41 > ☐ > 23·39

b 50·08 < ☐ < 50·1 < ☐ < 50·13

c 80·01 > ☐ > 79·98 > ☐ > 79·89

d 33·33 < ☐ < 33·36 < ☐ < 33·4

e 92·12 > ☐ > 92·1 > ☐ > 92

f 111·90 < ☐ < 111·93 < ☐ < 112

Challenge 3 Use the digits below to make ten 5-digit numbers, each with 2 decimal places. Use each digit only once in each number, for example, 305·17. Write the numbers in the grid. Then put the numbers in ascending order.

Ascending order:

Number

Lesson 4: **Rounding decimals**

- Round any number with 1 or 2 decimal places to the nearest whole number

Challenge 1

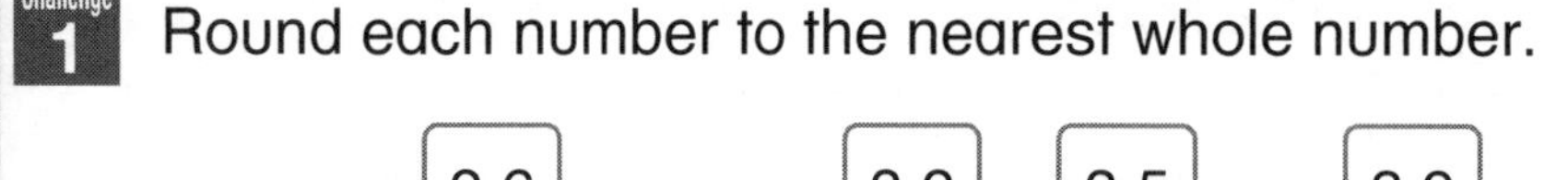

Round each number to the nearest whole number.

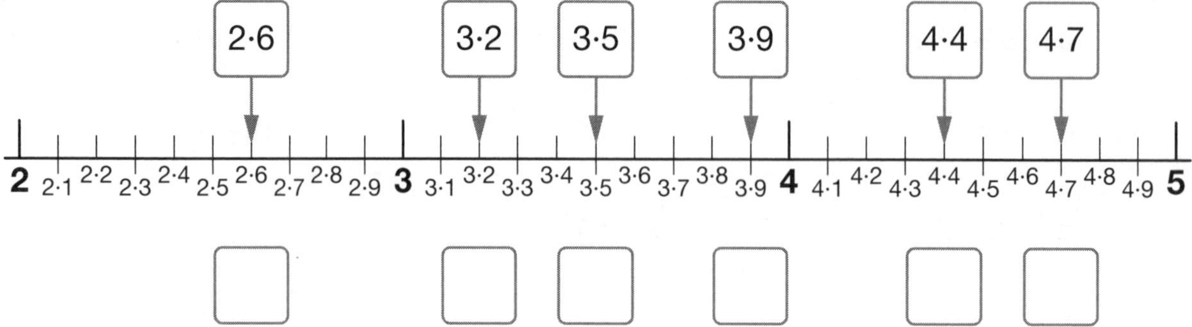

Challenge 2

1 Write the two whole numbers that each decimal comes between. Then circle the number that the decimal rounds to.

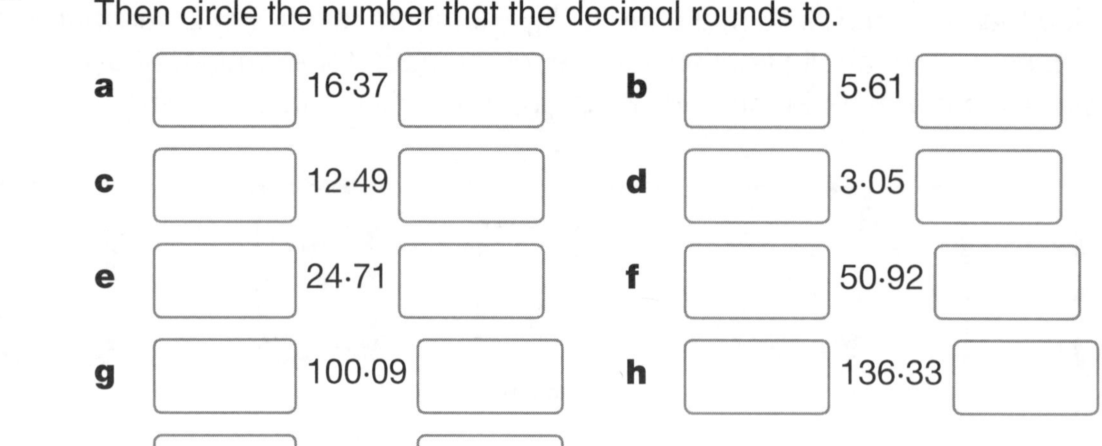

a ☐ 16·37 ☐

b ☐ 5·61 ☐

c ☐ 12·49 ☐

d ☐ 3·05 ☐

e ☐ 24·71 ☐

f ☐ 50·92 ☐

g ☐ 100·09 ☐

h ☐ 136·33 ☐

i ☐ 998·99 ☐

2 Round each measurement to the nearest whole number.

a 0·98 kg ☐ kg

b 6·05 m ☐ m

c 11·52 *l* ☐ *l*

d 32·01 km ☐ km

e 29·72 g ☐ g

f 85·55 cm ☐ cm

g 0·49 s ☐ s

h 149·61 m ☐ m

3 Round the prices to the nearest dollar.

a $7·07 ______ **b** $20·56 ______

c $59·61 ______ **d** $100·05 ______

e $237·37 ______ **f** $555·55 ______

Challenge 3

Use the clues to identify the correct number.
Circle the correct number.

a
- I am between 25 and 26.
- I am 26 rounded to the nearest whole number.
- My tenths digit is odd.

27·32	25·49	24·98	25·03
25·64	27·01	28·44	25·71

b
- I am between 210 and 211.
- I am 210 rounded to the nearest whole number.
- My tenths digit is the same as my tens digit.
- Add 0·39 to me and I would be 211 rounded to the nearest whole number.

210.19	209.48	211.44	210.67
211.11	212.06	210.11	210.51

c
- I am between 539 and 540.
- I am 540 rounded to the nearest whole number.
- My hundredths digit is the same as my units digit.
- Subtract 0·3 from me and I would be 539 rounded to the nearest whole number.

538.79	539.88	540.33	539.79
540.22	540.01	539.02	540.49

Number

Lesson 1: Equivalent fractions

- Identify, name and write equivalent fractions of a given fraction

You will need
- coloured pencils

Shade the bars to show the fractions equivalent to $\frac{1}{2}$.
Then complete the statements.

$\frac{1}{2}$	$\frac{1}{2}$

$\frac{1}{4}$	$\frac{1}{4}$	$\frac{1}{4}$	$\frac{1}{4}$

$\frac{1}{8}$	$\frac{1}{8}$	$\frac{1}{8}$	$\frac{1}{8}$	$\frac{1}{8}$	$\frac{1}{8}$	$\frac{1}{8}$	$\frac{1}{8}$

$$\frac{1}{2} = \frac{\square}{4} = \frac{\square}{8}$$

1 Shade the bars to show the fractions equivalent to $\frac{1}{5}$ and to $\frac{1}{3}$.
Then complete the statements.

$\frac{1}{5}$	$\frac{1}{5}$	$\frac{1}{5}$	$\frac{1}{5}$	$\frac{1}{5}$

$\frac{1}{10}$	$\frac{1}{10}$	$\frac{1}{10}$	$\frac{1}{10}$	$\frac{1}{10}$	$\frac{1}{10}$	$\frac{1}{10}$	$\frac{1}{10}$	$\frac{1}{10}$	$\frac{1}{10}$

a $\frac{1}{5} = \frac{\square}{10}$

$\frac{1}{3}$	$\frac{1}{3}$	$\frac{1}{3}$

$\frac{1}{6}$	$\frac{1}{6}$	$\frac{1}{6}$	$\frac{1}{6}$	$\frac{1}{6}$	$\frac{1}{6}$

b $\frac{1}{3} = \frac{\square}{6}$

2 Draw lines to match the equivalent fractions.

$\frac{1}{2}$	$\frac{1}{4}$
$\frac{2}{8}$	$\frac{2}{4}$
$\frac{4}{6}$	$\frac{2}{5}$
$\frac{4}{10}$	$\frac{2}{3}$

Challenge **3** Use the key to colour the picture.

- Colour $\frac{1}{2}$ and its equivalent fractions red.
- Colour $\frac{1}{3}$ and its equivalent fractions yellow.
- Colour $\frac{1}{5}$ and its equivalent fractions blue.

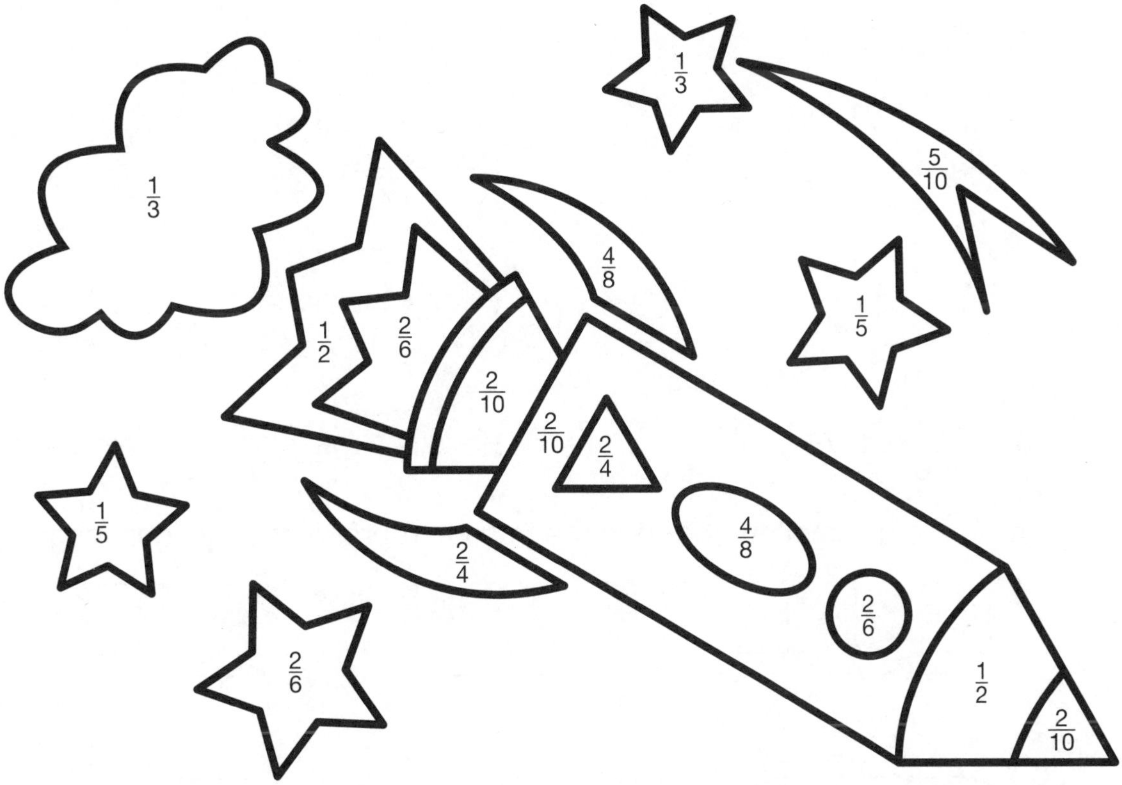

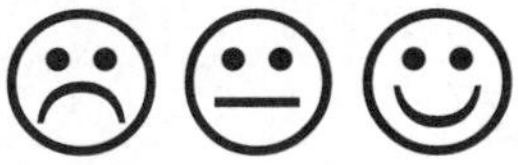

Lesson 2: **Fraction and decimal equivalents**

- Recognise fractions and decimals that are equivalent and use this to help order fractions.

Challenge 1

1 Draw lines to match each fraction with its decimal equivalent.

$\frac{7}{10}$	$\frac{1}{4}$	$\frac{3}{10}$	$\frac{1}{10}$	$\frac{3}{4}$	$\frac{9}{10}$	$\frac{1}{2}$
0·1	0·75	0·7	0·5	0·9	0·25	0·3

2 Now, order the seven fractions from Question 1, from smallest to largest.

Challenge 2

1 Complete the statements of equivalence.

a $0·4 = \frac{\square}{10}$

b $\frac{1}{\square} = 0·5$

c $0·25 = \frac{\square}{4}$

d $\frac{9}{\square} = 0·9$

e $0·\square = \frac{3}{4}$

f $\frac{7}{\square} = 0·7$

g $\frac{\square}{100} = 0·75$

h $0·\square = \frac{25}{100}$

2 Write the decimal number and the fraction represented by each diagram.

a 

b 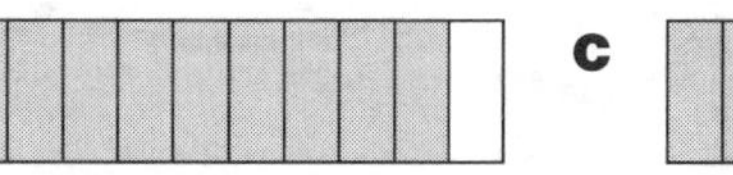

c 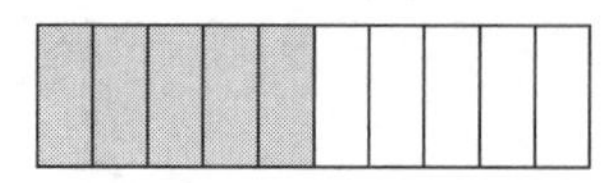

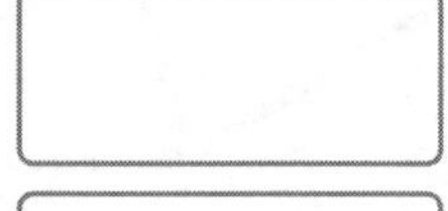

d 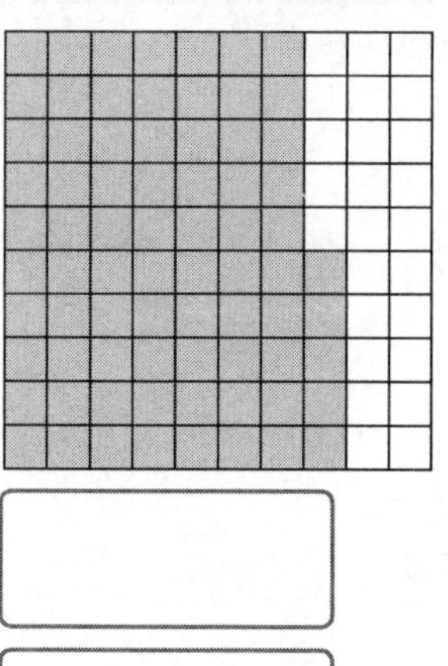

e 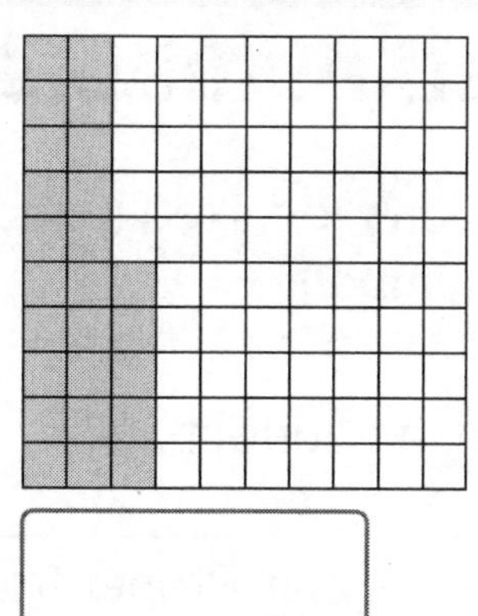

f 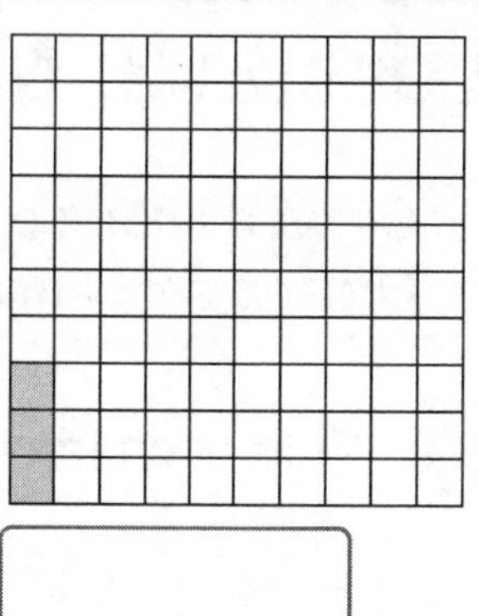

3 Put the fractions and decimals in each set in order, from smallest to largest.

a 0·3, $\frac{1}{4}$, 0·1, $\frac{1}{2}$

b $\frac{3}{4}$, 0·7, $\frac{1}{4}$, 0·2

c $\frac{25}{100}$, 0·8, $\frac{76}{100}$, $\frac{3}{4}$

Write the decimal equivalent of each mixed number.

a $2\frac{3}{4}$ =

b $3\frac{1}{2}$ =

c $7\frac{25}{100}$ =

d $5\frac{75}{100}$ =

e $9\frac{7}{10}$ =

f $12\frac{3}{10}$ =

g $15\frac{9}{100}$ =

h $17\frac{29}{100}$ =

i $16\frac{67}{100}$ =

j $20\frac{99}{100}$ =

k $35\frac{7}{100}$ =

l $100\frac{1}{100}$ =

Number

Lesson 3: **Mixed numbers**

- Convert improper fractions to mixed numbers.
- Order a set of mixed numbers

Write each fraction in the correct set.

$\frac{3}{5}$ $\frac{7}{10}$ $\frac{9}{4}$ $6\frac{2}{3}$ $11\frac{5}{8}$ $4\frac{1}{6}$ $\frac{10}{3}$ $8\frac{1}{4}$ $\frac{11}{9}$

Proper fractions

Improper fractions

Mixed numbers

1 Shade the circle model to help you convert each improper fraction to a mixed number. Use as many circles as you need.

a $\frac{13}{4} =$ ☐

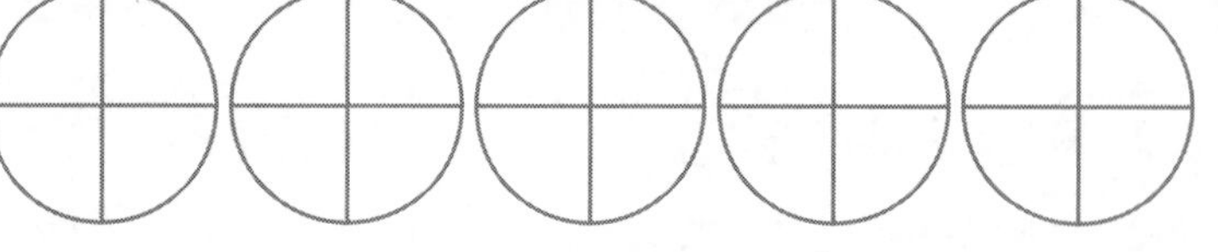

b $\frac{10}{3} =$ ☐

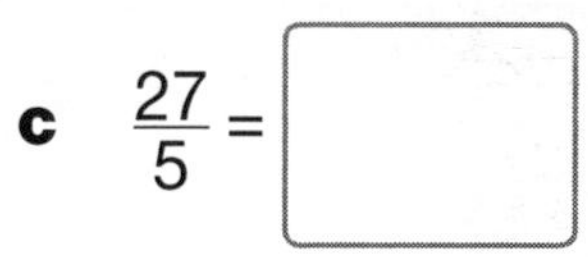

c $\frac{27}{5}$ =

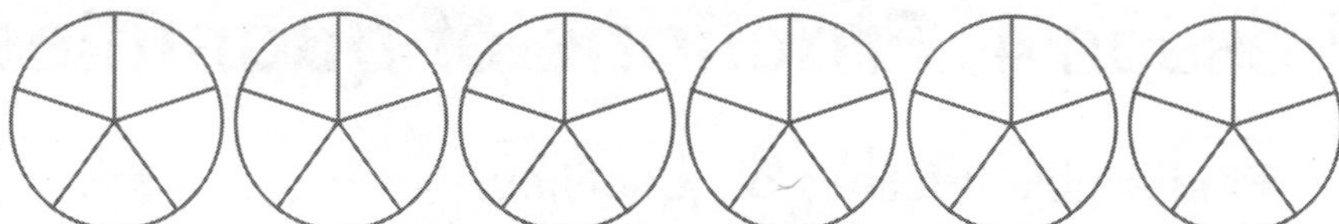

d $\frac{47}{8}$ =

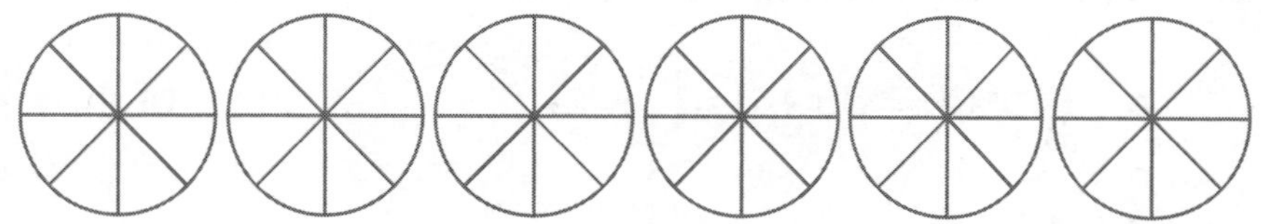

2 Put each set of mixed numbers in order, smallest to largest.

a $3\frac{3}{8}$, $4\frac{5}{8}$, $3\frac{1}{8}$, $4\frac{3}{8}$, $3\frac{7}{8}$

b $7\frac{3}{10}$, $8\frac{4}{5}$, $7\frac{1}{10}$, $8\frac{1}{5}$, $7\frac{7}{10}$

3 Order the set of fractions and place them on the number line.

$3\frac{2}{5}$, $2\frac{3}{5}$, $2\frac{1}{5}$, $3\frac{4}{5}$, $2\frac{2}{5}$

Challenge 3

Convert the mixed numbers to improper fractions.

a $3\frac{2}{3}$

b $2\frac{1}{2}$

c $4\frac{3}{4}$

d $8\frac{2}{5}$

e $9\frac{7}{10}$

f $5\frac{11}{12}$

Number

Lesson 4: **Fractions of quantities**

- Find simple fractions of quantities

Use division to help you find these fractions of quantities.

a $\frac{1}{3}$ of 30 = 30 ÷ 3 = ☐

b $\frac{1}{2}$ of 40 = 40 ÷ 2 = ☐

c $\frac{1}{4}$ of 32 = 32 ÷ 4 = ☐

d $\frac{1}{5}$ of 60 = 60 ÷ 5 = ☐

e $\frac{1}{8}$ of 48 = 48 ÷ 8 = ☐

f $\frac{1}{10}$ of 110 = 110 ÷ 10 = ☐

g $\frac{1}{7}$ of 35 = 35 ÷ 7 = ☐

h $\frac{1}{9}$ of 81 = 81 ÷ 9 = ☐

1 Use the fraction strips to help you find the non-unit fractions. Find the value of one part, then multiply to find the value of the parts required.

a Find $\frac{3}{4}$ of 80.

80			
$\frac{1}{4}$	$\frac{1}{4}$	$\frac{1}{4}$	$\frac{1}{4}$

$\frac{3}{4}$ of 80 = ☐ × ☐ = ☐

b Find $\frac{2}{5}$ of 45.

45				
$\frac{1}{5}$	$\frac{1}{5}$	$\frac{1}{5}$	$\frac{1}{5}$	$\frac{1}{5}$

$\frac{2}{5}$ of 45 = ☐ × ☐ = ☐

c Find $\frac{5}{8}$ of 72.

72							
$\frac{1}{8}$	$\frac{1}{8}$	$\frac{1}{8}$	$\frac{1}{8}$	$\frac{1}{8}$	$\frac{1}{8}$	$\frac{1}{8}$	$\frac{1}{8}$

$\frac{5}{8}$ of 72 = ☐ × ☐ = ☐

d Find $\frac{5}{6}$ of 42.

42					
$\frac{1}{6}$	$\frac{1}{6}$	$\frac{1}{6}$	$\frac{1}{6}$	$\frac{1}{6}$	$\frac{1}{6}$

$\frac{5}{6}$ of 42 = ☐ × ☐ = ☐

2 Work out these non-unit fractions.

a $\frac{2}{3}$ of 45 = ☐ **b** $\frac{4}{5}$ of 45 = ☐ **c** $\frac{7}{8}$ of 64 = ☐

d $\frac{9}{10}$ of 30 = ☐ **e** $\frac{8}{9}$ of 54 = ☐ **f** $\frac{5}{6}$ of 72 = ☐

Find the cost of these items after the discount (money off).
The first one has been done for you.

Item (original price)	**Offer**	**Discount (money off)**	**Sale price**
laptop ($1600)	$\frac{2}{5}$ off	$\frac{1}{5}$ of \$1600 = \$320 $\frac{2}{5}$ of \$1600 = \$320 × 2 = \$640	\$1600 – \$640 = \$960
handheld games console ($550)	$\frac{3}{5}$ off		
TV ($1900)	$\frac{7}{10}$ off		
bicycle ($707)	$\frac{3}{7}$ off		

Lesson 1: **Per cent symbol**

- Understand percentage as 'the number of parts in every hundred'

You will need
- coloured pencils

Challenge 1

The shaded part of each 100 grid represents a percentage. Write the percentage shown.

a

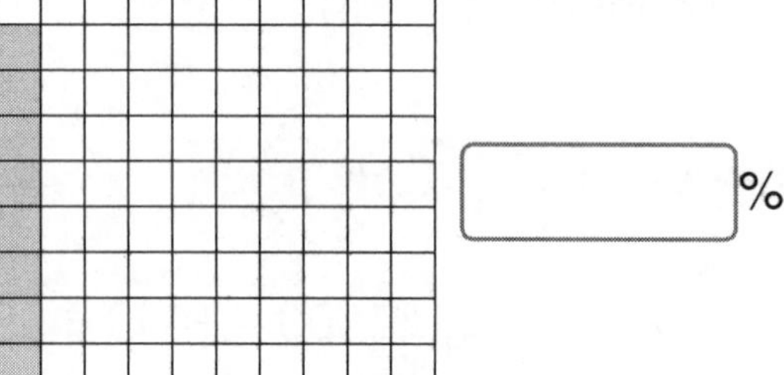

□ %

b

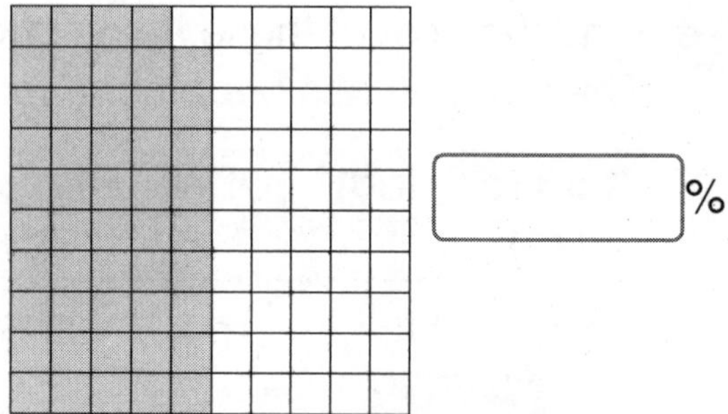

□ %

c

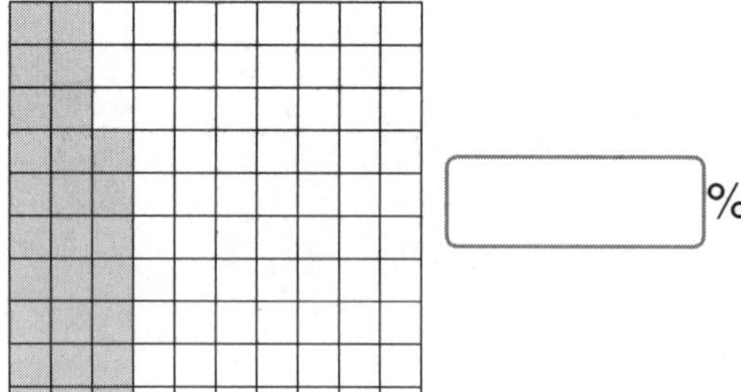

□ %

d

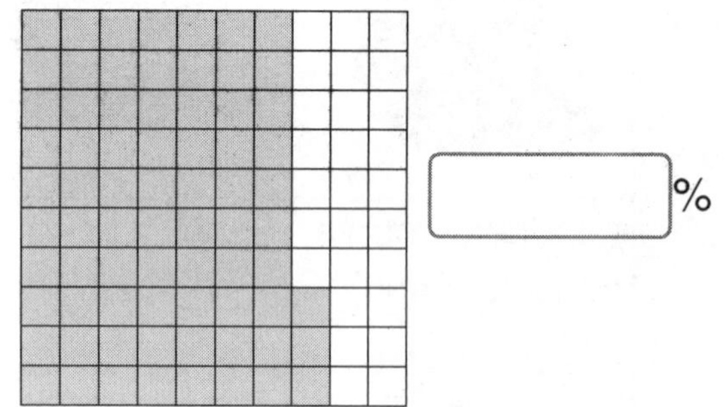

□ %

Challenge 2

1 Shade each grid to show the percentage given.

a

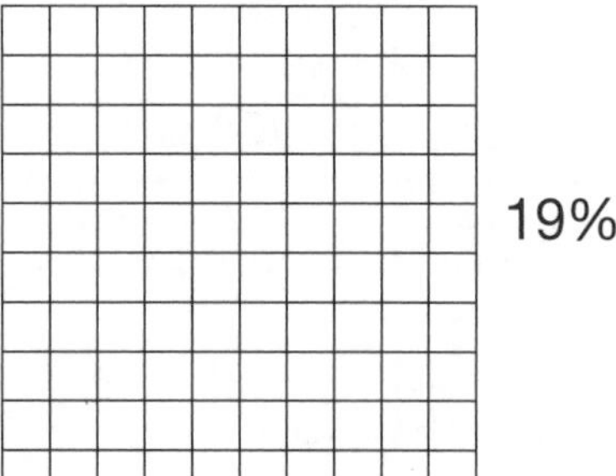

19%

b

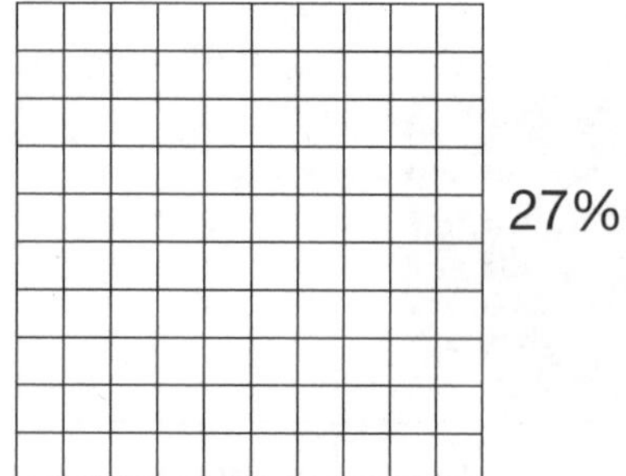

27%

c

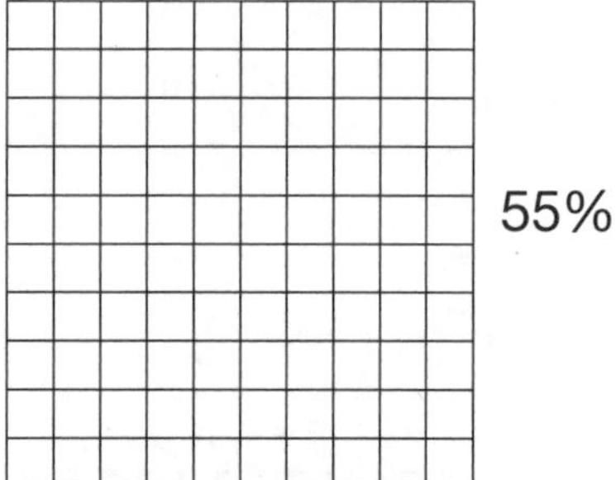

55%

d

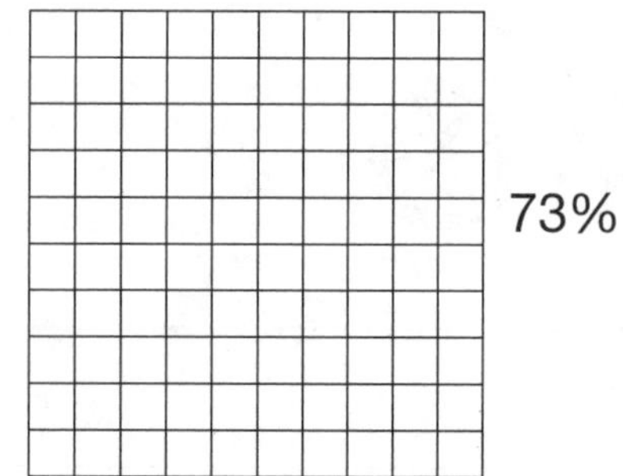

73%

2 Write each of these as a percentage.

a 13 out of 100 cars are grey.

b 29 out of 100 cakes are chocolate.

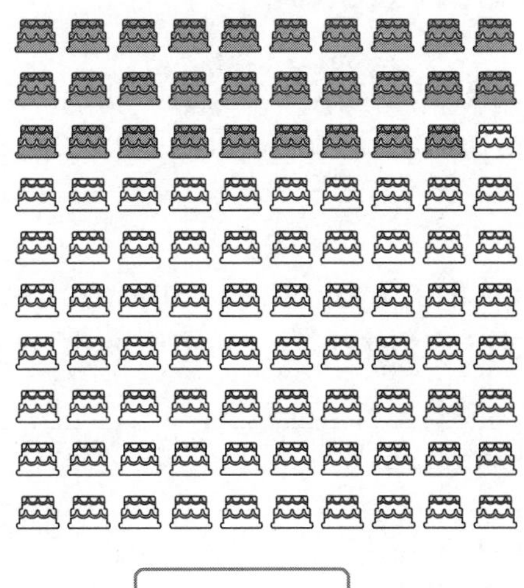

c 76 out of 100 days are sunny.

%

d 81 out of 100 people are happy.

%

Challenge 3 Write your own 'number of parts out of hundred' statement, similar to those in Challenge 2, and write the percentage you have described.

a

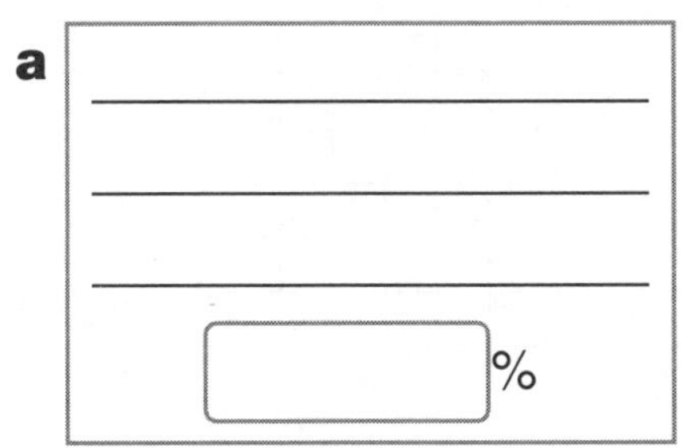

b

%

Number

Lesson 2: **Expressing fractions as percentages**

- Write percentages as a fraction with a denominator of 100
- Know percentage equivalents of certain fractions

Challenge 1

Write the fraction, in hundredths, that is represented by the shaded part of each 100 grid. Convert this to a percentage.

a

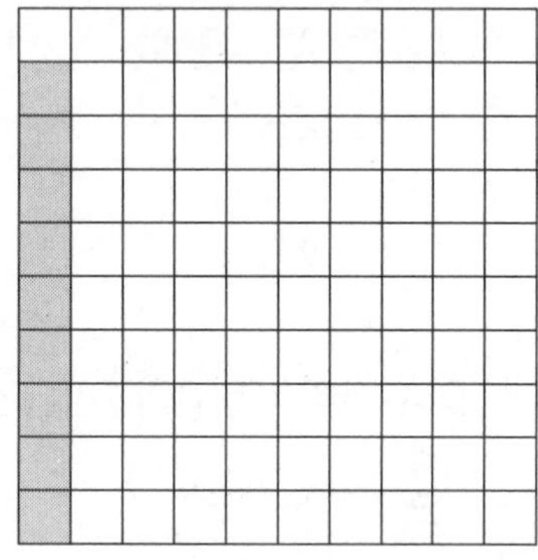

b

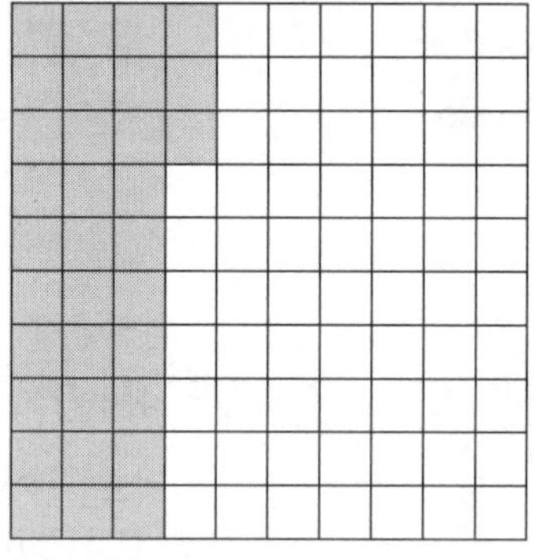

c

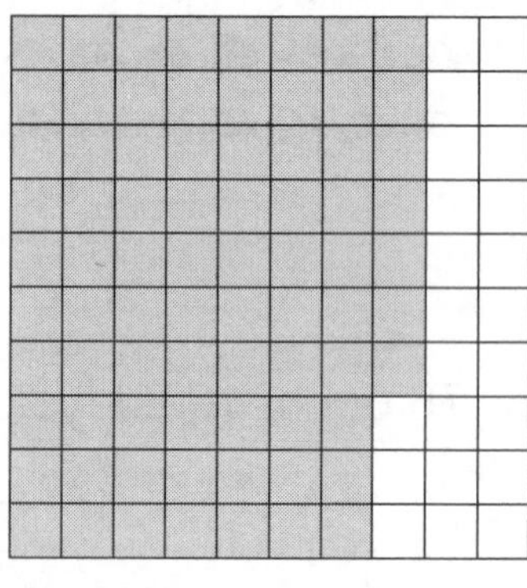

a $\frac{\square}{\square}$ = ☐%

b $\frac{\square}{\square}$ = ☐%

c 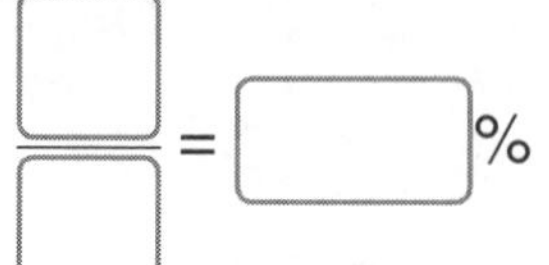

$\frac{\square}{\square}$ = ☐%

Challenge 2

1 Shade the fraction of the grid shown and write the percentage.

a $\frac{1}{2}$ = ☐%

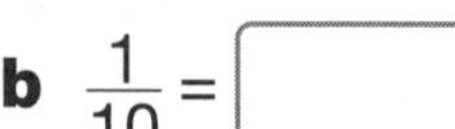

b $\frac{1}{10}$ = ☐%

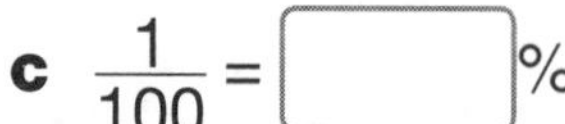

c $\frac{1}{100}$ = ☐%

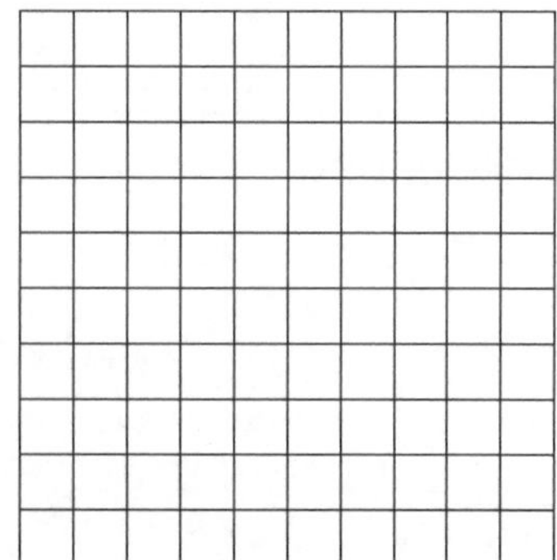

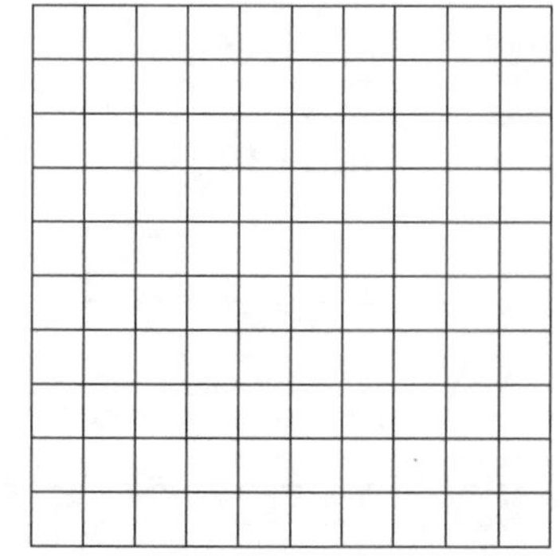

2 Write each of these as a percentage.

a 1 out of every 2 balls is green.

 %

b 23 out of every 100 vehicles are motorbikes.

 %

c 1 out of every 10 chocolates in a box is toffee flavoured.

 %

d 61 out of every 100 shapes are triangles.

 %

e 1 pair out of every 100 pairs of footwear are sandals.

 %

f 93 out of every set of 100 dishes are plastic.

 %

Challenge **3**

1 Write the equivalent fraction for these percentages. Simplify the fraction if possible.

a 23% **b** 67% **c** 59% 

d 10% **e** 1% **f** 50%

2 Write decimal and percentage equivalents for.

a $\frac{1}{2}$  % **b** $\frac{1}{4}$ %

c $\frac{3}{4}$ % **d** $\frac{7}{10}$ %

e $\frac{40}{100}$ % **f** $\frac{75}{100}$ %

Lesson 3: **Percentages of quantities**

- Find simple percentages of quantities

Challenge 1

Work out these percentages.

a 1% of 100 = ☐

b 50% of $300 = ☐

c 10% of 200 km = ☐

d 100% of 73 m = ☐

e 10% of 460 g = ☐

f 25% of $400 = ☐

g 25% of 800 litres = ☐

h 10% of 3500 years = ☐

Challenge 2

1 Work out these percentages. Use the boxes to show your working.

a 25% of $400 = ☐

b 10% of 875 km = ☐

c 50% of $1442 = ☐

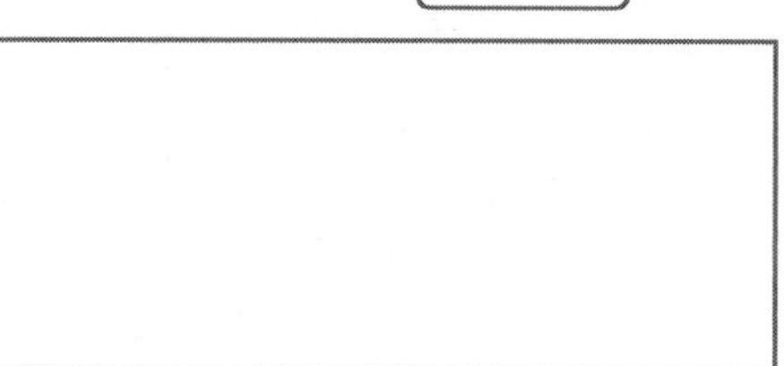

d 25% of 376 g = ☐

e 10% of $1345 = ☐

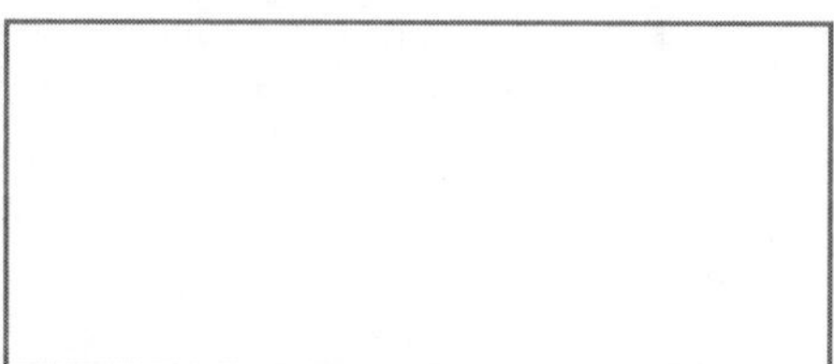

f 50% of 1368 hours = ☐

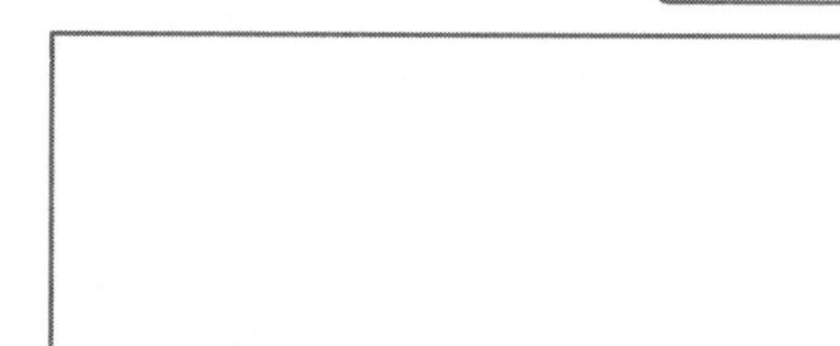

2 Solve these problems.

a 1% of the beetles living in a tree are orange. If there are 3200 beetles in the tree, how many are orange?

b In an experiment, 50% of coin flips were heads. The coin was flipped 384 times. How many times was heads flipped?

c 25% of learners travel to school by bus. There are 624 learners. How many travel by bus?

Challenge 3

Work out these percentages. Use what you know about finding 1%, 10%, 25% and 50% to help you.

a 1% of \$600 =

b 5% of 300 g =

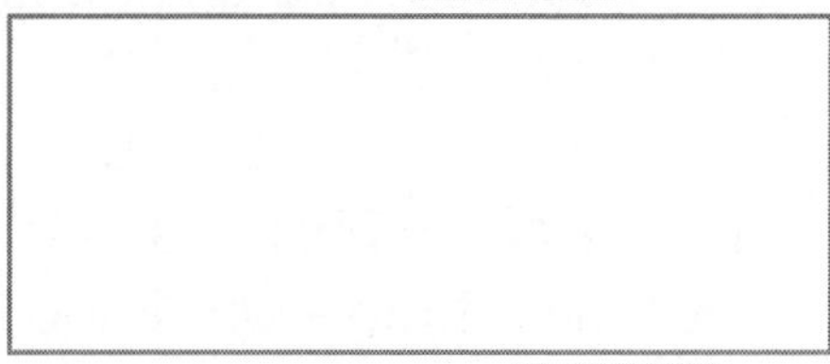

c 25% of \$5400 =

d 30% of 2300 kg =

e 60% of 4700 hours =

f 70% of \$1530 =

g 75% of \$2590 =

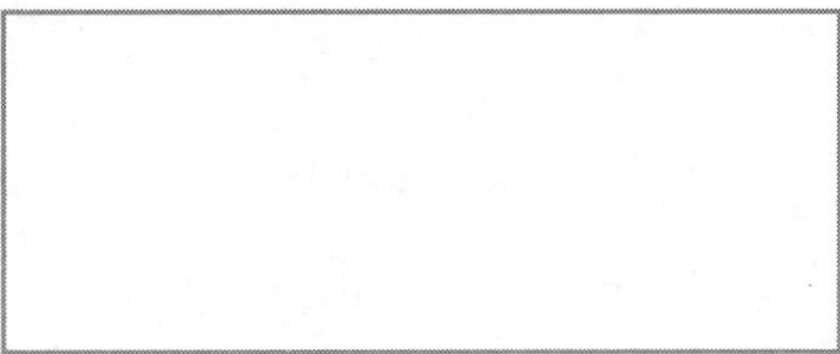

h 90% of \$7710 =

Lesson 4: **Percentage problems**

- Find simple percentages of quantities

Challenge 1

Solve these problems.

a 10% of the birds in a tree are green. If there are 270 birds in the tree, how many are green?

b 25% of the animals in a field are sheep. If there are 172 animals in the field, how many are sheep?

c 50% of the tiles in a shop have striped patterns. If 568 tiles are on sale, how many are striped?

d 1% of the balloons at a big party have smiley faces on them. If there are 2300 balloons, how many have smiley faces?

Challenge 2

1 Solve these problems.

a A cake costs $84. The price is reduced by 25%. How much is the new price?

b A car costs $24 000. 10% is taken off the price. By how much is the price of the car reduced?

c 3400 people visit a supermarket. The following week, 50% fewer people visit. How many people fewer is that?

d The money in a savings account increases by 25% every year. If there is $4200 in the account, what will the increase be after 3 years?

2 Solve these problems.

a 1% of the pages in a book have pictures. If the book has 500 pages, how many pages have pictures?

b A survey shows that 5% of visitors to an ice cream shop choose strawberry ice cream. If 700 people visit the shop, how many are likely to choose strawberry?

c 75% of the bicycles in a shop have a white frame. If there are 444 bicycles, how many are white?

d A garden centre sells 1300 plants of which 75% have yellow flowers. How many plants with yellow flowers are sold?

Challenge 3 Solve these two-step problems. You need to work out the percentage of the amount, then subtract it from the original price/amount.

a 50% of the books in a library are out on loan. If the library has 4322 books available for loan, how many books are actually in the library?

b An airline reduces the fare for one of its flights by 10%. If the price of a ticket is normally $1390, what is the new price?

c A TV is on offer with a sales sticker that says '25% off'. If the original price of the TV is $1440, what is the new sale price?

d 7% of the toys in a shop are board games. If the shop has 1400 toys for sale, how many toys will there be left if all the board games are sold?

Lesson 1: Proportion

- Use fractions to describe and estimate a simple proportion

Challenge 1

Continue the pattern, then complete the sentence.

a ○ △ ○ △ ○ △ ☐ ☐ ☐ ☐ ☐ ☐ ☐ ☐

In this pattern 1 in every ☐ shapes is a triangle.

b ○○○△○○○△ ☐ ☐ ☐ ☐ ☐ ☐ ☐ ☐

In this pattern 3 in every ☐ shapes is a circle.

c ○○△△△○○△△△ ☐ ☐ ☐ ☐ ☐

In this pattern 2 in every ☐ shapes is a circle.

Challenge 2

1 Angela and Toby have 12 biscuits between them. They share the biscuits in different ways. In each case, describe the amount of biscuits Angela has, compared to Toby, in as many ways as possible. The first one has been done for you.

a

Angela has half as many biscuits as Toby.
Out of a total of 12 biscuits, Toby has 8 biscuits.
Out of a total of 12 biscuits, Angela has 4 biscuits.
Out of a total of 12 biscuits, Toby has two thirds ($\frac{2}{3}$).
Out of a total of 12 biscuits, Angela has one third ($\frac{1}{3}$).

b

c

2 Describe each pattern using the phrase '… in every … '. Then write the proportion of spotted tiles as a fraction and the proportion of striped tiles as a fraction.

a

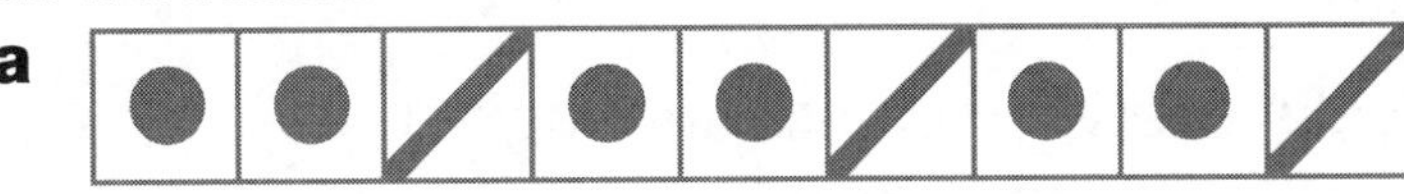

____

____

b

____

____

Challenge 3

Angela and Toby receive more biscuits in total, but they keep the same proportions you found in Challenge 2, Questions 1a, 1b and 1c. Complete the table with the new number of biscuits each of them will now have.

	1a	**1b**	**1c**
Fraction of plate that Toby has	$\frac{2}{3}$		
Fraction of plate that Angela has	$\frac{1}{3}$		
Number of biscuits Toby will have if the total is 24 biscuits			
Number of biscuits Angela will have if the total is 24 biscuits			
Number of biscuits Toby will have if the total is 36 biscuits			
Number of biscuits Angela will have if the total is 36 biscuits			

Lesson 2: **Proportion problems**

- Solve simple proportion problems

Challenge 1

Answer the questions. Assume the relationship between the numbers in the question is proportional.

a Daisy bakes 10 cakes in 5 days. How many cakes would Daisy make in 10 days?

b Ryan cycles a total of 12 kilometres in 4 trips to work. After 12 trips to work, how many kilometres will Ryan have cycled?

c Lucy reads 25 books every 3 months. After a year, how many books will Lucy have read?

Challenge 2

1 a The children attending an after-school club were divided into teams. In every team there were 2 girls and 3 boys. If there are 5 teams, how many boys are there? How many girls? Show your working in the box.

boys ☐ girls ☐

b In every box of chocolates, there are 4 dark chocolates and 7 white chocolates. In 6 boxes, how many dark chocolates are there? How many white chocolates?

dark ☐ white ☐

c In every small book, there are 10 pages and 8 pictures.
In 7 books, how many pages are there? How many pictures?

pages ☐ pictures ☐

2 a In every brick wall there are 40 yellow bricks and 60 red bricks.
For 9 walls, what is the total number of:

yellow bricks? ☐ red bricks? ☐

b In every pond, there are 50 frogs and 90 fish.
For 8 ponds, what is the total number of:

frogs? ☐ fish? ☐

Challenge 3 A recipe for 2 cupcakes requires 25 g of sugar and 50 g of flour.
What total amounts of sugar and flour are required to make:

a 4 cupcakes ☐ g sugar

☐ g flour

b 8 cupcakes ☐ g sugar

☐ g flour

c 12 cupcakes ☐ g sugar

☐ g flour

Lesson 3: **Ratio**

- Express parts of a whole as a ratio

Challenge 1

Write the ratios. The first one has been completed for you.

a In a sports team there are 4 girls for every 3 boys. The ratio of girls to boys is [4 to 3].

b In a jug of orange squash there are 2 parts juice for every 3 parts water. The ratio of juice to water is [to].

c In a purse there are 4 five-dollar bills for every 3 ten-dollar bills. The ratio of five-dollar bills to ten-dollar bills is [to].

d For every 2 sixes thrown with a dice, 7 fives were thrown. The ratio of sixes thrown to fives thrown is [to].

Challenge 2

1 Write the ratios given. Simplify them where possible.

a An animal charity centre has 60 animals. 15 of them are cats and the rest are dogs. What is the ratio of **cats to dogs**? [to].

b A pencil case holds 72 pencils. 12 of them are red and the rest are blue. What is the ratio of **blue to red pencils**? [to].

c There are 88 animals in a field. 22 of them are sheep and the rest are cows. What is the ratio of **cows to sheep**? [to].

2 a Finn shares out 12 bananas. He gives Lydia 1 banana for every 3 bananas he takes. How many bananas does Lydia get? [ ]

b In a school playground, there are 2 boys for every 3 girls. There are 30 children standing in the playground. How many boys are there? [ ]

c Mr. Jones mixes 1 tin of green paint with 2 tins of white to make a large tin. He needs 9 large tins of paint altogether. How many tins of green paint does he need?

d There are 5 green ducks to every 2 yellow ducks in a plastic duck race along a river. If there are 14 ducks altogether, how many of them are green?

Challenge 3

Lorries have 8 wheels and carry 12 large crates.

a What is the total number of crates carried by lorries that have a combined number of 24 wheels?

b What is the combined number of wheels for a set of lorries that carry a total of 36 crates?

c "Lorries that carry a total of 60 crates will have a total of 48 wheels." Is this statement correct? Explain your answer.

Lesson 4: **Ratio problems**

- Solve simple ratio problems

Challenge 1

Read the ingredients list for flapjacks. Scale the quantities up and down to make more flapjacks.

Ingredients	for 2 people	for 4 people	for 8 people	for 16 people
oats (g)	20			
butter (g)	10			
golden syrup (spoonfuls)	2			
sugar (g)	5			
ginger (teaspoons)	1			

Challenge 2

1 a The table shows the numbers of different flowers planted in 6 plots in a garden. Scale the quantities up or down for more or fewer plots.

Flowers	2 plots	3 plots	6 plots	12 plots	30 plots
daffodils			12		
crocuses			18		
roses			30		
pansies			6		
hyacinths			24		

b If 22 hyacinths had been planted in 6 plots, would it be possible to scale this number down for 2 plots? Explain your answer.

___

___

2 The table shows the numbers of different pieces found in 8 construction kits. Scale the quantities up or down for more or fewer kits.

Pieces	2 kits	4 kits	8 kits	32 kits	72 kits
longs			200		
shorts			128		
cogs			360		
wheels			288		
bases			184		

Challenge **3** The table shows the lengths of the sides of an irregular pentagon. The pentagon is scaled proportionally up or down to make smaller and larger pentagons. Use the information given to complete the table.

Side	Size 1: length (cm)	Size 2: length (cm)	Size 3: length (cm)	Size 4: length (cm)	Size 5: length (cm)
side A	3			30	
side B		14	42		
side C				40	72
side D	2		12		
side E		18		90	

Lesson 1: **Counting on or back (2)**

- Count on or back in thousands, hundreds, tens and units to add or subtract

Challenge 1 Fill in the missing numbers on the number lines.

a

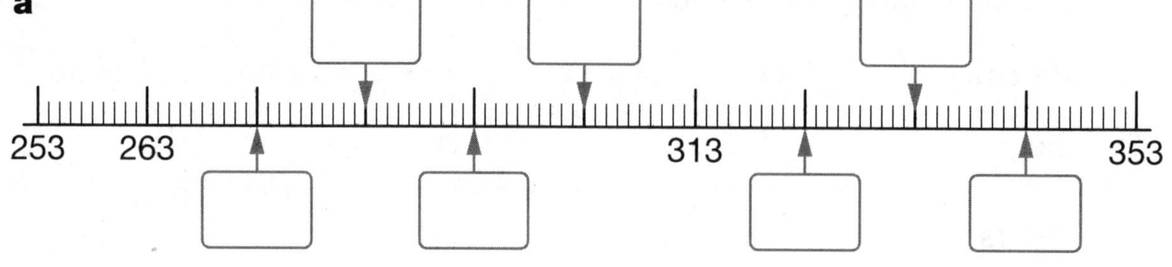

b

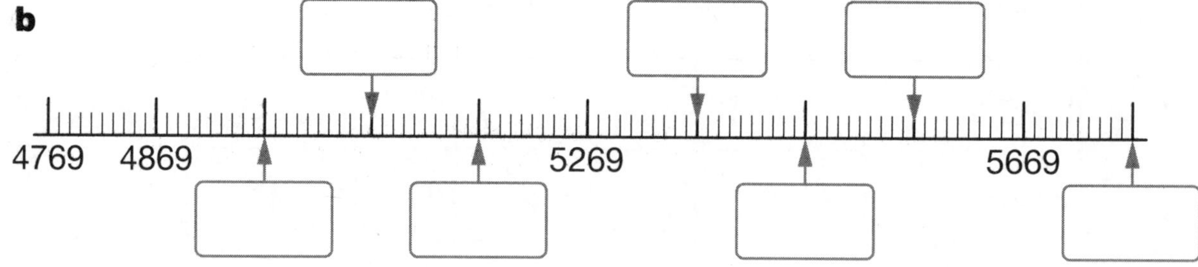

c

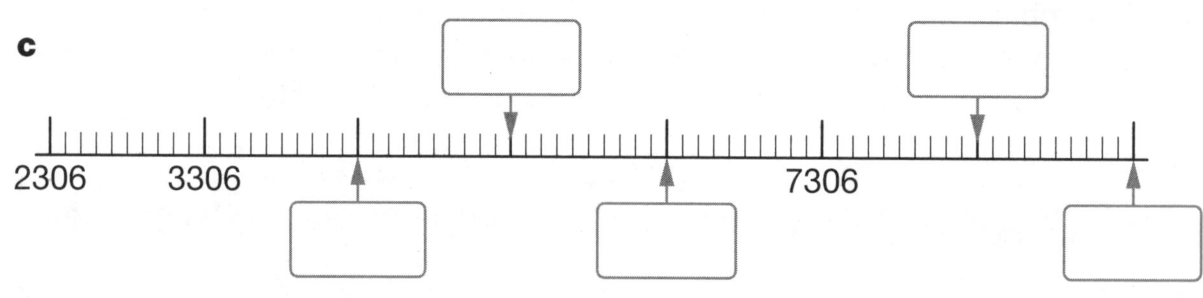

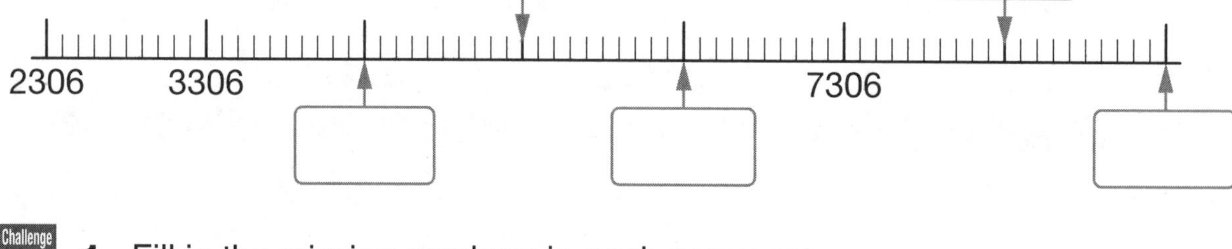

Challenge 2

1 Fill in the missing numbers in each sequence.

a 268, 278, 288, ☐, ☐, ☐, ☐, 338, ☐, ☐, ☐, 378

b 2153, 2163, 2173, ☐, ☐, ☐, 2213 ☐, ☐, ☐, 2253 ☐

c 43629, 44629, 45629 ☐, ☐, ☐, ☐, ☐, 51629 ☐, ☐, ☐,

2 Count on or back in multiples of 10, 100 or 1000 to complete the table. The first few answers have been done for you.

Number	+ 20	+ 50	+ 80	+ 300	+ 600	+ 900	+ 2000	+ 7000
3468	3488	3518	3548					
4987								
6209								
Number	**– 10**	**– 40**	**– 70**	**– 200**	**– 500**	**– 800**	**– 1000**	**– 3000**
4253								
5132								
8076								

Complete each number sentence by writing the operation and the number. The first one has been done for you.

a 473 [–10] = 463

b 2346 [ ] = 2446

c 6754 [ ] = 5754

d 78 [ ] = 178

e 5997 [ ] = 6007

f 8139 [ ] = 3139

g 881 [ ] = 281

h 4856 [ ] = 4916

I 3325 [ ] = 325

j 6363 [ ] = 5763

Number

Lesson 2: Adding 2- and 3-digit numbers

• Select and use effective strategies to add pairs of 2- and 3-digit numbers

Challenge 1

Choose an appropriate strategy to solve each calculation.

a 73 + 60 = ☐ **b** 98 + 70 = ☐ **c** 133 + 80 = ☐

d 267 + 60 = ☐ **e** 322 + 110 = ☐ **f** 446 + 120 = ☐

g 524 + 170 = ☐ **h** 739 + 250 = ☐ **i** 456 + 750 = ☐

j 621 + 620 = ☐ **k** 783 + 440 = ☐ **l** 818 + 890 = ☐

Challenge 2

1 The calculations are grouped together because they can be solved using the same strategy. However, you should use whichever strategy you prefer.

a **i** 75 + 25 = ☐ **ii** 275 + 325 = ☐

iii 460 + 340 = ☐ **iv** 635 + 265 = ☐

b **i** 67 + 24 = ☐ **ii** 444 + 28 = ☐

iii 96 + 97 = ☐ **iv** 654 + 237 = ☐

c **i** 47 + 36 = ☐ **ii** 277 + 46 = ☐

iii 76 + 48 = ☐ **iv** 586 + 247 = ☐

d **i** 98 + 83 = ☐ **ii** 298 + 44 = ☐

iii 68 + 35 = ☐ **iv** 533 + 498 = ☐

2 a Copy each problem into the column headed with the strategy that you would use to solve it. You may place a problem in more than one column.

259 + 198 | 97 + 48 | 56 + 70 | 67 + 76 | 354 + 423

198 + 243 | 44 + 53 | 676 + 286 | 476 + 347 | 271 + 600

Counting on	'Friendly' numbers	Partitioning	Compensation	Other

b For each of these problems, use your chosen strategy to solve it.

i 56 + 70 ______________________

ii 198 + 243 ______________________

iii 354 + 423 ______________________

Complete the number problems by filling in the missing numbers. Use your knowledge of addition strategies to help you.

a 83 + ________ = 153

b 298 + ________ = 684

c ________ + 66 = 143

d ________ + 367 = 537

e 78 + ________ = 133

f ________ + 694 = 1422

g 997 + ______ = 1764

h ________ + 69 = 156

i 777 + ________ = 1435

j 883 + ________ = 1221

k ________ + 96 = 293

l 998 + ________ = 1996

Number

Lesson 3: Subtracting 2- and 3-digit numbers

- Select and use effective strategies to subtract pairs of 2- and 3-digit numbers

Choose an appropriate strategy to solve each calculation.

a 73 + 60 = ☐ **b** 98 + 70 = ☐ **c** 133 + 80 = ☐

d 98 – 40 = ☐ **e** 63 – 30 = ☐ **f** 287 – 50 = ☐

g 596 – 90 = ☐ **h** 437 – 22 = ☐ **i** 761 – 44 = ☐

j 879 – 670 = ☐ **k** 952 – 840 = ☐ **l** 578 – 380 = ☐

m 737 – 550 = ☐ **n** 904 – 520 = ☐ **o** 883 – 790 = ☐

Challenge 2

1 The calculations are grouped together because they can be solved using the same strategy. However, you may use whichever strategy you prefer.

a **i** 50 – 25 = ☐ **ii** 75 – 25 = ☐

iii 745 – 525 = ☐ **iv** 965 – 425 = ☐

b **i** 97 – 54 = ☐ **ii** 576 – 42 = ☐

iii 869 – 543 = ☐ **iv** 924 – 811 = ☐

c **i** 384 – 288 = ☐ **ii** 594 – 78 = ☐

iii 772 – 488 = ☐ **iv** 986 – 516 = ☐

d **i** 489 – 98 = ☐ **ii** 687 – 97 = ☐

iii 893 – 498 = ☐ **iv** 996 – 699 = ☐

2 a Copy each problem into the column headed with the strategy that you would use to solve it. You may place a problem in more than one column.

779 – 398 | 98 – 50 | 678 – 353 | 987 – 398 | 575 – 225

95 – 35 | 888 – 777 | 892 – 616 | 467 – 220 | 405 – 299

Counting back	'Friendly' numbers	Partitioning	Compensation	Other

b For each of these problems, use your chosen strategy to solve it.

i 405 – 299 ______________________

ii 678 – 353 ______________________

iii 892 – 616 ______________________

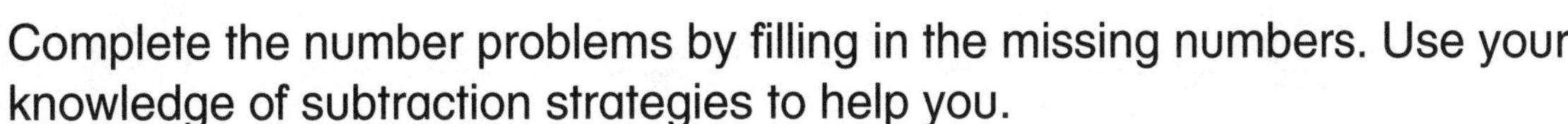

Challenge **3** Complete the number problems by filling in the missing numbers. Use your knowledge of subtraction strategies to help you.

a 163 – ________ = 93

b 347 – ________ = 187

c ________ – 98 = 376

d ________ – 432 = 147

e 676 – ________ = 248

f 972 – ________ = 584

g ________ – 311 = 313

h 575 – ________ = 250

i 789 – ________ = 491

j ________ – 399 = 397

k 569 – ________ = 326

l ________ – 325 = 640

Number

Lesson 4: **Adding more than two numbers**

- Use a written method to find the total of three or more 2- and 3-digit numbers

Challenge 1

Work out the sum of the numbers in each list, using a written method for addition.

a	23 37 38
b	75 68 52
c	23 228 242
d	309 258 26
e	504 37 426
f	194 87 99
g	86 89 198
h	794 521 856
i	668 775 983
j	979 968 999

Challenge 2

1 Estimate the sum of the prices on each receipt. Then find the totals.

a RECEIPT

.... $126
.... $243
.... $378
.... $184
Total ______

b RECEIPT

.... $464
.... $387
.... $499
.... $276
Total ______

c RECEIPT

.... $285
.... $698
.... $709
.... $867
Total ______

d RECEIPT

.... $656
.... $879
.... $758
.... $747
Total ______

e RECEIPT

.... $842
.... $774
.... $688
.... $959
Total ______

f RECEIPT

.... $989
.... $978
.... $969
.... $999
Total ______

2 Stage 5 learners count up their achievement points for the year. If a class has over 2850 points they win a prize. The class with the highest score wins a trophy.
What are the results?

Class scores

Red class	Blue class	Green class	Yellow class
868	697	443	956
754	886	975	647
679	769	556	462
552	527	874	783

______ ______ ______ ______

______ ______ ______ ______

____

Challenge 3 Scientists counted bugs on five trees. Find the total number of bugs on each tree and place the numbers in ascending order.

Tree A	Tree B	Tree C	Tree D	Tree E
135	685	414	394	495
712	547	316	672	711
931	142	131	945	967
612	815	737	576	312
967	289	742	895	387

Order: ☐ ☐ ☐ ☐ ☐

Number

Lesson 1: Near multiples of 10 or 100

- Add or subtract mentally near multiples of 10 or 100

You will need
- dice
- counters

Decrease each number by 9. | Increase each number by 11

a ☐ ← 47 → ☐

b ☐ ← 96 → ☐

c ☐ ← 153 → ☐

d ☐ ← 212 → ☐

e ☐ ← 477 → ☐

f ☐ ← 2582 → ☐

1 Write the missing numbers in the table.

	+ 19	– 29	+ 61	– 78	+ 299	– 202	+ 498	– 398
677								
951								
2617								
3421								
5886								
7043								

2 Play this game with a partner.

Each place a counter on the start square. Roll a dice to move along the path. You begin with 2997. Add or subtract the numbers that you land on. Compare your scores when you both finish. The winner is the person with the lower score. If a subtraction causes your score to become negative, you must go back to the start and begin the game again.

Start 2297		− 219	+ 237	− 251		− 499	+ 522	− 548
+ 9		+ 181		+ 289		+ 501		+ 538
− 29		− 158		− 291		− 479		− 562
+ 18		+ 142		+ 348		+ 481		+ 569
− 41		− 137		− 328		− 461		− 588
+ 59		+ 129		+ 369		+ 438		+ 599
− 68	+ 91	− 102		− 351	+ 399	− 412		Finish

Challenge 3 Complete each number sentence. The first two have been done for you.

a 178 ___+ 79___ = 257 **b** 1748 ___− 579___ = 1169

c 536 __________ = 625 **d** 888 __________ = 727

e 973 __________ = 1161 **f** 1791 __________ = 1013

g 1607 __________ = 3909 **h** 2683 __________ = 1725

i 2892 __________ = 2353 **j** 3177 __________ = 3475

k 5871 __________ = 5519

Lesson 2: **Near multiples of 1000**

- Calculate the difference between near multiples of 1000

You will need
- counters
- 1–3 spinner

Challenge 1

Use the number lines to calculate the differences between the numbers.

1900 2000 2100 2200 2300 2400 2500 2600 2700 2800 2900 3000 3100

a **i** 3007 – 1998 ____________ **ii** 3017 – 2001 ____________ **iii** 3026 – 1997 ____________

6900 7000 7100 7200 7300 7400 7500 7600 7700 7800 7900 8000 8100

b **i** 8005 – 6999 ____________ **ii** 8013 – 6996 ____________ **iii** 8027 – 7001 ____________

Challenge 2

1 Write the missing numbers in the table.

	– 999	**– 997**	**– 1998**	**– 2001**	**– 2998**	**– 2999**	**– 3997**	**–4002**
4003								
4021								
5006								
6022								
8013								
9016								

2 Play this game with a partner.

Place a counter on square 1. Spin 1–3 to move. If you meet a ladder, climb to the top. If you meet a snake, drop to the end of its tail. If you land on a number problem, solve it within 30 seconds. If you are unsuccessful, miss a go. The first player to reach square 30 is the winner.

21 4024 – 998	**22**	**23**	**24** 6021 – 1999	**25**	**26** 9017 – 4002	**27**	**28** 7006 – 5999	**29**	**30**
20 7002 – 4997	**19**	**18**	**17** 8026 – 6001	**16**	**15**	**14** 5011 – 2998	**13**	**12** 8012 – 4997	**11**
1	**2** 3017– 998	**3**	**4**	**5** 4003 – 999	**6**	**7**	**8** 2023 – 1997	**9**	**10**

Work out these calculations. Use either the 'finding the difference' method or compensation (rounding and adjusting).

a 39 134 – 11 998 = __________

b 56 416 – 27 997 = __________

c 43 263 – 19 001 = __________

d 212 376 – 19 999 = __________

e 304 663 – 47 998 = __________

f 451 007 – 113 999 = __________

g 634 313 – 458 997 = __________

h 742 193 – 580 002 = __________

Lesson 3: **Decimals that total 1 or 10**

- Know by heart one-place decimal pairs that total 1
- Find decimal pairs that total 10

Challenge 1

Use the number line to complete the number sentences. Each pair of decimals has a sum of 1.

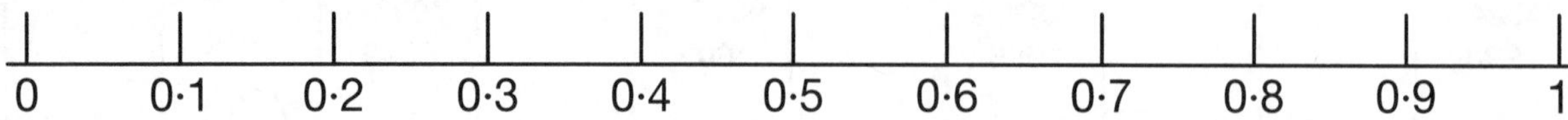

a 0·5 + ____ = 1

b ____ + 0·3 = 1

c 0·4 + ____ = 1

d 0·1 + ____ = 1

e ____ + 0·8 = 1

f 0·6 + ____ = 1

g ____ + 0·7 = 1

h 0·9 + ____ = 1

Challenge 2

1 What needs to be added to each number to give a total of 100? Write your answer in the blank card above or below the number.

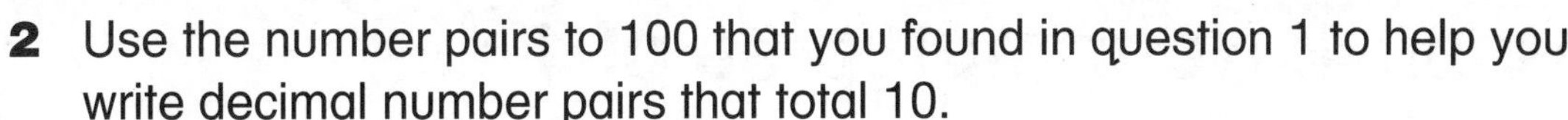

2 Use the number pairs to 100 that you found in question 1 to help you write decimal number pairs that total 10.

a 2·4 + ____ = 10 **b** 5·1 + ____ = 10

c 8·3 + ____ = 10 **d** 7·7 + ____ = 10

e 4·7 + ____ = 10 **f** 5·8 + ____ = 10

g 9·9 + ____ = 10 **h** 1·9 + ____ = 10

i 6·6 + ____ = 10 **j** 6·1 + ____ = 10

3 Write eight more decimal pairs that total 10.

a ________________ **b** ________________

c ________________ **d** ________________

e ________________ **f** ________________

g ________________ **h** ________________

Challenge **3**

Use your knowledge of number pairs that total 100 to work out pairs of numbers with 2 decimal places that together total 1.

a 0·78 + ____ = 1 **b** 0·13 + ____ = 1

c 0·94 + ____ = 1 **d** 0·57 + ____ = 1

e 0·65 + ____ = 1 **f** 0·48 + ____ = 1

g 0·26 + ____ = 1 **h** 0·31 + ____ = 1

i 0·88 + ____ = 1 **j** 0·97 + ____ = 1

k 0·02 + ____ = 1 **l** 0·09 + ____ = 1

Number

Lesson 4: **Near multiples of 1**

- Calculate the difference between near multiples of 1

You will need
- 0–9 number cards

Challenge 1

Use the number line to calculate the difference between each pair of numbers.

3·0 3·1 3·2 3·3 3·4 3·5 3·6 3·7 3·8 3·9 4·0 4·1 4·2 4·3 4·4 4·5 4·6 4·7 4·8 4·9 5·0 5·1 5·2 5·3 5·4 5·5 5·6 5·7 5·8 5·9 6·0

a 4·3 – 3·6 ________ **b** 4·2 – 3·7 ________

c 5·5 – 4·2 ________ **d** 5·3 – 3·1 ________

e 5·6 – 3·9 ________ **f** 5·1 – 3·3 ________

g 5·5 – 3·6 ________ **h** 5·4 – 3·8 ________

i 5·1 – 3·3 ________ **j** 5·7 – 3·9 ________

k 5·8 – 4·9 ________ **l** 5·2 – 4·6 ________

Challenge 2

1 Write the missing numbers in the table.

–	1·9	2·7	5·8	7·9	11·8	13·7
15·2						
17·3						
19·1						
21·4						
26·5						
29·6						

2 Describe the strategy you used to calculate the numbers missing from the table. What other strategy could you have used?

____

____

3 Shuffle the 0–9 number cards. Pick 3 cards to form a 3-digit number with 1 decimal place that is greater than 25, for example, 26·3. Write the decimal in the first box in the row and repeatedly subtract the number given. Do this for three different decimals.

a

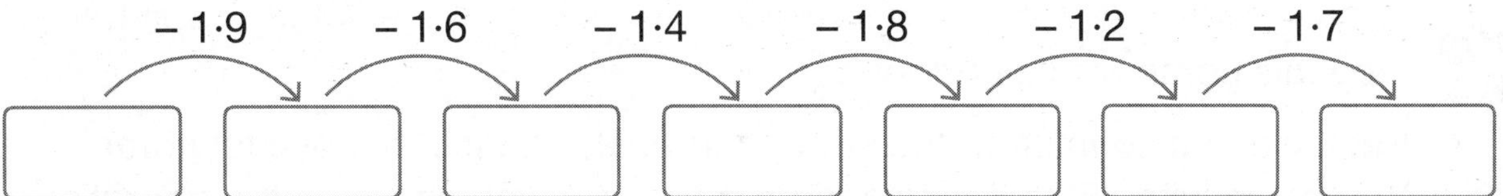

b

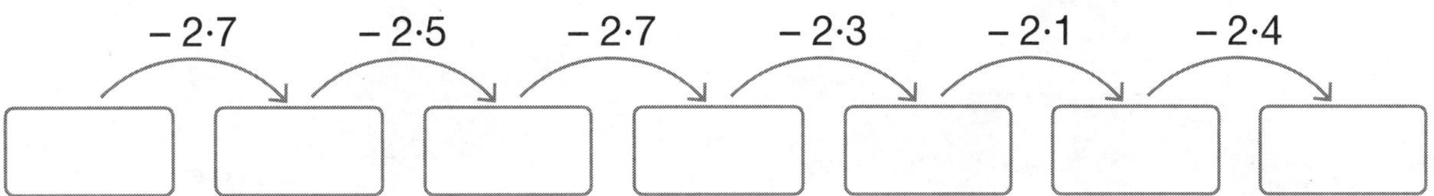

c

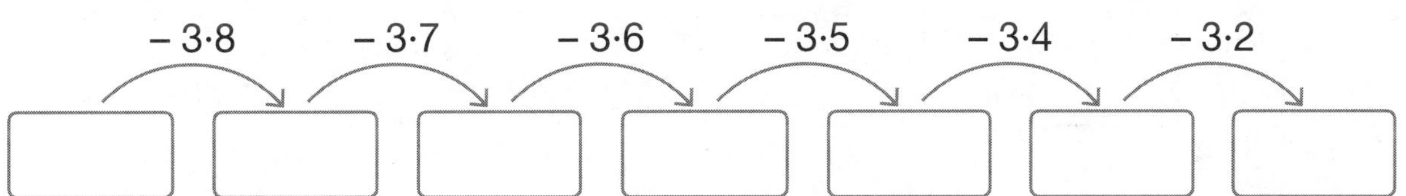

Challenge **3** Calculate the difference between each pair of numbers.

a 37·3 – 17·8 ☐ **b** 42·6 – 25·7 ☐

c 53·5 – 34·6 ☐ **d** 66·4 – 19·9 ☐

e 70·4 – 28·5 ☐ **f** 75·2 – 48·7 ☐

g 81·8 – 48·9 ☐ **h** 86·7 – 58·8 ☐

i 94·3 – 37·6 ☐ **j** 98·6 – 19·7 ☐

Number

Lesson 5: **Adding and subtracting 2- and 3-digit numbers**

- Select and use effective strategies to add and subtract pairs of 2- and 3-digit numbers

You will need
- dice
- counters
- 0–9 spinner

Play this game with a partner.

Each place a counter on the start square. Roll a dice to move forwards. You begin with 2500. If you land on a number, you carry out the operation shown (addition or subtraction). The winner is the person with the lower score at the finish.

Start 2500

– 30

– 70

– 50

– 90

– 40

+ 80

– 200

– 500

+ 300

– 240

+ 170

– 330

– 290

– 185

Finish

1 Complete each calculation. Use whichever strategy you prefer.

a	80 – 39 = ______	**b**	75 – 25 = ______	**c**	96 + 23 = ______
d	70 – 31 = ______	**e**	147 + 28 = ______	**f**	186 – 152 = ______
g	261 – 152 = ______	**h**	384 + 298 = ______	**i**	425 + 275 = ______
j	510 – 365 = ______	**k**	603 – 368 = ______	**l**	844 – 323 = ______
m	745 + 85 = ______	**n**	923 – 297 = ______	**o**	998 + 798 = ______

2 Link each subtraction to its answer. Clue: Some of the problems have the same answer.

561 – 536

807 – 649

87 – 59

96 – 68

37 + 198

255 + 179

733 – 498

682 – 524

75 – 50

473 – 445

434 235 28 25 158

Challenge 3 Choose a number from the cards below and write it in the answer space of an addition calculation. Spin a 0–9 spinner and write the number in the first space of the calculation. Work out the missing number.

a ______ + ______ = ☐ **b** ______ + ______ = ☐

c ______ + ______ = ☐ **d** ______ + ______ = ☐

e ______ + ______ = ☐ **f** ______ + ______ = ☐

g ______ + ______ = ☐ **h** ______ + ______ = ☐

i ______ + ______ = ☐ **j** ______ + ______ = ☐

Lesson 6: **Adding more than two numbers**

- Use a written method to find the total of three or more 2- or 3-digit numbers

1 Use a mental or written method to solve each addition problem. Show your working in the box.

a 23 + 42 + 31 = ☐

b 65 + 22 + 11 = ☐

c 24 + 33 + 42 = ☐

d 41 + 26 + 33 = ☐

Challenge 2

1 Use a mental or written method to work out these calculations. The sum of the calculation to the left becomes the first number to add in the set of figures to the right.

a 56 + 33 + 22 → ☐ + 241 + 132 → ☐ + 356 + 127 = ☐

b 46 + 27 + 19 + 22 → ☐ + 138 + 109 + 147 →

☐ + 202 + 113 + 163 = ☐

2 Use the formal written method to work out the answers to these word problems. Show your working in the box.

a Alex bought 4 packets of stickers. The packets contain 346, 482, 517 and 358 stickers. How many stickers does Alex have in total?

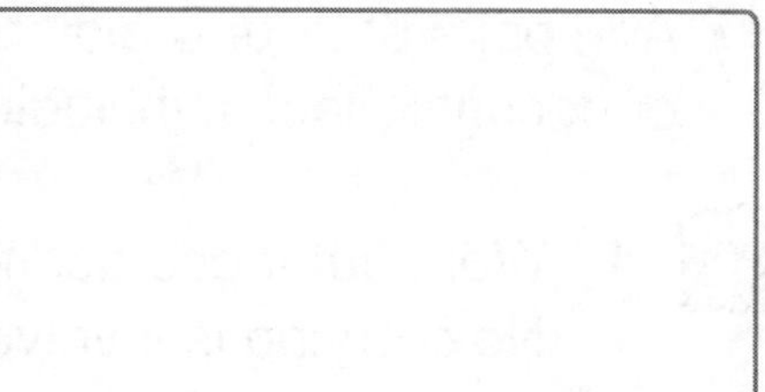

____

b A running track is divided into four sections, 682 m, 437 m, 594 m and 729 m. What is the total length of the track?

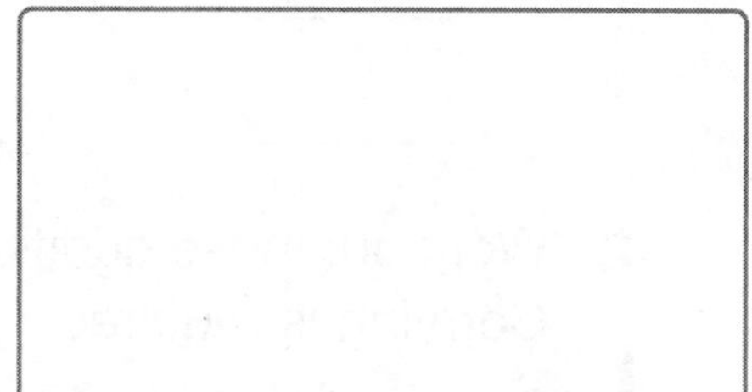

____

c Four containers of juice are poured into a larger container. The containers hold 509 ml, 893 ml, 654 ml and 786 ml. What is the combined volume in the larger container?

____

Challenge 3 Use the numbers on the stars to write three addition calculations, each with 5 numbers. Work out the answer to each. Show your working out.

Number

Lesson 7: **Adding decimals**

- Add pairs of 3- or 4-digit numbers, with the same number of decimal places, including amounts of money

1 Work out these addition calculations using the formal written method. No carrying is involved.

a 2·4 + 4·2 = ______

b 43·6 + 55·3 = ______

c 3·65 + 2·14 = ______

d 37·76 + 42·13 = ______

2 Work out these addition calculations using the formal written method. Carrying is required.

a 4·8 + 3·7 = ______

b 35·3 + 18·4 = ______

c 6·28 + 5·36 = ______

d 43·47 + 53·82 = ______

1 Work out these calculations using the formal written method. Write an estimate for each calculation before you work it out. Write your working in the box.

a 6·6 + 7·8 **b** 45·4 + 82·7 **c** 7·84 + 8·95 **d** 48·69 + 28·29

Estimate:

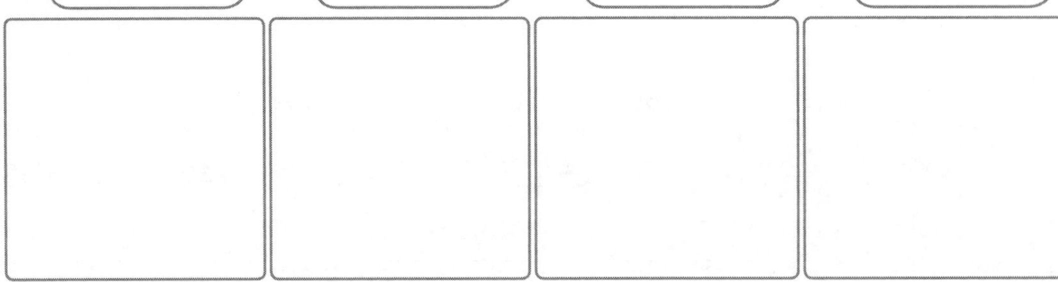

e 9·3 + 9·8 **f** 65·6 + 28·7 **g** 7·42 + 8·79 **h** 58·39 + 67·84

Estimate:

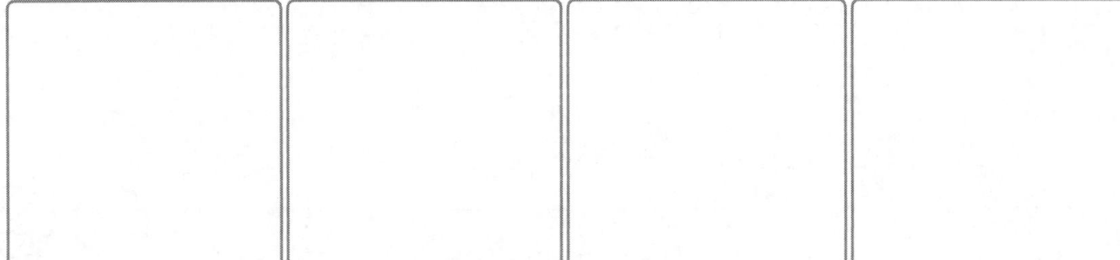

2 Use the formal written method to work out each calculation. Write the letter for each answer in the box below the question to reveal the secret phrase.

46·8 + 37·1	25·74 + 39·26	7·38 + 5·47	5·86 + 8·39	6·3 + 2·8	63·29 + 28·97	8·88 + 8·18

9·6 + 7·7	55·67 + 48·28	31·66 + 47·93	3·29 + 4·66	4·67 + 6·93	7·37 + 9·79

12·85	92·26	79·59	83·9	11·6	9·1	103·95	65	7·95	17·06	14·25	17·16	17·3
I	E	T	W	O	T	E	R	H	N	T	D	M

Challenge 3

1 All the prices in a shop have risen by $37.29. Use the formal written method to calculate the new prices.

______ ______ ______ ______ ______

2 In another shop, all the prices have risen by $58.78. Use the formal written method to calculate the new prices.

______ ______ ______ ______ ______

Lesson 8: **Subtracting decimals**

- Subtract pairs of 3- or 4-digit numbers, with the same number of decimal places, including amounts of money

Challenge 1

1 Use the formal written method to work out these subtraction calculations. No renaming is involved.

a $\begin{array}{r} 8 \cdot 4 \\ -\ 4 \cdot 2 \\ \hline \end{array}$ **b** $\begin{array}{r} 73 \cdot 6 \\ -\ 51 \cdot 3 \\ \hline \end{array}$ **c** $\begin{array}{r} 3 \cdot 65 \\ -\ 2 \cdot 14 \\ \hline \end{array}$ **d** $\begin{array}{r} 97 \cdot 76 \\ -\ 42 \cdot 13 \\ \hline \end{array}$

2 Use the formal written method to work out these subtraction calculations. Renaming is required.

a $\begin{array}{r} 6 \cdot 5 \\ -\ 2 \cdot 9 \\ \hline \end{array}$ **b** $\begin{array}{r} 82 \cdot 7 \\ -\ 45 \cdot 4 \\ \hline \end{array}$ **c** $\begin{array}{r} 7 \cdot 55 \\ -\ 3 \cdot 39 \\ \hline \end{array}$ **d** $\begin{array}{r} 59 \cdot 65 \\ -\ 16 \cdot 81 \\ \hline \end{array}$

Challenge 2

1 Use the formal written method to work out these subtraction calculations. Write an estimate for each calculation before you work it out. Remember to use the inverse operation to check your answer to a calculation. Write your working in the box.

a 9·4 – 6·8 **b** 56·4 – 23·7 **c** 8·67 – 3·95 **d** 92·96 – 48·29

Estimate:

e 8·3 – 5·7 **f** 37·4 – 25·8 **g** 8·36 – 4·29 **h** 33·61 – 28·17

Estimate:

2 Using the formal written method to work out each calculation. Write the letter for each answer in the box below the question to reveal the secret phrase.

64·4 – 27·2	34·26 – 18·19	47·37 – 28·29	7·63 – 2·91	8·3 – 5·5	78·63 – 59·27	9·39 – 6·88

8·3 – 4·6	86·38 – 57·27	73·08 – 52·65	8·34 – 4·18	8·67 – 4·96	7·33 – 2·77

19·08	19·36	3·7	4·72	20·43	37·2	3·71	2·51	16·07	4·16	29·11	4·56	2·8
C	A	P	I	A	D	E	L	E	C	L	S	M

Challenge 3

1 The prices in a shop have fallen by $19.78. Use the formal written method to calculate the new prices.

$53.52 $94.38 $76.47 $81.08 $90.03

________ ________ ________ ________ ________

2 The prices in another shop have fallen by $33.34. Use the formal written method to calculate the new prices.

$75.12 $84.23 $91.13 $90.05

________ ________ ________ ________ ________

Lesson 1: **Adding and subtracting decimals mentally**

- Use a range of strategies to add and subtract decimals mentally

Add and subtract the decimals mentally.

a 3·3 + 3·2 = ____________ **b** 4·6 + 2·2 = ____________

c 3·4 + 2·4 = ____________ **d** 5·7 + 3·2 = ____________

e 7·6 + 2·3 = ____________ **f** 8·1 + 1·6 = ____________

g 4·5 + 5·5 = ____________ **h** 7·8 + 1·2 = ____________

i 6·3 – 4·2 = ____________ **j** 5·7 – 3·6 = ____________

k 8·9 – 5·7 = ____________ **l** 6·3 – 4·1 = ____________

m 9.7 – 8·2 = ____________ **n** 8·8 – 7·7 = ____________

o 7.5 – 4·5 = ____________ **p** 9·3 – 8·3 = ____________

1 Add and subtract the decimals mentally.

a 7·3 + 11·9 = ____________ **b** 23·6 + 24·5 = ____________

c 48·7 + 21·5 = ____________ **d** 20·8 + 21·4 = ____________

e 33·8 + 45·5 = ____________ **f** 46·7 + 45·7 = ____________

g 39·8 + 46·7 = ____________ **h** 73·9 + 22·9 = ____________

i 9·2 – 6·8 = ____________ **j** 27·3 – 9·9 = ____________

k 48·6 – 19·8 = ____________ **l** 56·5 – 17·9 = ____________

m 31·4 – 17·7 = ____________ **n** 74·2 – 25·4 = ____________

o 81·3 – 19·5 = ____________ **p** 91·1 – 37·3 = ____________

2 a Complete the addition pyramids. Each number in the pyramid is the sum of the numbers in the two bricks directly below it.

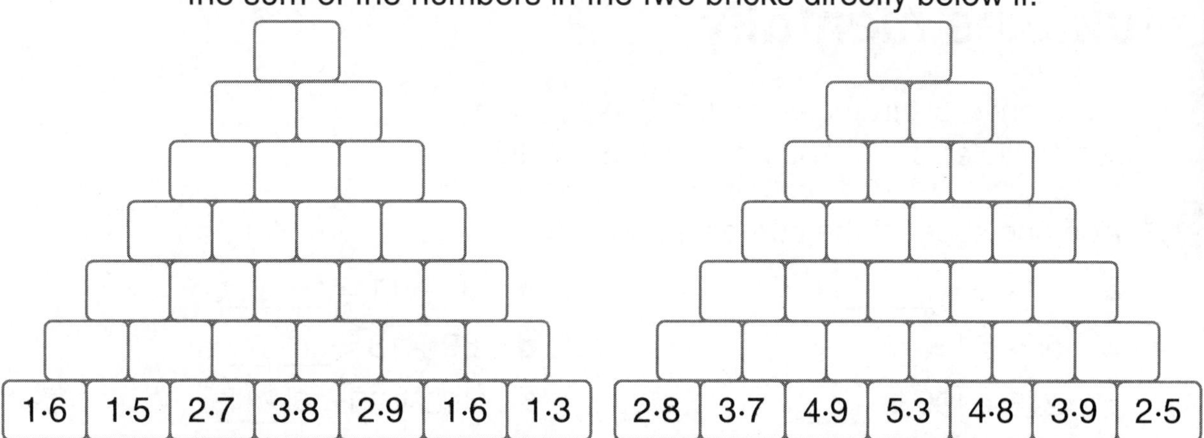

b Write the missing numbers in these addition pyramids.

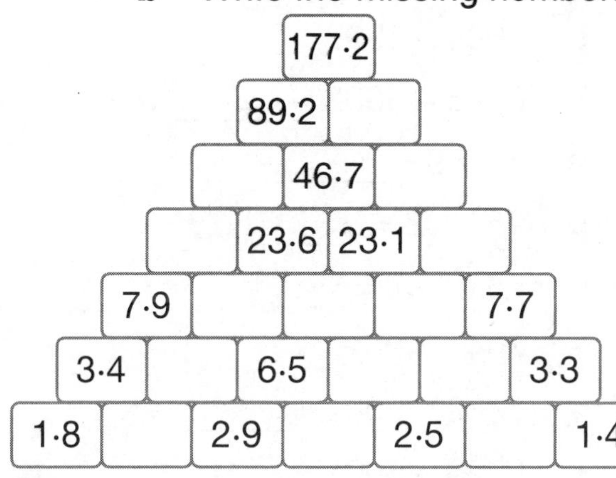

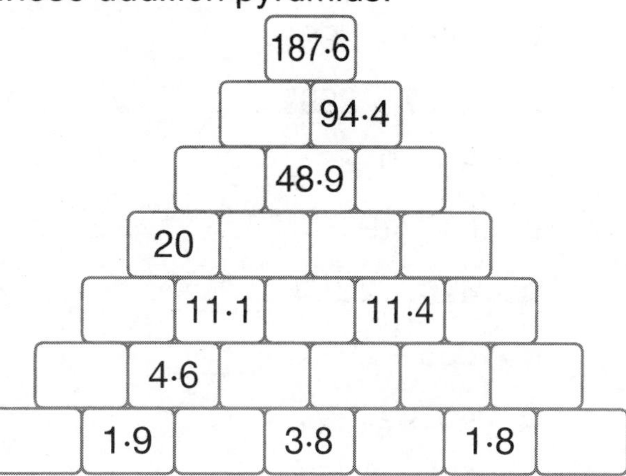

Challenge 3 Fill in the missing numbers.

a 8·3 + ______ = 22·2

b ______ + 14·8 = 41·4

c 57·7 + ______ = 86·3

d ______ + 33·5 = 53·3

e 43·8 + ______ = 89·5

f ______ + 25·8 = 82·5

g 59·9 + ______ = 79·8

h ______ + 16·7 = 81·6

i 29·2 – ______ = 12·4

j ______ – 29·9 = 19·4

k 87·6 – ______ = 68·8

l ______ – 28·9 = 50·6

m 58·4 – ______ = 38·7

n ______ – 35·4 = 28·8

o 91·3 – ______ = 41·8

p ______ – 29·3 = 38·8

Number

Lesson 2: **Adding and subtracting near multiples mentally**

- Use a range of strategies to add and subtract near multiples of 10, 100 and 1000 mentally

Challenge 1

Add and subtract the numbers mentally.

a 18 + 9 = ______ **b** 37 + 11 = ______

c 55 + 21 = ______ **d** 68 + 18 = ______

e 213 + 199 = ______ **f** 456 + 99 = ______

g 612 + 201 = ______ **h** 737 + 198 = ______

i 1453 + 999 = ______ **j** 2684 + 1999 = ______

k 4367 + 2999 = ______ **l** 6626 + 3002 = ______

m 83 – 9 = ______ **n** 72 – 9 = ______

o 64 – 19 = ______ **p** 95 – 22 = ______

q 424 – 201 = ______ **r** 682 – 99 = ______

s 836 – 299 = ______ **t** 704 – 498 = ______

u 4534 – 999 = ______ **v** 7886 – 2002 = ______

w 8033 – 3999 = ______ **x** 9923 – 6001 = ______

Challenge 2

1 Fill in the missing numbers by adding and subtracting mentally.

a

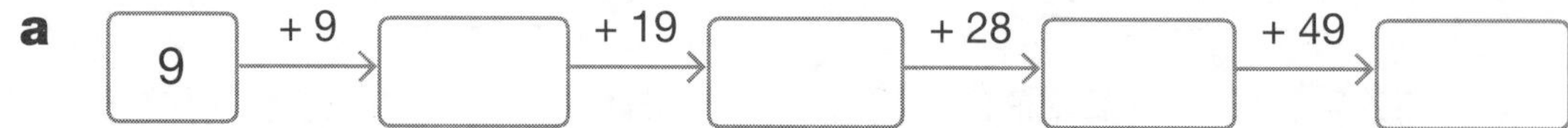

b 314 → – 9 → ☐ → – 28 → ☐ → – 39 → ☐ → – 58 → ☐

c 76 → + 299 → ☐ → + 398 → ☐ → + 298 → ☐ → + 197 → ☐

d 996 → – 99 → ☐ → – 297 → ☐ → – 98 → ☐ → – 199 → ☐

e 23 → + 999 → ☐ → + 2998 → ☐ → + 1999 → ☐ → + 997 → ☐

f

2 Create and solve as many addition and subtraction problems as you can, by choosing different pairs of cards.

7467  499 6997 4002 32 846 95 3482 1999

754 27 5001 73 297 22 302 8223 198

Challenge 3 Fill in the missing numbers.

a 39 →(+ ____) 68 →(+ ____) 97 →(+ ____) 132 →(+ ____) 179

b 356 →(+ ____) 317 →(+ ____) 278 →(+ ____) 219 →(+ ____) 156

c 439 →(+ ____) 528 →(+ ____) 577 →(+ ____) 661 →(+ ____) 749

d 886 →(+ ____) 827 →(+ ____) 768 →(+ ____) 729 →(+ ____) 636

e 3789 →(+ ____) 4328 →(+ ____) 4777 →(+ ____) 6212 →(+ ____) 7899

f 9876 →(+ ____) 8227 →(+ ____) 7438 →(+ ____) 5229 →(+ ____) 3016

Lesson 3: **Adding more than two numbers**

- Use a written method to find the total of more than two numbers

You will need
- dice

Challenge 1

1 Use the formal written method to work out these calculations.

a
```
  44
  36
  23
+ 33
----
```

b
```
  28
  18
  39
+ 41
----
```

c
```
  14
  28
  65
+ 55
----
```

d
```
  77
  77
  26
+ 46
----
```

e
```
  38
  28
  48
  34
+ 46
----
```

f
```
  23
  17
  43
  27
+ 55
----
```

g
```
  36
  24
  27
  47
+ 66
----
```

h
```
  85
  85
  93
  93
+ 79
----
```

Challenge 2

1 Use the formal written method to add each set of numbers. Arrange the numbers in the columns to make mental addition as easy as possible.

a 347, 284, 37, 246, 428 +

b 229, 87, 572, 353, 349 +

c 84, 561, 606, 749, 46 +

2 Work out the answers to these word problems using the formal written method. Show your working in the box next to each question.

a Rufus bought items in five different shops, spending \$527, \$648, \$438, \$93 and \$236. How much did he spend in total?

b A lorry delivers five loads of sand to a construction site. The masses of the loads are 746 kg, 5 kg, 857 kg, 654 kg and 899 kg. How much sand was delivered in total?

c The times taken for five competitors to complete a race were 99 min, 138 min, 266 min, 231 min, 194 min. How much time did the five competitors spend running altogether?

Challenge **3** Roll the dice to create 20 three-digit numbers and record them in the box below. You are going to find the sum of all the numbers. Do this by adding 4 sets of 5 numbers together using column addition. Choose the numbers you want in each set to make mental addition of the columns as easy as possible.

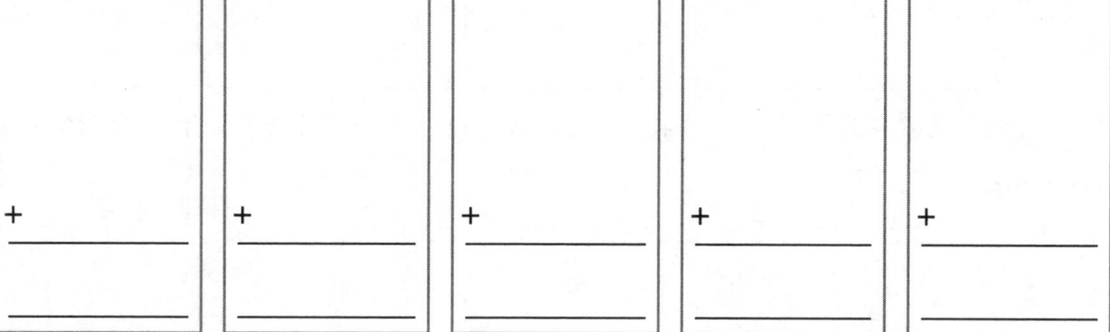

Total of the 20 numbers is

Number

Lesson 4: **Adding and subtracting decimals**

- Add and subtract pairs of 3- or 4-digit numbers, with the same number of decimal places, including amounts of money

Challenge 1

1 Use the formal written method to work out these addition calculations.

a 3·7 + 3·8 = ______ **b** 25·8 + 42·4 = ______ **c** 6·83 + 2·75 = ______ **d** 64·94 + 53·53 = ______

2 Use the formal written method to work out these subtraction calculations.

a 8·5 − 2·6 = ______ **b** 63·8 − 38·5 = ______ **c** 9·33 − 5·27 = ______ **d** 72·38 − 57·12 = ______

Challenge 2

1 Write an estimate for each calculation before you work it out. Write your working in the box. If needed, put in zeros so the numbers have the same number of digits.

a 9·8 + 5·9 **b** 37·7 + 92·8 **c** 6·46 + 7·8 **d** 77·28 + 58·37

Estimate:

e 8·4 − 5·7 **f** 49.3 − 26·8 **g** 7·48 − 3·87 **h** 94·94 − 68·68

Estimate:

2 Work out these money calculations.

a $4.80 + $3.90 = ______

b $67.80 + $72.70 = ______

c $6.98 + $7.65 = ______

d $72.86 + $75.87 = ______

e $7.40 + $3.60 = ______

f $86.10 + $33.80 = ______

g $8.22 + $3.55 = ______

h $71.94 + $27.38 = ______

A shop increases its prices by $39.48 one week, then decreases them by $61.61 the following week. Write the new price labels below the original ones and show your working.

a 

b 

c 

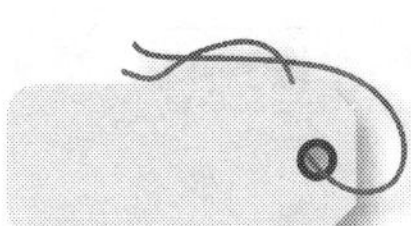

d 

e 

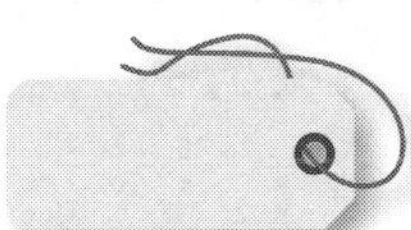

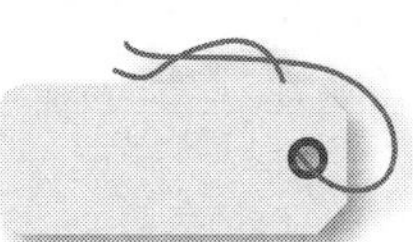

Lesson 1: Multiples

- Recognise the multiples of 6, 7, 8 and 9
- Know whether a number is divisible by 2, 5, 10 and 100 by applying a test

Challenge 1

a Which of these numbers are divisible by 5? Circle them.

91 45 70 111 155 230 336 572 680 423 795 1253

b Which of these numbers are divisible by 10? Circle them.

180 75 93 270 155 410 332 565 700 1498 2920 3825

c Which of these numbers are divisible by 100? Circle them.

490 320 600 850 905 1100 2400 5050 6000 4320 8500

Challenge 2

1 Write the numbers in the correct places in the Venn diagram.

6

788

11

725

5

9

23

930

2485

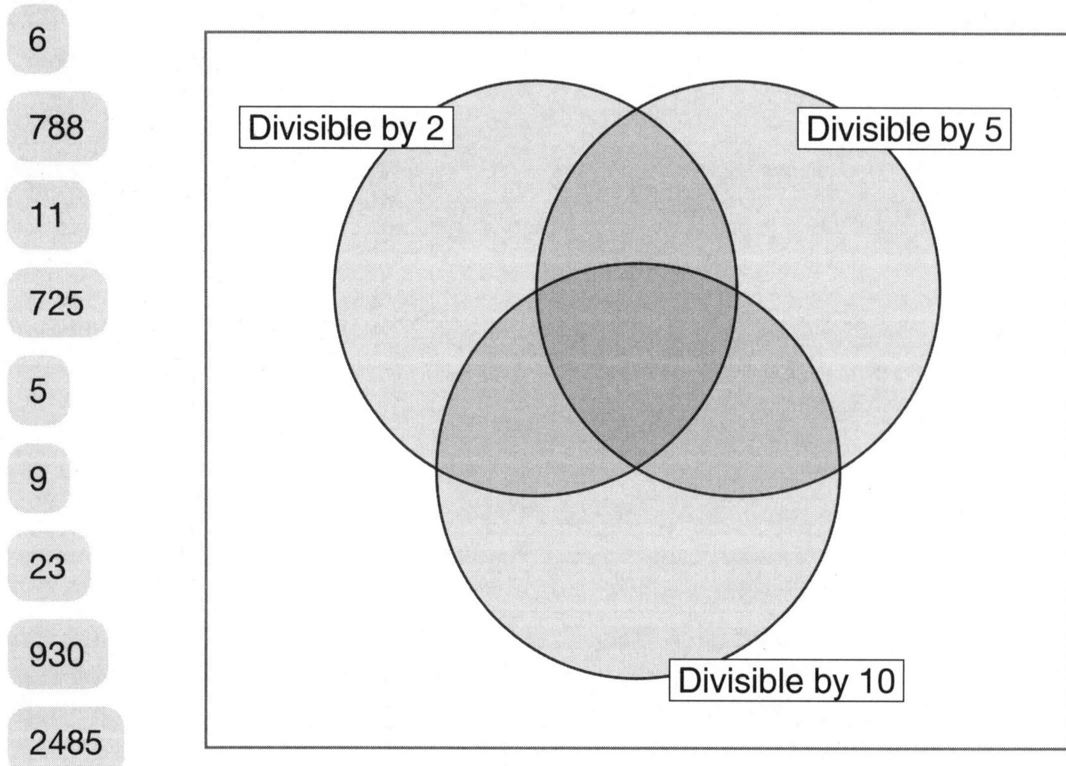

Explain why there are no numbers in the region that represents numbers divisible by 10 only. ______________________________

2 Use the numbers in the cloud to complete the table.
A number may appear in the table more than once.
Which is the only number to appear in the table three times? ☐

28 6 21 14 30 81 64 18 35 32 27 54
49 16 70 8 48 60 72 63
12 40 80 45 36 24 9 56 42 7

	80 or less but greater than 59	40 or less but greater than 19	60 or less but greater than 39	100 or less but greater than 79	20 or less
Multiple of 6					
Multiple of 7					
Multiple of 8					
Multiple of 9					

Challenge 3 Complete the diagram for the numbers from 1 to 200.

	Multiple of 6	**Multiple of 7**
Multiple of 8		
Multiple of 9		

Which of the numbers from 1 to 200 would be members of the set of:

a multiples of 6, 7 and 8? ____________________

b multiples of 6, 7 and 9? ____________________

Number

Lesson 2: **Factors**

- Find factors of 2-digit numbers

a Write a multiplication fact and a division fact for each multiple of 3.

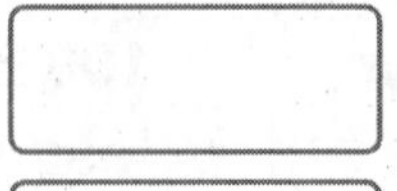
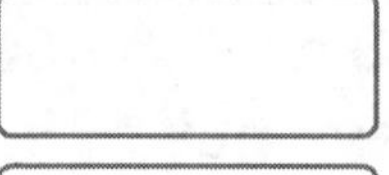
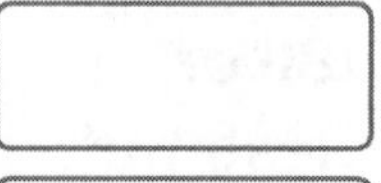

b Write a multiplication fact and a division fact for each multiple of 8.

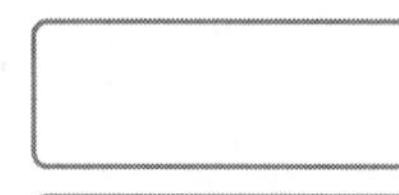
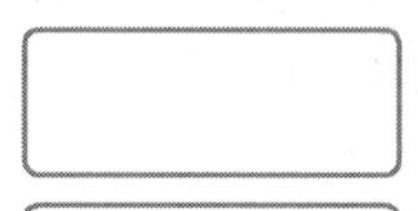
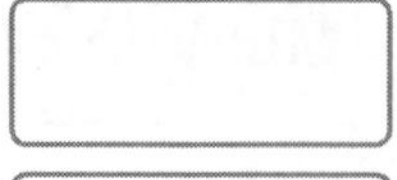

Challenge 2

1 For each problem, find the missing factor and write it in the box.

a ☐ × 4 = 16 **b** 3 × ☐ = 18 **c** ☐ × 7 = 21

d 2 × ☐ = 16 **e** ☐ × 2 = 20 **f** 5 × ☐ = 30

g ☐ × 6 = 24 **h** 9 × ☐ = 27 **i** ☐ × 4 = 40

j ☐ × 3 = 15 **k** 4 × ☐ = 12 **l** ☐ × 8 = 80

m ☐ × 9 = 54 **n** 6 × ☐ = 36 **o** 7 × ☐ = 63

2 Write all the factor pairs for each number.
The first one has been done for you.

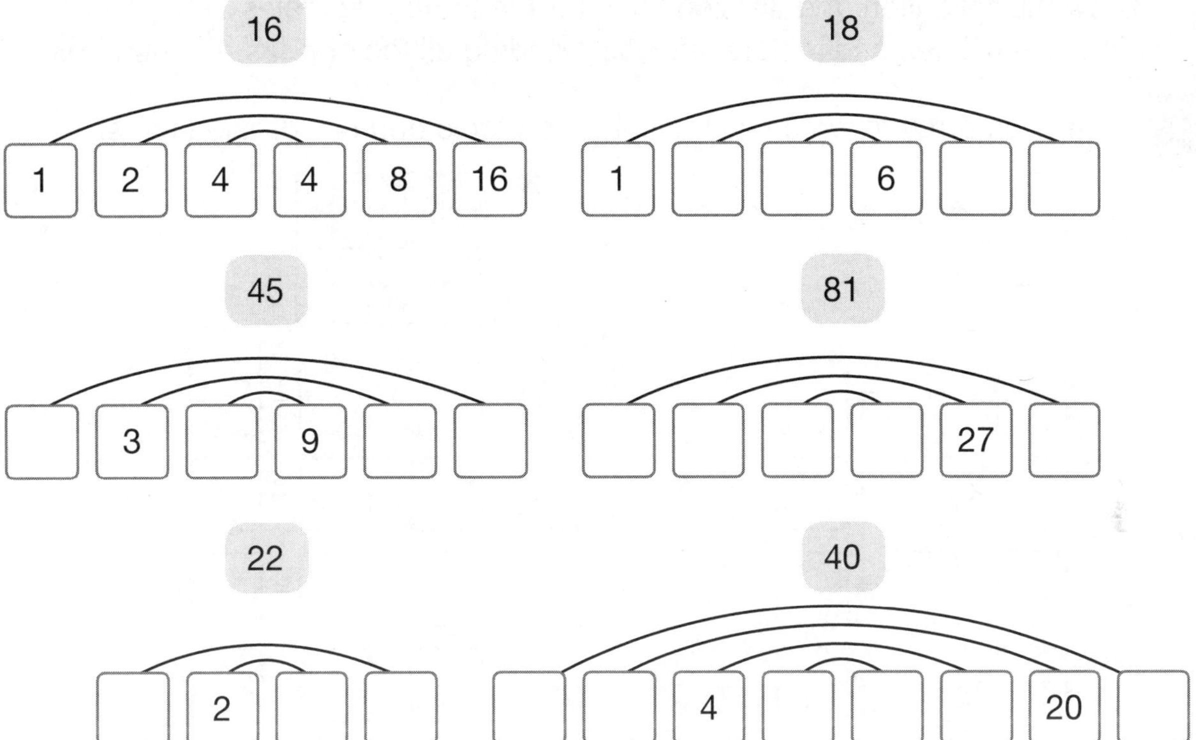

Challenge 3 Write the factors of the numbers in the Venn diagram. Write the factors shared by both numbers in the overlapping space.

a

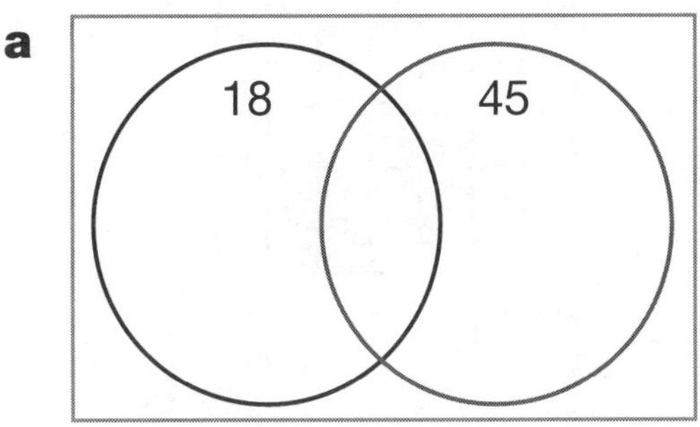

b

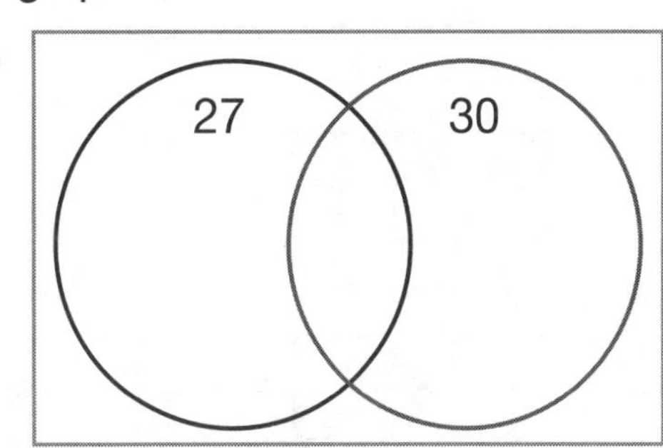

c

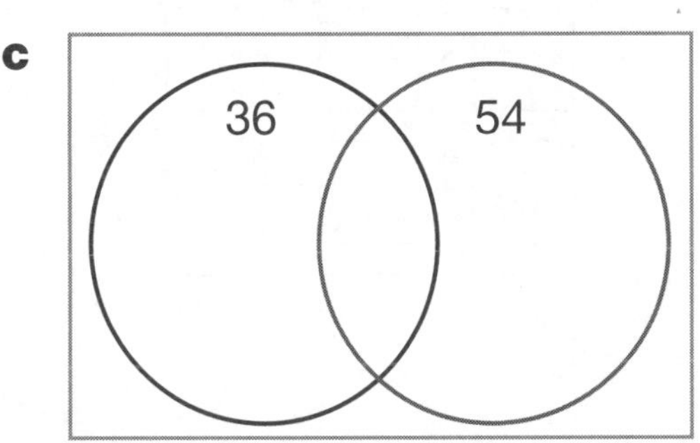

d

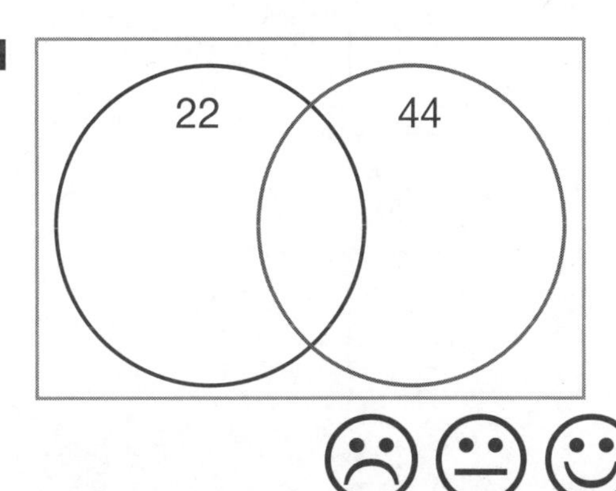

Number

Lesson 3: **Multiples and factors**

- Know multiplication and division facts for the 2× to 10× tables
- Identify multiples and factors, including finding all factor pairs of a number

Challenge 1

Use each array to write two multiplication facts and two division facts.

a

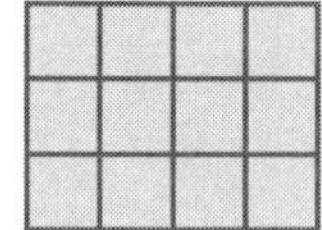

□ × □ = □

□ × □ = □

□ ÷ □ = □

□ ÷ □ = □

b

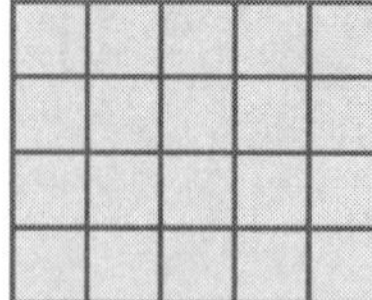

□ × □ = □

□ × □ = □

□ ÷ □ = □

□ ÷ □ = □

c

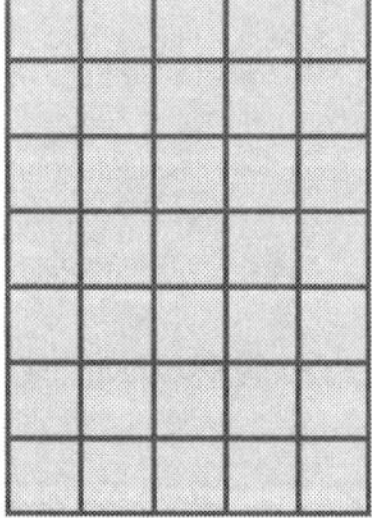

□ × □ = □

□ × □ = □

□ ÷ □ = □

□ ÷ □ = □

d

□ × □ = □

□ × □ = □

□ ÷ □ = □

□ ÷ □ = □

1 Draw arrays to help you find all the factor pairs of each number. Your teacher will give you some squared paper.

a 32 ______________________________

b 28 ______________________________

c 30 ______________________________

2 Circle the numbers that are **not** factors of the given number.

a **34** 1, 2, 6, 13, 17, 34

b **46** 1, 2, 4, 10, 12, 23, 46

c **64** 1, 2, 4, 8, 16, 18, 32, 64

d **72** 1, 2, 3, 4, 6, 7, 8, 9, 12, 16, 18, 24, 36, 72

How many factor pairs does each number have? Write them in the boxes, or draw a factor rainbow for each.

a 68 ☐

b 54 ☐

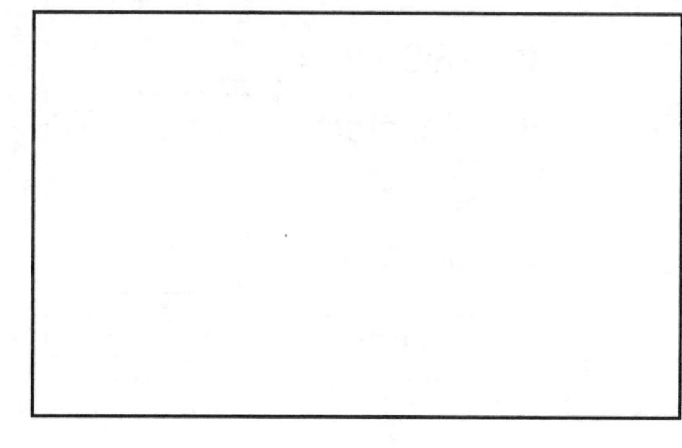

c 84 ☐

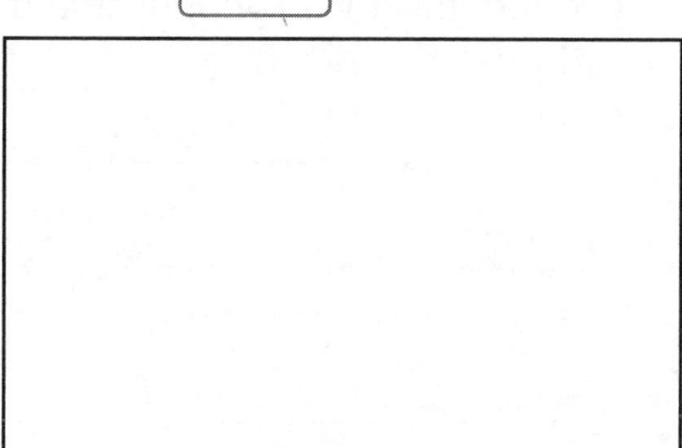

d 88 ☐

Number

Lesson 4: **Multiplying a 3-digit number by a single-digit number (1)**

- Multiply a 3-digit number by a single-digit number

Challenge 1

Partition each number into hundreds, tens and units.

a 427 = ☐ + ☐ + ☐ **b** 249 = ☐ + ☐ + ☐

c 508 = ☐ + ☐ + ☐ **d** 726 = ☐ + ☐ + ☐

e 915 = ☐ + ☐ + ☐ **f** 838 = ☐ + ☐ + ☐

Challenge 2

1 For each calculation, estimate first, then use partitioning to work out the answer. Show your working. Check your answer with your estimate.

a 437 × 2 = ______
Estimate: ☐

b 698 × 4 = ______
Estimate: ☐

c 808 × 6 = ______
Estimate: ☐

2 For each calculation, estimate first, then use the grid to work out the answer. Show your working. Check your answer with your estimate.

a 197 × 3 = ______
Estimate: ☐

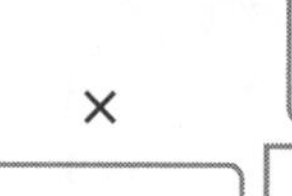
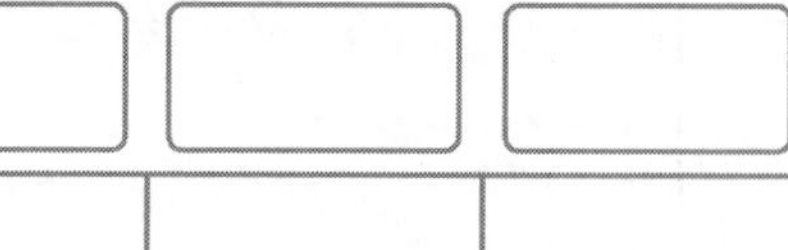

b 839 × 8 = ______
Estimate: ☐

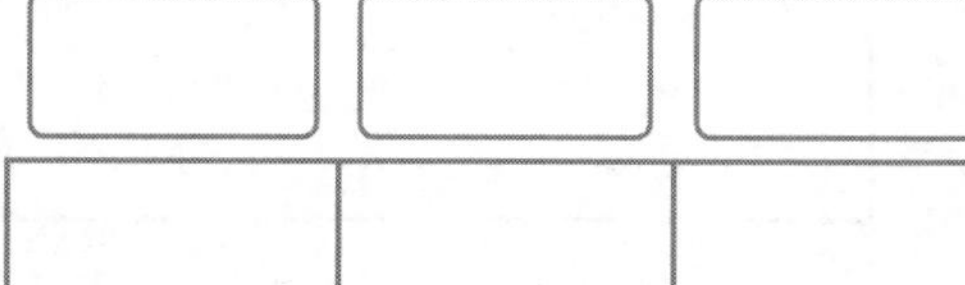

Challenge 3

For each calculation, estimate first, then use the expanded written method to work out the answer. Show your working. Check your answer with your estimate.

a 326 × 3 =

Estimate:

×

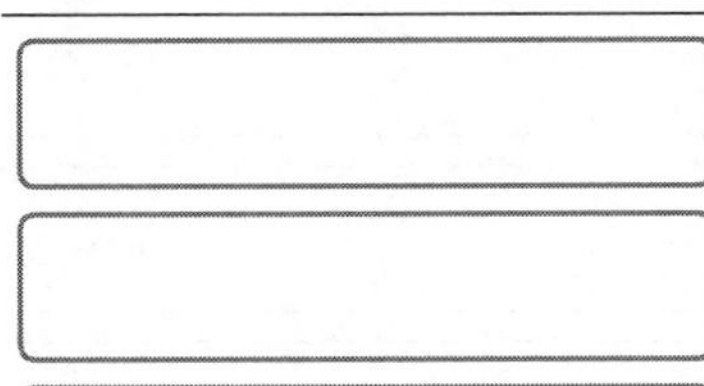

b 574 × 5 =

Estimate:

×

c 781 × 7 =

Estimate:

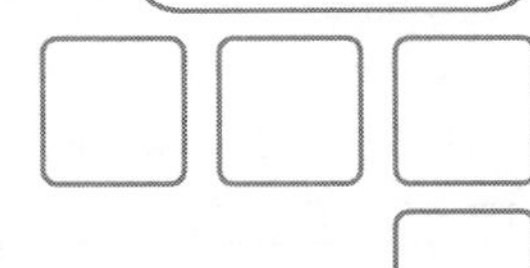

×

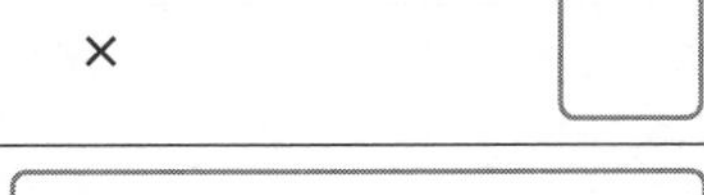

d 908 × 8 =

Estimate:

×

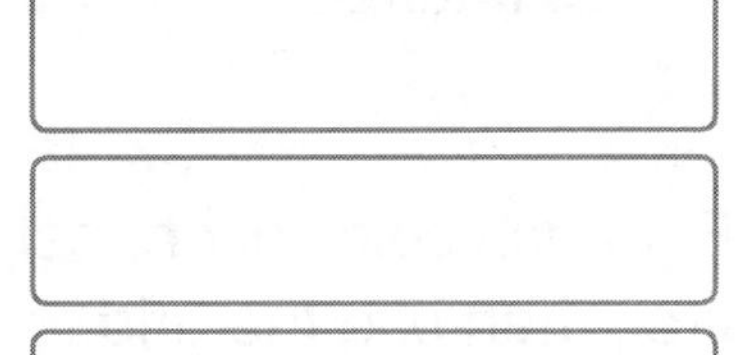

Number

Lesson 5: **Multiplying a 2-digit number by a 2-digit number (1)**

- Multiply a 2-digit number by a 2-digit number

For each calculation, estimate first, then use partitioning to work out the answer. The first one has been completed for you.

a 23 × 3 = (20 × 3) + (3 × 3) = 60 + 9 = 69

b 34 × 4 =

c 39 × 3 =

d 29 × 6 =

1 For each calculation, estimate first, then use partitioning to work out the answer. Show your working. Check your answer against your estimate.

a 29 × 23 =

Estimate:

b 49 × 34 =

Estimate:

c 63 × 46 =

Estimate:

2 For each calculation, estimate first, then use the grid to work out the answer. Show your working. Check your answer against your estimate.

a 57 × 48 = ________

Estimate:

×			

b 66 × 53 = ______

Estimate:

×

c 89 × 69 = ______

Estimate:

×

Challenge 3

Estimate first, then use the expanded written method to work out the answer. Show your working. Check your answer against your estimate.

a 26 × 29 =

Estimate:

×

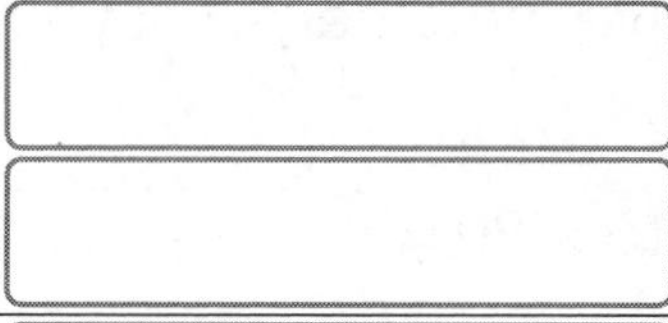

b 59 × 37 =

Estimate:

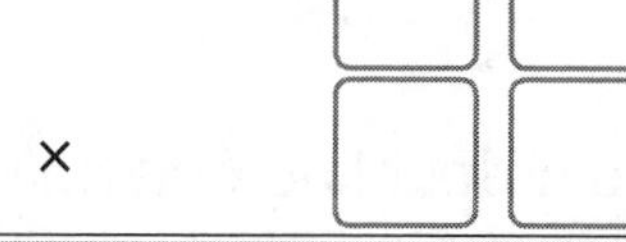

×

c 63 × 67 =

Estimate:

×

d 93 × 98 =

Estimate:

×

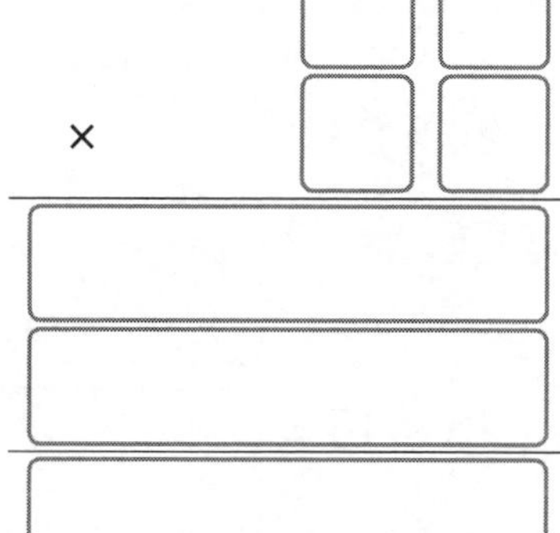

Lesson 6: **Multiplying a 2-digit number by a 2-digit number (2)**

- Use a halving and doubling strategy to multiply a 2-digit number by a 2-digit number

Halve and double the numbers in the tables.

Halved	Number	Doubled
	24	
	16	
	36	
	22	
	44	
	38	
	26	

Halved	Number	Doubled
	18	
	56	
	32	
	46	
	28	
	34	
	48	

Challenge 2

1 Use a doubling and halving strategy to find the answers to these calculations. Double one number and halve the other, until you get a multiplication that's easier to solve.

a 36 × 16 =

b 15 × 80 =

c 18 × 24 =

d 40 × 32 =

e 24 × 28 =

f 46 × 24 =

g 25 × 16 =

h 18 × 40 =

2 Play a game with a partner.

- Decide whether to play as Player 1 or Player 2.
- Take turns to choose two numbers from the middle of the board. Multiply them, using a doubling and halving strategy.
- If the answer is on your side of the board, cross it off. However, if the answer is on your partner's side of the board, they can cross it off.
- The first player to cross out all of their numbers is the winner.

Player 1

1900	896	504
306	1152	420
221	950	408
576	520	476

36	26	13	28
40	16	34	15
17	25	50	38
24	32	56	18

Player 2

480	728	800
1040	578	672
1064	2800	1000
640	1904	234

Challenge **3** Use doubling and halving to multiply a decimal and a whole number.

a 16 × 2·5 = 

b 22 × 2·5 = 

c 8 × 4·5 = 

d 12 × 3·5 = 

e 44 × 7·5 = 

f 36 × 7·5 = 

Lesson 7: **Dividing a 3-digit number by a single-digit number (1)**

- Use mental strategies to divide a 3-digit number by a single-digit number

Use known division facts to solve these problems.

1 a $6 \div 2 =$ ☐ **b** $60 \div 2 =$ ☐ **c** $600 \div 2 =$ ☐

2 a $12 \div 3 =$ ☐ **b** $120 \div 3 =$ ☐ **c** $1200 \div 3 =$ ☐

3 a $28 \div 7 =$ ☐ **b** $280 \div 7 =$ ☐ **c** $2800 \div 7 =$ ☐

4 a $40 \div 8 =$ ☐ **b** $400 \div 8 =$ ☐ **c** $4000 \div 8 =$ ☐

1 Use known number facts or partitioning to complete each division.

a $250 \div 5 =$ ☐ **b** $306 \div 3 =$ ☐ **c** $260 \div 2 =$ ☐

d $780 \div 6 =$ ☐ **e** $108 \div 4 =$ ☐ **f** $246 \div 3 =$ ☐

g $357 \div 7 =$ ☐ **h** $416 \div 8 =$ ☐ **i** $558 \div 9 =$ ☐

j $646 \div 2 =$ ☐ **k** $472 \div 4 =$ ☐ **l** $498 \div 6 =$ ☐

2 Use the mental partitioning method of division to work out each calculation. Show your working, then write the letter for each answer in the box below the question to reveal the secret phrase.

252 ÷ 3	396 ÷ 4	423 ÷ 9	144 ÷ 6	665 ÷ 7	552 ÷ 8

265 ÷ 5	154 ÷ 2	492 ÷ 6	518 ÷ 7	316 ÷ 4	639 ÷ 9	249 ÷ 3	792 ÷ 8

99	79	24	83	77	84	69	71	47	53	74	82	95	99
E	T	T	G	T	M	L	E	N	S	A	R	A	Y

Challenge 3 Some of the inputs and outputs for each function machine are missing. Find the missing numbers.

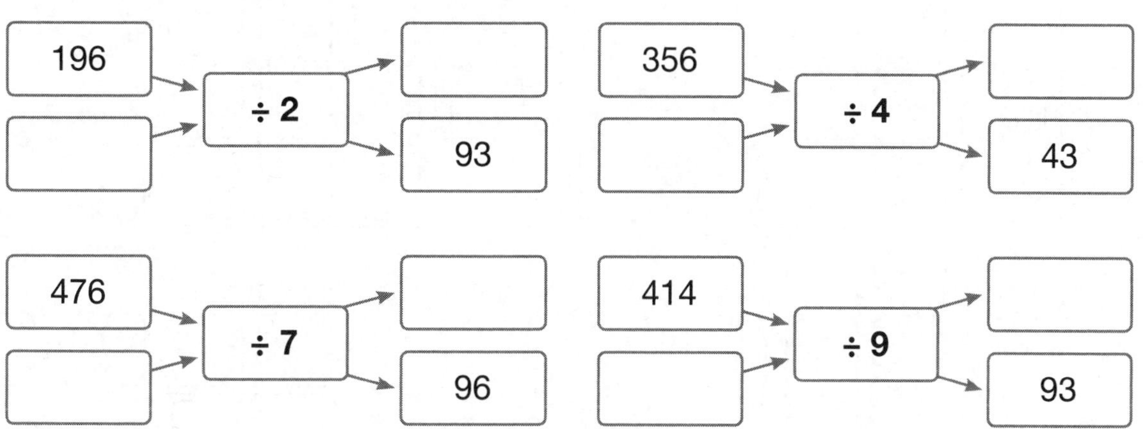

Number

Lesson 8: **Dividing a 3-digit number by a single-digit number (2)**

- Use mental and written strategies to divide a 3-digit number by a single-digit number

1 Write the multiples of 8 from 8 to 80. Use your list to write the multiple of 8 that comes before each number.

a ☐ 27 **b** ☐ 22 **c** ☐ 77

d ☐ 51 **e** ☐ 69 **f** ☐ 35

1 Estimate first, then use the expanded written method of division to work out the answer to each calculation. Remember to use multiplication to check the results of the division. There is no remainder in the answer.

a 258 ÷ 6 **b** 539 ÷ 7 =

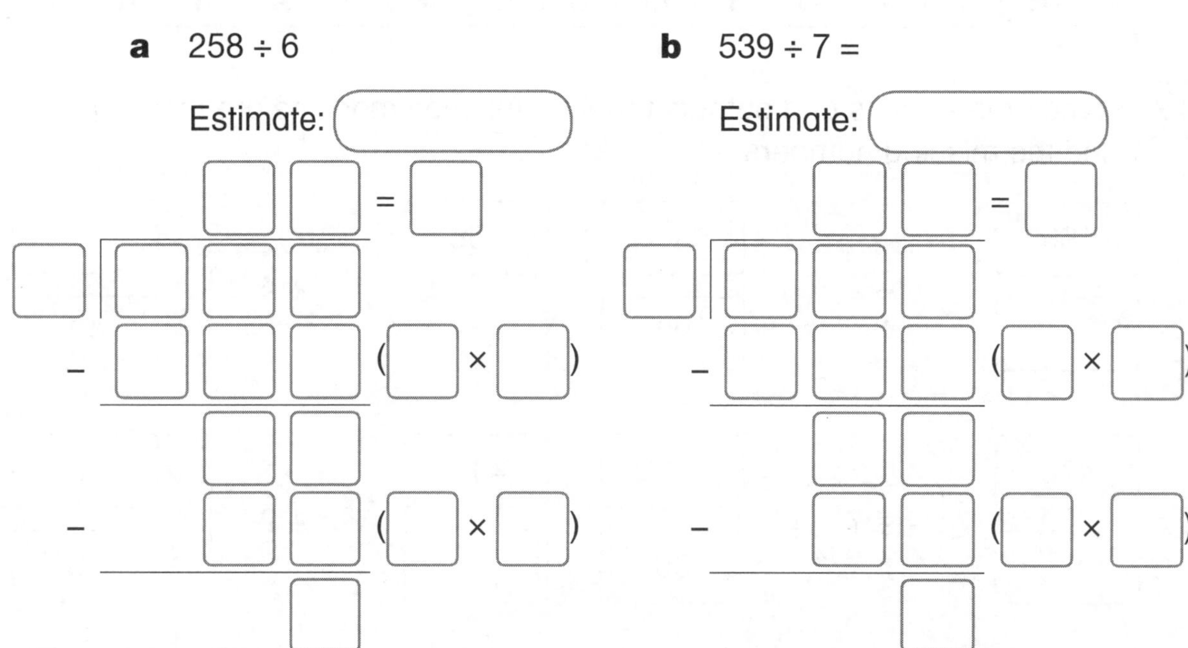

2 Estimate first, then use the expanded written method of division to work out the answer to each calculation. There is a remainder in the answer.

a 187 ÷ 8

Estimate:

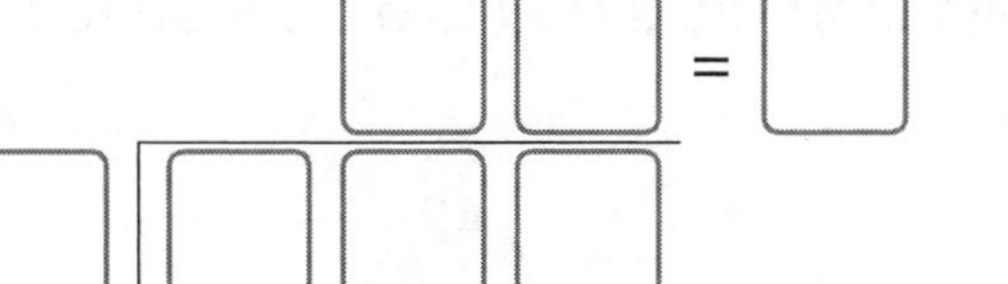

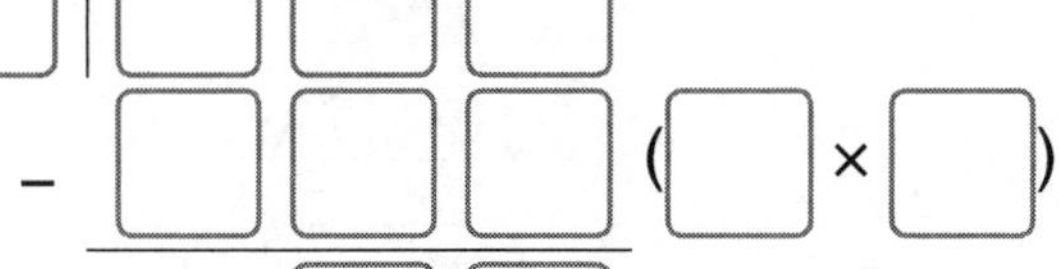

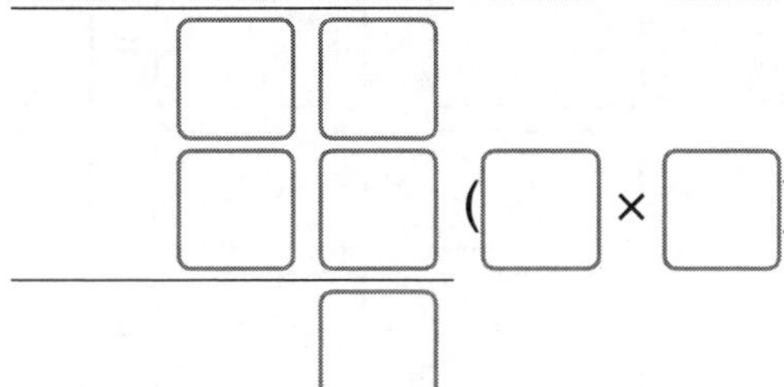

b 249 ÷ 9

Estimate:

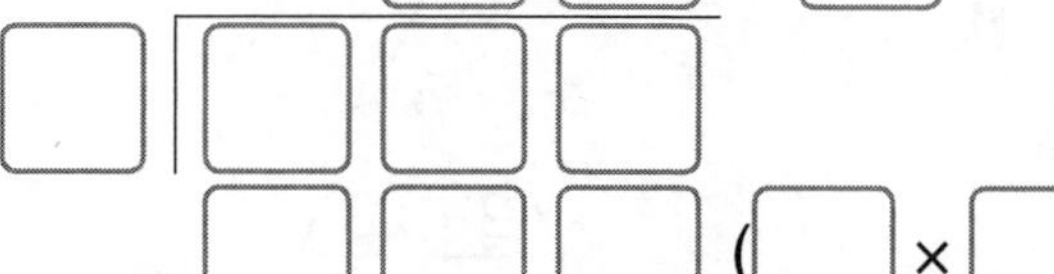

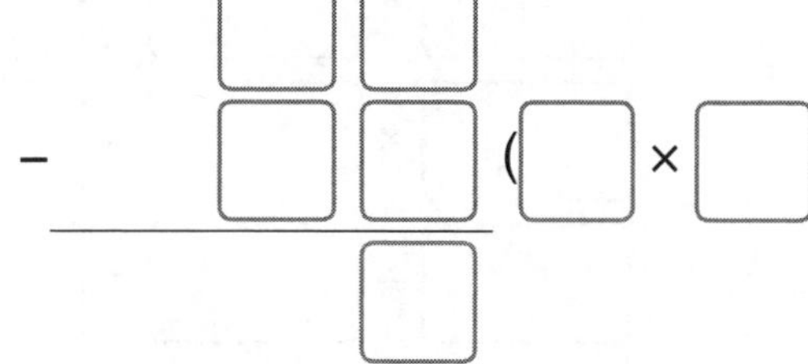

Challenge 3

Solve the word problems. Use the expanded written method of division.

1 A shop stocks 534 pairs of jeans. If the jeans are stored in piles of 6, how many piles should the shop make?

2 Amy wants to buy 483 cookies for a party. If the cookies come in boxes of 7, how many boxes of cookies should she buy?

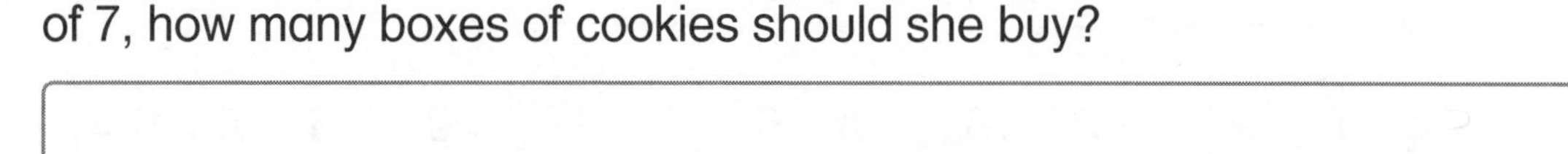

3 A school has $547 to buy new books. If each book costs $8, how many books can the school buy? How much money is left over?

4 A restaurant is hosting a party for 533 guests. If each table can seat 6 people how many people will NOT be seated at a table of 6?

Lesson 1: **Multiplication and division facts**

- Know multiplication and division facts for the 2× to 10× tables
- Know squares of all numbers to 10 × 10

Use each fact triangle to write two multiplication facts and two division facts.

a

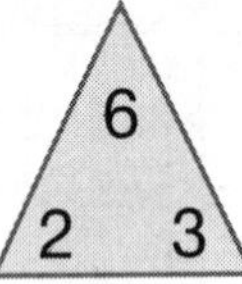

☐ × ☐ = ☐

☐ × ☐ = ☐

☐ ÷ ☐ = ☐

☐ ÷ ☐ = ☐

b

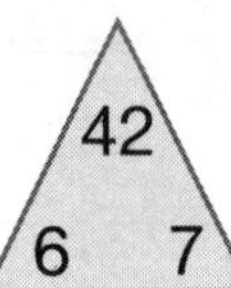

☐ × ☐ = ☐

☐ × ☐ = ☐

☐ ÷ ☐ = ☐

☐ ÷ ☐ = ☐

1 Fill in the missing numbers.

a ☐ × 3 = 9 **b** 7 × ☐ = 28 **c** 2 × 6 = ☐

d ☐ × 10 = 80 **e** 4 × ☐ = 32 **f** 7 × 7 = ☐

g ☐ × 2 = 18 **h** 9 × ☐ = 9 **i** 6 × 6 = ☐

2 Fill in the missing numbers.

a 8 ÷ ☐ = 4 **b** 81 ÷ 9 = ☐ **c** ☐ ÷ 2 = 6

d 12 ÷ ☐ = 3 **e** 16 ÷ 4 = ☐ **f** 72 ÷ 8 = ☐

g ☐ ÷ 10 = 6 **h** 45 ÷ ☐ = 5 **i** ☐ ÷ 10 = 10

3 Play this game with a partner.

- Take turns to choose any two numbers from the grid to multiply or divide. Cross through the numbers in the middle section.
- Say the answer and write it in your grid. For division, double the answer before adding it to your grid.
- The game ends after 14 rounds, or when all players can't say a number fact. Each players finds the total of all their scores. The winner is the player with the higher total score.

Player 1		4	2	21	6	20	25	20	30	24	12	Player 2	
		5	40	42	14	30	15	54	60	30	16		
		18	50	12	8	10	16	56	3	54	18		
		35	6	45	4	27	14	24	18	28	24		
		36	15	72	70	36	16	40	48	10	35		
		6	7	8	24	12	45	48	9	21	32		
		63	40	28	81	9	42	64	32	49	56		
		18	36	8	72	20	12	63	80	90	27		

Challenge 3 Use the table to work out the scores for each hoop thrown. Write the score next to each hoop. Then add all the hoops to find the total score.

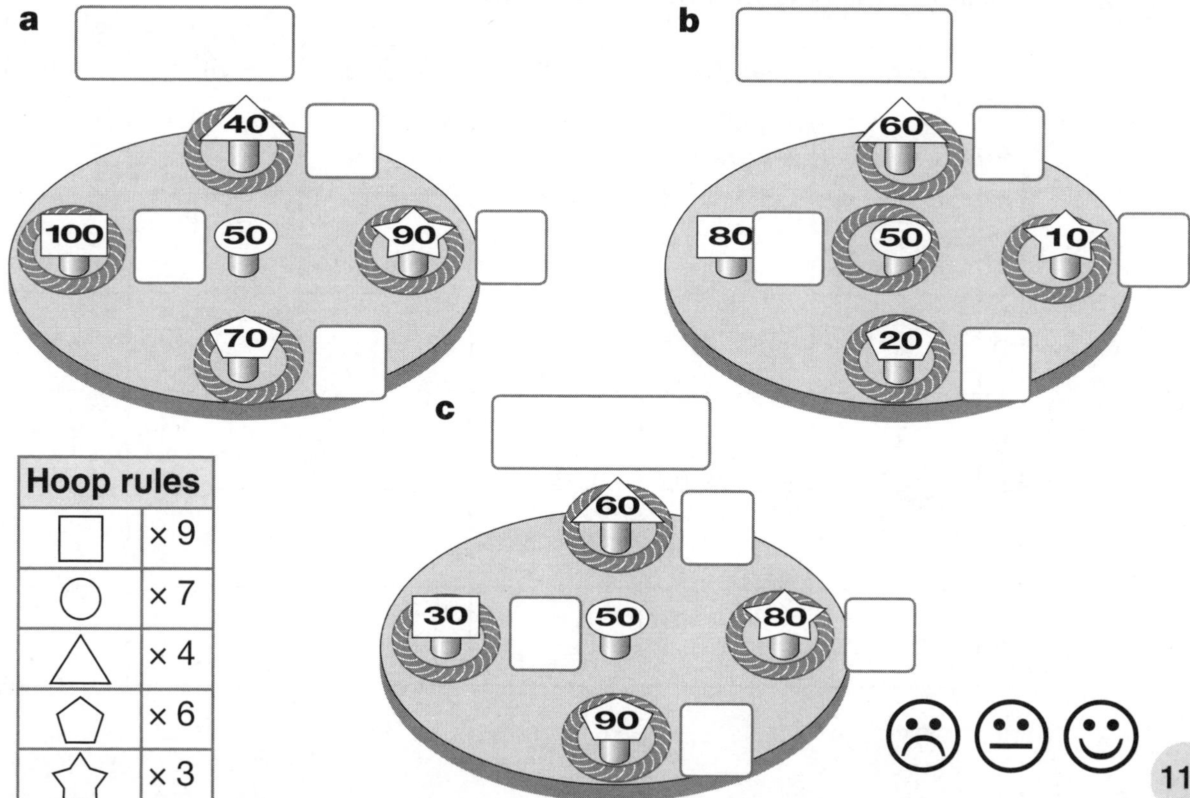

Lesson 2: **Multiplying multiples of 10 and 100 (1)**

- Multiply multiples of 10 to 90, and multiples of 100 to 900, by a single-digit number

Challenge 1

Fill in the missing numbers.

a 10 × 7 = ☐ **b** 3 × ☐ = 30 **c** 10 × 9 = ☐

d ☐ × 10 = 80 **e** 100 × ☐ = 700 **f** 3 × 100 = ☐

g 9 × ☐ = 900 **h** ☐ × 100 = 800 **i** ☐ × 10 = 50

j 6 × ☐ = 60 **k** 10 × 4 = ☐ **l** ☐ × 10 = 20

m 5 × 100 = ☐ **n** ☐ × 100 = 600 **o** ☐ × 4 = 400

Challenge 2

1 Fill in the missing numbers in the table.

	× 40	**× 70**	**× 90**	**× 300**	**× 500**	**× 800**
3						
7						
5						
9						
2						
4						

2 Calculate the total price for each set of purchases.

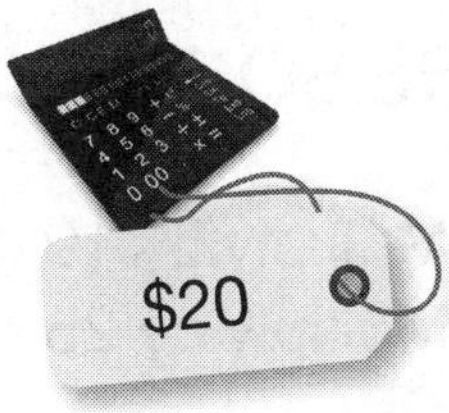

a

3 calculators
7 cars
6 DVD players
9 music systems

$

b

8 cameras
4 laptops
2 DVD players
7 music systems

$

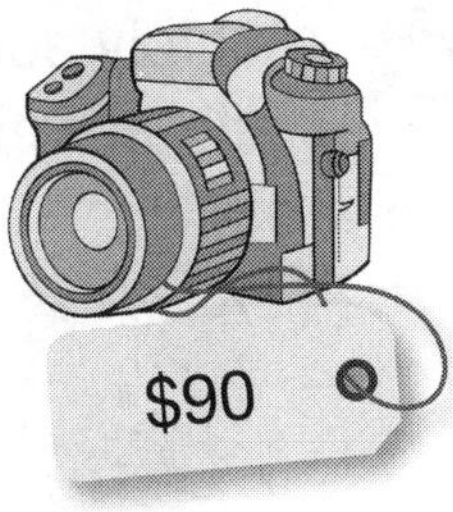

c

6 cameras
4 calculators
7 laptops
5 cars
3 music systems

$

d

6 cars
9 music systems
5 laptops
7 DVD players
9 calculators

$

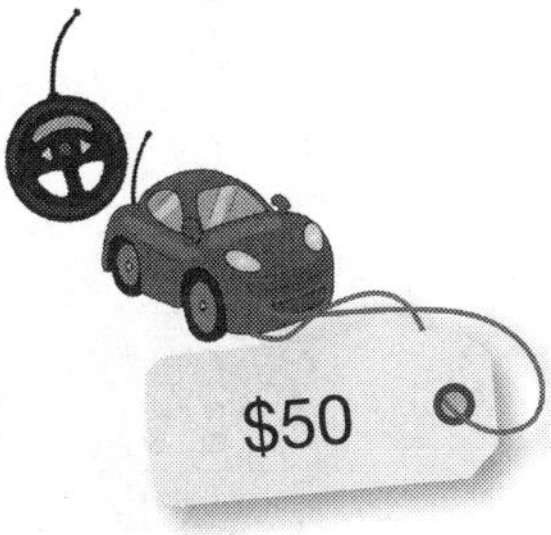

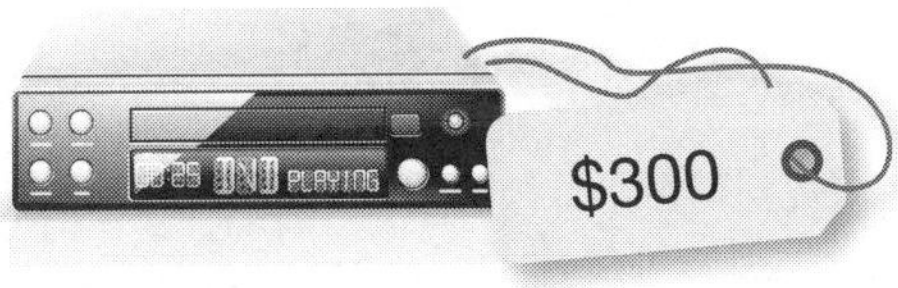

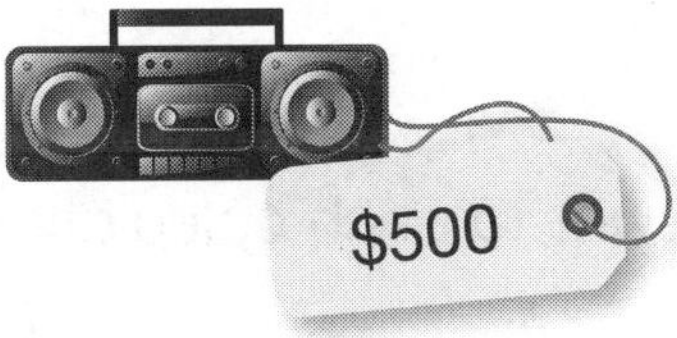

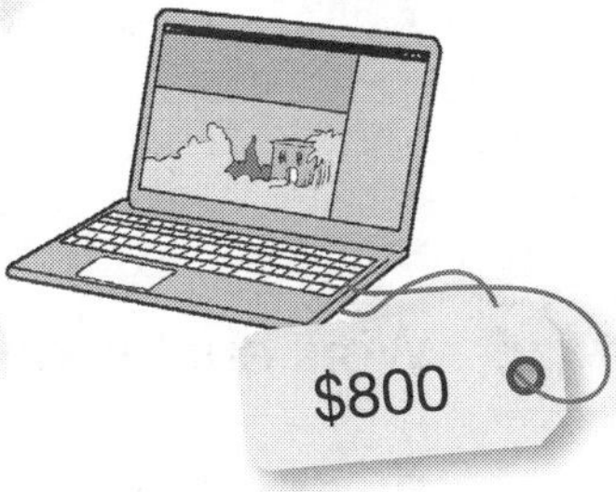

$20

$90

$50

$300

$500

$800

Challenge 3 Each shop receipt shows the total costs of a set of some of the items pictured above. Work out how many of each item was purchased.

a

b

$5000 = ☐ DVD players and ☐ music systems

c

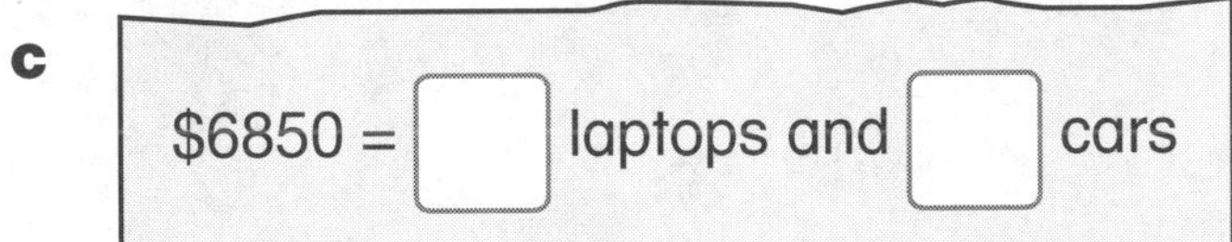

Lesson 3: **Multiplying by 19, 21 or 25 (1)**

- Multiply by 19 or 21 by multiplying by 20 and adjusting
- Multiply by 25 by multiplying by 100 and dividing by 4

Challenge 1 Multiply each number in the top row of balloons by 20. Then link it to the balloon with the answer.

Challenge 2

1 Work out the answer to each calculation.

a 3 × 19 = ☐ **b** 8 × 21 = ☐ **c** 5 × 25 = ☐

d 7 × 19 = ☐ **e** 4 × 21 = ☐ **f** 8 × 25 = ☐

g 6 × 19 = ☐ **h** 9 × 21 = ☐ **i** 6 × 25 = ☐

2 Calculate the price of each set of magazines purchased.

a

19 'Fun' magazines
21 'Jump' magazines

$

b

25 'Kids' magazines
21 'Bubble' magazines

$

c

21 'Party' magazines
19 'Jump' magazines
25 'Fun' magazines

$

d

19 'Party' magazines
21 'Fun' magazines
25 'Jump' magazines
19 'Kids' magazines

$

Challenge 3 Each shop receipt shows the total cost of buying multiple copies of the magazines shown in Challenge 2. The multiples may be 19, 21 or 25.

Work out how many of each item was purchased.

a \$320 = ☐ FUN and ☐ JUMP

b \$278 = ☐ BUBBLE and ☐ KIDS

c \$280 = ☐ PARTY and ☐ FUN

d \$321 = ☐ BUBBLE and ☐ JUMP

Lesson 4: **Multiplication by factors (1)**

- Use factors to multiply

You will need
- dice

- Play this game with a partner.
- Each player rolls a dice to create nine 2-digit numbers. Write six of your numbers in the circles and the remaining three of your numbers in the 'spares' area.
- Take turns to find a factor pair for one of your numbers. Cross out the pair on the grid and the number you chose.
- If you cannot go, you can choose a spare number instead but you will have to miss a turn. The first player to cross out six numbers is the winner.

PLAYER 1	1	1	1	1	1	1	2	2	PLAYER 2
	2	2	2	2	2	2	2	3	
	3	3	3	4	4	4	4	4	
	5	5	5	5	6	6	6	6	
	7	7	7	7	8	8	8	8	
	9	9	9	9	10	10	10	10	
	11	11	11	11	12	12	12	12	
	12	13	13	14	14	15	15	16	
	16	17	17	18	18	19	19	20	
	20	21	21	22	22	23	24	25	
	26	27	28	29	30	31	32	33	

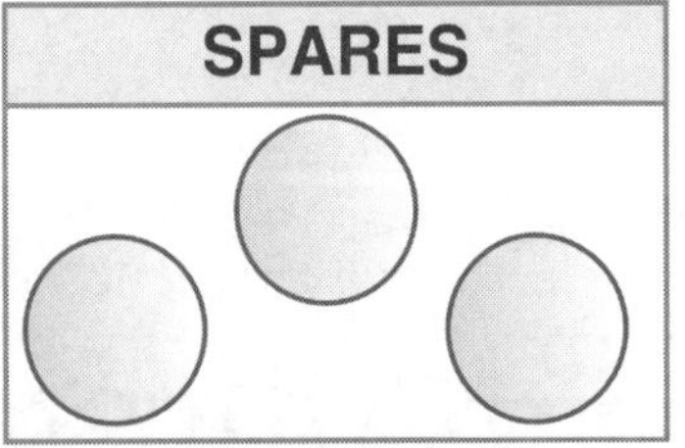

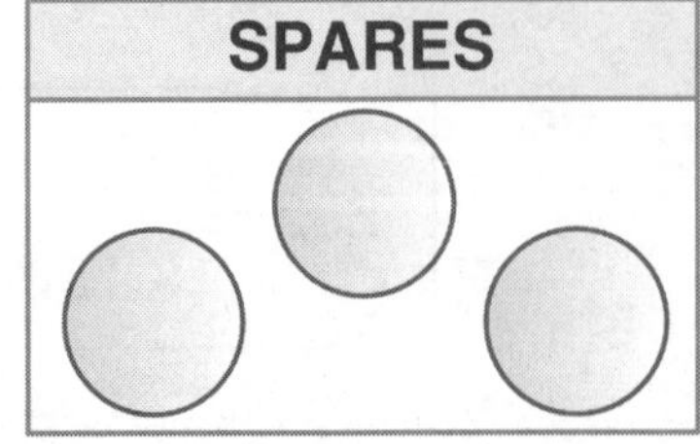

Challenge 2

1 Solve each problem by splitting the second number into its factors.

a $17 \times 15 =$

b $39 \times 15 =$

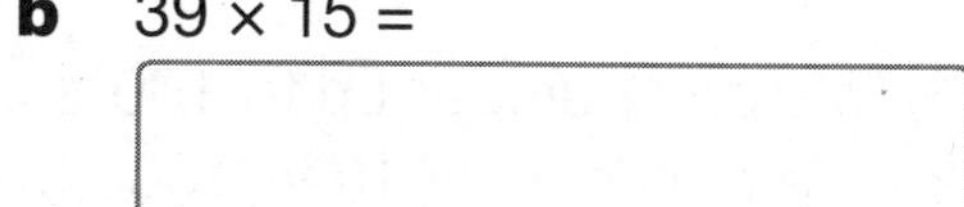

c $45 \times 18 =$

d $57 \times 18 =$

e $29 \times 36 =$

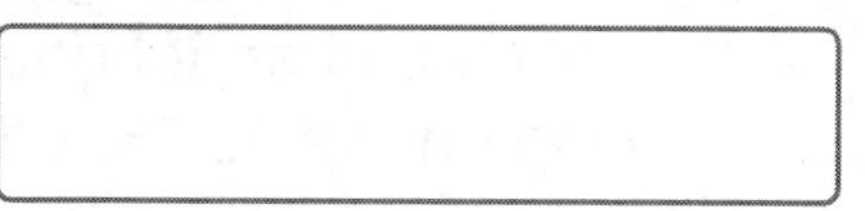

f $63 \times 36 =$

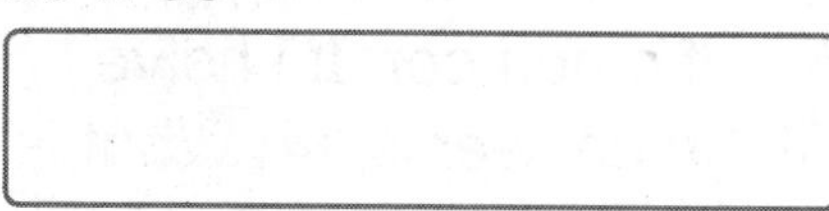

2 Link each bag of sweets to a number and multiply. Write the answer in the box below the number.

24

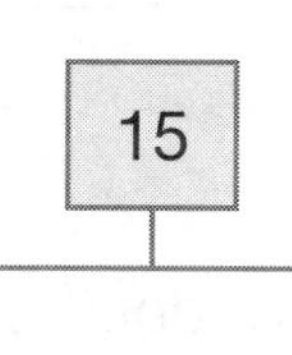

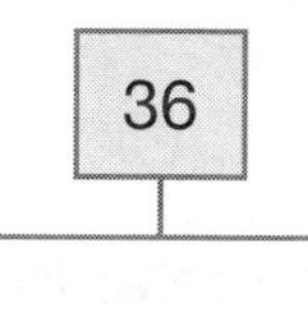

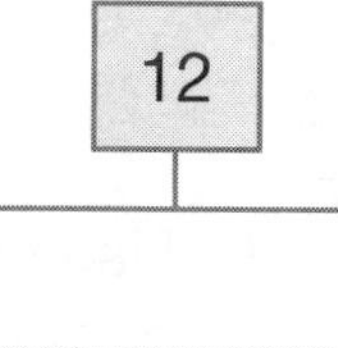

Challenge 3

Solve each problem by splitting both numbers into their factors.

a $36 \times 36 =$

b $48 \times 36 =$

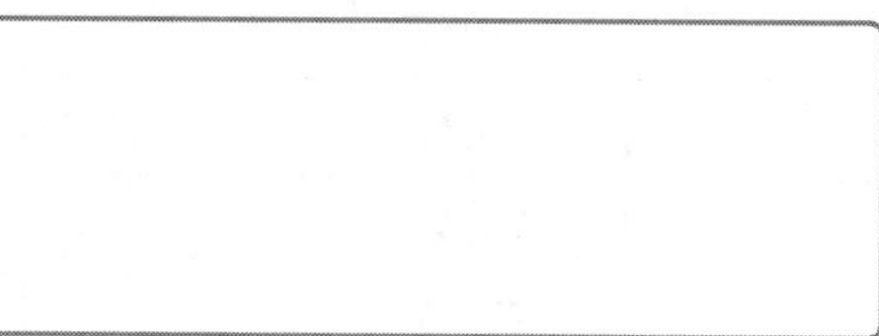

c $64 \times 64 =$

d $72 \times 64 =$

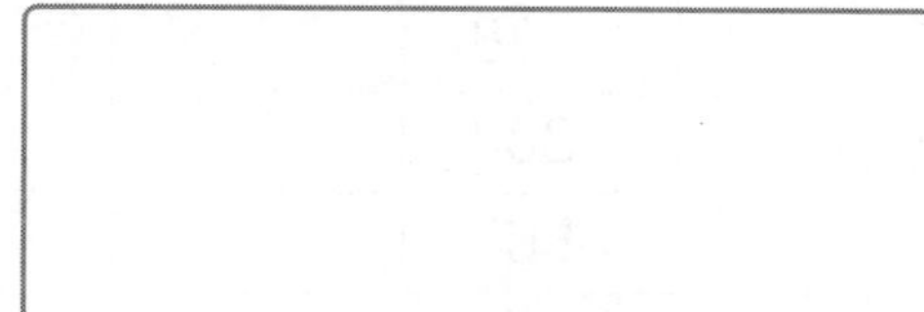

Lesson 5: **Doubles and halves (1)**

- Double any number up to 100 and halve even numbers to 200
- Double multiples of 10 to 1000 and multiples of 100 to 10 000

Challenge 1

Guess the number. Write the answer in the empty thought bubble.

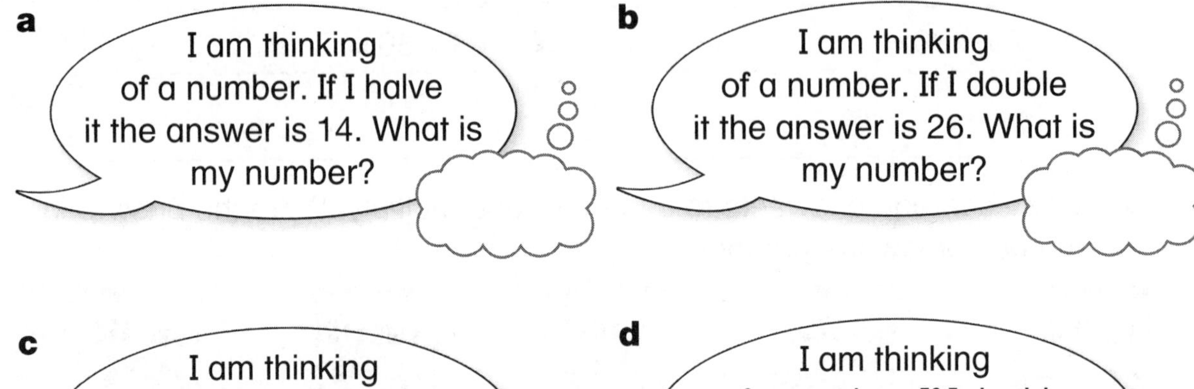

c

I am thinking of a number. If I halve it the answer is 8. What is my number?

d

I am thinking of a number. If I double it the answer is 34. What is my number?

Challenge 2

1 Use whichever strategy you prefer to halve or double the numbers in the table.

Halved	Number	Doubled
	44	
	440	
	4400	
	62	
	620	
	6200	
	38	
	380	
	3800	

Halved	Number	Doubled
	46	
	460	
	4600	
	78	
	780	
	7800	
	96	
	960	
	9600	

Number	Doubled
97	
970	
9700	
89	
890	
8900	
99	
990	
9900	

2 Fill in the missing numbers. One has been done for you.

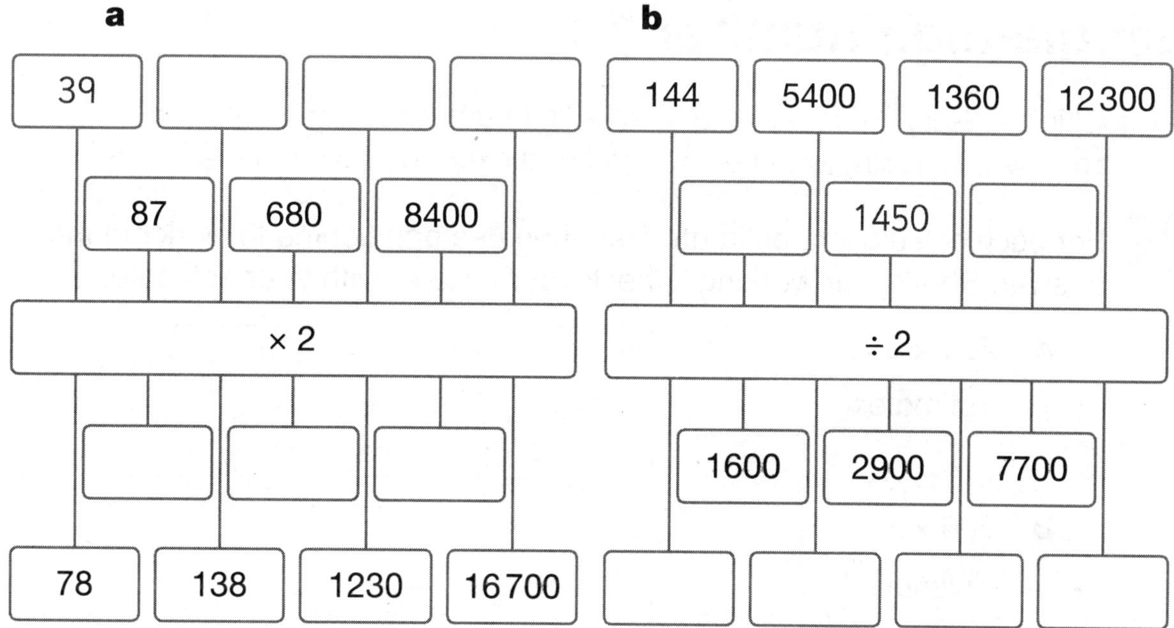

Challenge **3** Solve these word problems.

a 78 passengers board a boat. At the first stop, half the passengers get off and 218 get on. At the second stop, more passengers get on, and this doubles the number of passengers on board. How many passengers are on the boat now?

b 986 passengers get on a train. At the first stop, half the passengers get off and 912 more get on. At the second stop, more passengers get on board, and this doubles the number of passengers on board. How many passengers are on the train now?

Lesson 6: **Multiplying a 3-digit number by a single-digit number (2)**

- Multiply a 3-digit number by a single-digit number using a range of strategies, including partitioning, grid and expanded written methods

Challenge 1

For each calculation, estimate first, then use partitioning to work out the answer. Show your working. Check your answer with your estimate.

a 234 × 2 =

Estimate:

b 366 × 4 =

Estimate:

c 537 × 6 =

Estimate:

Challenge 2

1 For each calculation, estimate first, then use the grid to work out the answer. Show your working. Check your answer with your estimate.

a 587 × 6 =

Estimate:

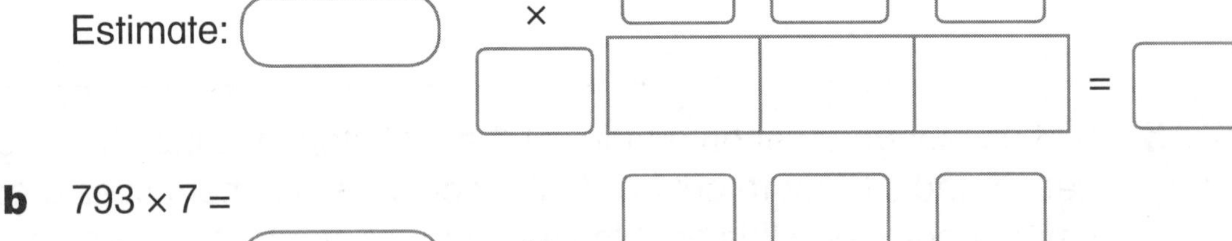

b 793 × 7 =

Estimate:

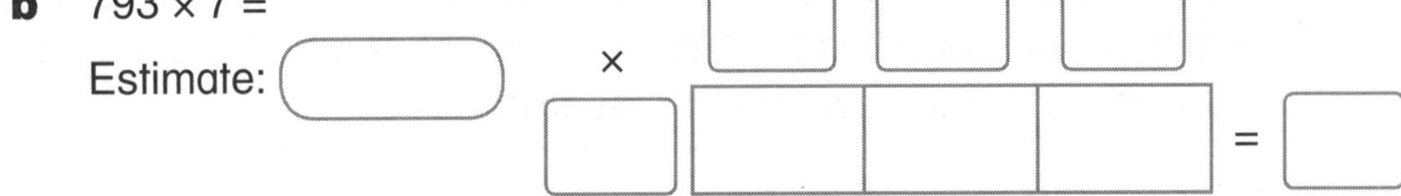

c 946 × 9 =

Estimate:

× =

2 For each calculation, estimate first, then use the expanded written method to work out the answer. Show your working. Check your answer with your estimate.

a 483 × 6 =

Estimate:

×

b 763 × 8 =

Estimate:

×

Challenge 3

- Play this game with a partner. Decide whether to play as Player 1 or Player 2.
- Take turns to choose two numbers from the middle of the board. One should be a 3-digit number and the other a 1-digit number.
- Multiply them, using the expanded written method. If the answer is on your side of the board, cross it off. However, if the answer is on your partner's side of the board, they can cross it off.
- The first player to cross off all their numbers is the winner.

5159	**5328**	**3766**
2646	**5802**	**2532**
5336	**4002**	**1749**

737	3	583	4
9	289	7	667
976	6	888	8
844	294	538	967

2601	**6633**	**3552**
3228	**6752**	**2023**
6003	**1176**	**2646**

Number

Lesson 7: **Multiplying a 2-digit number by a 2-digit number (3)**

- Use a range of strategies, including partitioning, grid and expanded written methods, to multiply a 2-digit number by a 2-digit number

Challenge 1

For each calculation, estimate first, then use partitioning to work out the answer. The first one has been done for you.

a 56 × 3 = (50 × 3) + (6 × 3) = 150 + 18 = 168

b 43 × 3 =

c 59 × 3 =

d 37 × 6 =

Challenge 2

1 For each calculation, estimate first, then use partitioning to work out the answer. Show your working. Check your answer against your estimate.

a 47 × 27 =

Estimate:

b 59 × 43 =

Estimate:

c 78 × 56 =

Estimate:

2 For each calculation, estimate first, then use the grid to work out the answer. Show your working. Check your answer against your estimate.

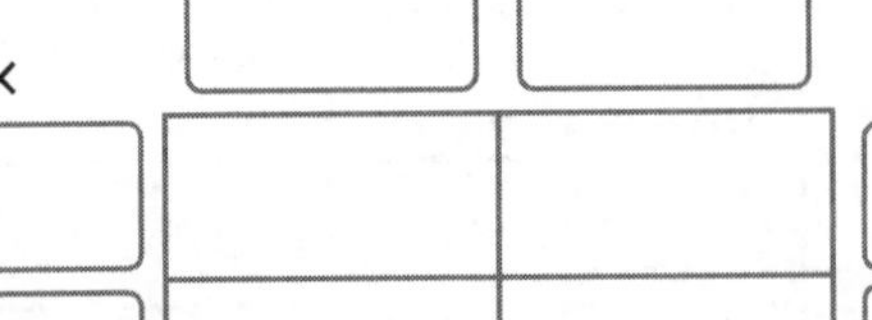

a 63 × 49 =

Estimate: 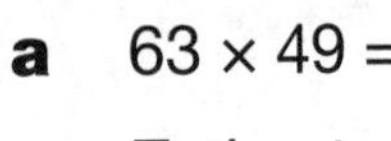

b 76 × 69 =

Estimate:

×

c 94 × 93 =

Estimate:

×

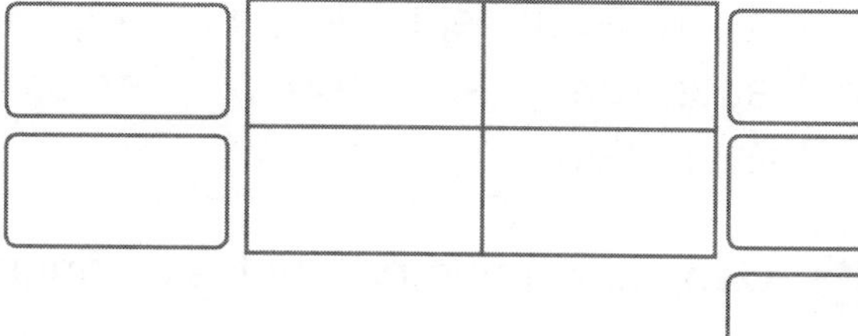

Challenge 3

Estimate first, then use the expanded written method to work out the answer. Show your working. Check your answer against your estimate.

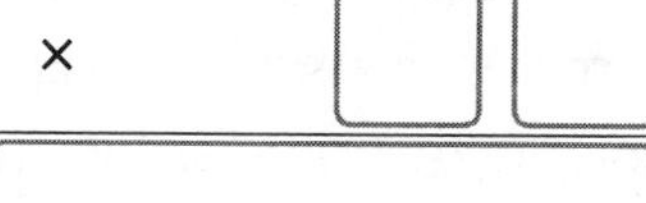
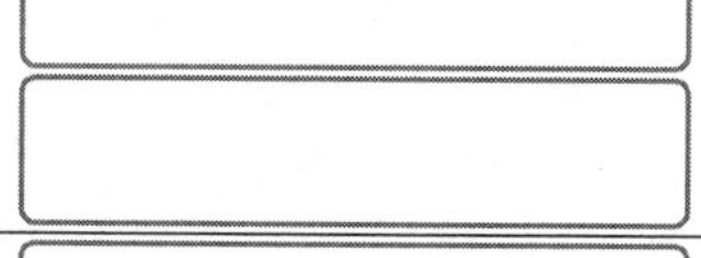

a 33 × 37 =

Estimate:

×

b 63 × 42 =

Estimate:

×

c 71 × 89 =

Estimate:

×

d 94 × 97 =

Estimate:

×

Number

Lesson 8: **Dividing a 3-digit number by a single-digit number (3)**

- Use a range of strategies, including partitioning, grouping and expanded written methods, to divide a 3-digit number by a single-digit number
- Recognise when to round up or down after division, depending on the problem

Challenge 1

Use known number facts or partitioning to complete each division.

a 440 ÷ 4 = ☐ **b** 315 ÷ 3 = ☐ **c** 296 ÷ 4 = ☐

d 280 ÷ 2 = ☐ **e** 721 ÷ 7 = ☐ **f** 324 ÷ 6 = ☐

g 630 ÷ 3 = ☐ **h** 832 ÷ 8 = ☐ **i** 448 ÷ 7 = ☐

Challenge 2

1 Estimate first, then use the expanded written method of division to work out the answer to each calculation. Remember to use multiplication to check the results of the division. There are no remainders in the first two answers.

a 665 ÷ 7 =

Estimate ☐

b 744 ÷ 8 =

Estimate ☐

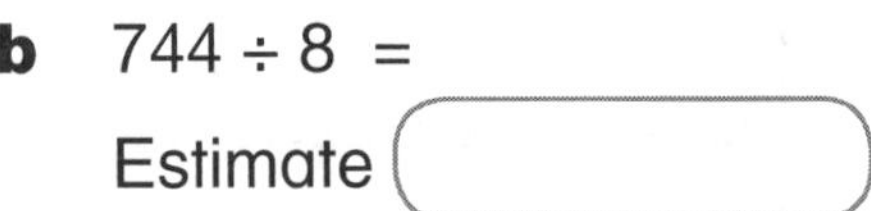

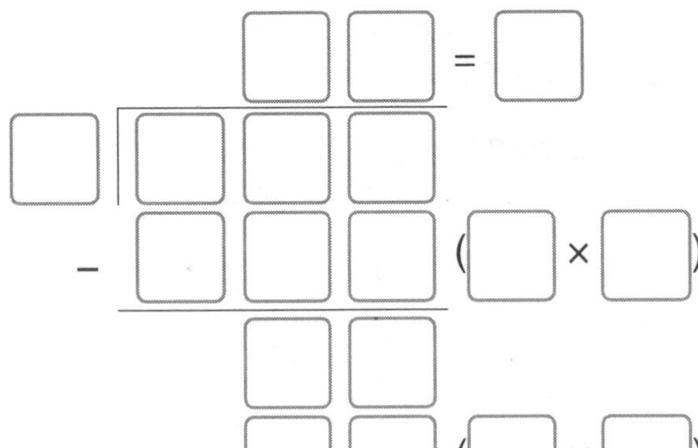

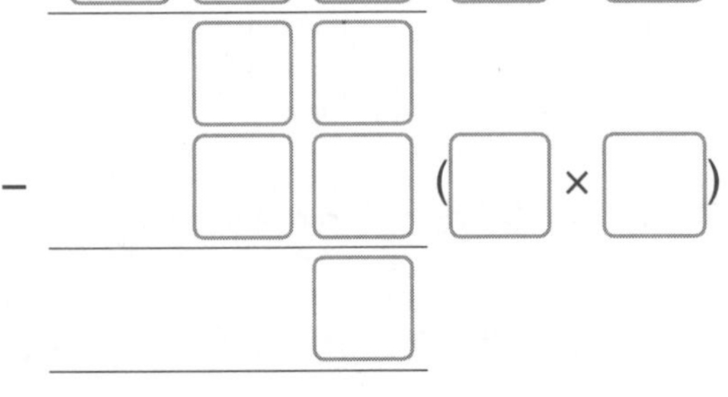

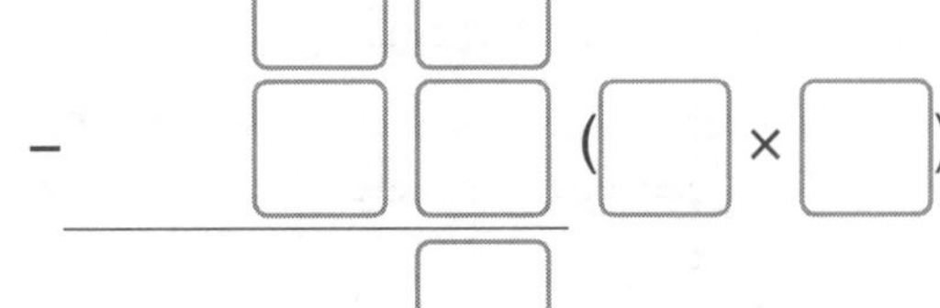

c $235 \div 8$

d $149 \div 9$

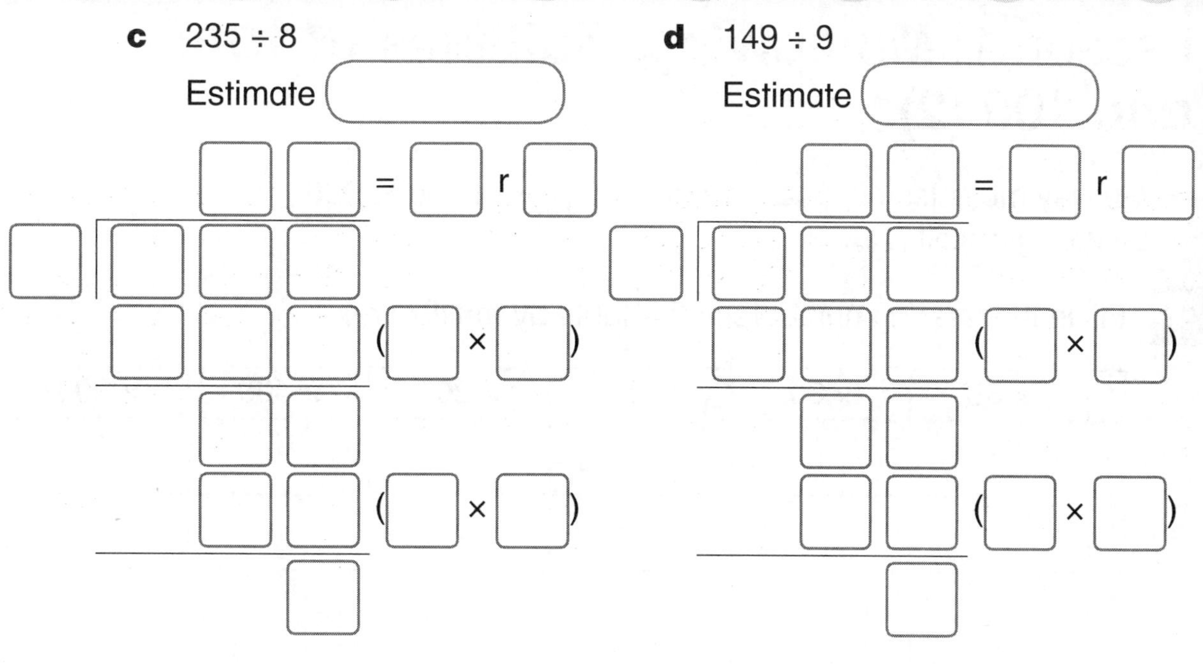

2 Answer the word problems. Decide whether to round any remainders up or down.

a Nathan's book has 184 pages. He reads 7 pages every day. How many days does it take him to finish the book?

b Ella has 477 magazines to deliver to shops. They are collected together in packs of 8. How many complete packs does she have?

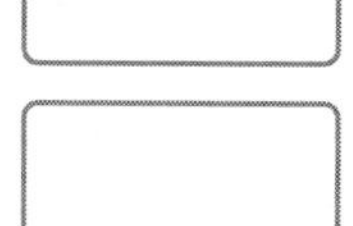

c A gardener has $672. He wants to buy plants that cost $9 each. How many can he buy?

Challenge 3 Answer the word problems. Decide whether to round any remainders up or down.

1 2420 people want to ride a rollercoaster. The cars hold 7 people each. How many cars will be full?

2 1760 large boxes are loaded into vans that each have a capacity of 9 boxes. How many vans will be needed to transport all of the boxes?

3 3250 kg of sand needs to be shipped in containers that can each carry a maximum weight of 950 kg. How many containers will the sand fill?

Number

Lesson 1: **Multiplying multiples of 10 and 100 (2)**

- Multiply multiples of 10 to 90, and multiples of 100 to 900, by a single-digit number

Challenge 1 Fill in the missing numbers in the table by multiplying.

	× 30	× 60	× 80	× 200	× 400	× 900
7						
9						
2						
4						

Challenge 2 **1** Calculate the total mass of each set of items.

a 3 tins of peas
5 boxes of Sunny Flakes
4 cartons of milk  g

Peas
90 g

b 6 trays of tomatoes 
3 packs of kebabs
7 tins of peas
5 boxes of eggs  g

c 9 tins of peas 
9 boxes of eggs
8 trays of tomatoes
7 boxes of Sunny Flakes
6 cartons of milk 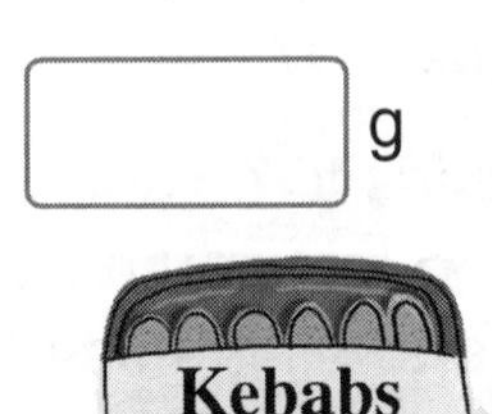 g

70 g

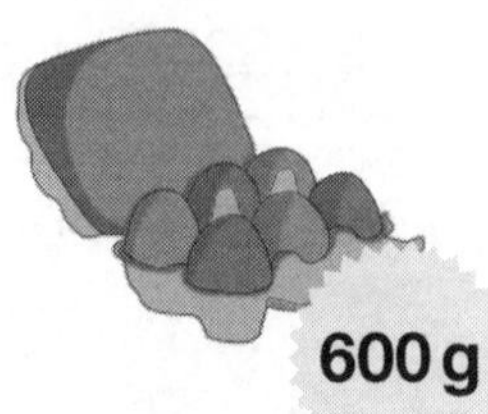

2 Use rounding to find an estimate for each multiplication.

a 47 × 4 Estimate [ ] **b** 56 × 7 Estimate [ ]

c 83 × 6 Estimate [ ] **d** 68 × 6 Estimate [ ]

e 94 × 8 Estimate [ ] **f** 77 × 9 Estimate [ ]

g 317 × 5 Estimate [ ] **h** 288 × 4 Estimate [ ]

Challenge 3

Look back at the items for sale in question 1 of Challenge 2.

Calculate the combined mass of each large order.

a
40 trays of tomatoes
60 boxes of Sunny Flakes
30 boxes of eggs
70 cartons of milk
[ ] g

b
50 boxes of eggs
20 packets of kebabs
70 boxes of Sunny Flakes
40 trays of tomatoes
[ ] g

c
60 packets of kebabs
40 tins of peas
80 trays of tomatoes
70 boxes of eggs
[ ] g

d
70 cartons of milk
50 tins of peas
80 boxes of Sunny Flakes
60 trays of tomatoes
90 boxes of eggs
[ ] g

Number

Lesson 2: **Multiplying by 19, 21 or 25 (2)**

- Multiply by 19 or 21 by multiplying by 20 and adjusting
- Multiply by 25 by multiplying by 100 and dividing by 4

Calculate the total costs.

a \$4 × 19 = ☐ **b** \$3 × 21 = ☐ **c** \$7 × 25 = ☐

d \$5 × 19 = ☐ **e** \$6 × 21 = ☐ **f** \$8 × 25 = ☐

g \$8 × 19 = ☐ **h** \$9 × 21 = ☐ **i** \$6 × 25 = ☐

j \$9 × 19 = ☐ **k** \$8 × 21 = ☐ **l** \$9 × 25 = ☐

Challenge 2

1 For the balloons in the top row, multiply a light balloon by 19, and a dark balloon by 21.

Link each balloon in the top row to the balloon with the answer in the bottom row.

70

80

90

1710

840
1260
1520

2 Calculate the total distance run by each team.

TRACK A

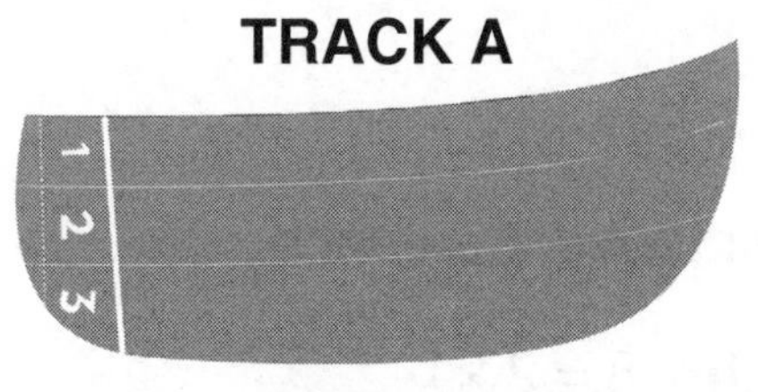

90 m

TRACK B

400 m

TRACK C

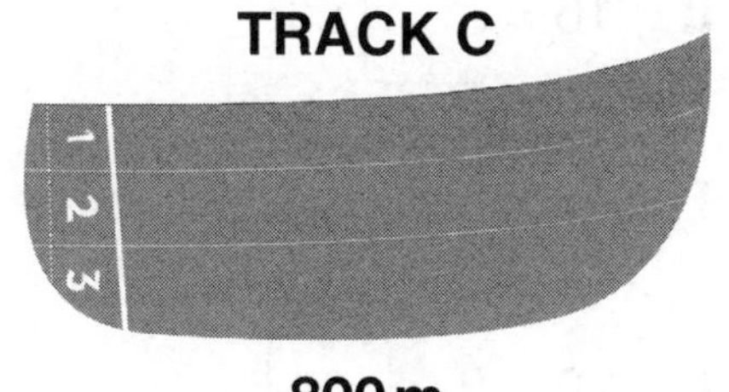

800 m

TRACK D

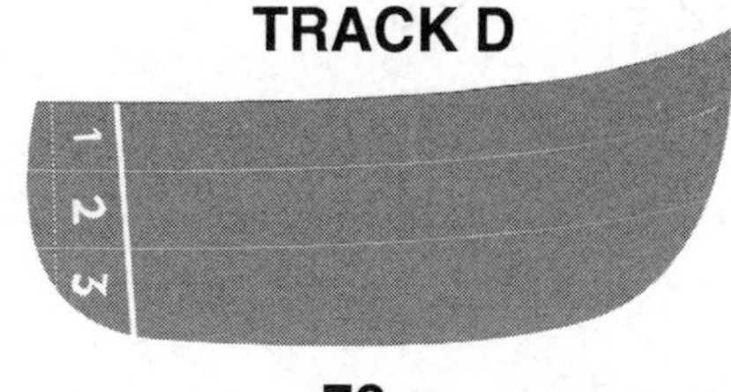

70 m

a TEAM 1
19 laps of Track A

b TEAM 2
21 laps of Track D

c TEAM 3
25 laps of Track B

d TEAM 4
19 laps of Track C

Calculate the total costs.

a $150 × 19 =

b $190 × 21 =

c $230 × 25 =

d $260 × 19 =

e $320 × 21 =

f $380 × 25 =

Number

Lesson 3: Multiplication by factors (2)

- Use factors to multiply

Challenge 1

Complete the missing numbers in each number sentence.

a 6 = ☐ × 3

b 8 = 2 × ☐

c 12 = ☐ × 6

d 16 = ☐ × 2

e 14 = 7 × ☐

f 18 = 2 × ☐

g 24 = 12 × ☐

h 30 = 2 × ☐

Challenge 2

1 Solve each multiplication by splitting one of the numbers into its factors. Show your working in the box.

a 17 × 6 = ☐

b 14 × 13 = ☐

c 19 × 12 = ☐

d 18 × 21 = ☐

2 Connect each car to the house with the answer to the calculation.

Challenge 3 Solve each problem by splitting the smaller number into its factors.

a $230 \times 6 =$ 

b $14 \times 130 =$ 

c $170 \times 8 =$

d $18 \times 210 =$ 

e $240 \times 12 =$ 

f $16 \times 420 =$ 

Lesson 4: **Doubles and halves (2)**

- Double multiples of 10 to 1000 and multiples of 100 to 10 000

Challenge 1

For each number fact you are given, write three more related facts. The first one has been done for you.

a Double 2 is 4.

Double 20 is 40.

Double 200 is 400.

Double 2000 is 4000.

b Double 9 is 18.

___

___

___

c Half 16 is 8.

___

___

___

d Double 6 is 12.

___

___

___

e Half 8 is 4.

___

___

___

f Half 18 is 9.

___

___

___

Challenge 2

1 Draw lines to link each double to its half.

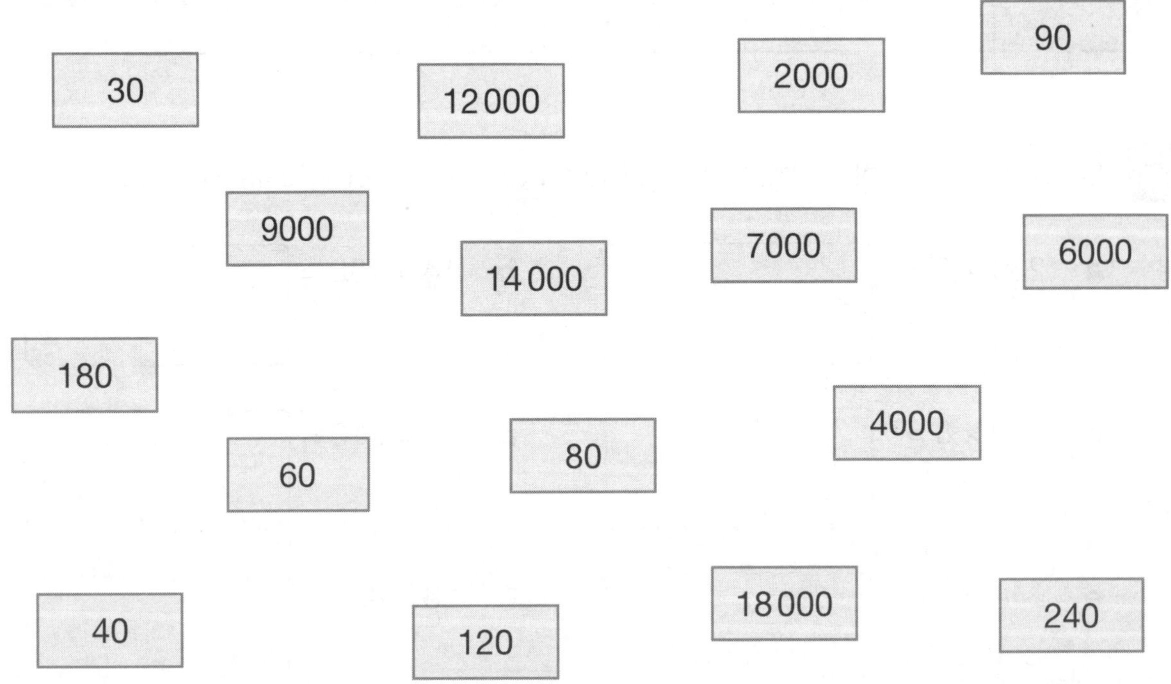

2 Double each number.

a	110		**b**	480
c	4200		**d**	220
e	590		**f**	5500
g	350		**h**	660
i	6200		**j**	440
k	770		**l**	6600

3 Halve each number.

a	120		**b**	720
c	3200		**d**	360
e	340		**f**	5400
g	240		**h**	160
i	7600		**j**	480
k	580		**l**	3400

Halve each number.

a	490		**b**	2710		**c**	6634
d	370		**e**	7350		**f**	8378
g	610		**h**	8970		**i**	18 964
j	850		**k**	5262		**l**	11 376

Number

Lesson 5: **Doubles and halves (3)**

- Find the double or half of a decimal by doubling or halving a related whole number and adjusting

Challenge 1

For each number fact you are given, write a related decimal fact. The first one has been done for you.

a Double 26 is 52.

Double 2·6 is 5·2.

b Double 48 is 96.

____

c Half 74 is 37.

____

d Double 19 is 38.

____

e Half 36 is 18.

____

f Half 96 is 48.

____

Challenge 2

1 Draw lines to link each double to its half.

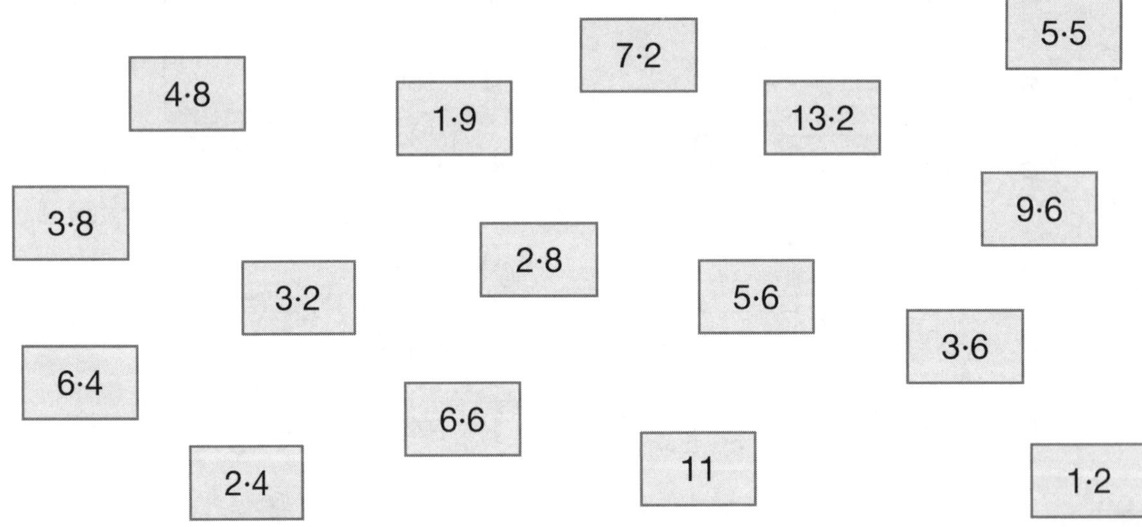

2 Double each number.

a	0·4		**b**	1·7		**c**	4·8	
d	0·9		**e**	2·6		**f**	5·9	
g	1·3		**h**	3·4		**i**	6·7	
j	8·6		**k**	3·11		**l**	2·27	
m	1·33		**n**	4·45		**o**	2·48	

3 Halve each number.

a	2·2		**b**	5·6	
c	12·46		**d**	1·4	
e	7·8		**f**	3·28	
g	6·2		**h**	4·36	
i	7·72		**j**	1·6	
k	6·48		**l**	9·94	
m	8·34		**n**	10·06	

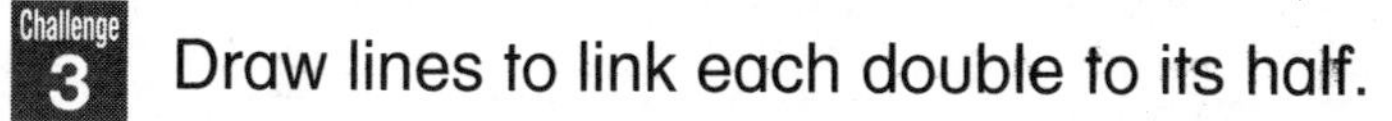

Challenge 3 Draw lines to link each double to its half.

5·29

1·715

7·61

4·37

3·43

5·33

3·57

4·19

2·645

3·805

2·095

7·77

1·785

2·665

2·185

3·885

Number

Lesson 6: **Multiplying a decimal by a single-digit number**

- Multiply a 2-digit number with 1 decimal place by a single-digit number

Challenge 1

For each number fact you are given, write a related decimal fact. The first one has been done for you.

a 24 × 3 = 72 — 2·4 × 3 = 7·2

b 73 × 7 = 511 ______

c 78 × 8 = 624 ______

d 37 × 4 = 148 ______

e 62 × 9 = 558 ______

f 95 × 9 = 855 ______

Challenge 2

1 Work out the answer to each multiplication by using a related whole number calculation. Show your working in the box.

a 2·7 × 4 = ☐

b 4·8 × 6 = ☐

c 6·6 × 7 = ☐

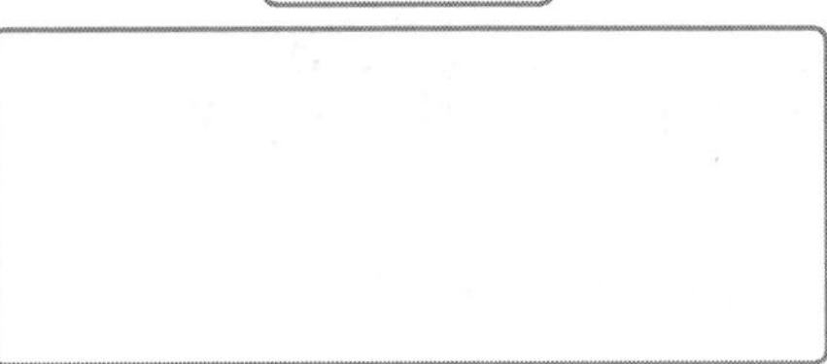

d 8·9 × 8 = ☐

2 Work out the answer to each multiplication. Use partitioning. The first one has been done for you.

a 2·6 × 6 = (2 × 6) + (0·6 × 6) = 12 + 3·6 = 15·6

b 3·7 × 4 = ______

c 7·8 × 7 = ______

d 9·4 × 9 = ______

3 Work out the answer to each multiplication. Use the grid method.

a 4·6 × 3 = __________

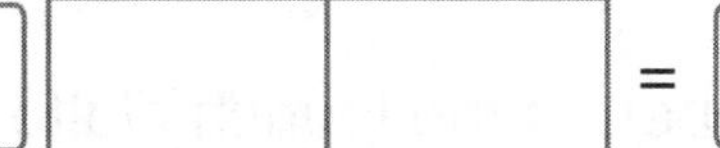

b 8·7 × 9 = __________

c 6·9 × 7 = __________

A 5·7 kg

B 3·9 kg

C 8·8 kg

4 Work out the combined mass of each set of crates.

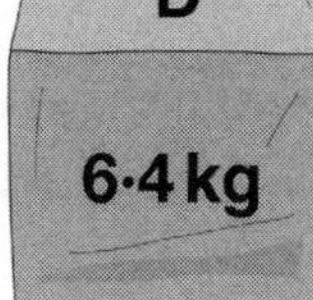

a 5 of crate A and 3 of crate B ______ kg

b 4 of crate C and 7 of crate D ______ kg

c 6 of crate B and 9 of crate C ______ kg

Challenge 3

Work out the total distance jumped by each athlete for each event and write it inside the brackets. Use this to find the total distance jumped for each athlete for all three events.

	Distance of jump (metres)			
	3·7 m	**4·9 m**	**5·3 m**	**Total distance jumped**
Femi	6 jumps (22.2)	5 jumps (24.5)	3 jumps (15·9)	62·6
Dalia	3 jumps ( )	4 jumps ( )	7 jumps ( )	
Jasper	9 jumps ( )	3 jumps ( )	4 jumps ( )	
Carina	8 jumps ( )	2 jumps ( )	5 jumps ( )	

Who jumped the furthest distance in total? ____________________

Number

Lesson 7: **Writing a remainder as a fraction**

- Divide a 2-digit number by a single-digit number, writing any remainder as a fraction

Challenge 1

Divide the number on each rocket by the number on the launch platform. Write the remainder as a fraction. Simplify the fraction if you can.

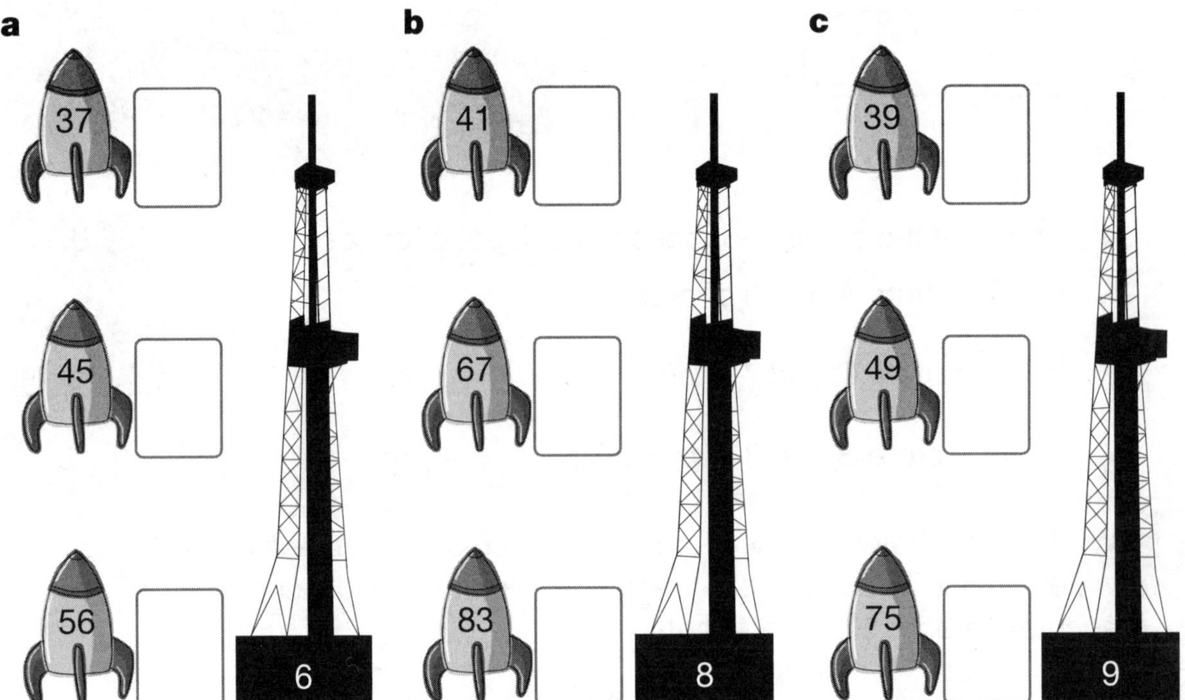

Challenge 2

1 Work out the answer to each division calculation. Write the remainder as a fraction. Simplify the fraction where possible.

a $32 \div 3 =$ ______

b $34 \div 4 =$ ______

c $67 \div 5 =$ ______

d $64 \div 6 =$ ______

e $65 \div 7 =$ ______

f $68 \div 8 =$ ______

2 Squash is poured equally between several containers. What amount of squash will there be in each container? Write the remainder as a fraction.

a 95 ml

b 98 ml

c 98 ml

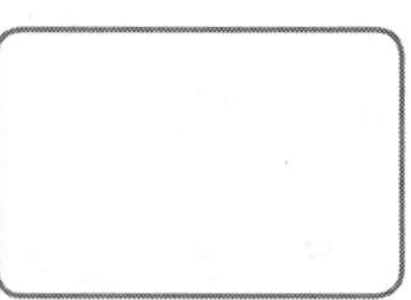

Challenge **3** Write a calculation for each instruction.

a Divide a 2-digit number by 4 to give a remainder of $\frac{1}{4}$.

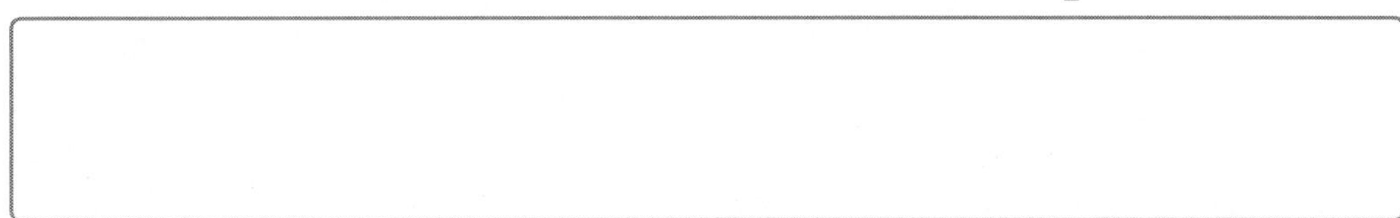

b Divide a 2-digit number by 8 to give a remainder of $\frac{1}{2}$.

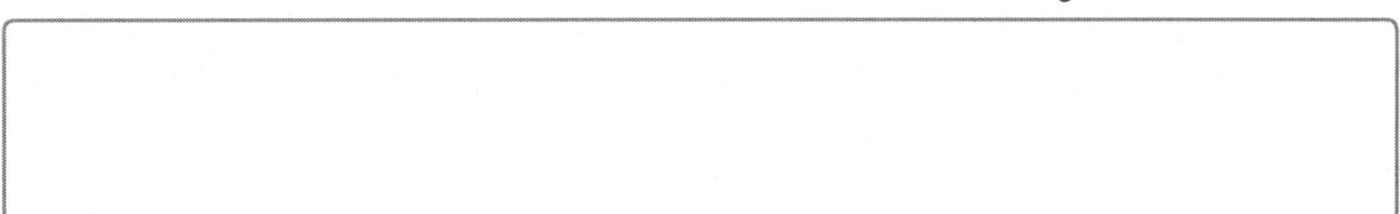

c Divide a 3-digit number by 5 to give a remainder of $\frac{2}{5}$.

d Divide a 3-digit number by 6 to give a remainder of $\frac{1}{3}$.

Number

Lesson 8: Order of operations

- Use brackets to order operations and understand the relationship between the four operations and how the laws of arithmetic apply to multiplication

Use the BODMAS rule to work out the answers to these calculations.

a $8 + 3 \times 2 =$ ☐

b $42 \div 7 - 4 =$ ☐

c $6 \times 5 + 7 =$ ☐

d $14 + 45 \div 5 =$ ☐

e $9 \div 3 + 7 =$ ☐

f $47 - 27 \div 3 =$ ☐

g $16 - 10 \div 2 =$ ☐

h $99 - 72 \div 9 + 24 =$ ☐

1 Use the BODMAS rule to work out the answers to these calculations.

a $72 \div 9 + 7 \times 5 =$ ☐

b $80 - (32 \div 8) =$ ☐

c $14 + 35 \div 7 - 10 =$ ☐

d $23 + (7 \times 9) - 12 =$ ☐

e $7 \times 9 \div 3 - 20$ ☐

f $160 \div 2 - (8 \times 9) =$ ☐

g $36 + 18 \times 2 - 4 =$ ☐

h $(49 - 13) \div 2 \times 5 - 45 =$ ☐

i $96 \div 4 \times 6 + 18 =$ ☐

j $3 \times (16 \div 2) + 16 \times 5 =$ ☐

k $12 \times 8 - 57 \div 3 =$ ☐

l $15 \times (73 - 54) + 39 \div 13 =$ ☐

2 Work out each calculation using the BODMAS rule. Write the letter for each answer in the box below the question to reveal the secret phrase.

10 + 3 × 6	54 – 4 × 3 × 2	6 + 35 ÷ 7 – 10	82 – 15 ÷ 5	8 + 60 ÷ 5 – 3

(41 + 11) × 2	21 × 2 + 1	(26 + 6) ÷ 2	99 ÷ 3 – 3 × 2	8 + 9 – 2 × 3

9 × 3 + 8	(18 + 10) – 2 × 3	16 + 7 × 4	12 ÷ 2 × 6 + 4 – 3

10 × 8 + 52 ÷ 4	67 – 27 ÷ 9	8 + (7 × 9) – 12	22 + 18 × 2 + 4

38 + (9 × 6) ÷ 3	27 ÷ 9 + 12 ÷ 4	(10 + 5) × 3 – 25	34 ÷ 2 + 4

98 ÷ (2 × 7) + 79 – 41	12 ÷ 2 – 5 + 17	54 – 16 ÷ 4

43	30	104	28	17	16	50	11	62	22	79	59	20	27
O	D	I	A	T	N	N	E	T	O	I	B	C	B

56	64	18	35	1	93	21	37	44	45	6
R	U	O	F	D	S	T	E	R	I	A

Challenge **3** Put brackets in each statement to make it correct.

a 88 – 8 ÷ 2 = 40

b 68 ÷ 2 + 2 × 8 + 31 – 42 = 39

c 81 ÷ 53 – 44 = 9

d 9 × 48 ÷ 3 + 5 – 13 = 41

e 38 + 10 – 2 × 6 = 36

f 64 –16 ÷ 3 + 2 × 6 = 28

g 8 + 8 × 9 – 11 = 69

h 64 ÷ 16 × 4 + 12 – 7 + 5 = 1

Geometry

Lesson 1: Triangles

- Identify equilateral, isosceles and scalene triangles

You will need
- coloured pencils

Challenge 1 Use the key to colour each triangle.

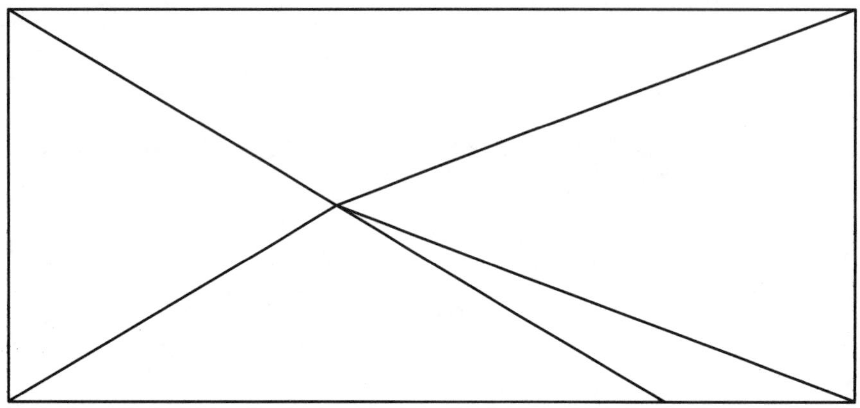

Key
Red – equilateral
Green – scalene
Blue – isosceles

Challenge 2

1 Complete the table, putting the letter of each shape in the correct column.

Equilateral triangles	Isosceles triangles	Scalene triangles

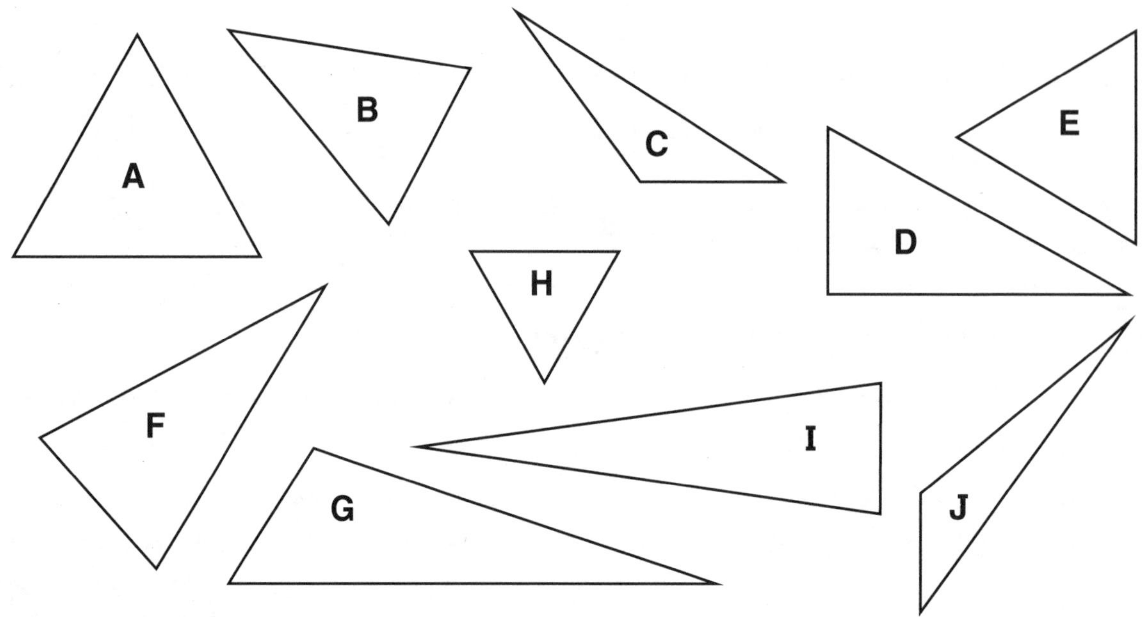

2 Complete the table. Write ✓ for yes and ✗ for no.

Triangle	Equilateral	Isosceles	Scalene
all sides equal, all angles equal			
two sides equal, two angles equal			
no sides equal, no angles equal			
can have a right angle			
can have an angle greater than 90°			
has two or more angles less than 90°			
regular shape			
irregular shape			

Challenge **3** Divide each quadrilateral by drawing a diagonal. Name the triangles it makes. The first one has been done for you.

parallelogram

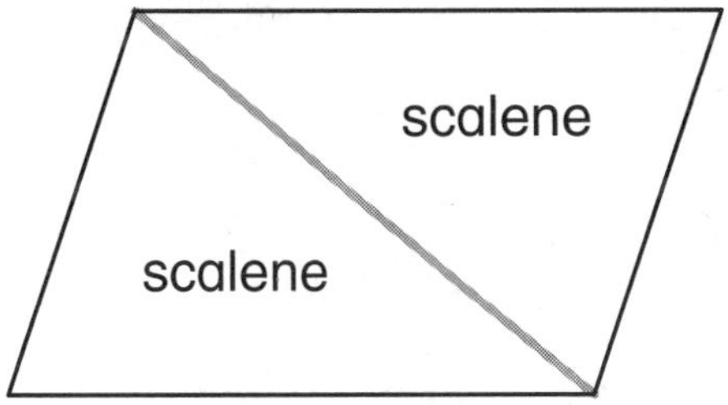

scalene

scalene

square

rhombus

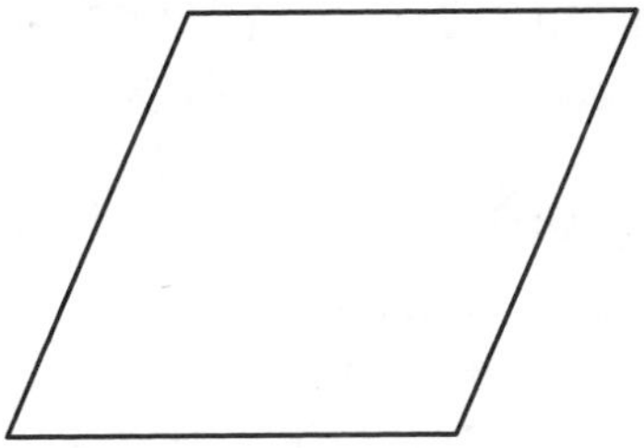

rectangle

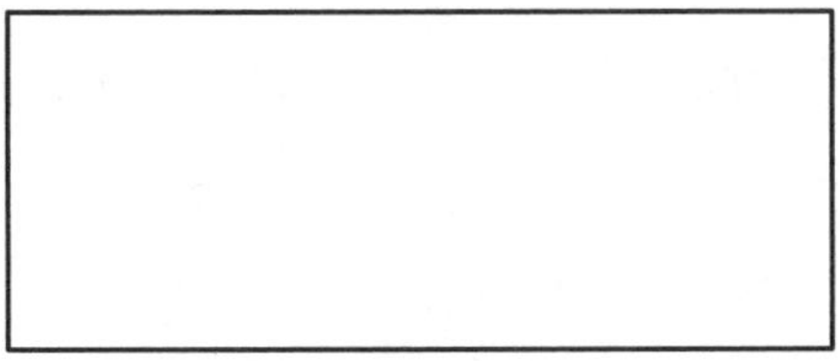

trapezium

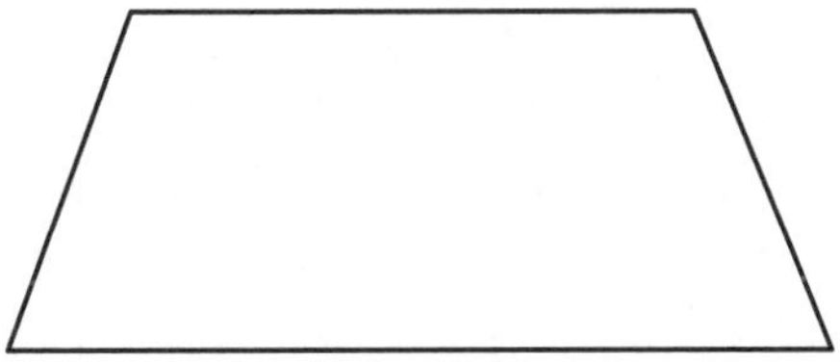

kite

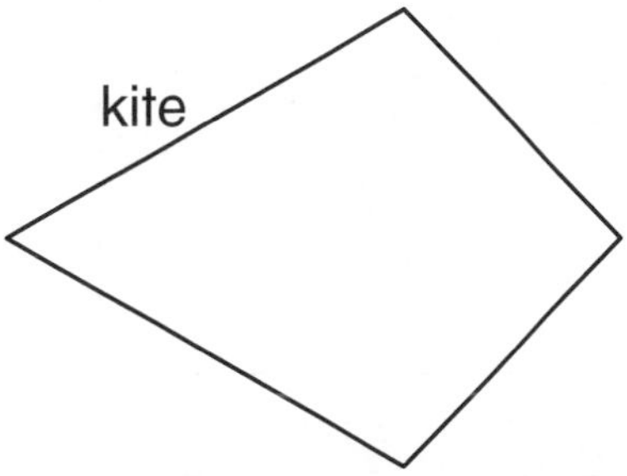

Lesson 2: **Symmetry in regular polygons**

- Recognise reflective symmetry in a regular polygon
- Identify lines of symmetry in a regular polygon
- Recognise rotational symmetry in a regular polygon

You will need
- coloured pencils

Place a tick (✓) in the boxes to indicate whether each shape has reflective symmetry, rotational symmetry or both.

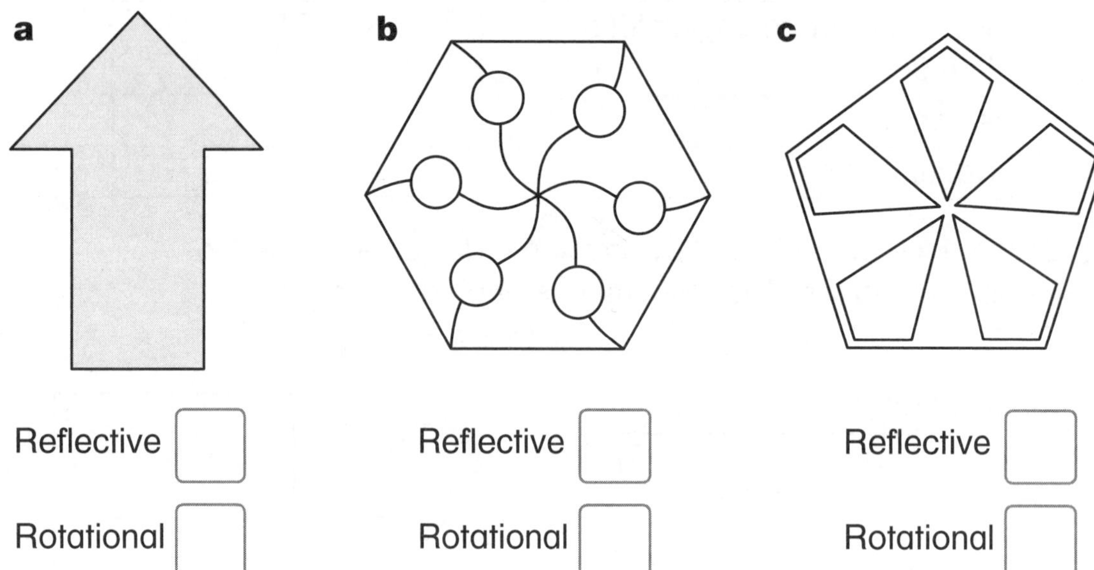

1 Draw dotted lines to indicate lines of symmetry in each shape. Write the number of lines of symmetry in the box.

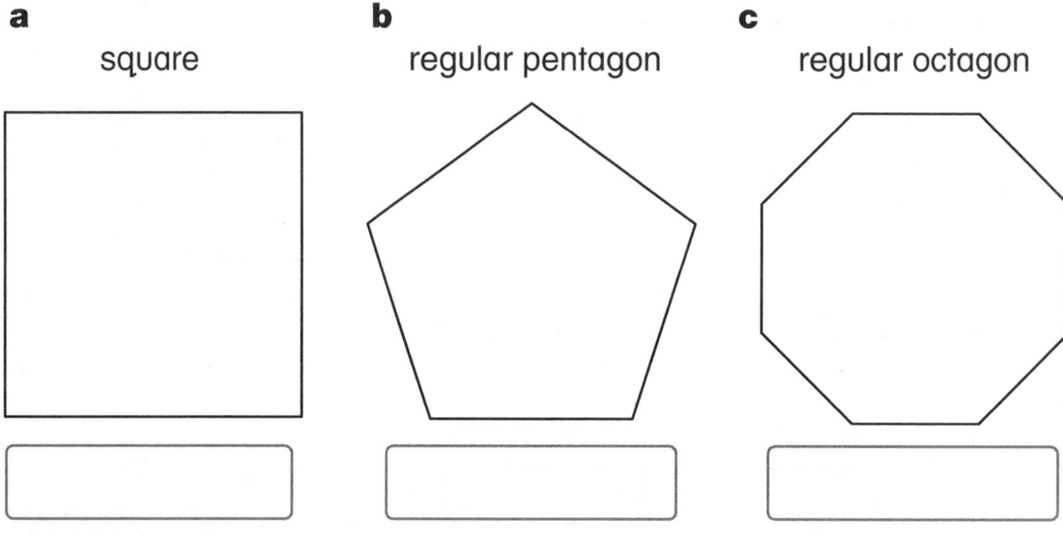

2 How many times can each logo be rotated around its centre so that it fits on top of itself? Write the number in the box.

a

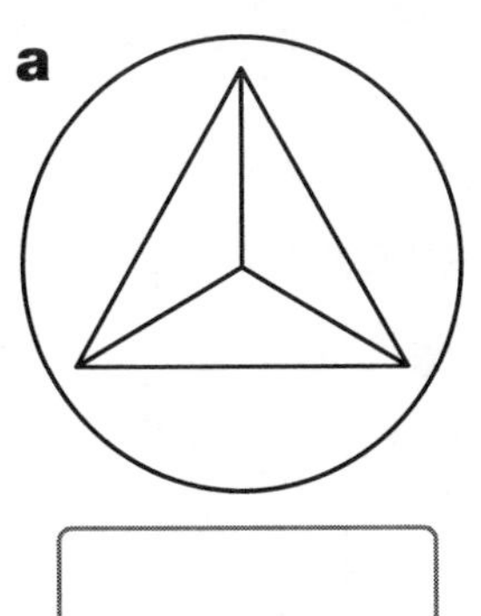

b

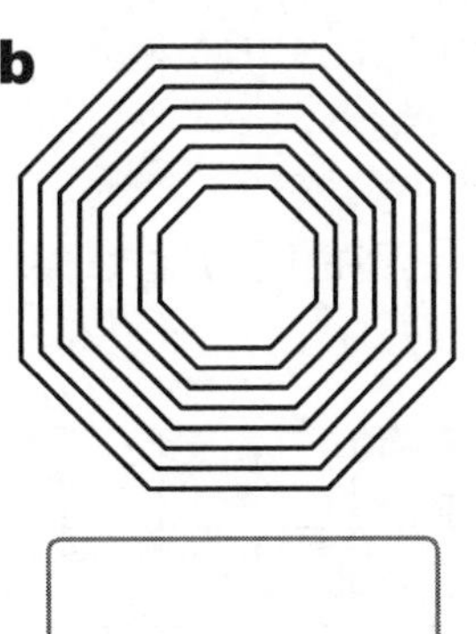

c

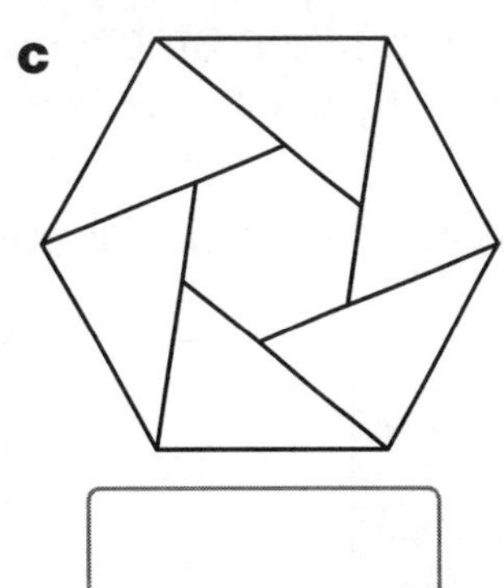

3 Draw a logo of your own that has both reflective and rotational symmetry.

Challenge **3** Colour each shape so that, when rotated about its centre, it will fit on top of itself the number of times given. A full turn does not count.

a

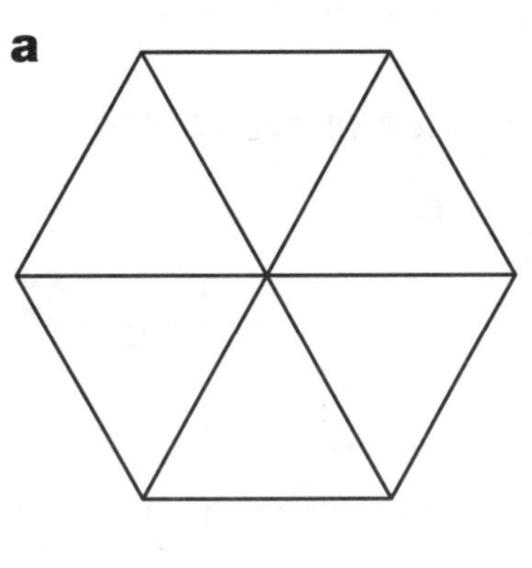

3

b

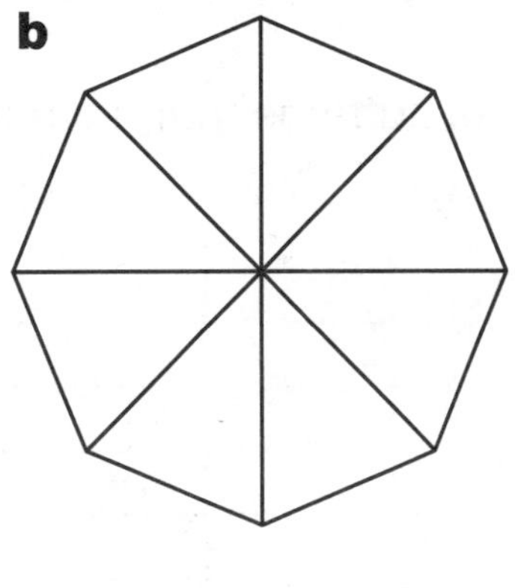

2

c

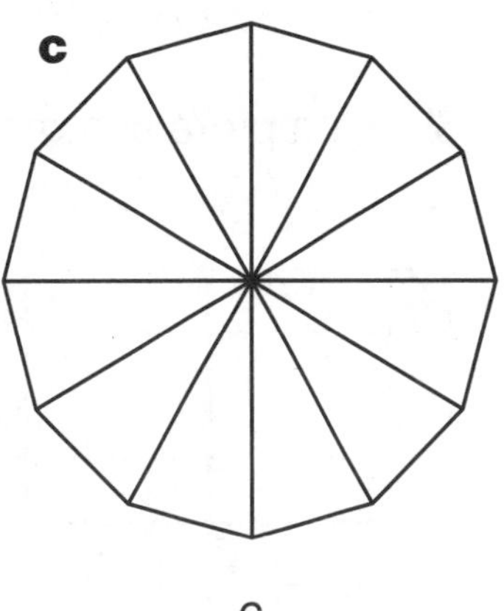

6

Lesson 3: **Symmetrical patterns**

- Complete a symmetrical pattern on squared paper that has two lines of symmetry

Challenge 1

Complete symmetrical patterns that have one line of symmetry.

a

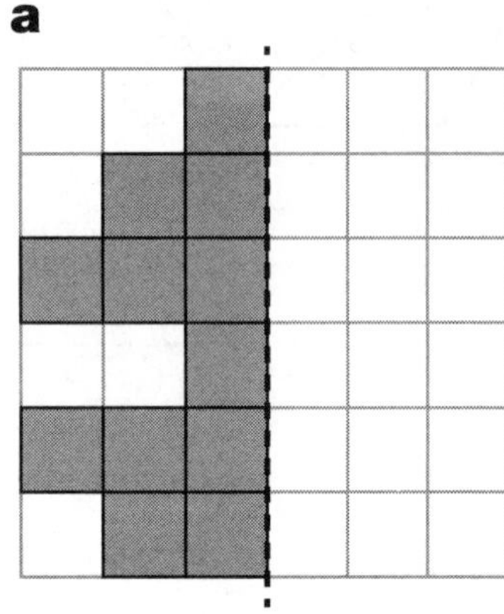

b

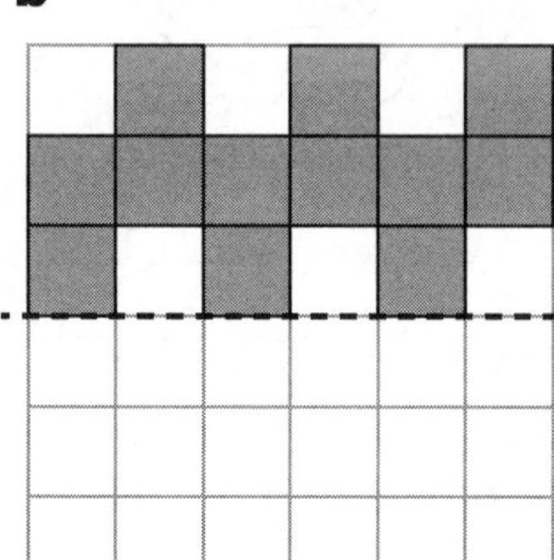

c

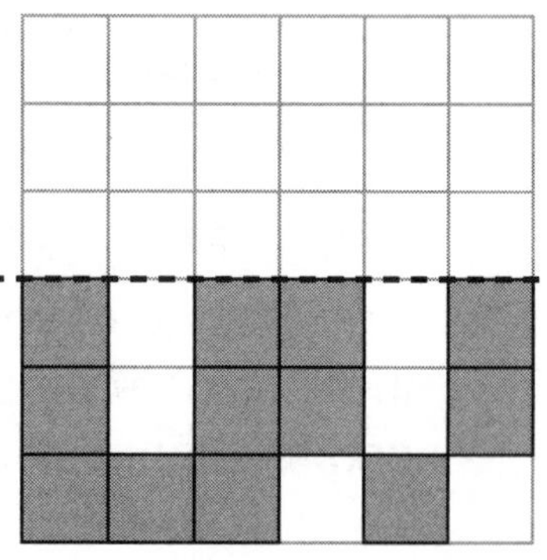

Challenge 2

1 Complete symmetrical patterns that have one line of symmetry.

a

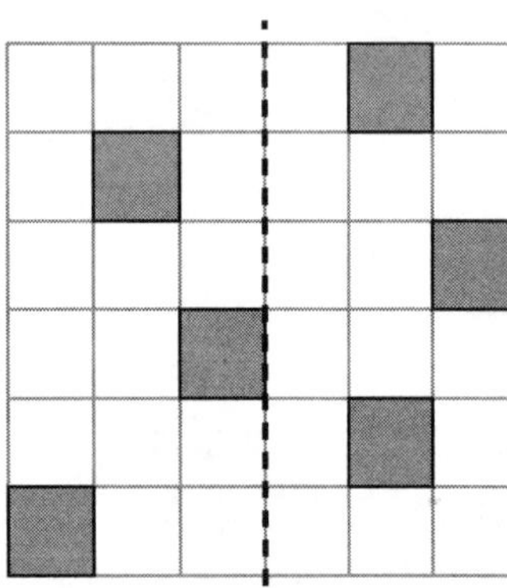

b

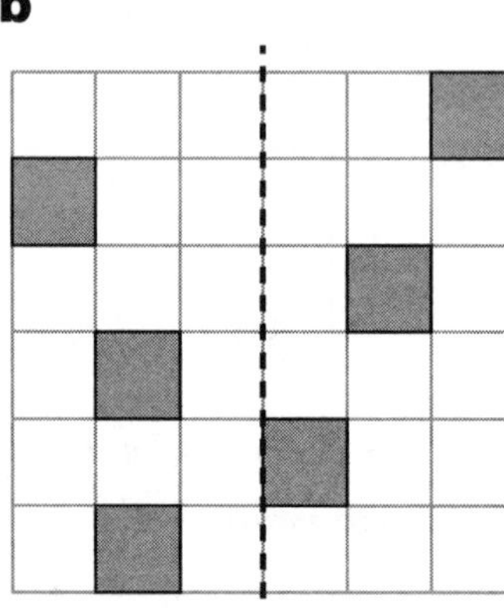

c

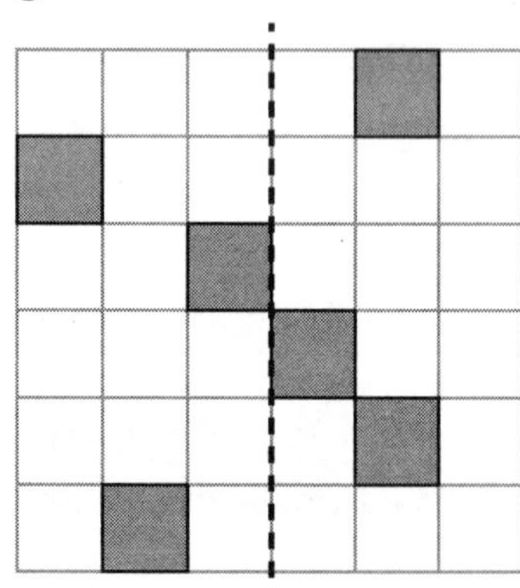

2 Complete symmetrical patterns that have two lines of symmetry.

a

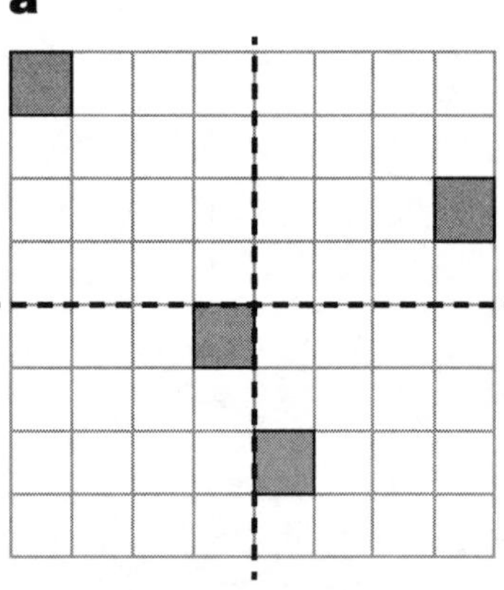

b

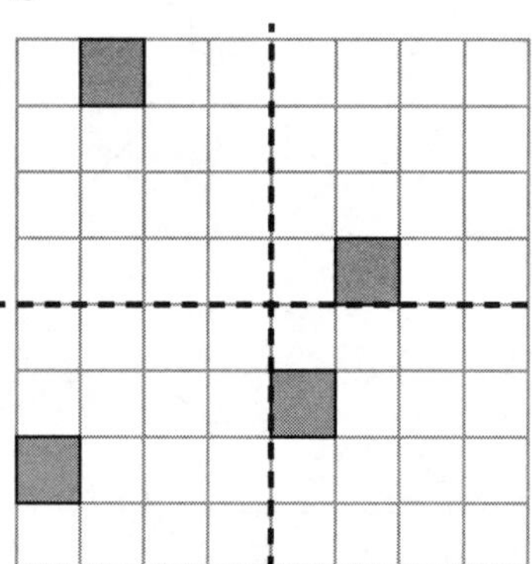

c

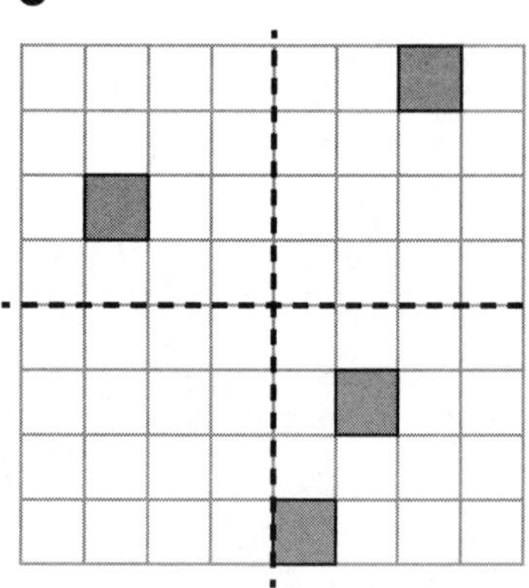

3 Create your own symmetrical patterns with the pegboards below. The first two have been done for you.

a

b

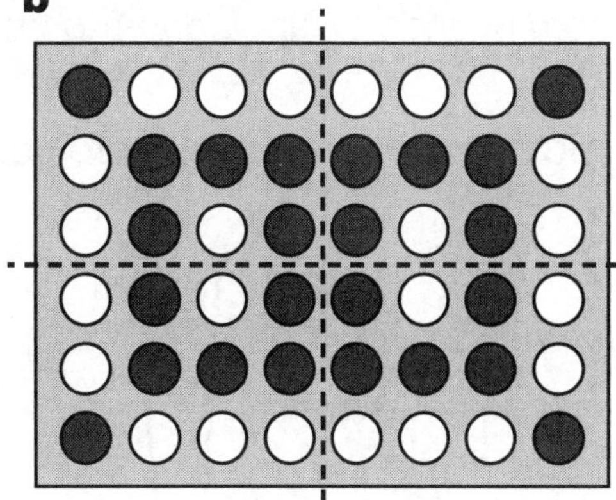

c

d

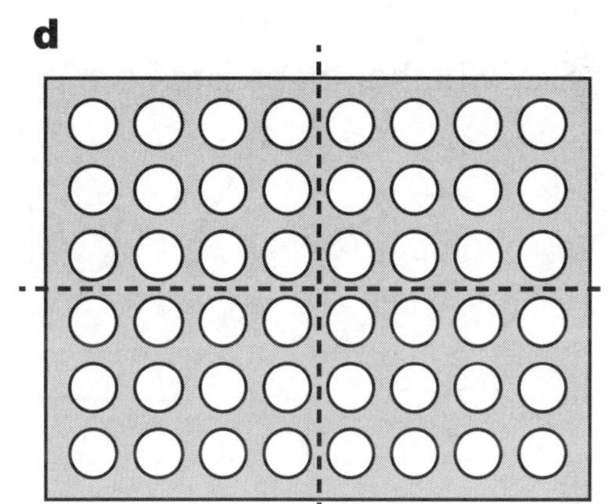

Challenge 3 Complete the grid designs to give them rotational symmetry. Make up your own design using the empty grid.

a

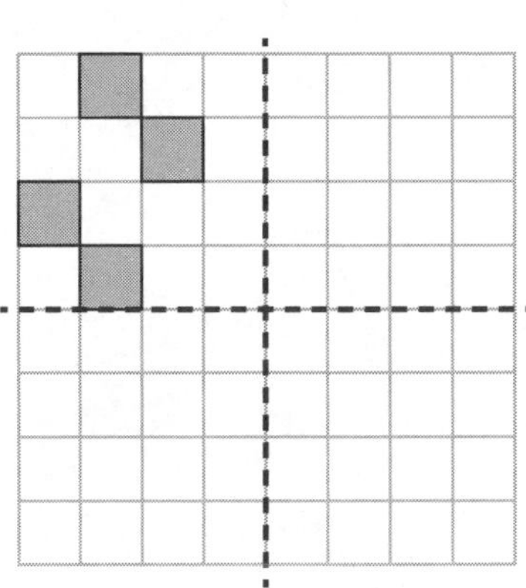

b

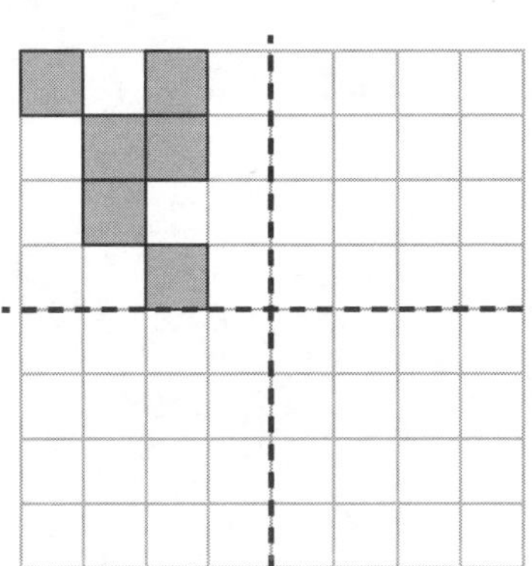

c

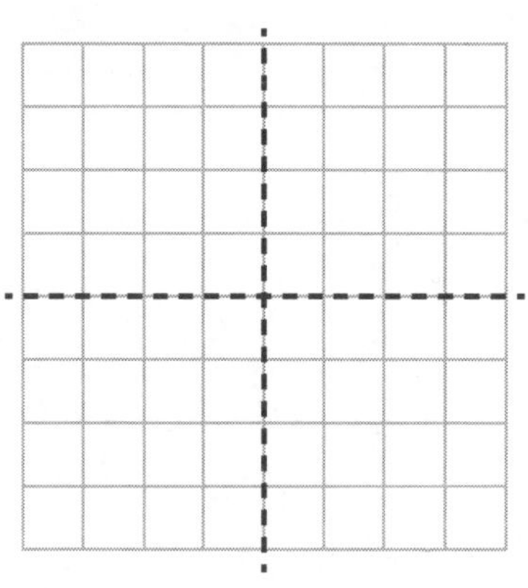

Lesson 4: **Perpendicular and parallel lines**

- Describe parallel and perpendicular lines and recognise them in grids, shapes and the environment

You will need
- red pencil

Challenge 1

Say whether these lines are parallel or not.

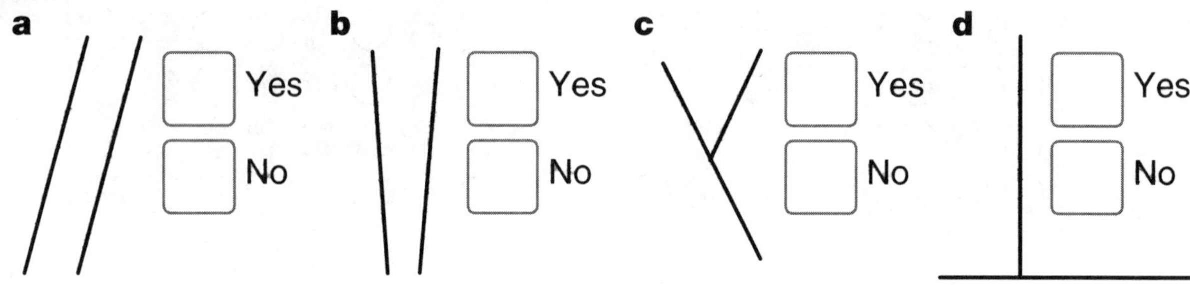

Say whether these lines are perpendicular or not.

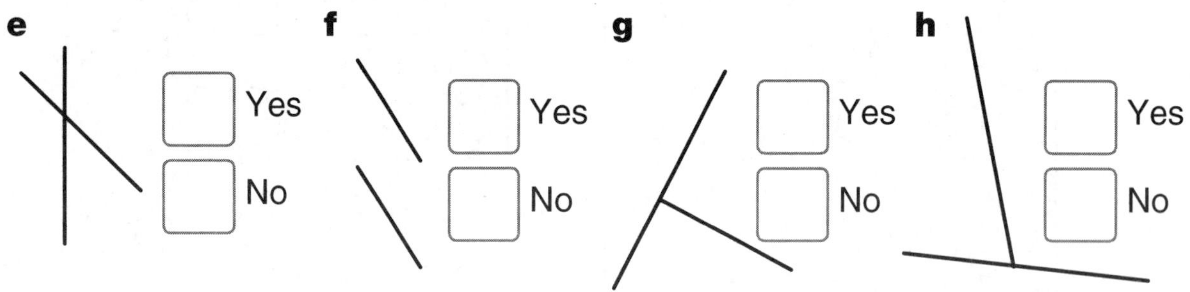

Challenge 2

1 Say whether each set of lines is parallel, perpendicular or neither.

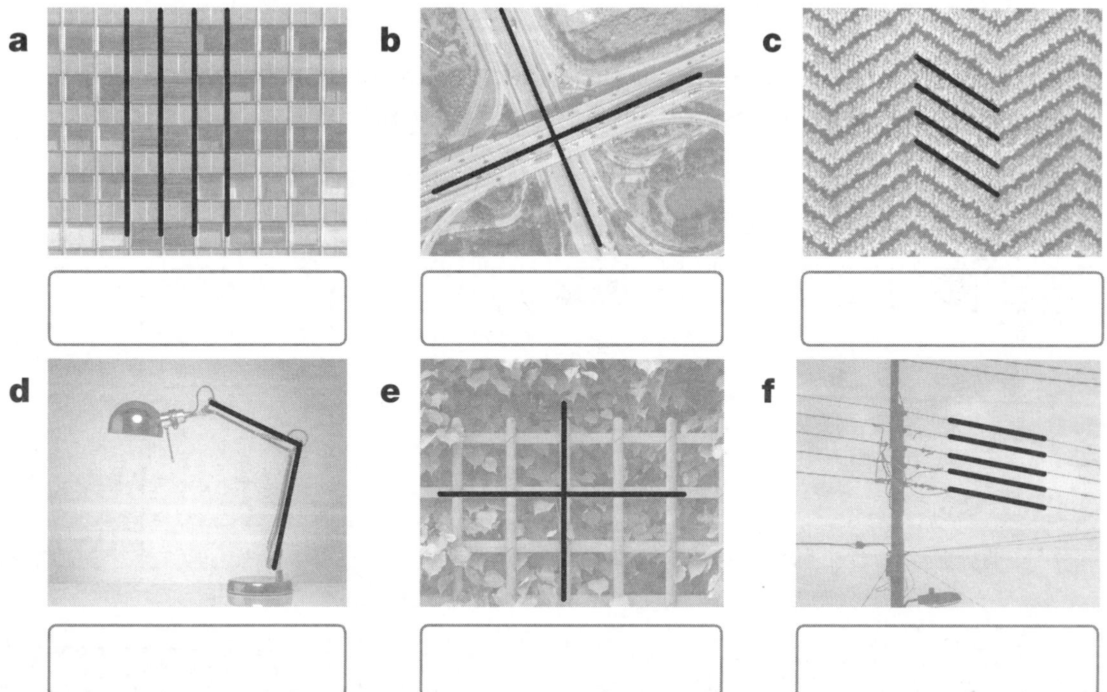

2 Find two lines in each picture that match the description. Highlight them in red. The first one has been done for you.

a Perpendicular

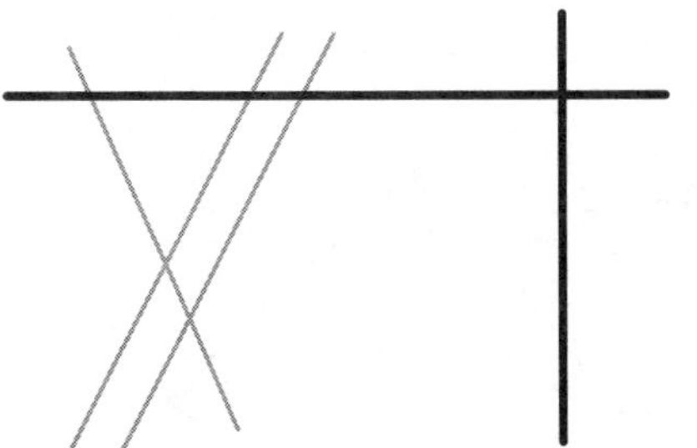

b Parallel

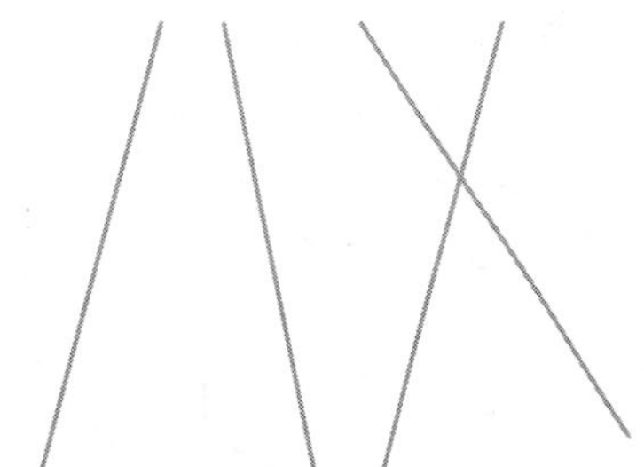

c Perpendicular

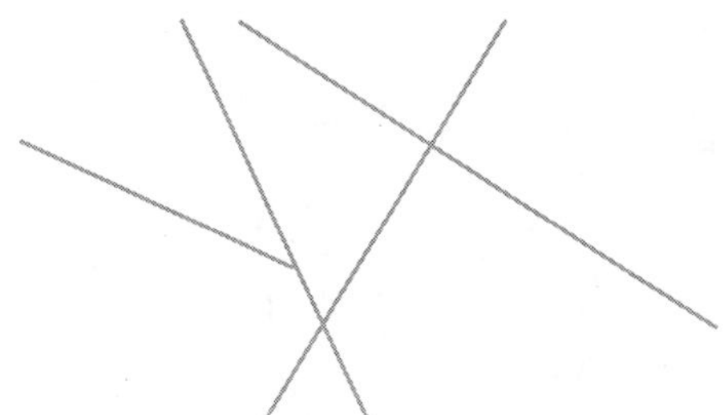

d Parallel

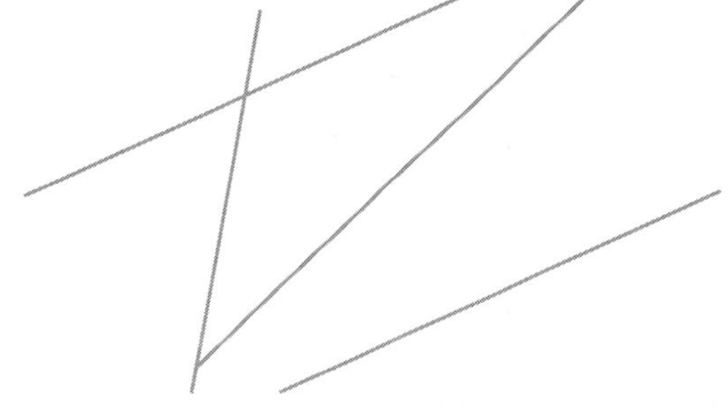

Challenge **3** Join the black dots to make parallel lines and join the white dots to make perpendicular lines. Use a ruler to help you draw straight lines.

a
- Draw a pair of parallel lines.
- Draw a line perpendicular to one of them.

b
- Draw a pair of parallel lines.
- Draw a pair of lines perpendicular to them.

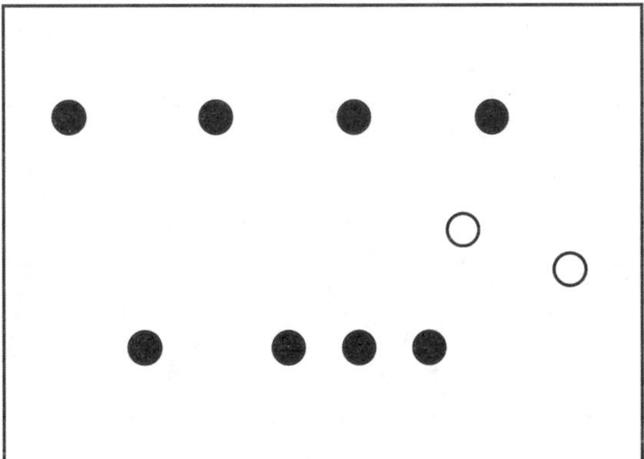

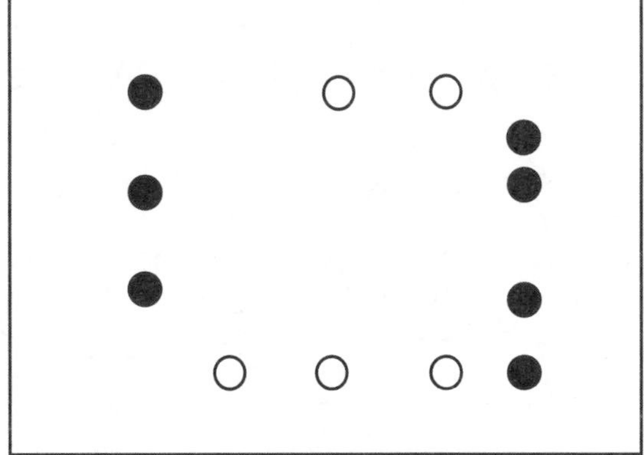

Lesson 1: **Visualising 3D shapes**

- Imagine what a 3D shape would look like from a 2D drawing

Challenge 1 Name the 3D shape.

a

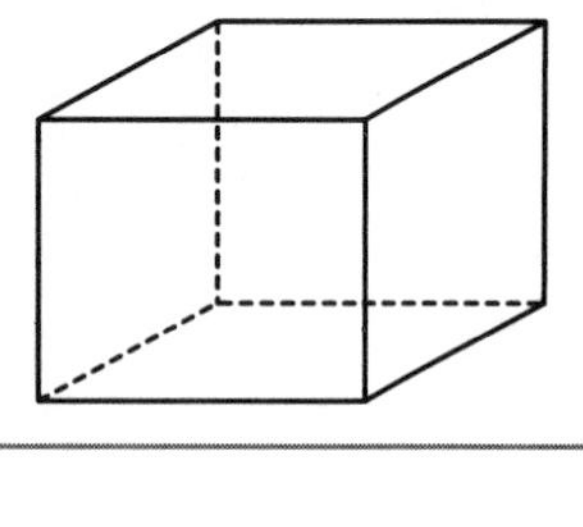

b

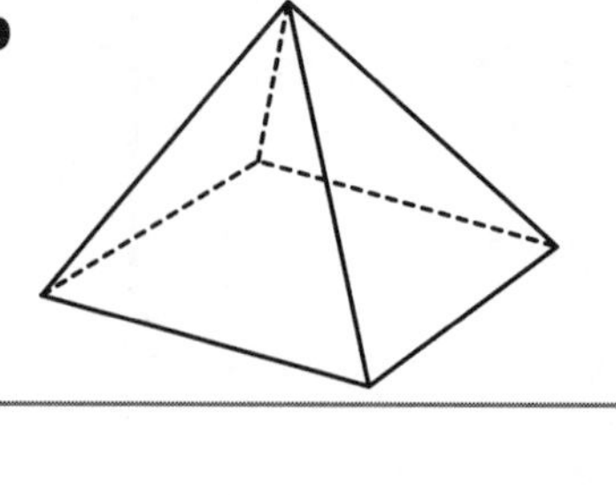

c

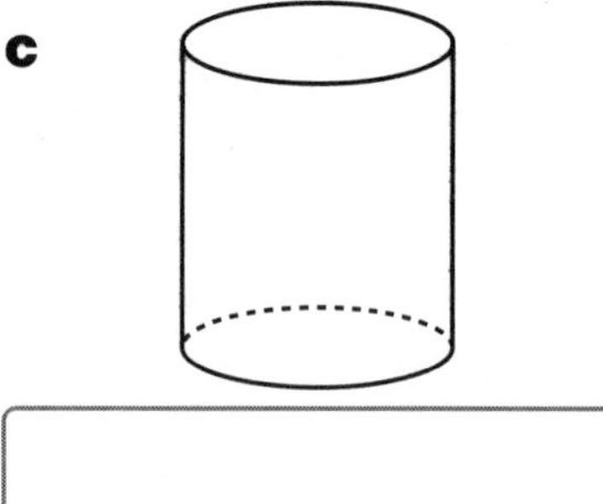

d

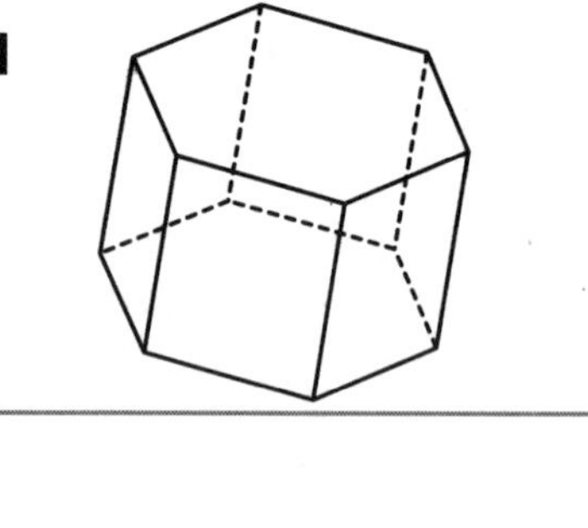

Challenge 2 **1** Choose the correct name for each shape.

pentagonal prism	hexagonal pyramid	cone	tetrahedron

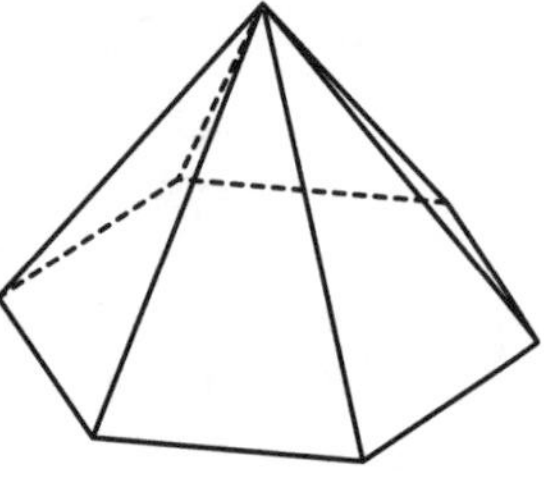

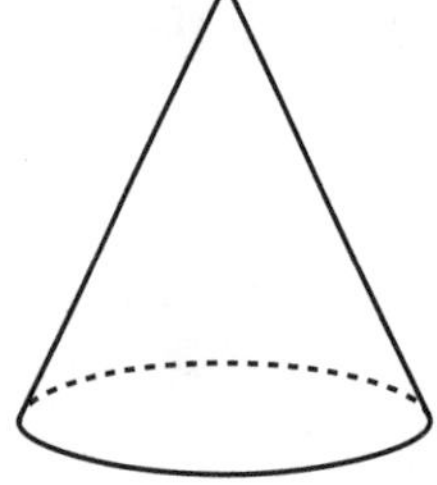

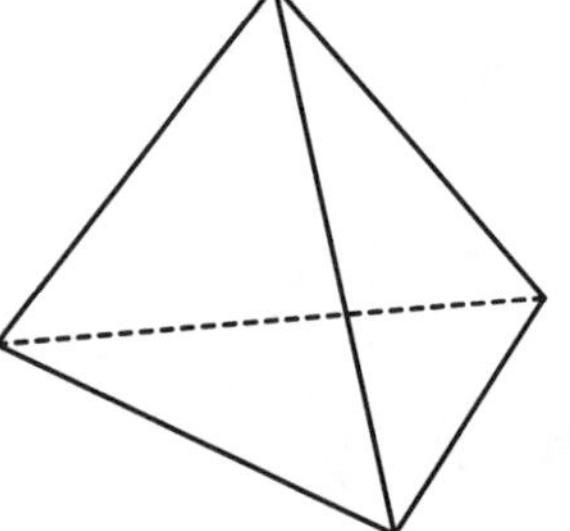

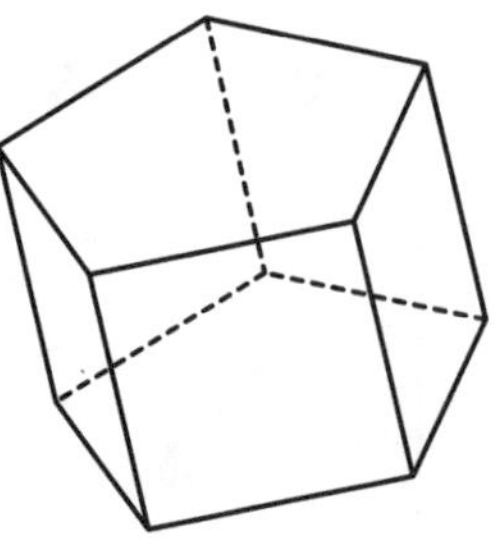

2 Draw the 3D shapes named in each box.

a cube	**b** cuboid
c cylinder	**d** cone

Challenge 3 Draw dotted lines to show the edges and faces of the shapes that are hidden from view. The first one has been completed for you.

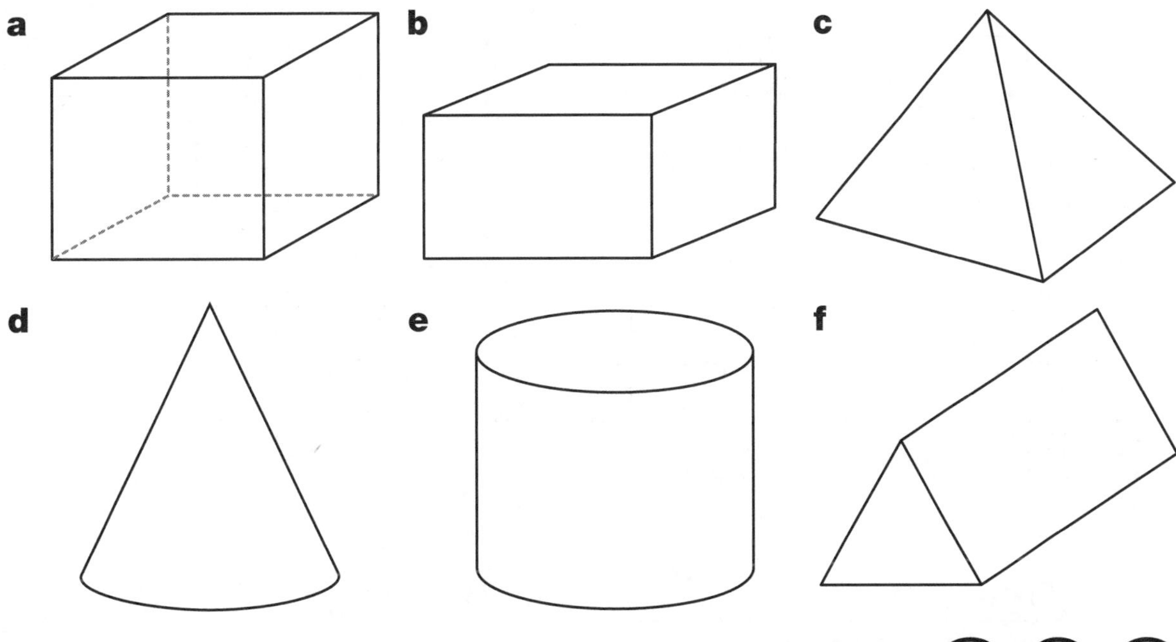

Lesson 2: **Nets**

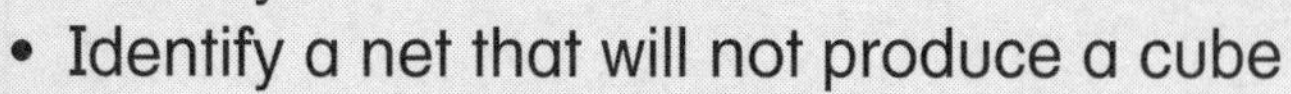

- Imagine what a 3D shape would look like from its net
- Identify and build different nets for a cube
- Identify a net that will not produce a cube

You will need
- coloured pencils
- squared paper

Challenge 1

Circle the correct net for each cube.

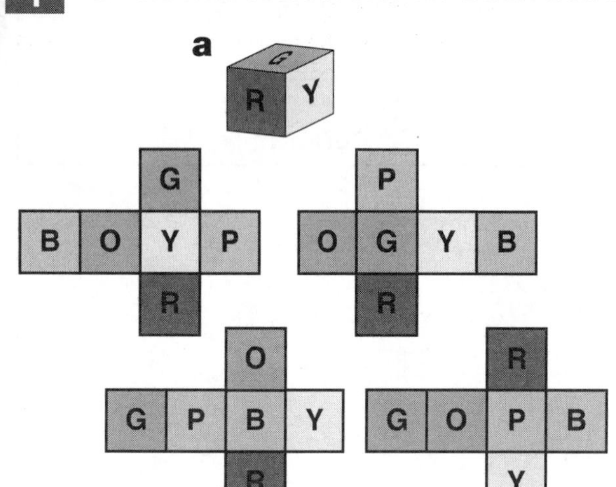

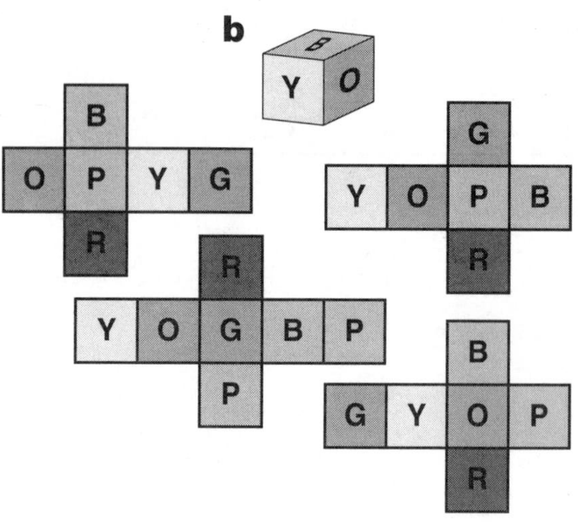

Challenge 2

1 Some of the shapes below are nets of open or closed cubes. For each shape, put ✓ in the table if the shape is a net of an open or closed cube and ✗ if it is not. If you are not sure, copy the shape onto squared paper, cut it out and try to fold it into a cube to check.

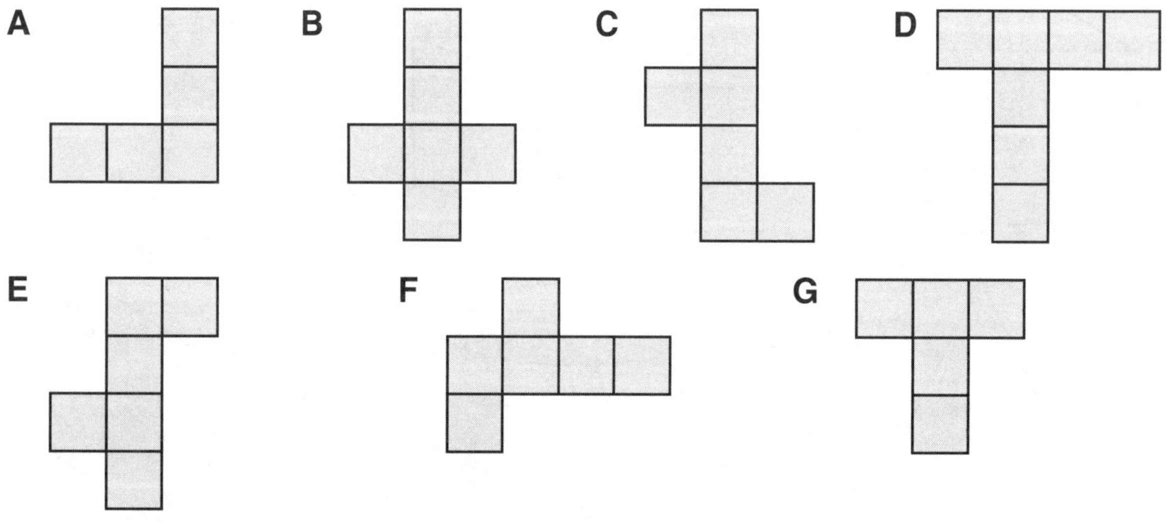

Shape	A	B	C	D	E	F	G
Net of an open or closed cube							

2 Look at the three views of each closed cube. Work out where the faces are in relation to each other and colour in the faces of the net.

Views of cube	Net of cube
B, O, G · Y, G, O · B, P, R	
O, R, Y · O, G, B · P, B, G	

Challenge 3 Circle the net that has the vertices of the cube correctly labelled.

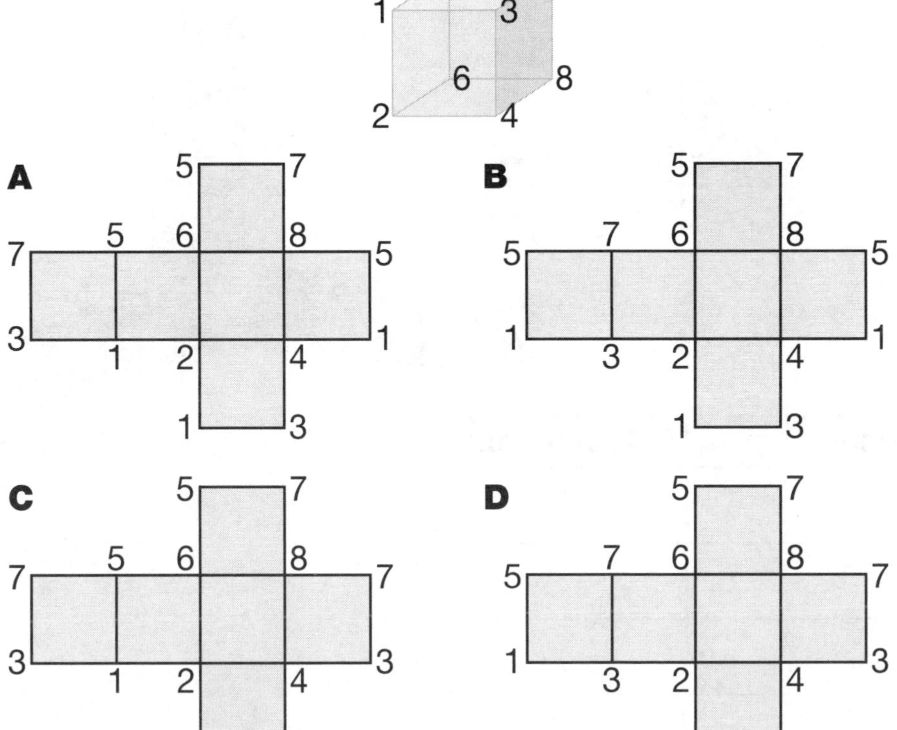

Lesson 3: **Constructing 3D shapes**

- Build 3D shapes from different materials
- Build and use skeleton shapes to spot edges and vertices

You will need
- interlocking cubes
- modelling materials

Challenge 1

How many cubes are needed to make each shape? You can construct the shapes to check your answers. Write the number in the box.

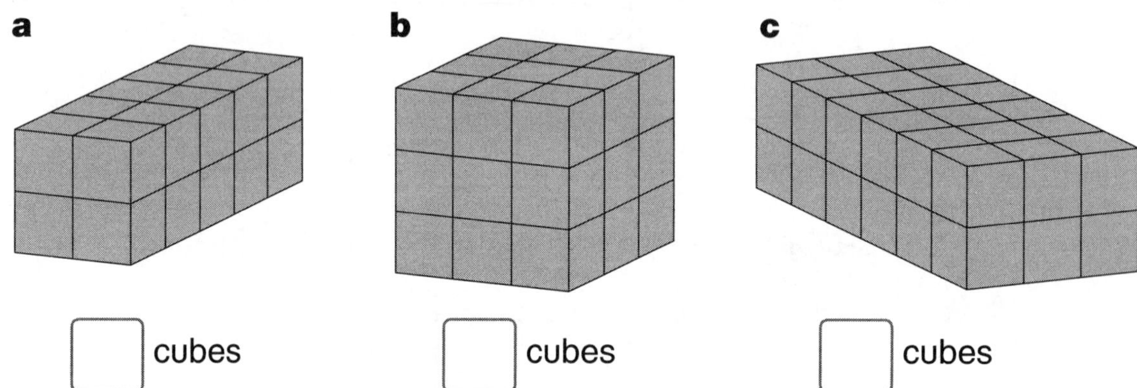

a ☐ cubes **b** ☐ cubes **c** ☐ cubes

Challenge 2

1 What is the smallest number of cubes that need to be added to each shape for it to become a cuboid? Estimate first, then make the model and count the number of cubes used to check your answer.

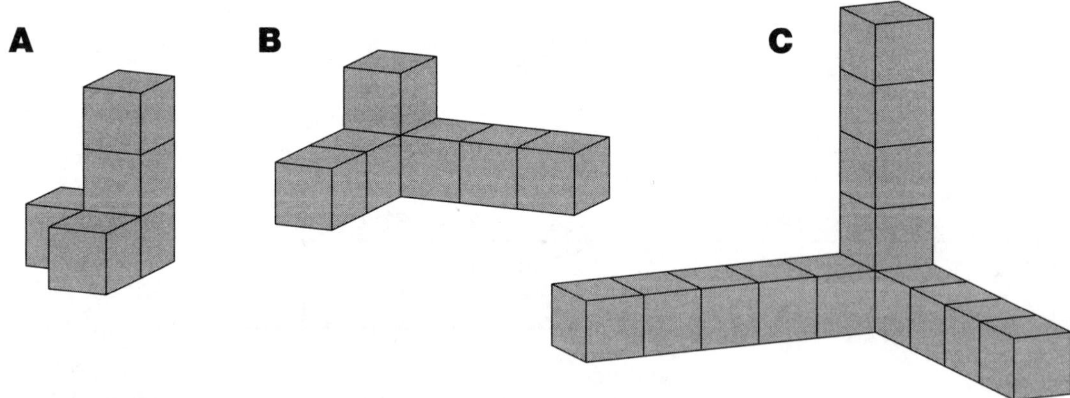

Shape	Estimate	Actual number
A		
B		
C		

2 Construct the shapes using any modelling material you like. Draw your models and complete the answer boxes.

Cube	**Triangular-based pyramid**	**Square-based pyramid**
Shape of faces ______	Shape of faces ______	Shape of faces ______
Number of faces ☐	Number of faces ☐	Number of faces ☐
Number of vertices ☐	Number of vertices ☐	Number of vertices ☐
Number of edges ☐	Number of edges ☐	Number of edges ☐

Challenge **3** Construct more complex shapes using your choice of modelling materials. Draw your models and complete the answer boxes.

Pentagonal prism	**Hexagonal prism**	**Octahedron**
Shape of faces ______	Shape of faces ______	Shape of faces ______
Number of faces ☐	Number of faces ☐	Number of faces ☐
Number of vertices ☐	Number of vertices ☐	Number of vertices ☐
Number of edges ☐	Number of edges ☐	Number of edges ☐

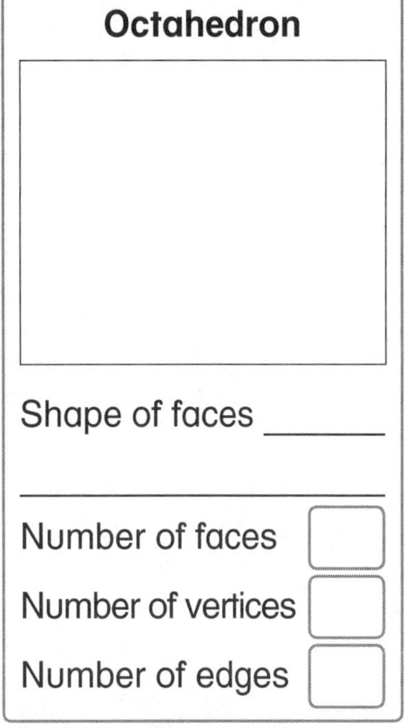

Geometry

Lesson 4: **Relationships between 3D shapes**

- Know that prisms and pyramids are named according to the shape of their base.
- Recognise the relationships between different 3D shapes

You will need
- coloured pencils

Challenge 1

Colour all the prisms in red and all the pyramids in blue.

Challenge 2 Use the shape of the base to name each solid.

a

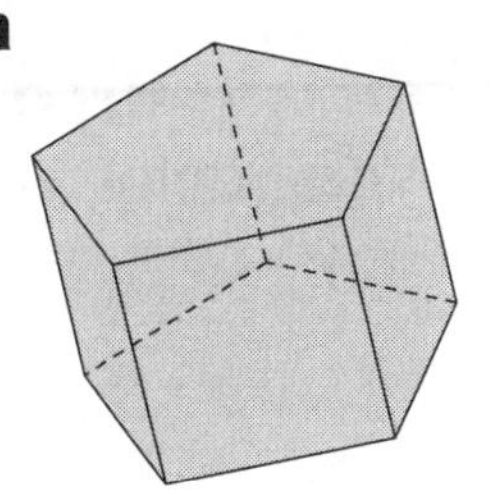

b

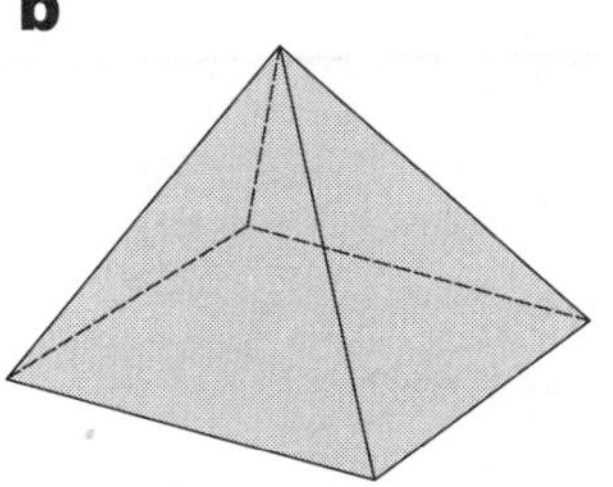

c

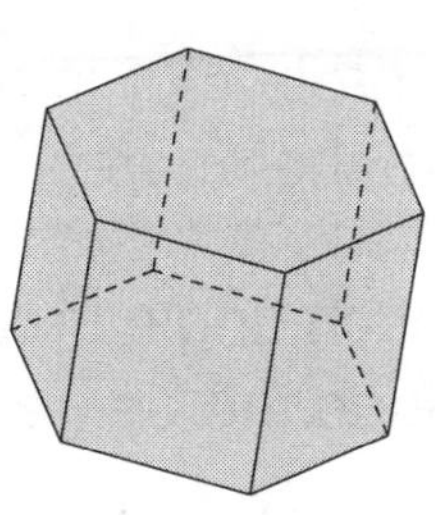

d

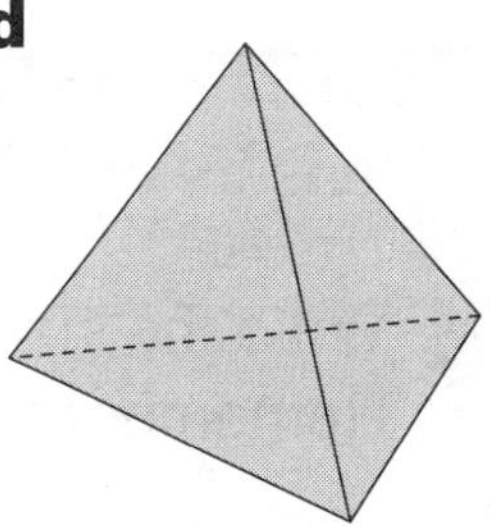

______________________ ______________________ ______________________ ______________________

______________________ ______________________ ______________________ ______________________

Challenge 3 Complete the table.

Shape	Number of faces	Number of vertices	Number of edges
triangular-based pyramid			
square-based pyramid			
triangular prism			
pentagonal prism			
hexagonal prism			
tetrahedron			
octahedron			

Geometry

Lesson 1: Measuring angles

- Know how to use a protractor to measure an angle
- Measure an angle to the nearest 5°

You will need
- protractor

Challenge 1 Write the size of each angle in degrees.
Remember to include the degrees symbol °.

a

b

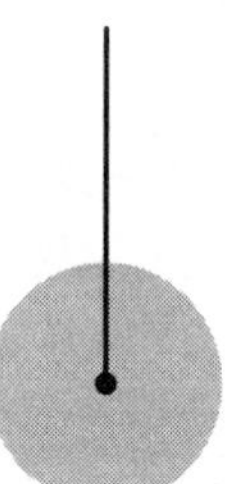

c

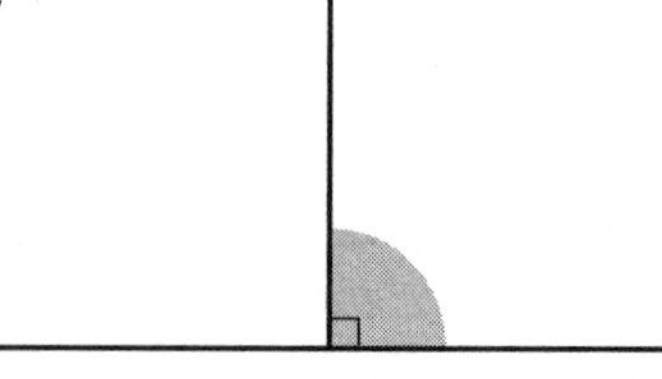

Challenge 2 **1** Read the scale and write the size of the angle.

a

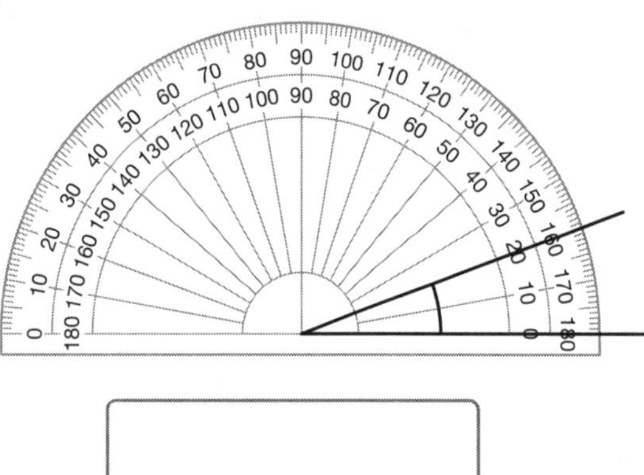

b

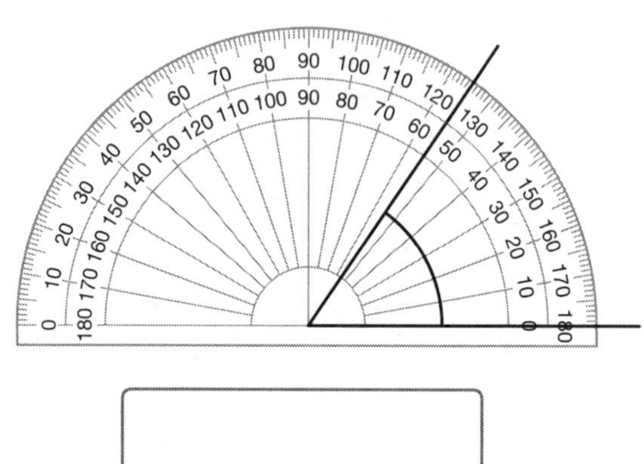

c

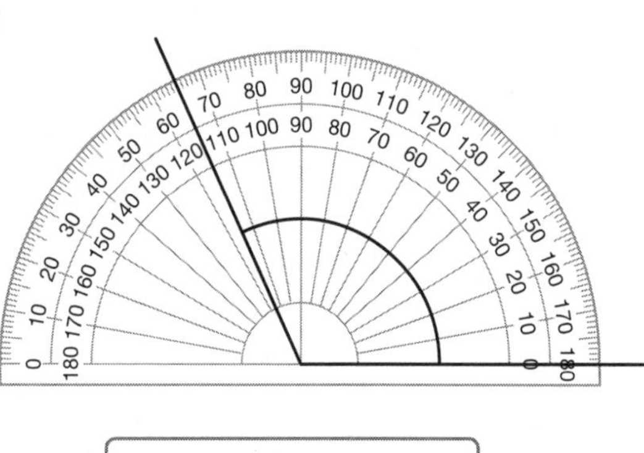

d

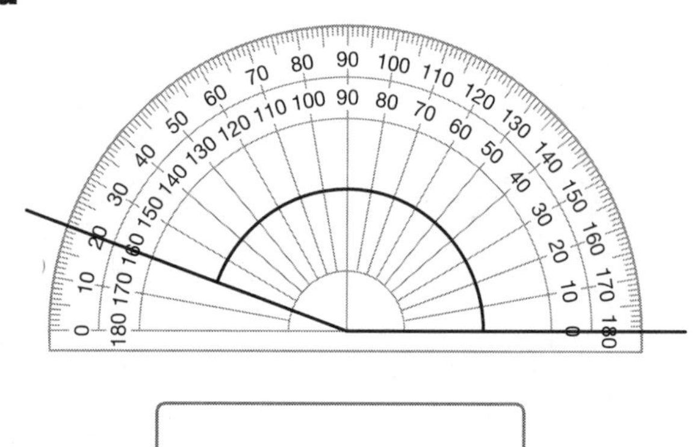

2 Use a protractor to measure each angle to the nearest 5°.

a

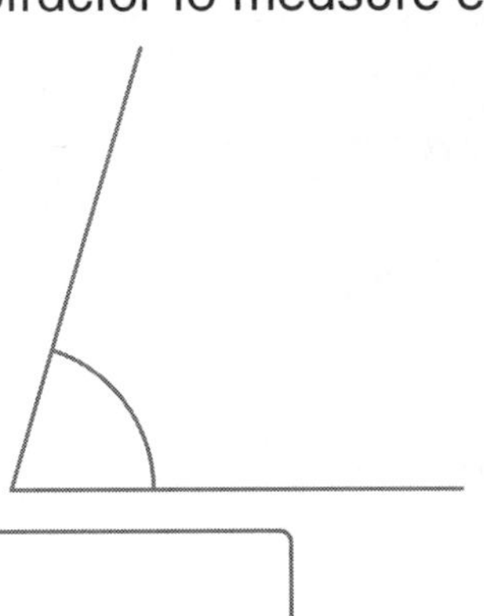

b

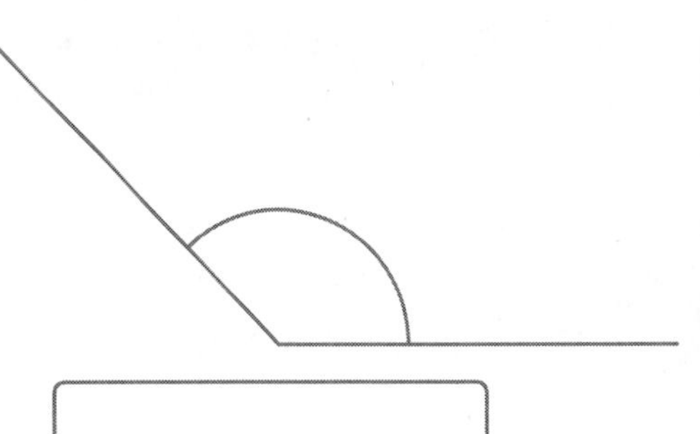

c

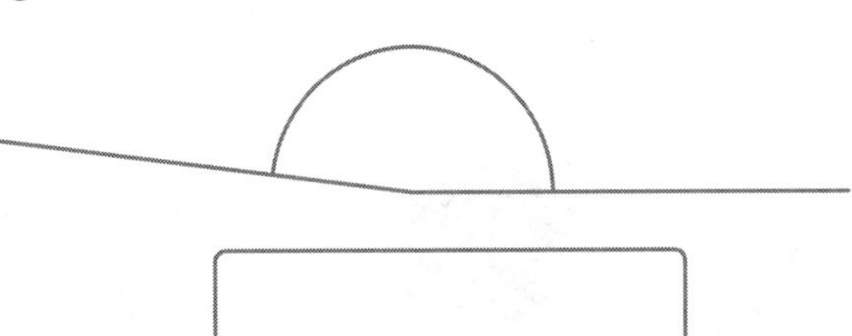

d

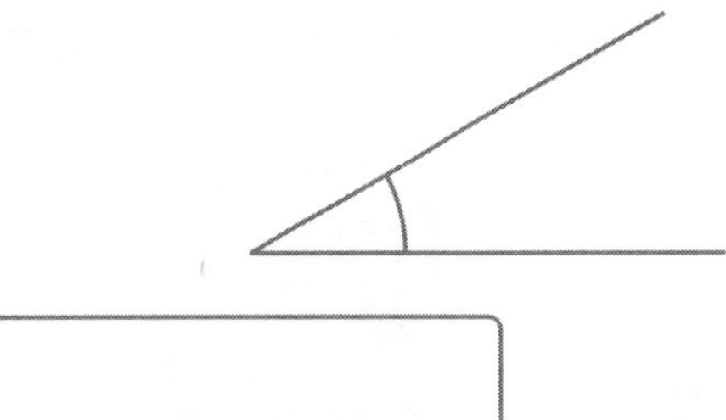

Challenge **3** Use a protractor to measure each angle to the nearest degree.

a

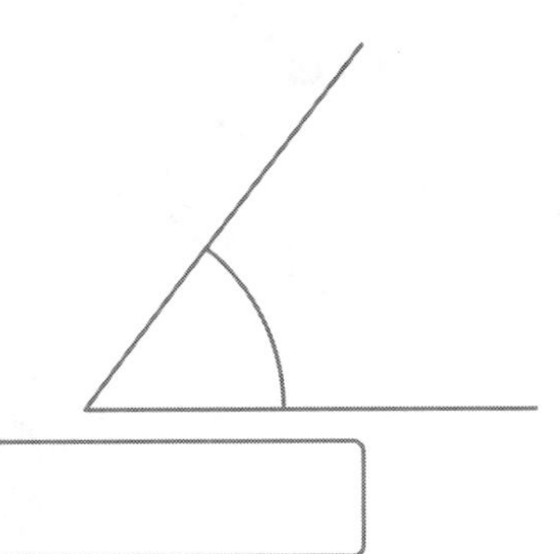

b

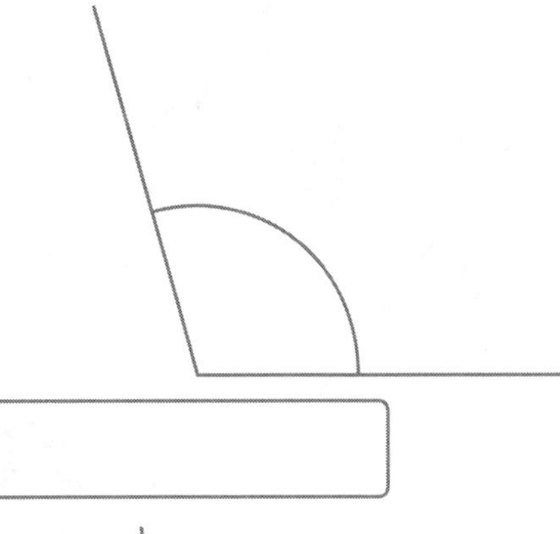

c

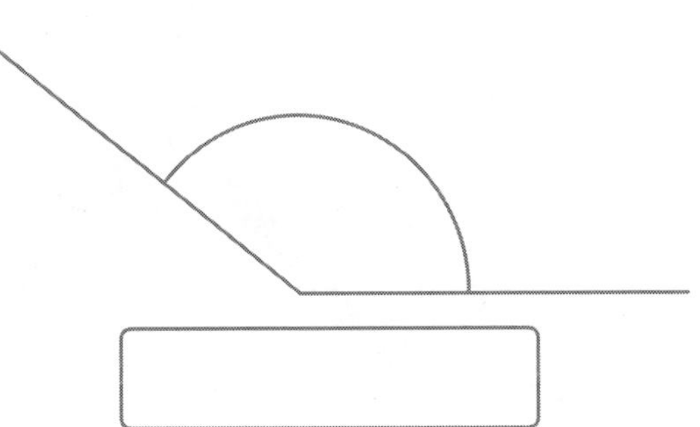

d

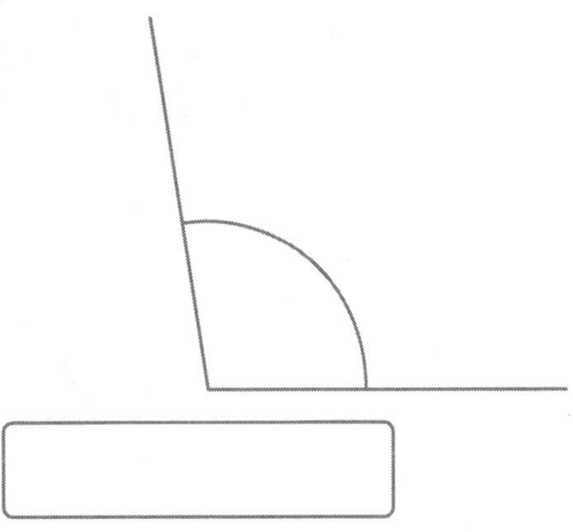

Lesson 2: **Angle size**

- Identify and describe angles less than, equal to or greater than a right angle (90°)
- Estimate the size of an angle and place angles in order

You will need
- pencil
- ruler
- protractor

Challenge 1

Write a letter inside each shaded angle.

L = less than a right angle
R = right angle
G = greater than a right angle

Challenge 2

Each angle has a letter. Place the set of angles in ascending and descending order, by writing the letters in the boxes provided.

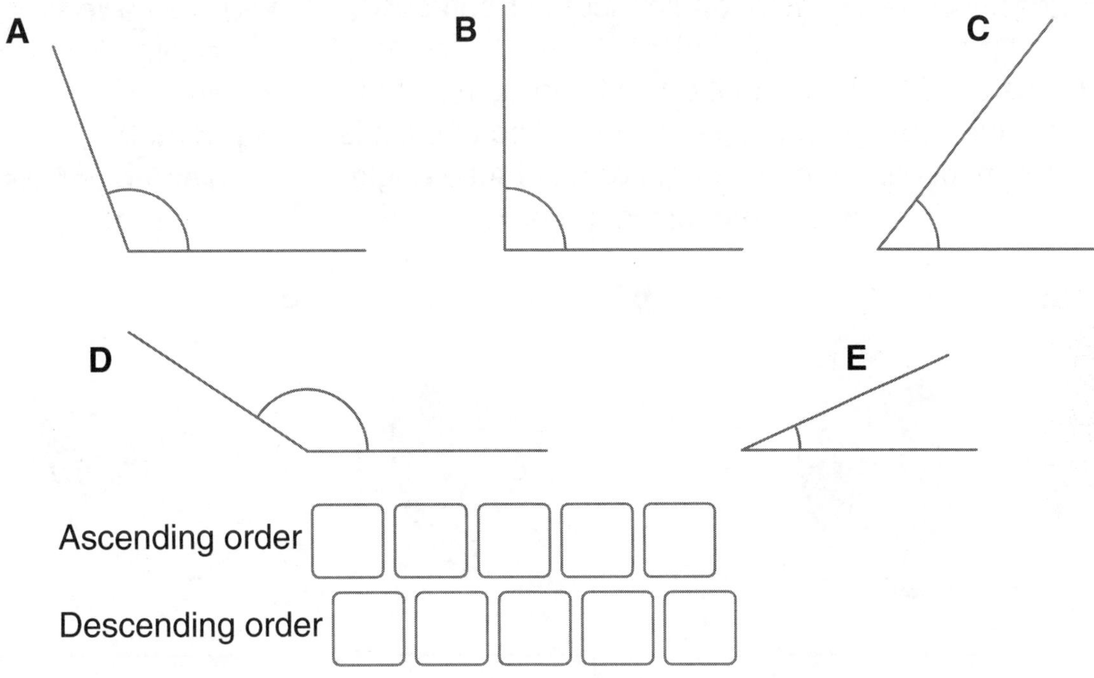

Ascending order ☐ ☐ ☐ ☐ ☐

Descending order ☐ ☐ ☐ ☐ ☐

Challenge 3

Look at the metro map below. Identify and label as many angles as you can find.

☹ 😐 ☺

Geometry

Lesson 3: **Classifying angles**

- Classify angles as right angle, acute or obtuse

You will need
- pencil
- ruler
- protractor
- coloured pencils

Use a protractor or right angle finder to help you decide whether the angle of each slice of cake is a right angle, an acute angle or an obtuse angle. Write the name of the angle in the box.

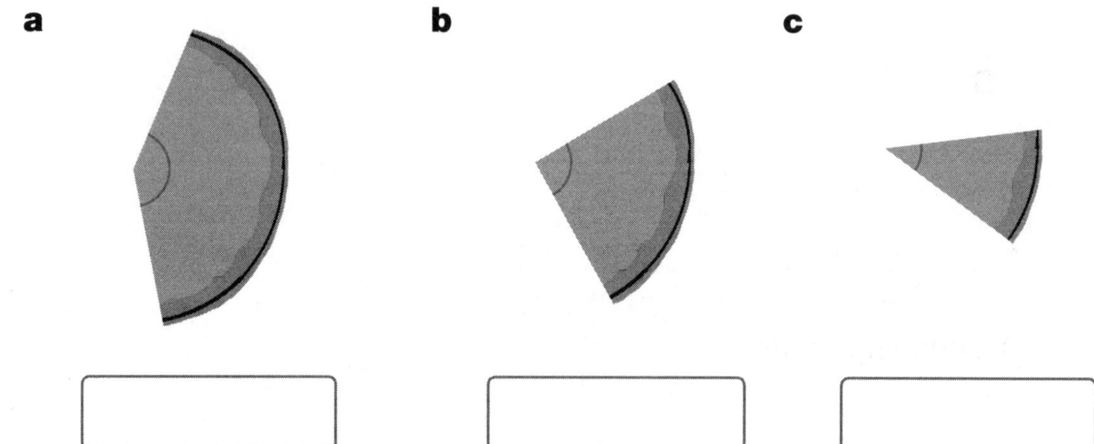

Challenge 2

1 Use a protractor or right angle finder to help you decide whether each angle is right, acute or obtuse. Write the name of the angle in the box.

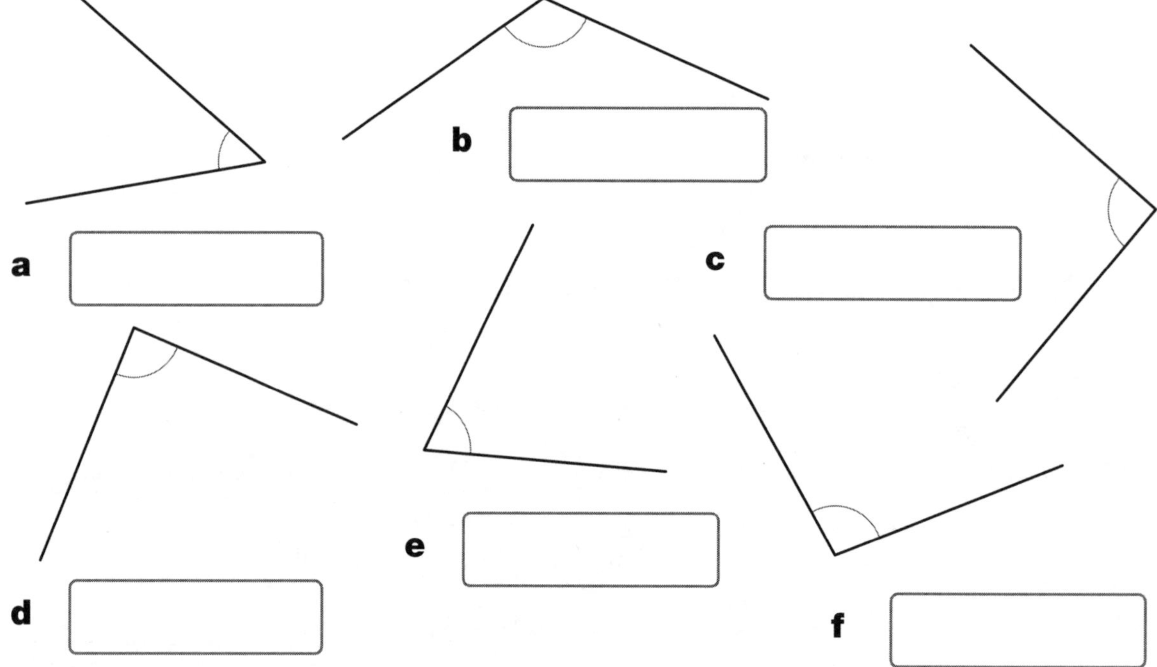

2 The shape contains many angles. Use the key to colour the angles. One of the acute angles has been shaded for you.

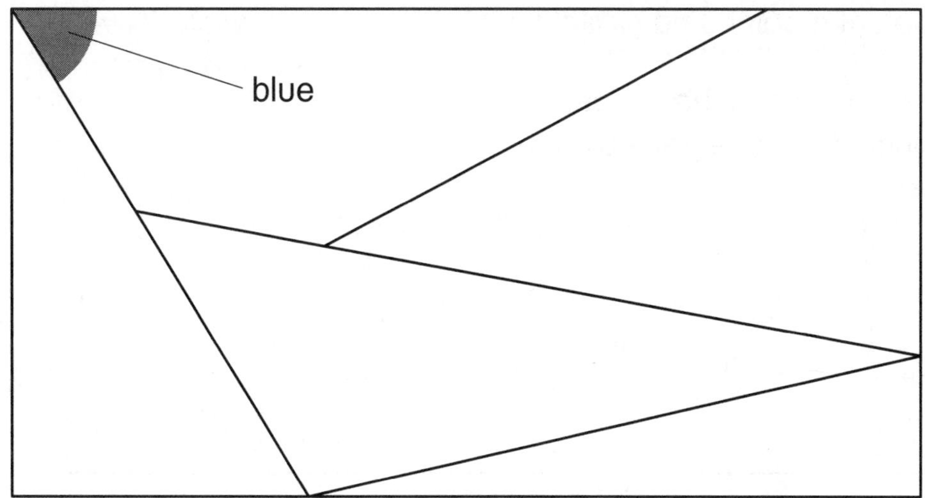

blue	acute
green	right
red	obtuse

Challenge 3 Use a ruler to divide a circle into sectors, four of which are acute angles and three of which are obtuse angles.

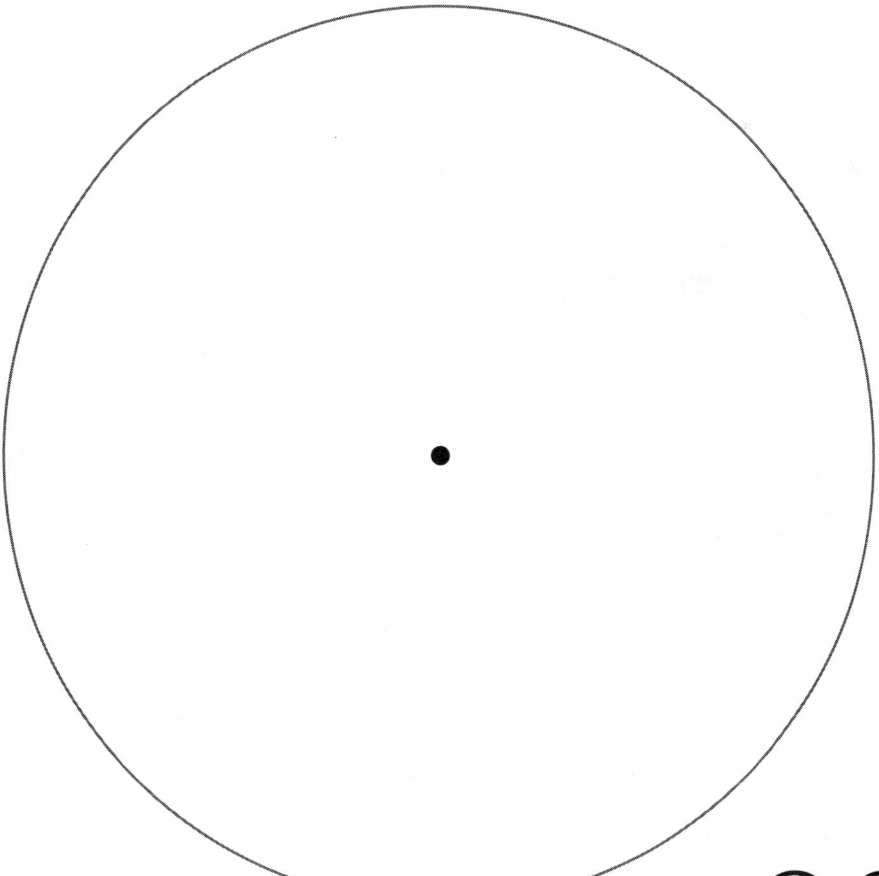

Geometry

Lesson 4: Angles on a straight line

- Identify two angles at a point on a straight line

You will need
- protractor

Challenge 1

Write the missing angles in the boxes.
Remember to include the degrees symbol °.

a

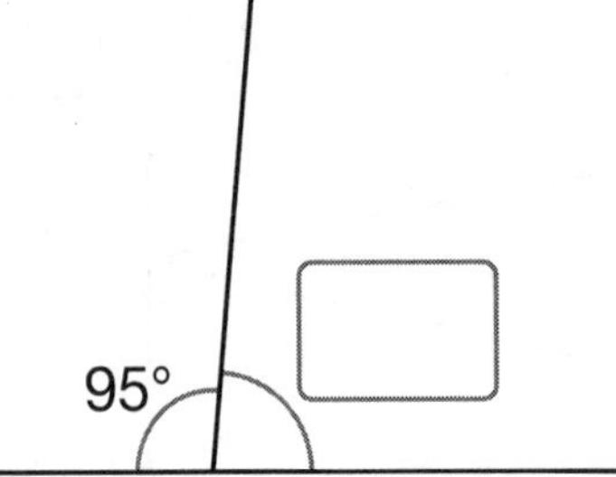

b

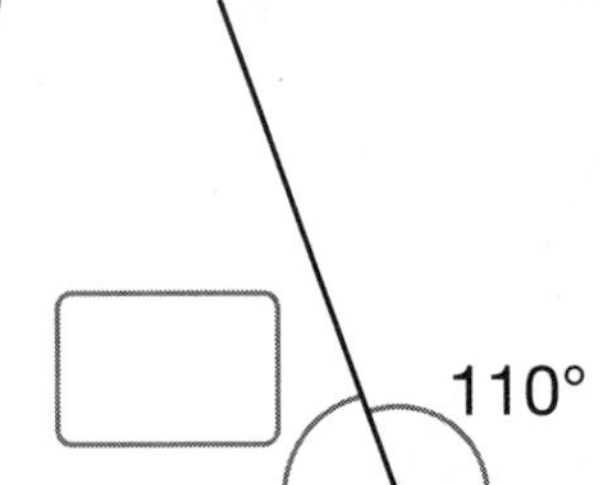

c

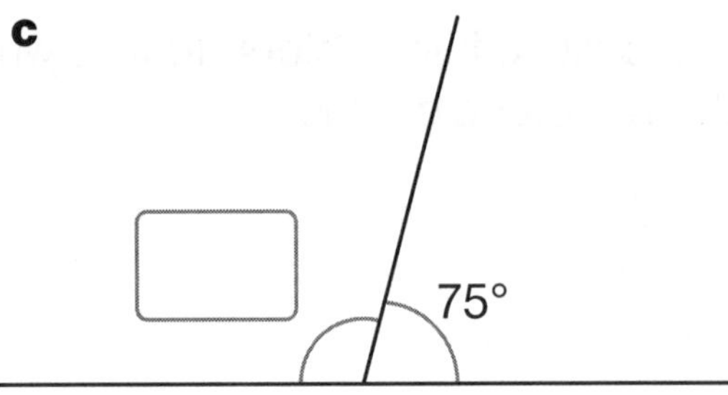

Challenge 2

1 Write the missing angles in the boxes.

a

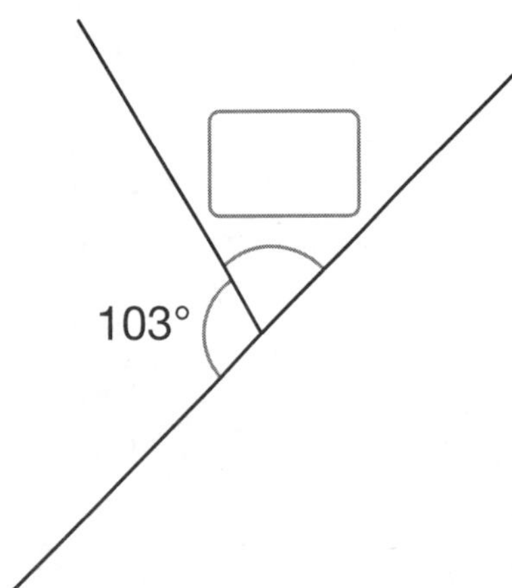

b

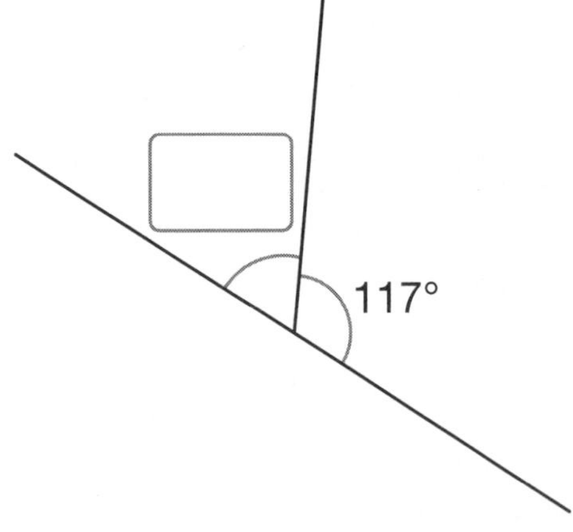

c

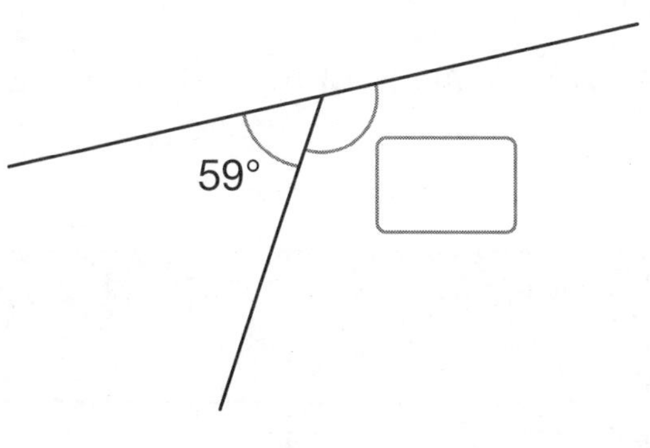

d

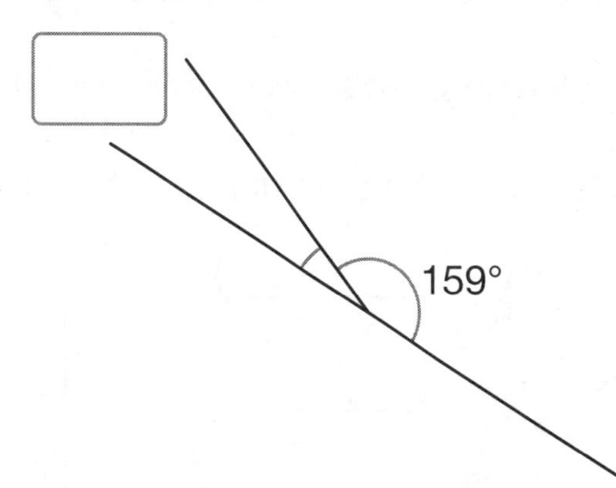

Challenge 3 Write the missing angles in the boxes.

a

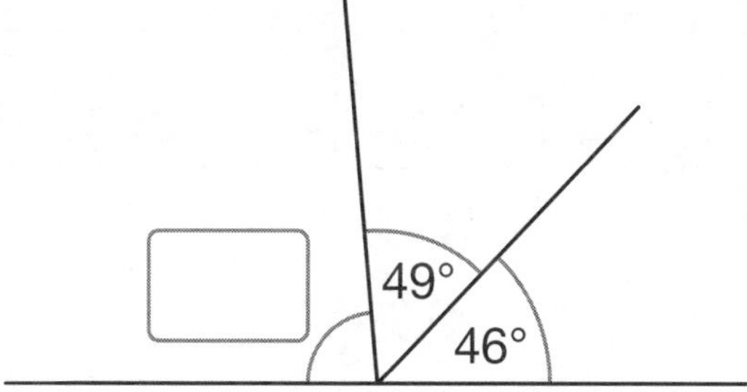

b

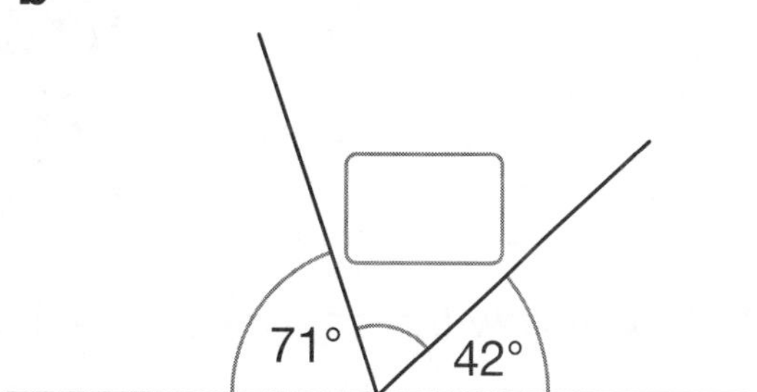

c

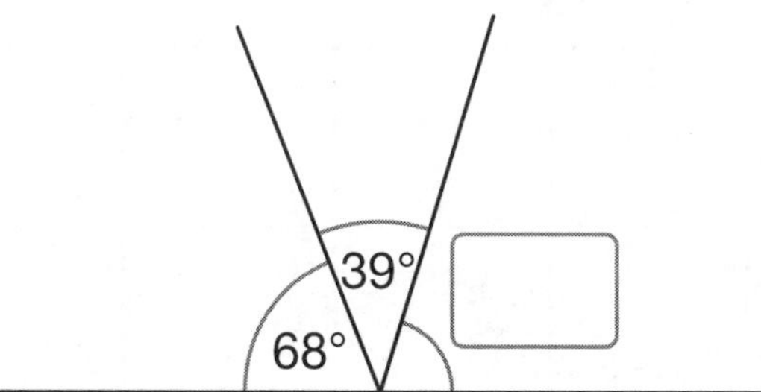

d

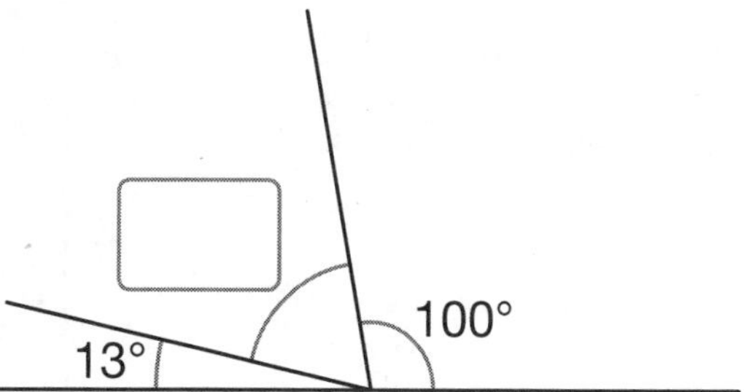

Lesson 1: Reading and plotting co-ordinates

- Understand that co-ordinates show the exact position of a point on a grid

Challenge 1

Write the co-ordinates of each object.

a 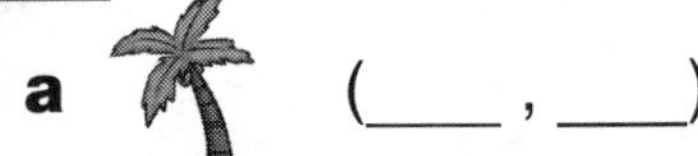

b 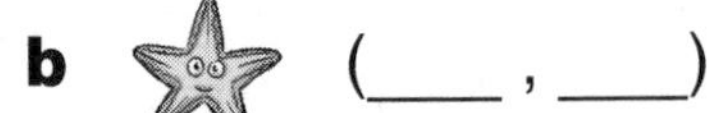

c 

d 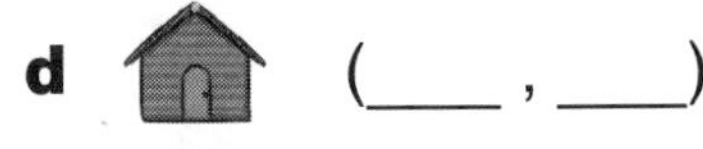

e 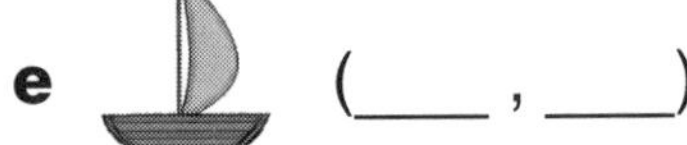

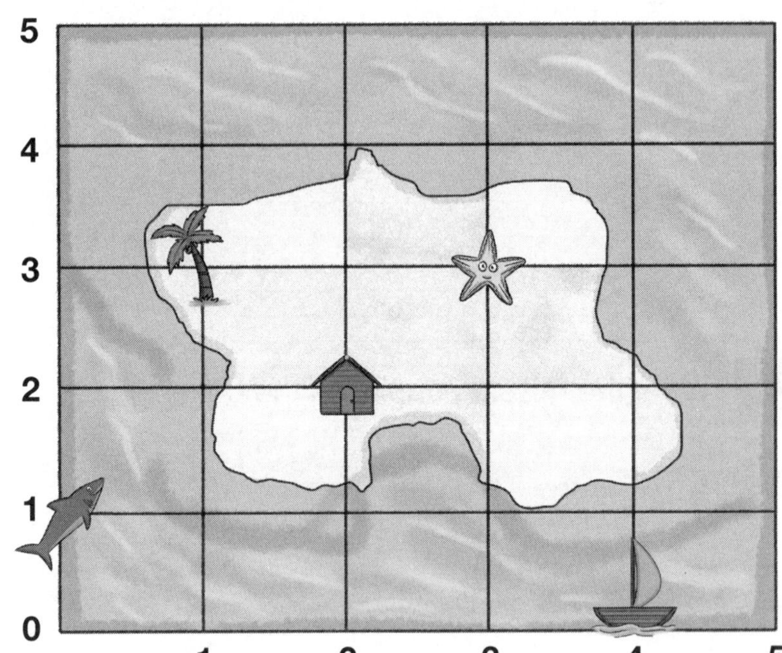

Challenge 2

1 Draw the objects on the map at the co-ordinates given.

a A shark at (1, 4)

b A boat at (0, 3)

c A hut at (3, 3)

d A starfish at (4, 2)

e A mountain at (3, 2)

f A cave at (1, 3)

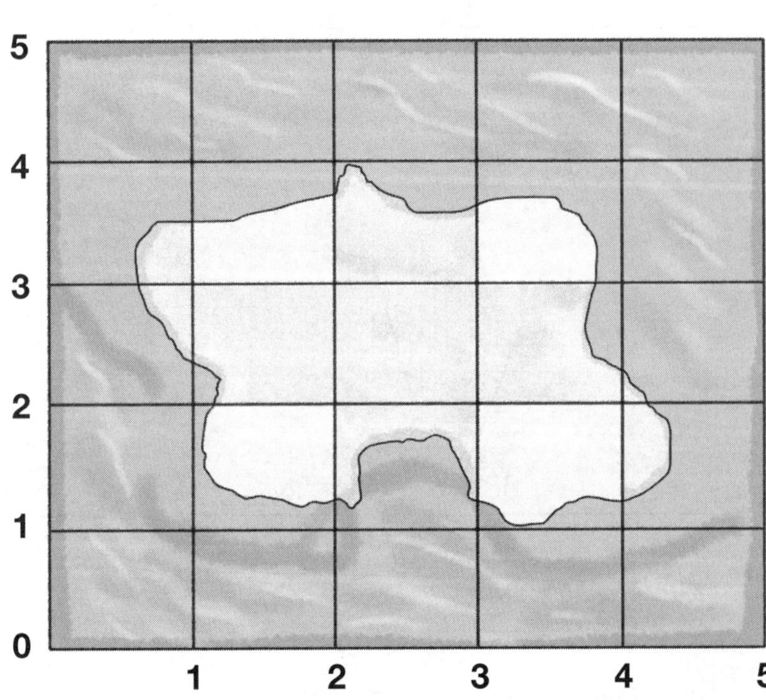

2 a Which objects share the same x-co-ordinate? [ ] and [ ]

b Which objects have a y-co-ordinate of 2? [ ] and [ ]

c What do you notice about the map positions of the boat and the hut?

____

d What do you notice about the map positions of the cave and the mountain?

____

e How do you explain these positions?

____

Draw the objects on the map using the clues.

a An octopus at (1, 4)

b A lake at an x-co-ordinate double that for the octopus and a y-co-ordinate half that for the octopus.

c A boat at the same x-co-ordinate as the lake, but at a y-co-ordinate 3 greater than the lake.

d A dolphin halfway between the co-ordinates for the octopus and the boat.

e A pair of mountains that are 2 squares apart on the x-axis and 1 square apart on the y-axis.

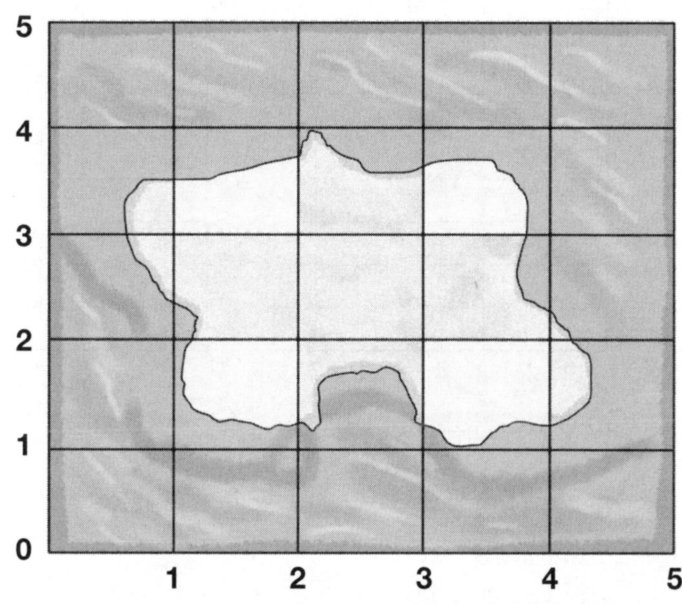

Lesson 2: **Shapes from co-ordinates**

- Plot specific points on a co-ordinate grid to form a shape

You will need
- ruler

Challenge 1 Use the co-ordinates to plot each shape.

(3, 3), (8, 3), (8, 8), (3, 8)

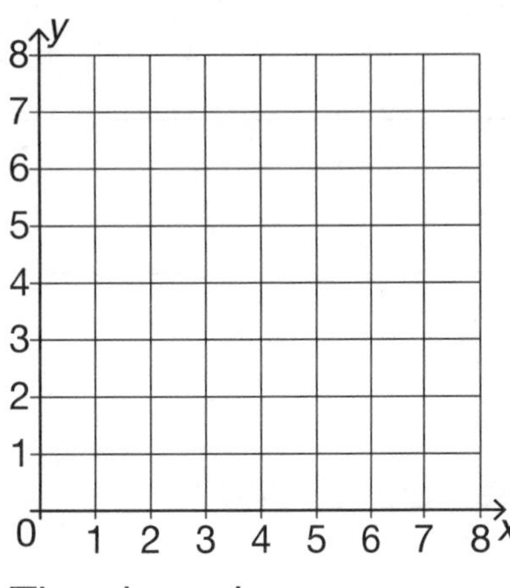

The shape is a ______.

(2, 6), (7, 6), (7, 3)

The shape is a ______.

(1, 1), (1, 6), (8, 6), (8, 1)

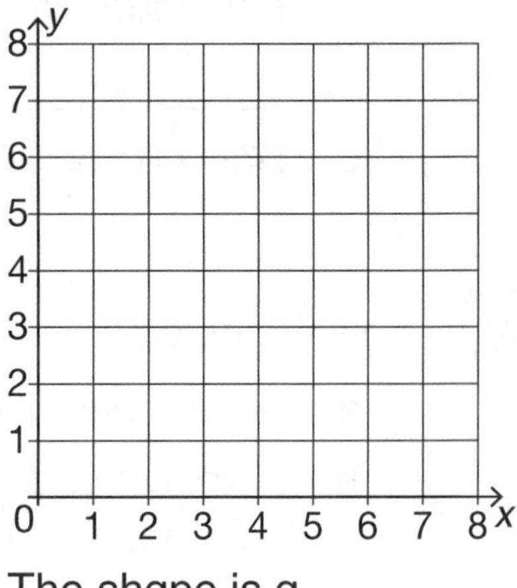

The shape is a ______.

Challenge 2

1 Draw each shape on the grid. Write the co-ordinates of each vertex of the shape.

Draw a right-angled triangle. Start at point (5, 2).

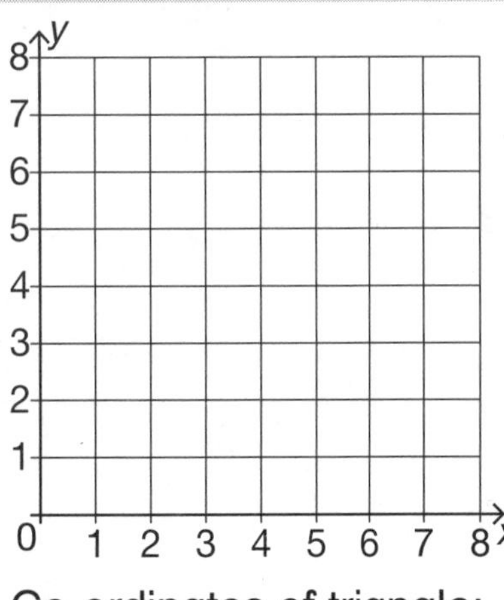

Co-ordinates of triangle:

(_, _) (_, _) (_, _)

Draw a square. Start at point (7, 7).

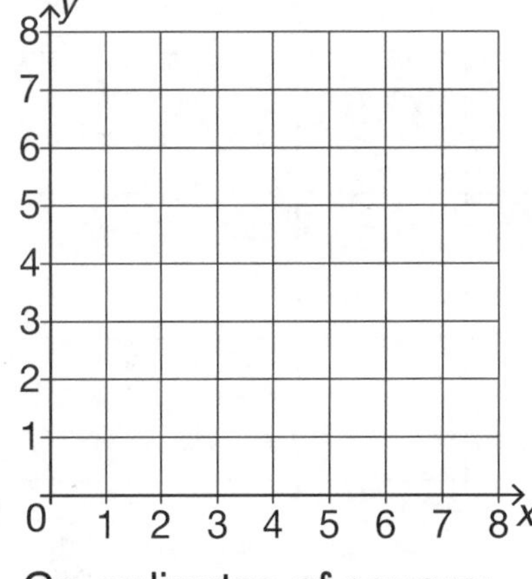

Co-ordinates of square:

(_, _) (_, _)
(_, _) (_, _)

Draw a rectangle. Start at point (0, 6).

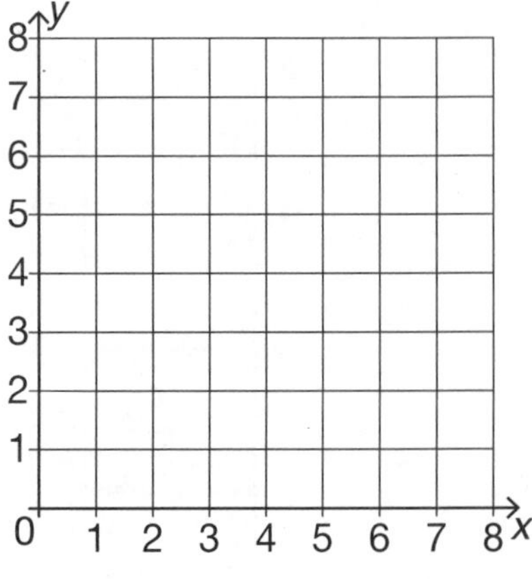

Co-ordinates of a rectangle:

(_, _) (_, _)
(_, _) (_, _)

2 Draw the shape and identify the co-ordinates of the missing vertex.

Plot these points:
A (2, 2) B (2, 7) C (7, 7)
ABCD is a rectangle.

What are the co-ordinates of D? (__, __)

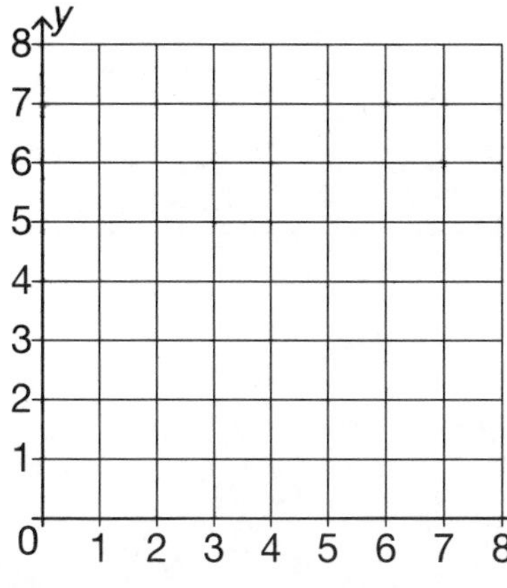

Plot these points:
A (2, 7) B (8, 5)
ABC is an isosceles triangle.

What are the co-ordinates of C? (__, __)

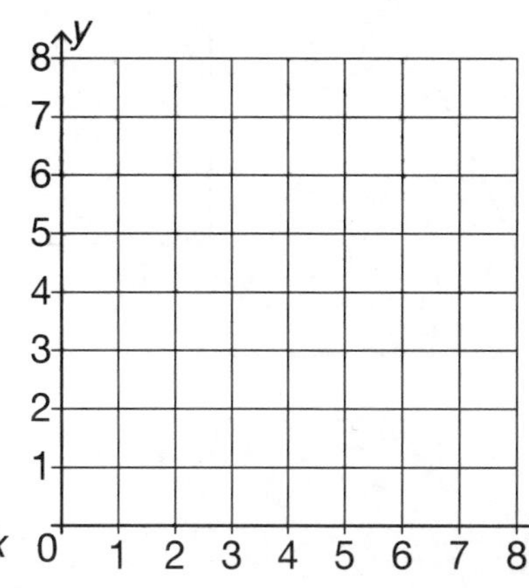

Plot these points:
A (8, 7) B (6, 3) C (1, 3)
ABCD is a parallelogram.

What are the co-ordinates of D? (__, __)

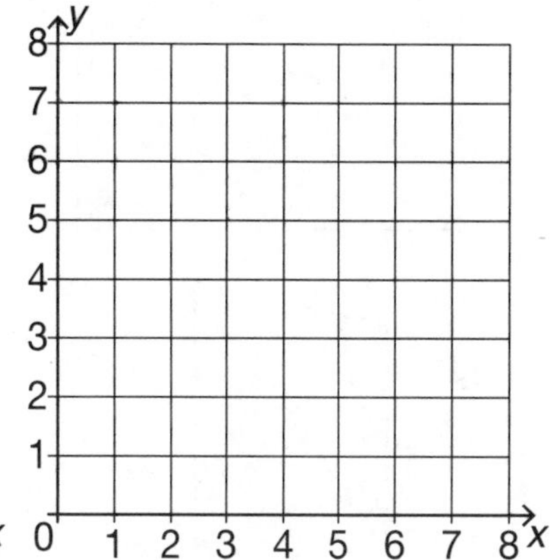

Challenge **3** Draw the shape and identify the co-ordinates of the missing vertex.

Plot these points:
A (1, 2) B (3, 5) C (7, 5)
ABCD is a trapezium.

What are the co-ordinates of D? (__, __)

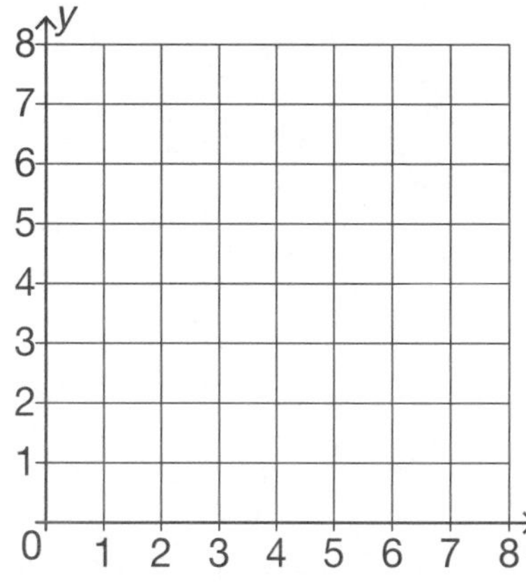

Plot these points:
A (5, 7) B (8, 5) C (5, 3)
ABCD is a rhombus.

What are the co-ordinates of D? (__, __)

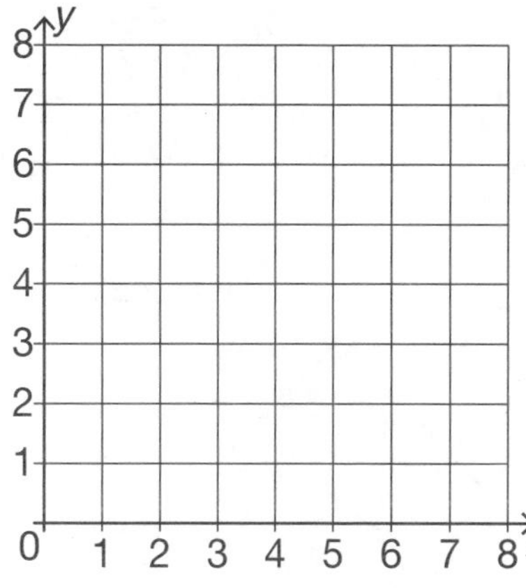

Plot these points:
A (2, 8) B (6, 7) C (7, 5)
D (6, 3)
ABCDE is a symmetrical pentagon.

What are the co-ordinates of E? (__, __)

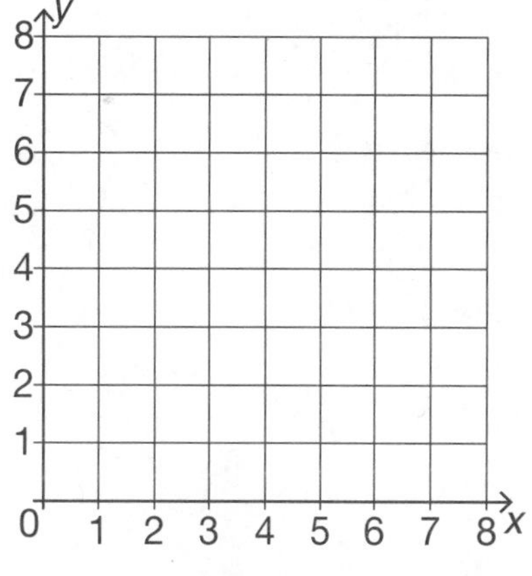

Geometry

Lesson 3: **Testing for symmetry**

- Fold paper shapes or use mirrors to test shapes for symmetry

You will need
- mirror
- ruler

Place a mirror on each shape to check for symmetry.
Circle the shapes that are symmetrical.

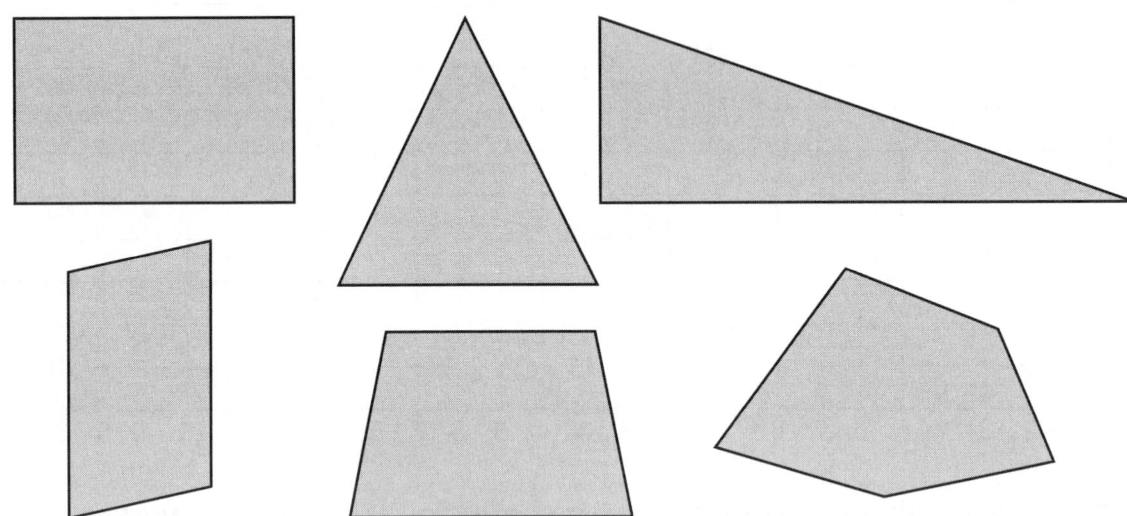

1 Use your mirror to test each shape for symmetry. Write the letters of the 2D shapes to complete the table.

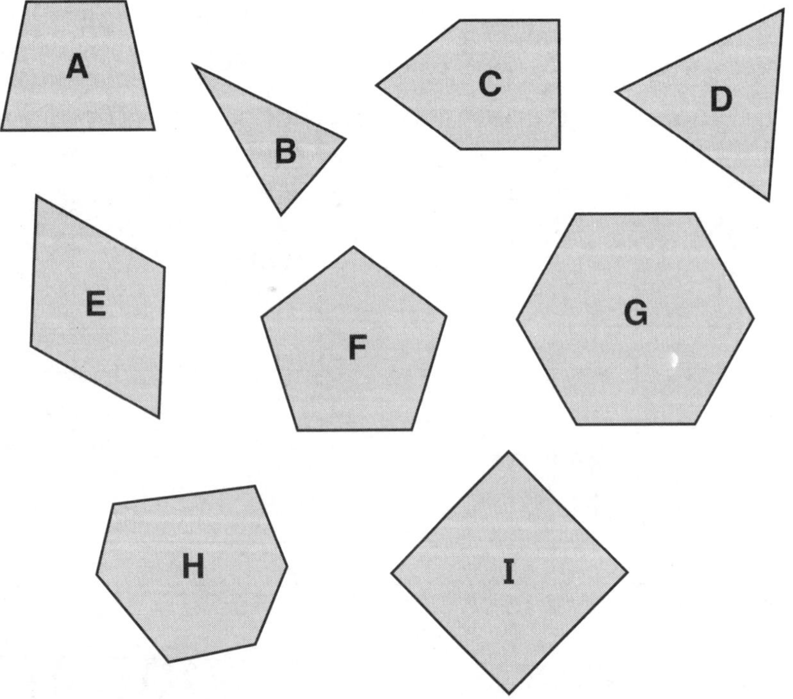

Lines of symmetry	Shape
none	
1	
2	
3	
4	
5	
6	

2 Complete the shapes to make them symmetrical.

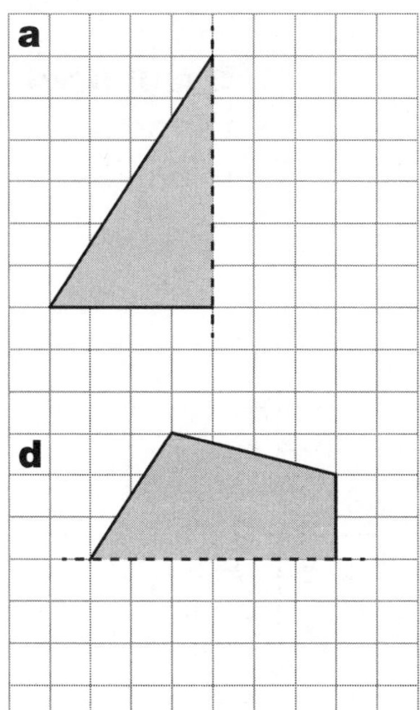

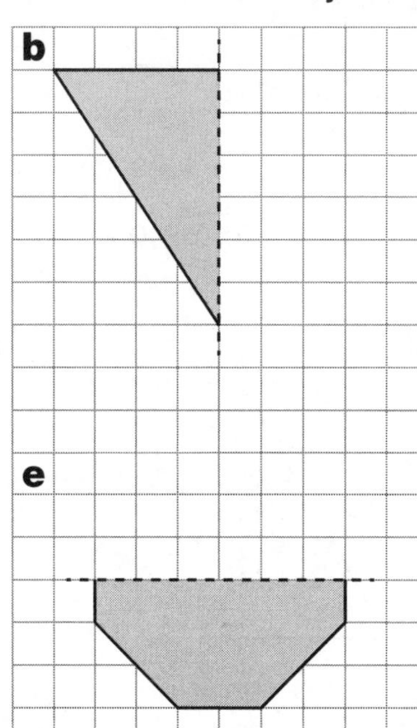

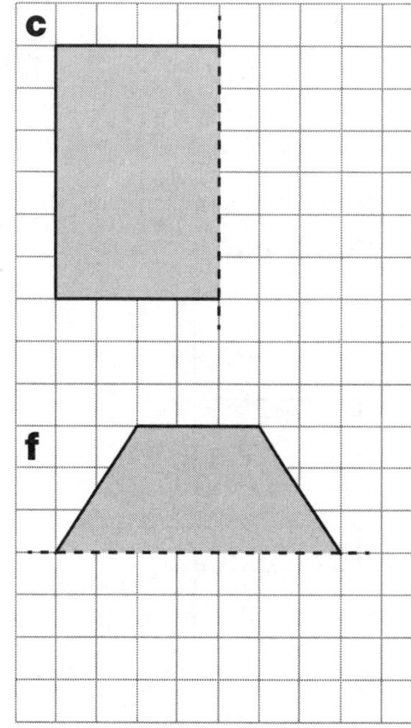

Challenge 3 Use the dotted grids to draw the shapes described.

A quadrilateral with 2 pairs of equal sides, with 1 line of symmetry only.

A kite with one line of symmetry.

A pentagon that has no lines of symmetry.

A triangle with 2 equal sides and one line of symmetry only.

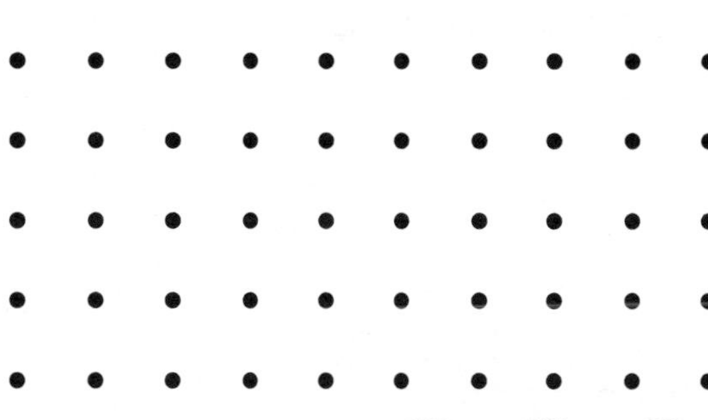

Geometry

Lesson 4: **Reflection (1)**

- Identify and describe the position of a shape following a reflection

You will need
- mirror
- ruler

Challenge 1

Place your mirror along the line of symmetry. Draw the reflection.

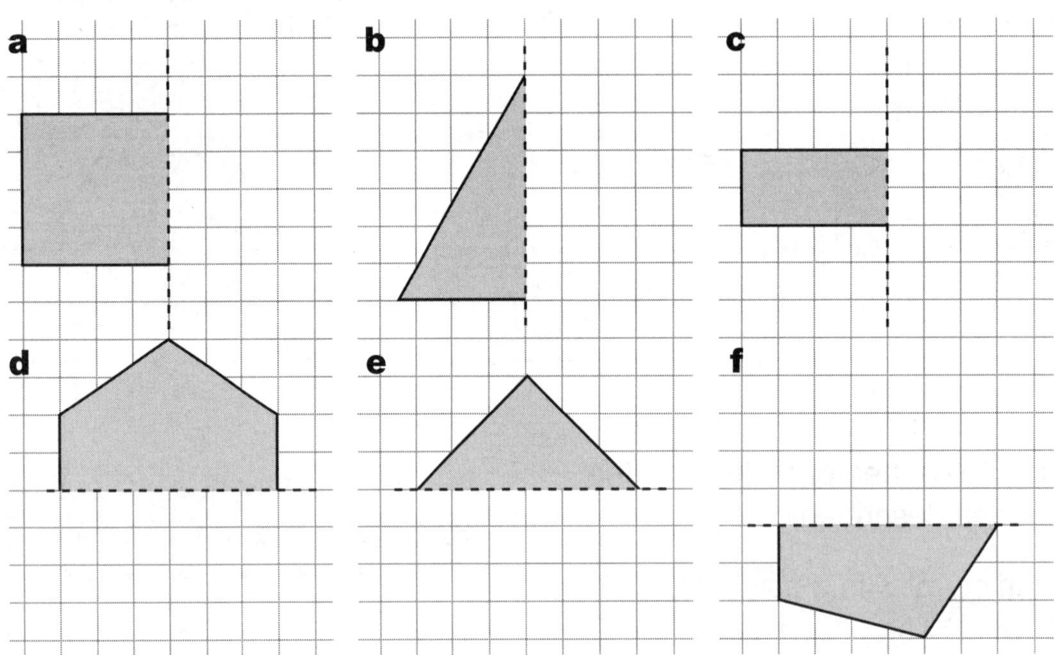

Challenge 2

1 Reflect each shape in the mirror line.

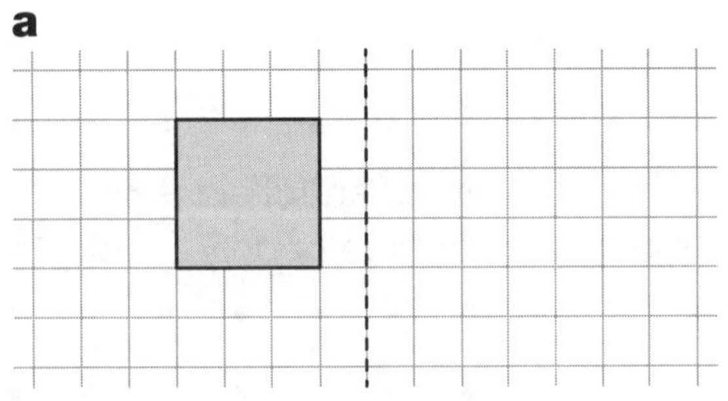

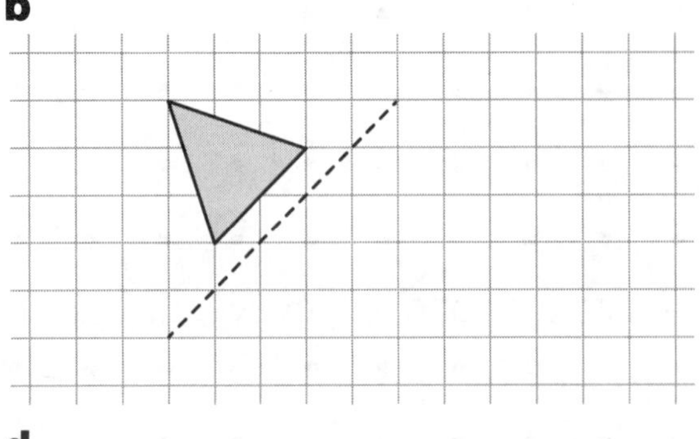

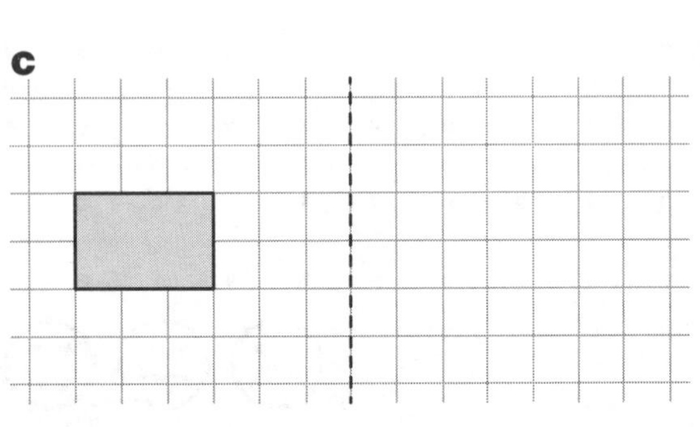

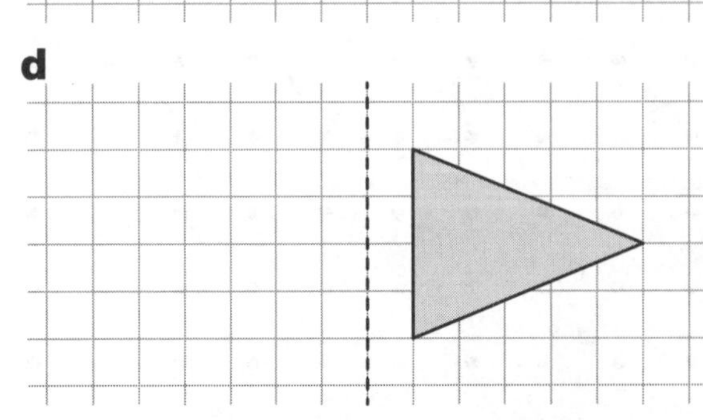

2 Draw the shape described. Reflect each shape in the mirror line.

a Scalene triangle

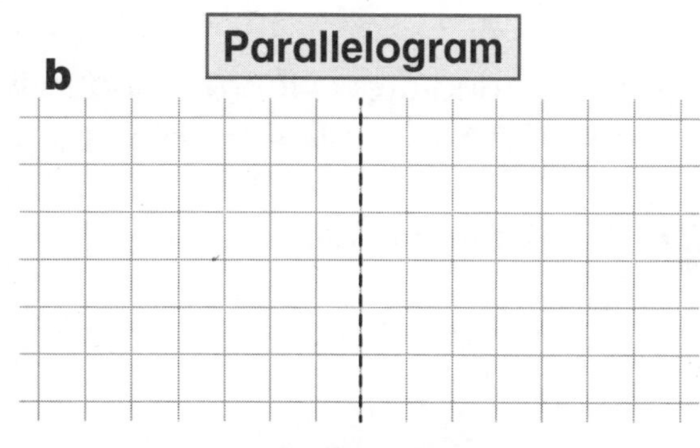

b Parallelogram

c Hexagon

Challenge **3** Reflect the irregular shapes in the mirror lines.

a

b

c

d

e

f

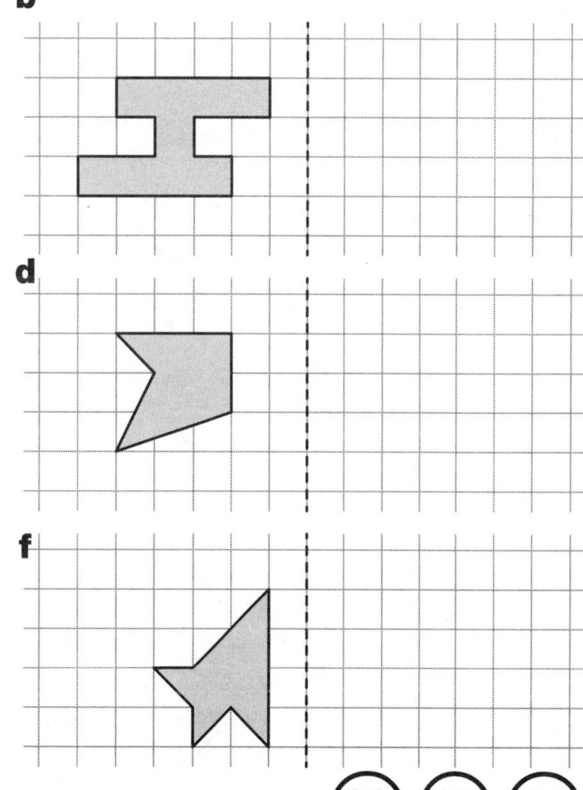

Geometry

Lesson 5: **Reflection (2)**

- Predict and draw where a shape will be after reflection where the mirror line is not vertical or horizontal

You will need
- mirror
- ruler

Challenge 1

Draw the reflection of the point in the mirror line.

a

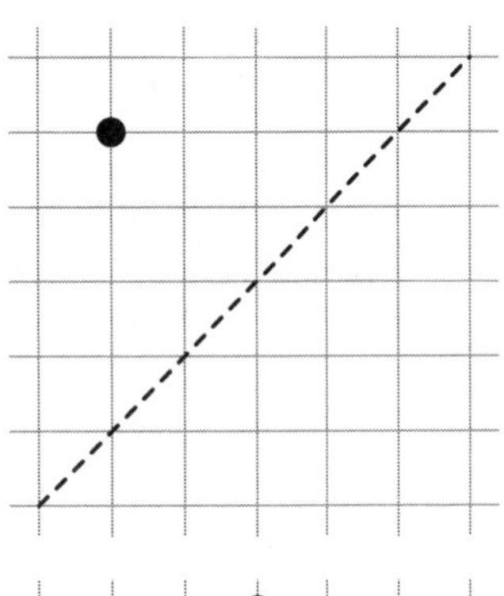

b

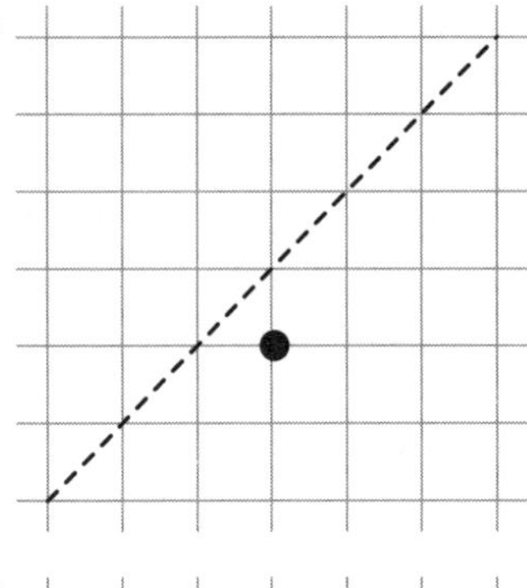

c

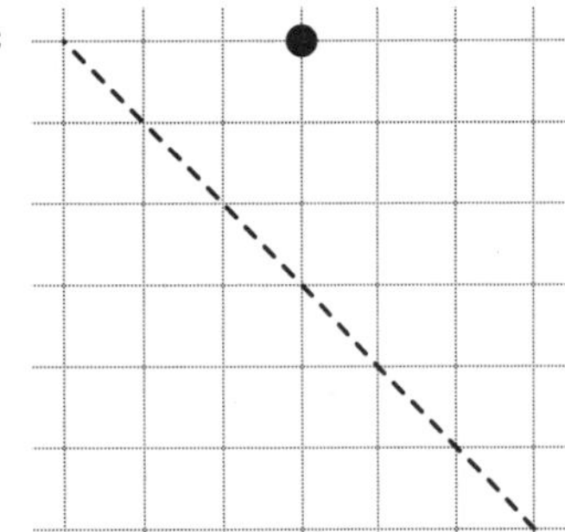

d

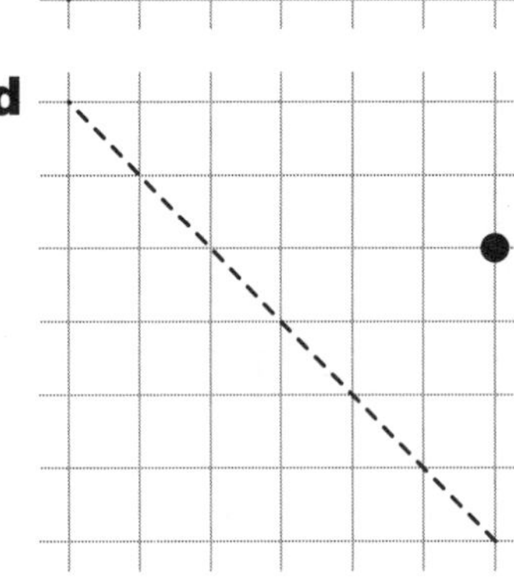

Challenge 2

1 Mark in the vertices of each shape and reflect them across the mirror line. Connect up the dots to form the reflected image.

a

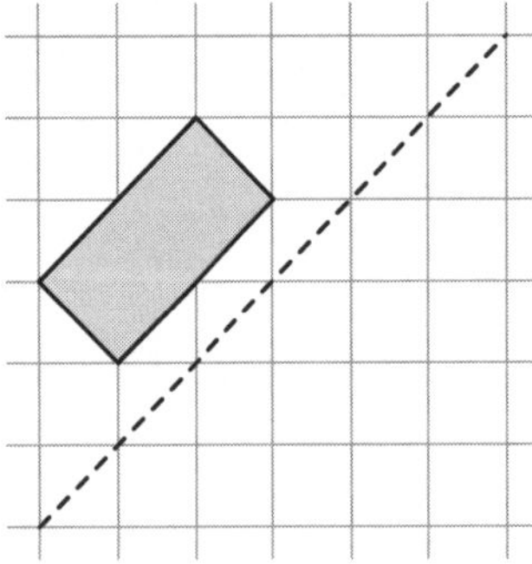

b

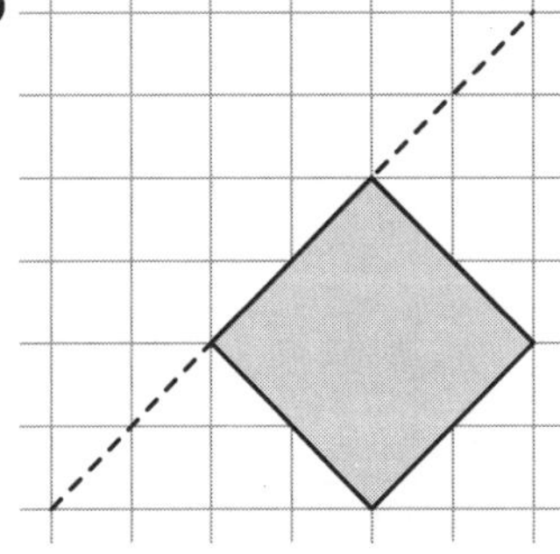

c

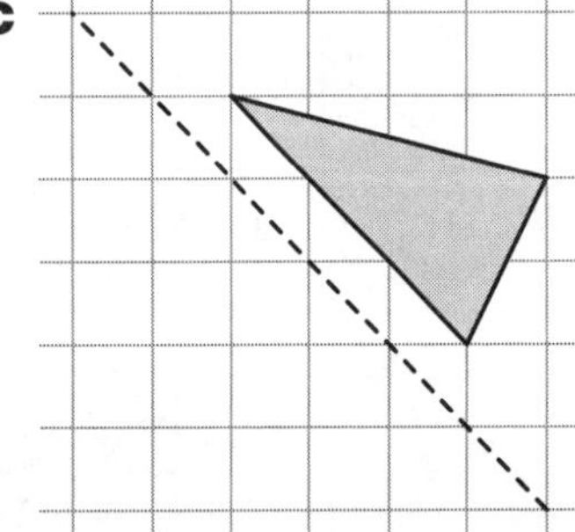

d

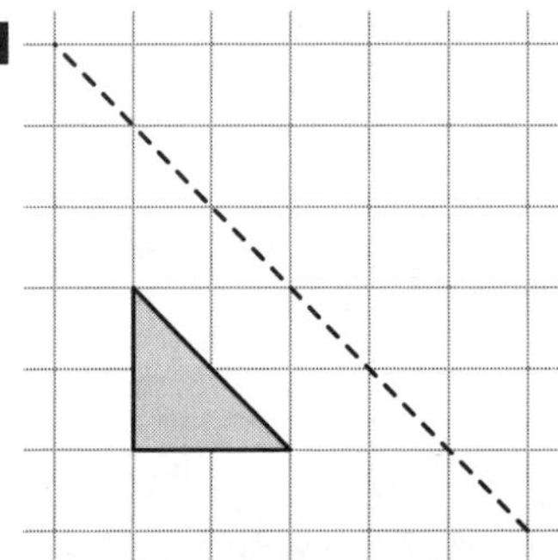

2 Reflect each irregular polygon and draw the image.

a

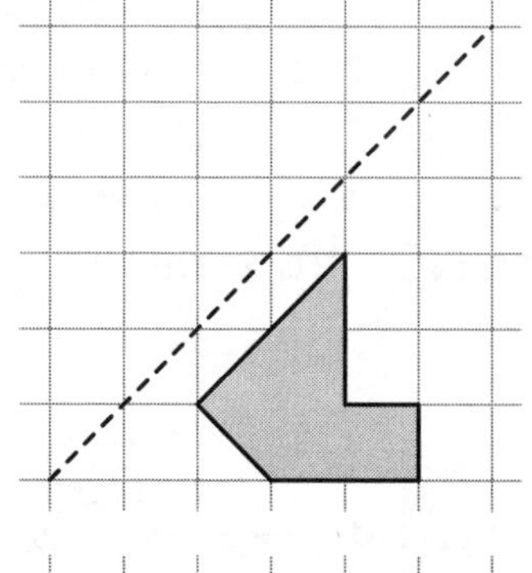

b

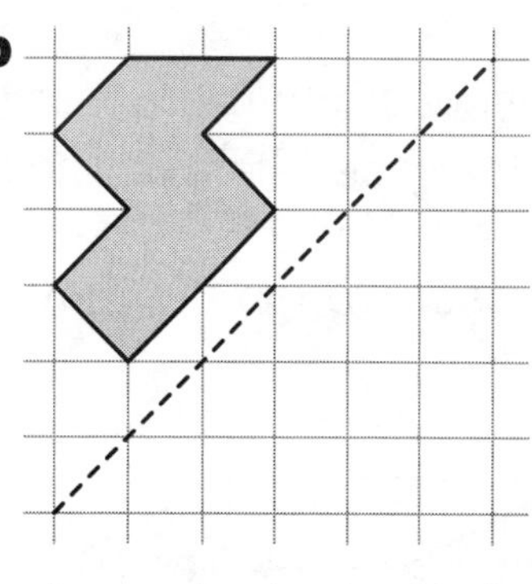

c

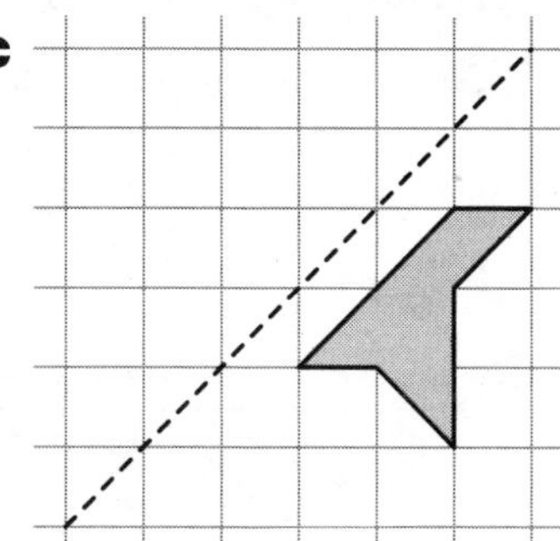

d

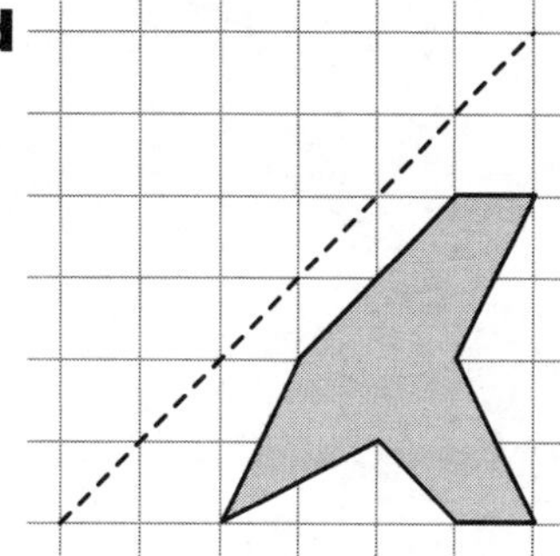

Challenge 3

Each shape has been reflected across a mirror line. Mark the mirror line on each grid.

a

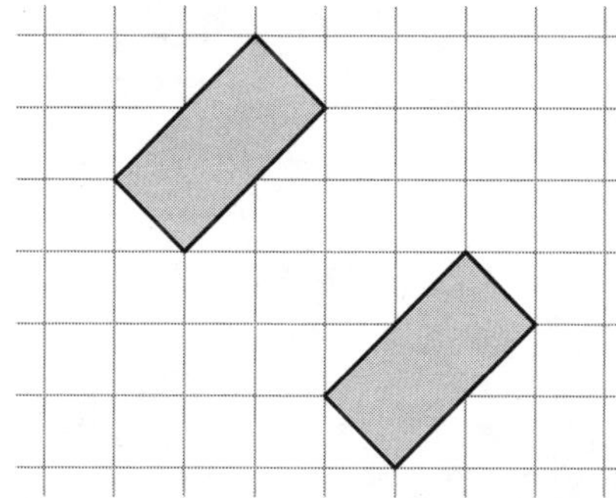

b

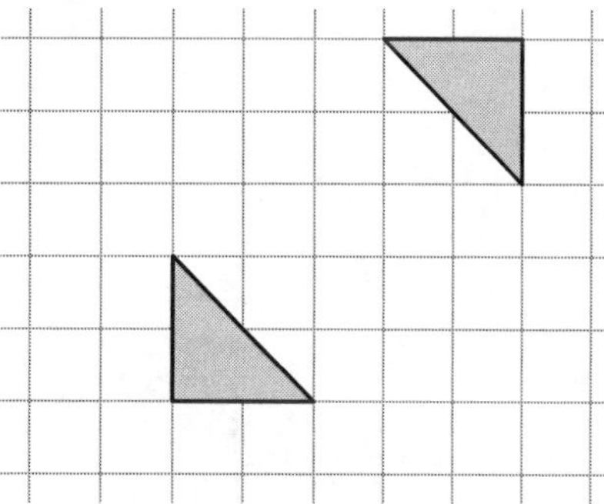

c

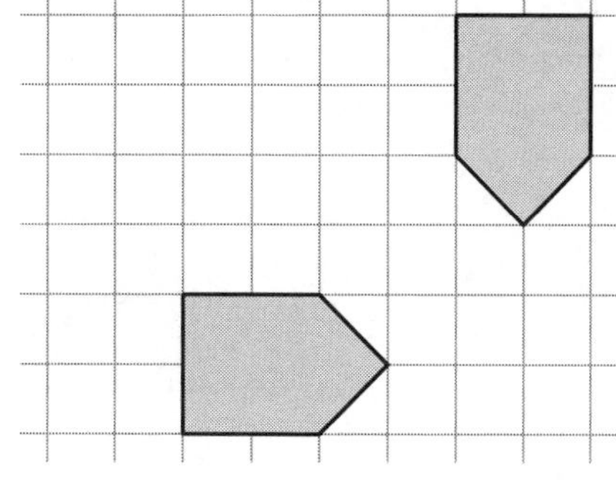

d

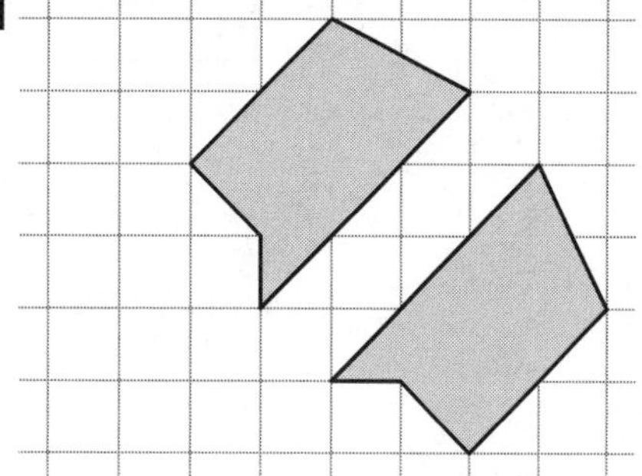

Geometry

Lesson 6: Understanding translation

- Identify, describe and represent the position of a shape after a translation

You will need
- ruler

Draw a cross through the movements that are NOT translations.

a
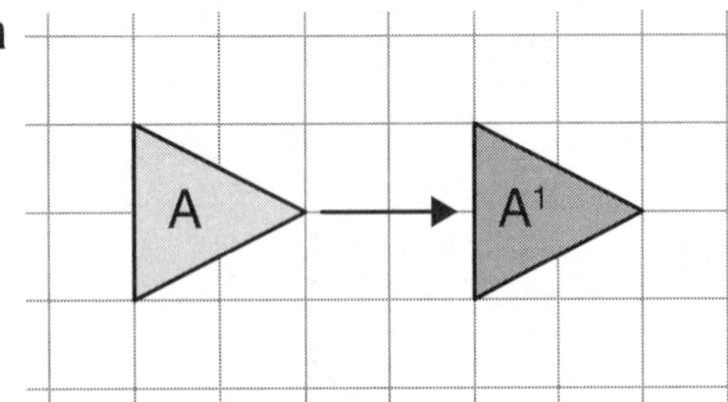

b
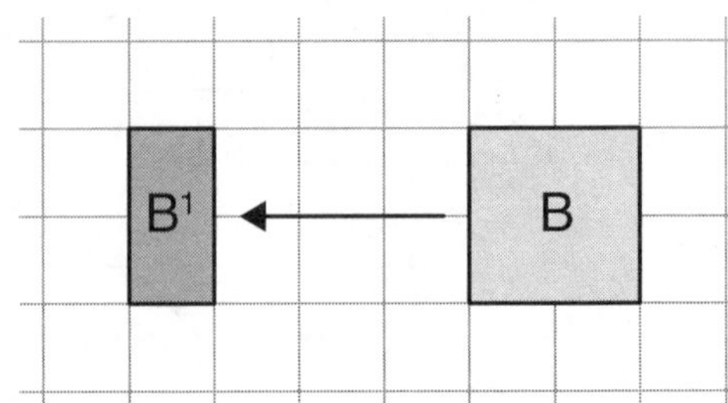

c
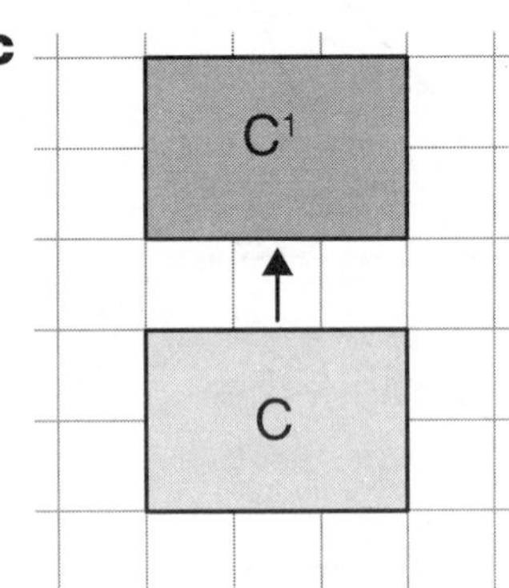

d
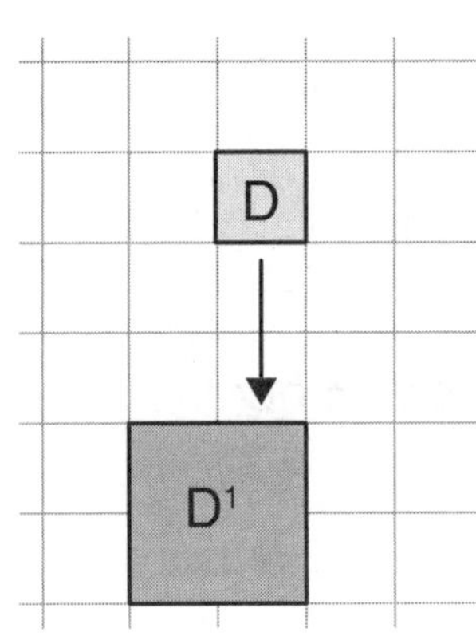

e
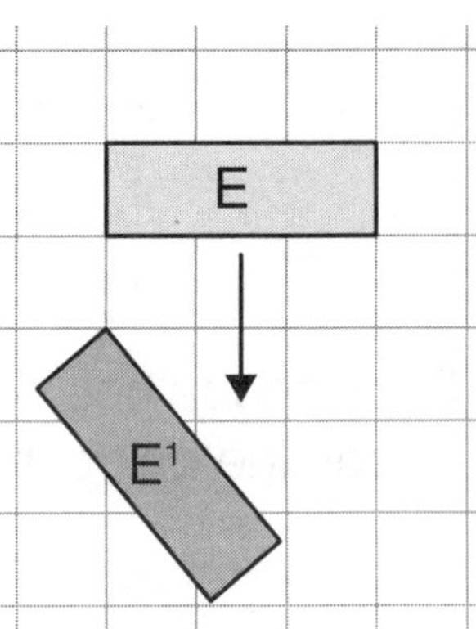

Challenge 2

1 Complete each sentence.

a
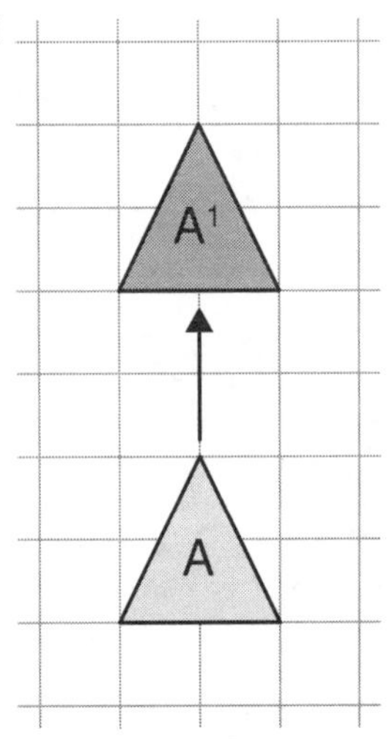

The triangle has been translated ☐ squares ☐.

b
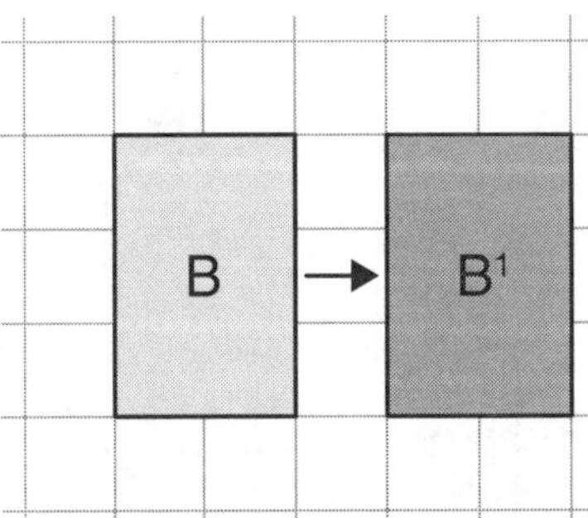

The rectangle has been translated ☐ squares to the ☐.

c
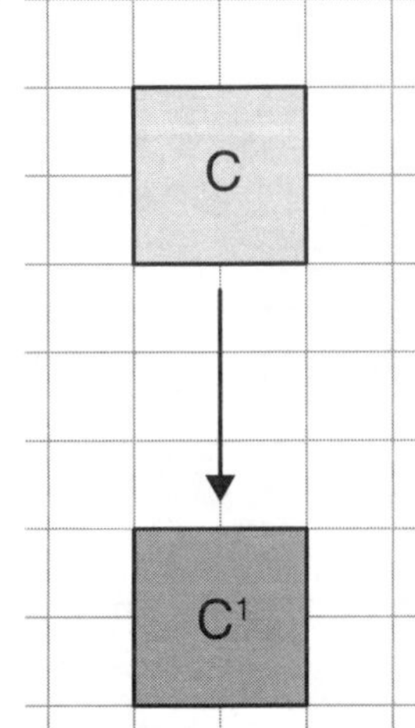

The square has been translated ☐ squares ☐.

2 Translate each shape as follows:

a

A

Four squares to the right

b

B

Five squares to the left

Challenge **3** The table shows the translations that move shape A via images B, C, D and E back to its original position, A. The total number of grid squares involved in the moves is given. Complete the blank table with a similar set of translations that return shape A back to its original position, but moving through fewer grid squares.

Translation	Grid squares moved		Total
	Up or down	Left or right	
A to B	1	8	9
B to E	13	9	22
E to D	5	12	17
D to C	4	9	13
C to A	5	20	25
			86

Translation	Grid squares moved		Total
	Up or down	Left or right	
A to ☐			
☐ to ☐			
☐ to ☐			
☐ to ☐			
☐ to ☐			

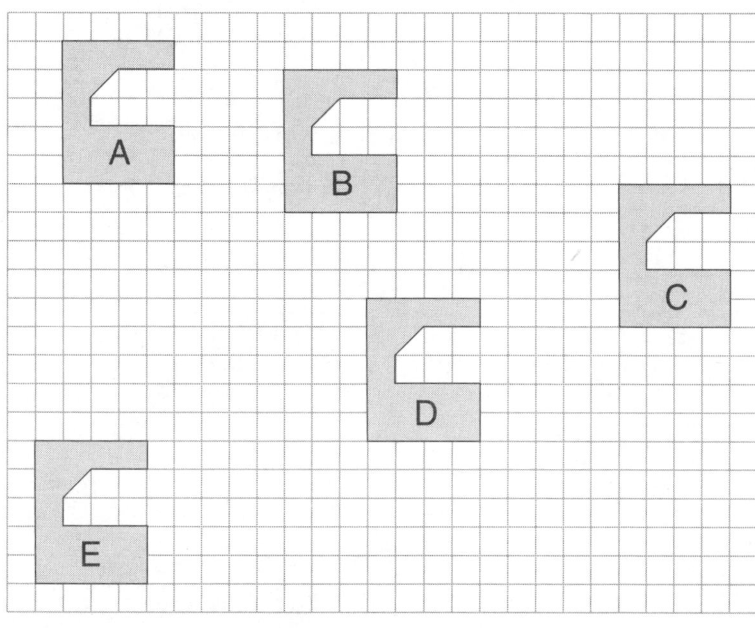

Lesson 7: **Shape translation (1)**

- Know where a shape will be after a translation and know that the shape has not changed

You will need
- ruler

Draw a line to match each translation to its description.

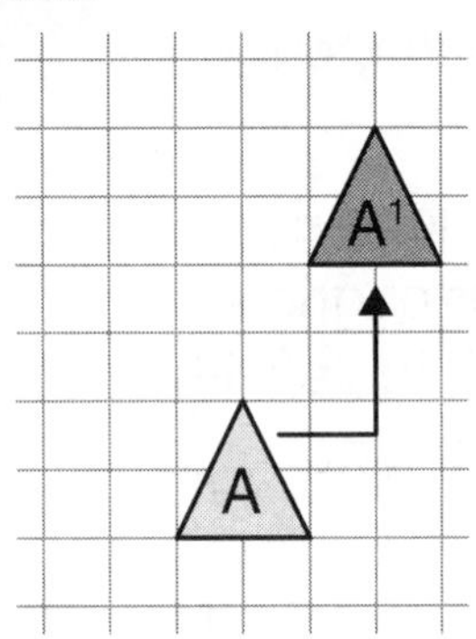

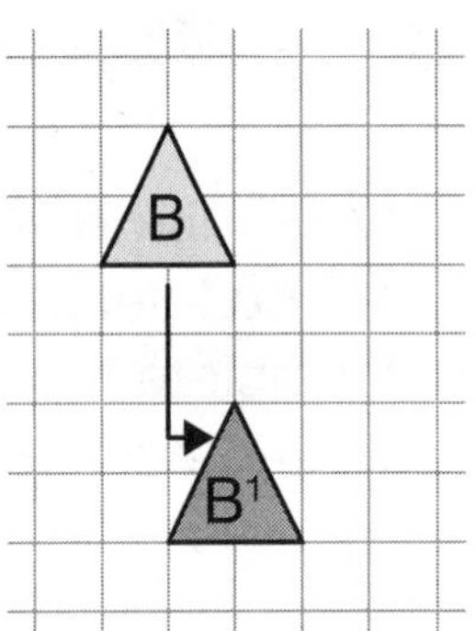

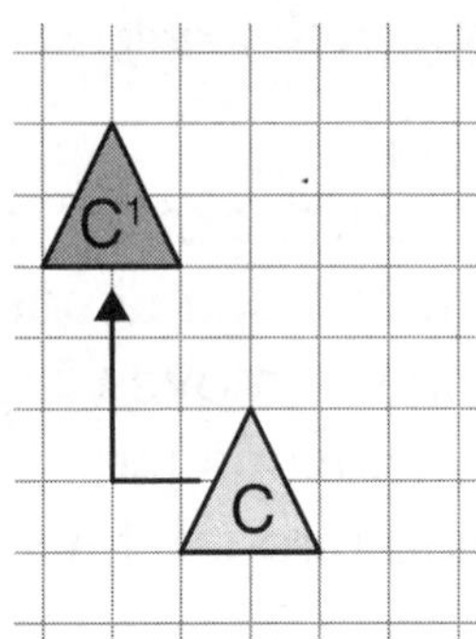

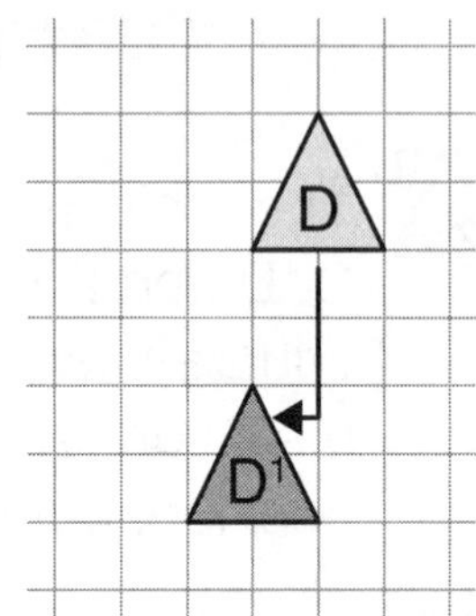

Left 2 squares, up 4 squares.

Down 4 squares, right 1 square.

Down 4 squares, left 1 square.

Right 2 squares, up 4 squares.

1 Translate each shape as follows:

a

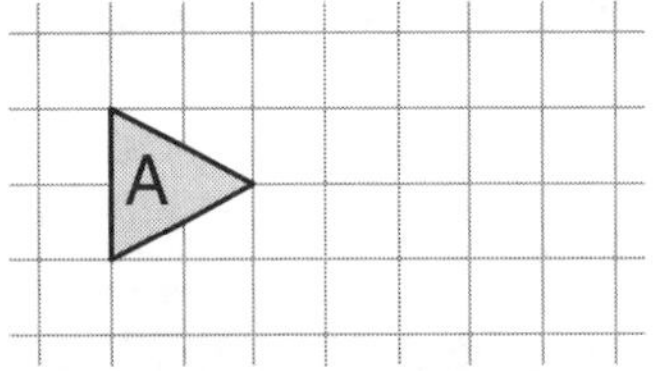

Right 5 squares, up 1 square

b

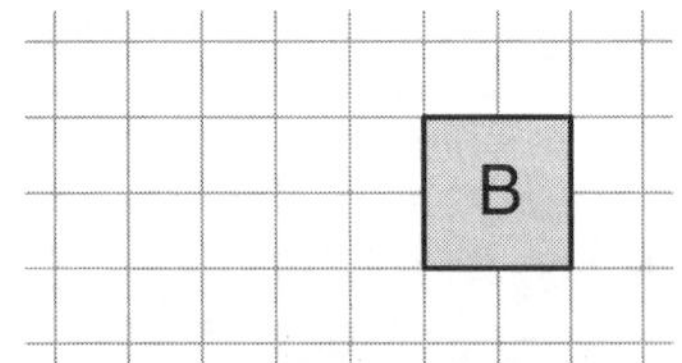

Down 1 square, left 4 squares

c

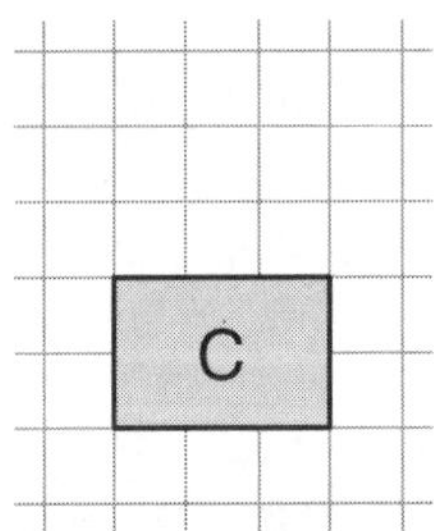

Up 3 squares, right 1 square

d

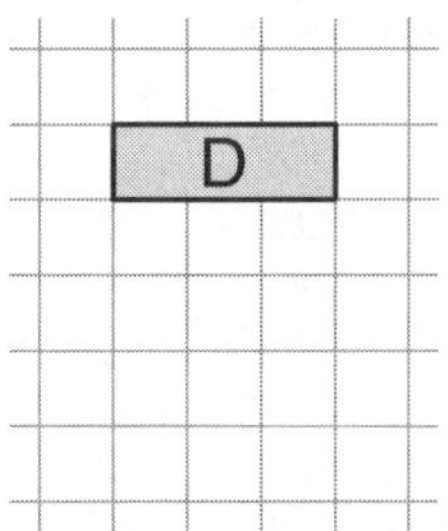

Down 4 squares, left 1 square

2 Complete each sentence.

a

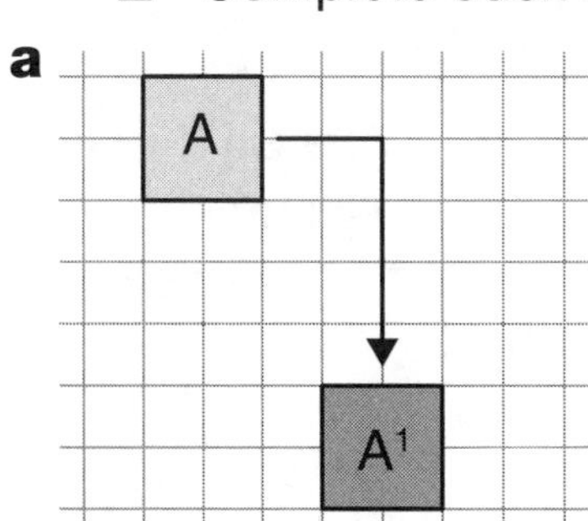

Shape A has been translated ______________

____

____

b

B
B1

Shape B has been translated ______________

____

____

c

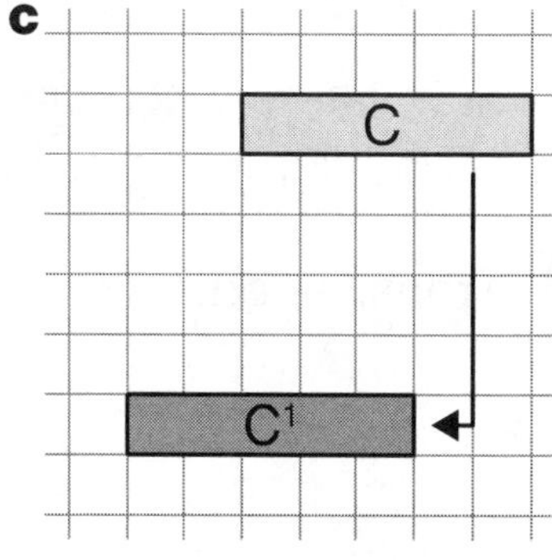

Shape C has been translated ______________

____

____

Challenge 3 Make patterns by translating the shape.

a

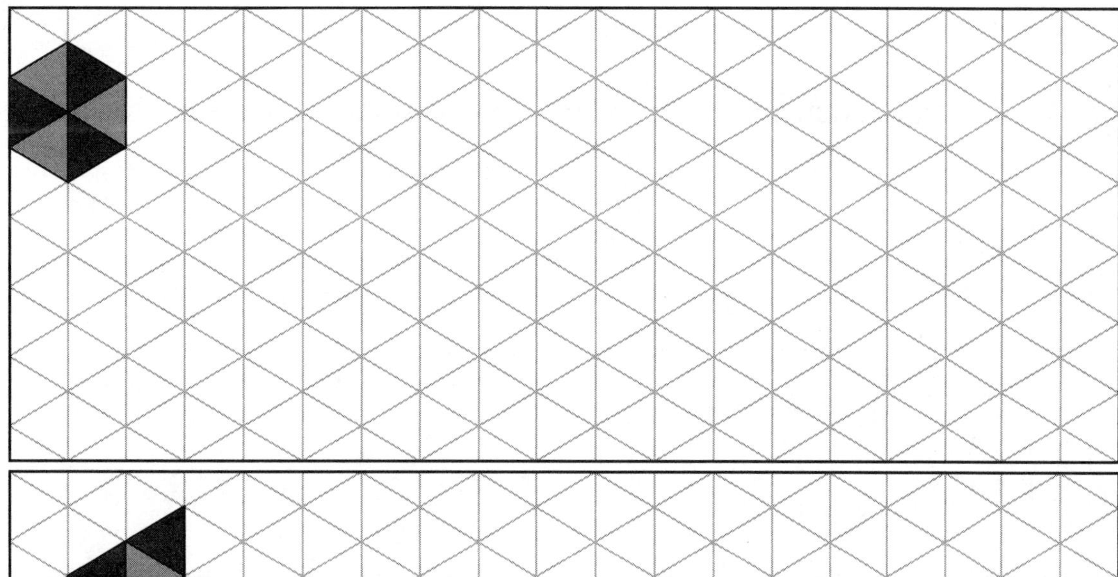

b

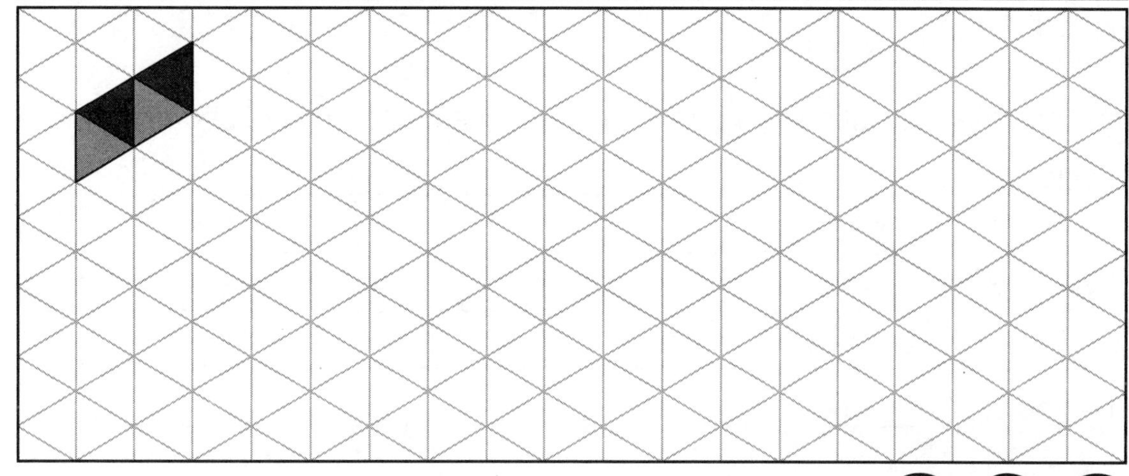

Lesson 8: **Shape translation (2)**

- Know where a compound shape will be after two translations

You will need
- ruler

Challenge 1 Translate each compound shape to create a tiling pattern.

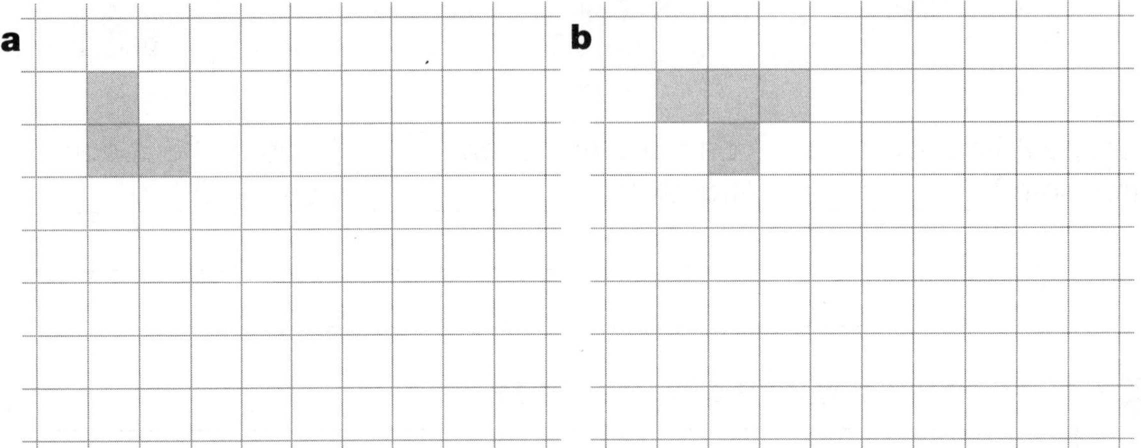

Challenge 2 **1** Translate each shape three times in the smaller 3 by 3 grids.

a

1

3 2

b

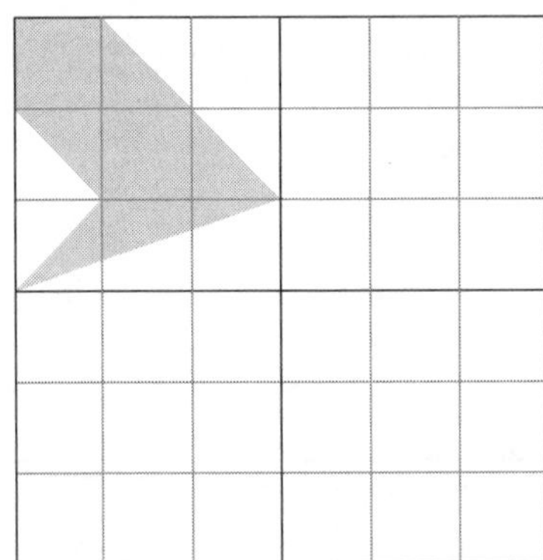

c

Describe the translation that moves the vertices of the original shape in part a to:

Position 1: ______________________________

____

Position 2: ______________________________

____

Position 3: ______________________________

____

2 Place a cross through the diagrams that show an incorrect translation.

a

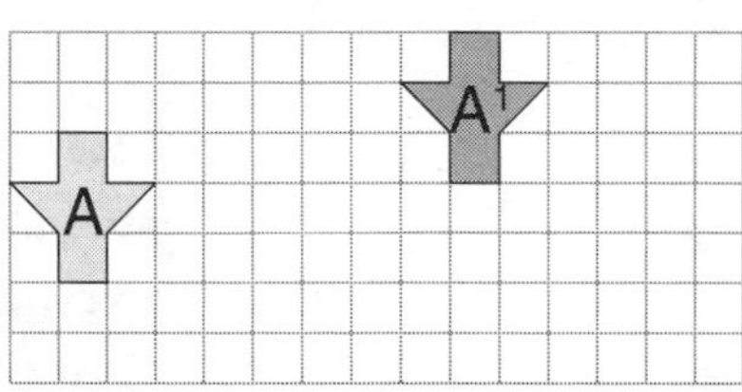

Right 8 squares,
up 3 squares

b

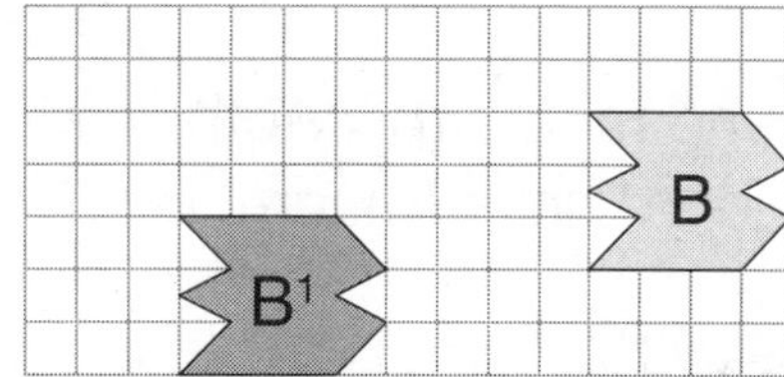

Left 7 squares,
down 2 squares

Reflect each shape in the mirror line, then complete the translation.

a

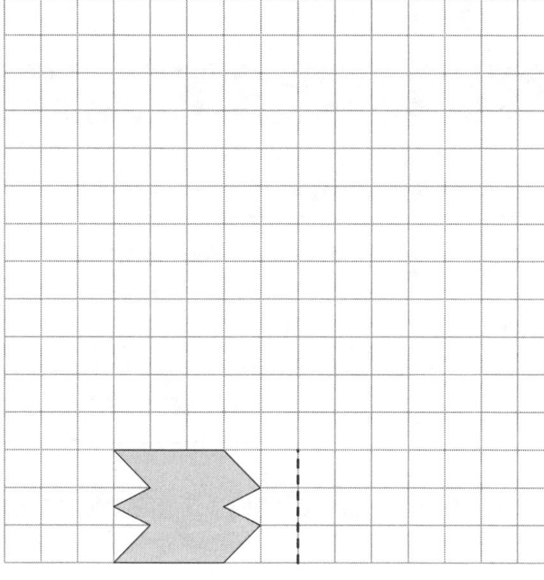

Translation following reflection: up 9 squares, left 8 squares.

b

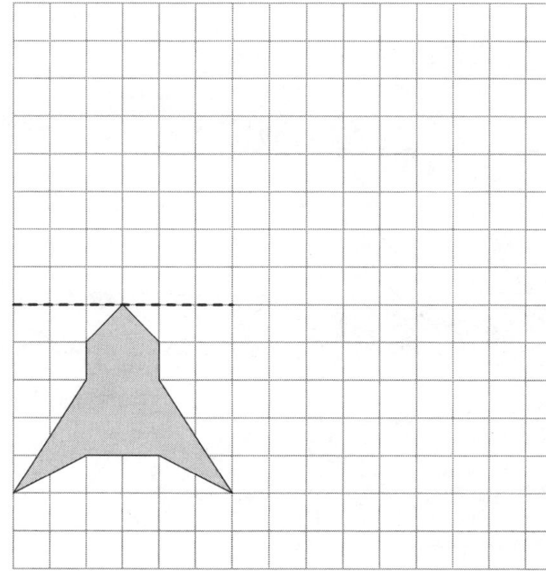

Translation following reflection: right 7 squares, down 8 squares.

Measure

Lesson 1: **Measuring length**

- Estimate and measure length or height using standard units (m, cm, mm)

You will need
- ruler
- 4 classroom objects

Estimate the length of each object in the unit shown. Then measure the object with a ruler.

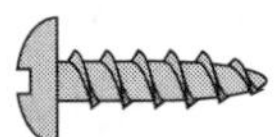

CRAYON

Object	Estimate	Measurement
screw	_____ millimetres (mm)	_____ millimetres (mm)
crayon	_____ centimetres (cm)	_____ centimetres (cm)
pencil	_____ centimetres (cm)	_____ centimetres (cm)

1 Measure the length of each crayon in millimetres. Circle the three crayons that are the same length.

2 Label four objects A to D and place them in a straight line in order on the classroom floor. The objects should be placed at the distances given in the table. Measure the actual distances and complete the table.

Distance	Approximate distance apart	Actual distance apart
A to B	less than 50 cm	
B to C	greater than 50 cm, less than 1 metre	
C to D	greater than 1 metre	

Challenge 3 Draw a plan of your school playground in the box below. Mark four features, for example, a tree, a hut or a wall, and label them A to D. Estimate the distance in metres between the features, then go outside and measure the distances to complete the table.

Estimated distance apart

	A	B	C	D
A				
B				
C				

Actual distance apart

	A	B	C	D
A				
B				
C				

Lesson 2: **Converting units**

- Know the relationships between kilometres, metres, centimetres and millimetres
- Use multiplication to convert from larger to smaller units of length

Draw lines to match the measurements in the top row to their equivalent measurements in the bottom row.

3 km	23 m	77 cm	8·4 km	6·7 m
8400 m	770 mm	3000 m	670 cm	2300 cm

1 Complete the conversions.

a 6 km = ☐ m

b 8 m = ☐ cm

c 9 cm = ☐ mm

d 46 km = ☐ m

e 19 m = ☐ cm

f 83 cm = ☐ mm

g 5·2 km = ☐ m

h 9·1 m = ☐ cm

i 35·7 cm = ☐ mm

2 Complete the conversions for each relationship.

a

6 m

☐ mm ⟷ ☐ cm

b

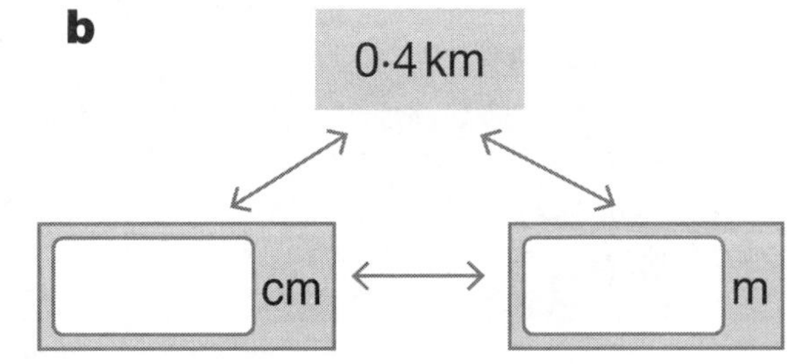

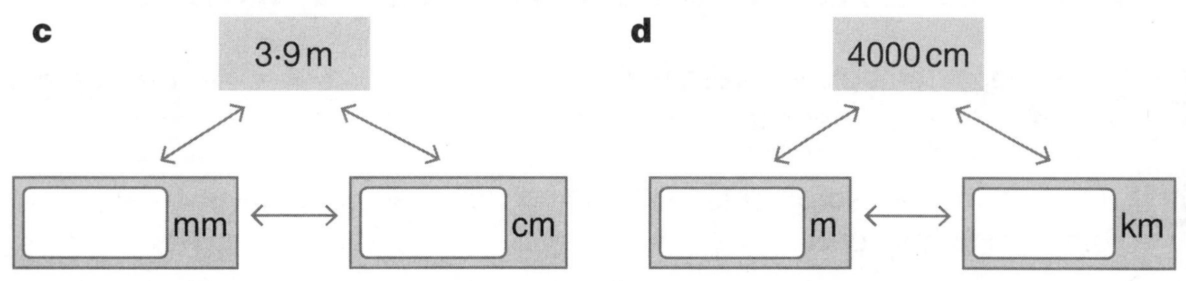

1 **a** Carla is measuring the lengths of two pieces of wood. The first piece is 85 cm long. The second is 620 mm long. How long are the two pieces together? Give your answer in centimetres.

b Finn rode 4·5 kilometres on his bike. His friend Drake rode 3250 metres on his bike. How much farther did Finn travel than Drake? Give your answer in metres.

c Molly has a toy storage box 1·3 m by 99 cm. How many more centimetres is the length of the box than the width? Give your answer in centimetres.

d Julia goes for a run and stops at drink fountain 3350 m from her home. She continues her run and stops at a second fountain 5·1 km from her home. What is the distance between the fountains? Give your answer in metres.

2 The width of each envelope is double its height. Complete the table of widths and perimeters (in millimetres) for the envelopes given in the table.

Height (cm)	Width (mm)	Perimeter (mm)
15		
22·3		
27·4		
31·2		

Measure

Lesson 3: **Ordering and rounding length**

- Order measurements in mixed units
- Round units to the nearest whole unit

You will need
- ruler

Challenge 1

Convert the measurements to the unit given, then put them in order, smallest to largest.

a

7·3 m	817 cm	8 m	870 cm
☐ cm		☐ cm	
☐	☐	☐	☐

smallest → largest

b

96 mm	8·9 cm	95·9 mm	9·1 cm
	☐ mm		☐ mm
☐	☐	☐	☐

smallest → largest

Challenge 2

1 Convert the measurements to the same unit, then put them in order, smallest to largest.

a

66·1 cm	659 mm	66 cm	0·6 m	690 mm
☐	☐	☐	☐	☐

smallest → largest

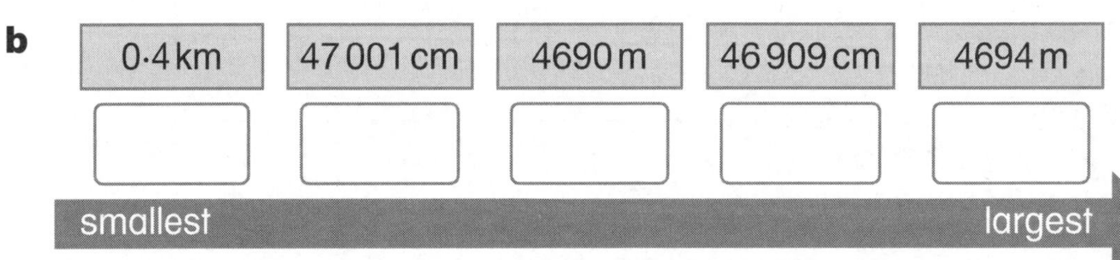

b

0·4 km	47 001 cm	4690 m	46 909 cm	4694 m
☐	☐	☐	☐	☐

smallest → largest

2 Use a ruler to measure the lengths of the caterpillars. Round each measurement to the nearest centimetre and complete the table.

A 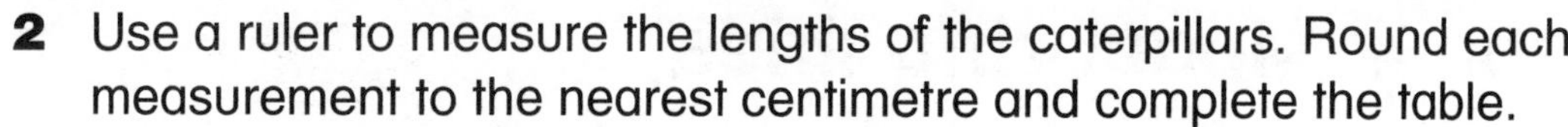

B 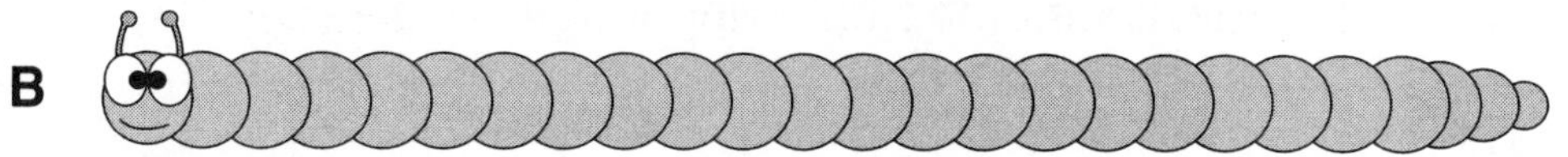

C 

Caterpillar	Actual length (cm)	Rounded length (cm)
A		
B		
C		

Challenge **3** Round the height of the towers to the nearest tenth (1 decimal place). Then write them in ascending order of rounded height.

A 370·49 m
Rounded: ☐ m

B 371·04 m
Rounded: ☐ m

C 370·55 m
Rounded: ☐ m

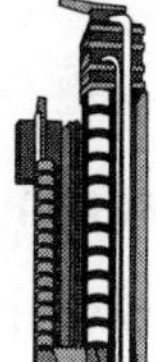

D 371·05 m
Rounded: ☐ m

☐ ☐ ☐ ☐

smallest → largest

Measure

Lesson 4: **Measuring lines**

- Draw lines to a required length (cm or mm)
- Measure lines to the nearest centimetre or millimetre

You will need
- ruler

Use a ruler to draw lines of the following lengths.

a 4 cm

b 7 cm

c 66 mm

1 Use a straight edge (not a ruler) to draw lines that you estimate to be the lengths given. Measure each length with a ruler. Calculate the difference between your estimate and the actual length.

a 5 cm

Actual length: Difference:

b 44 mm

Actual length: Difference:

c 72 mm

Actual length: Difference:

2 Measure the length of each line to the level of accuracy given.

a To the nearest centimetre.

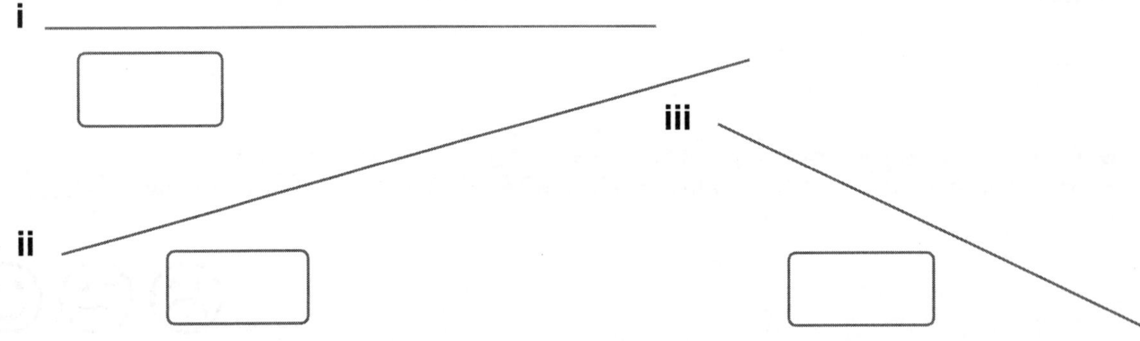

i **b** To the nearest millimetre.

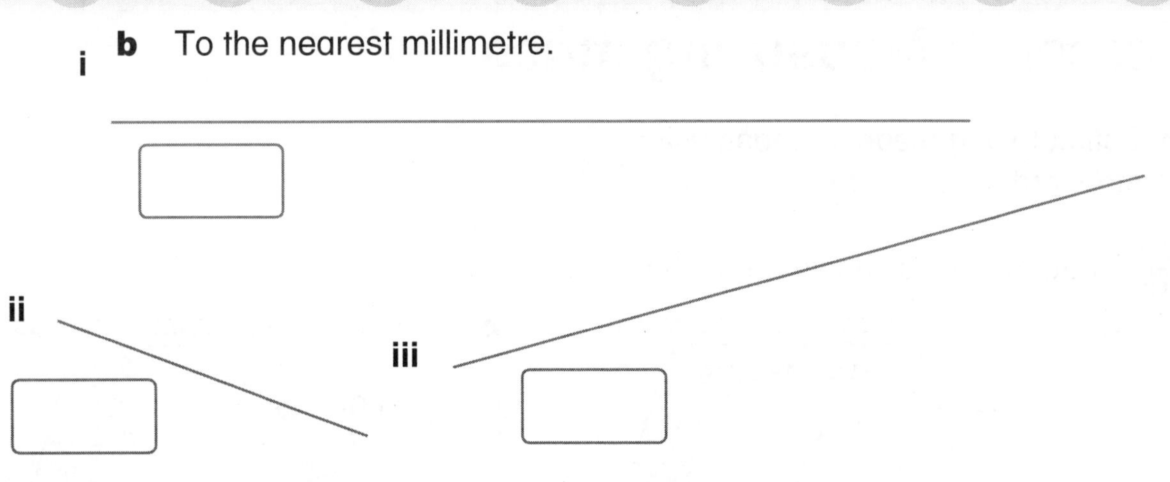

ii

iii

Challenge 3 Draw the following:

a Line A is 89 mm. Line B is 63 mm. A and B are parallel lines 1·4 cm apart.

b Draw a scalene triangle ABC with the following sides:
AB – 42 mm
BC – 28 mm
Measure side CA:

CA – ☐ mm

c Draw a square with sides 4·6 cm long.

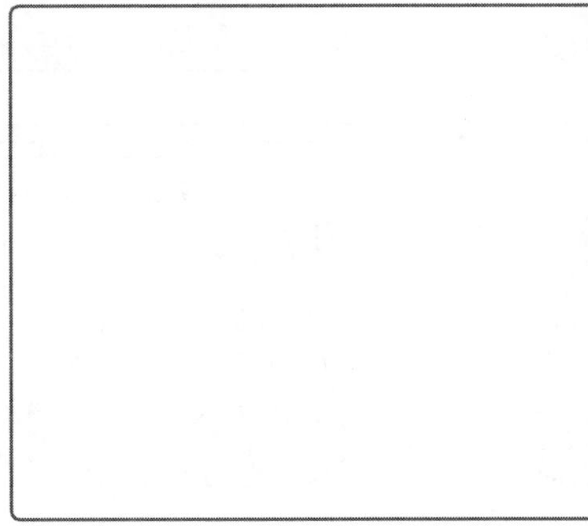

Measure

Lesson 1: **Measuring mass**

- Estimate and measure mass using standard units (g, kg)

Challenge 1

Write the mass shown on each scale.

a

☐ kg

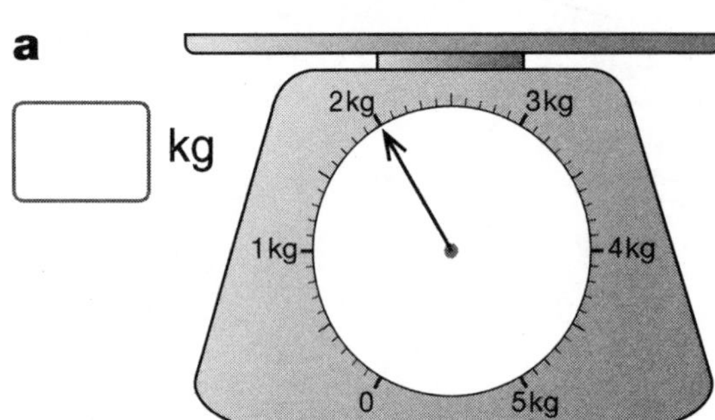

b

☐ kg

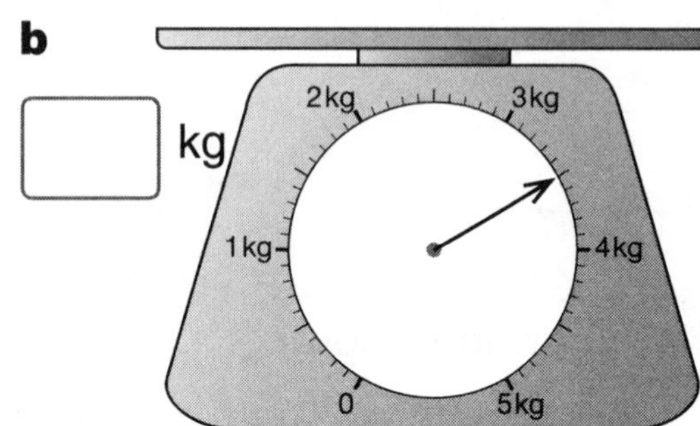

c

☐ kg

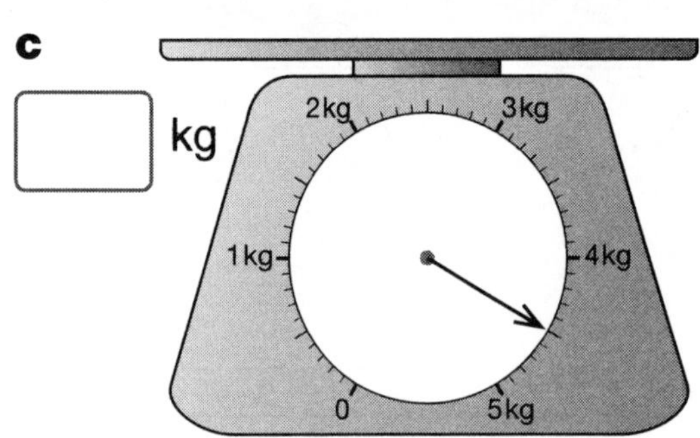

d

☐ kg

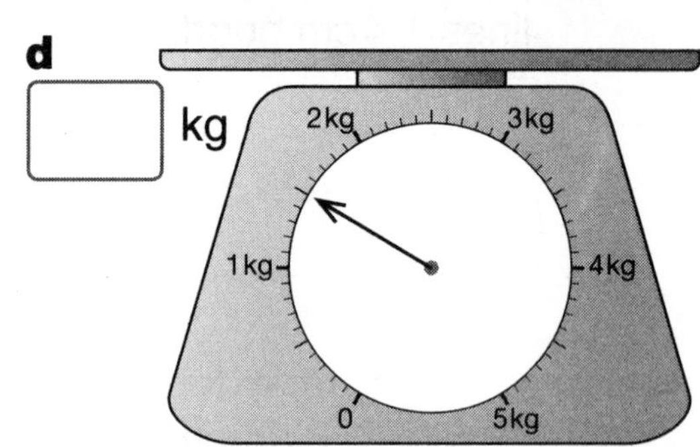

Challenge 2

1 Write the mass shown on each scale to the nearest 10 g.

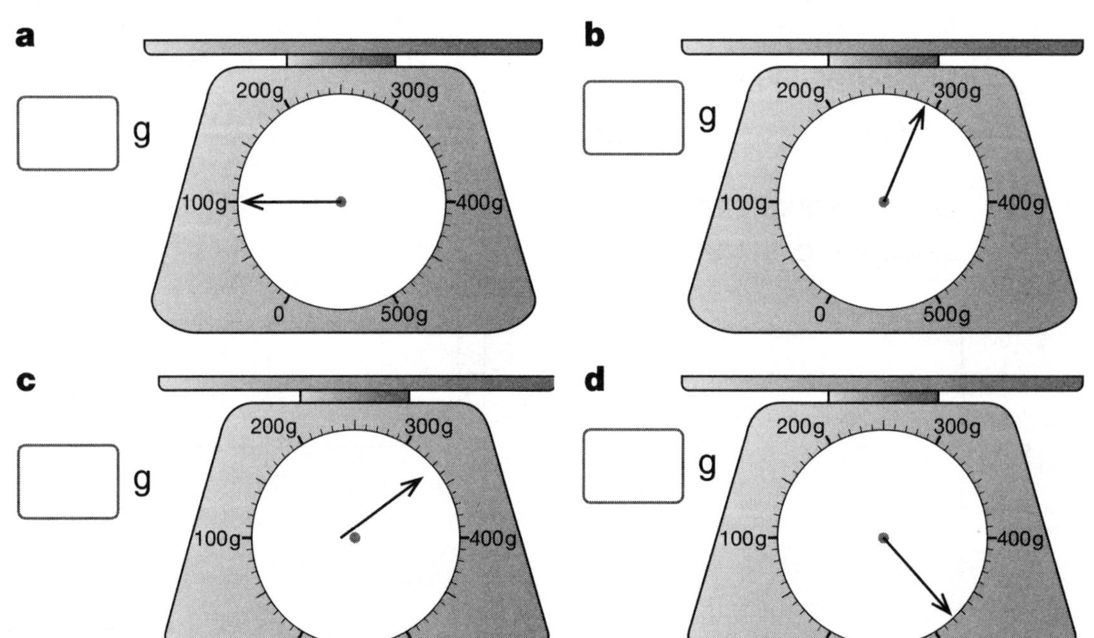

2 Write the mass shown on each scale to the nearest 100 g.

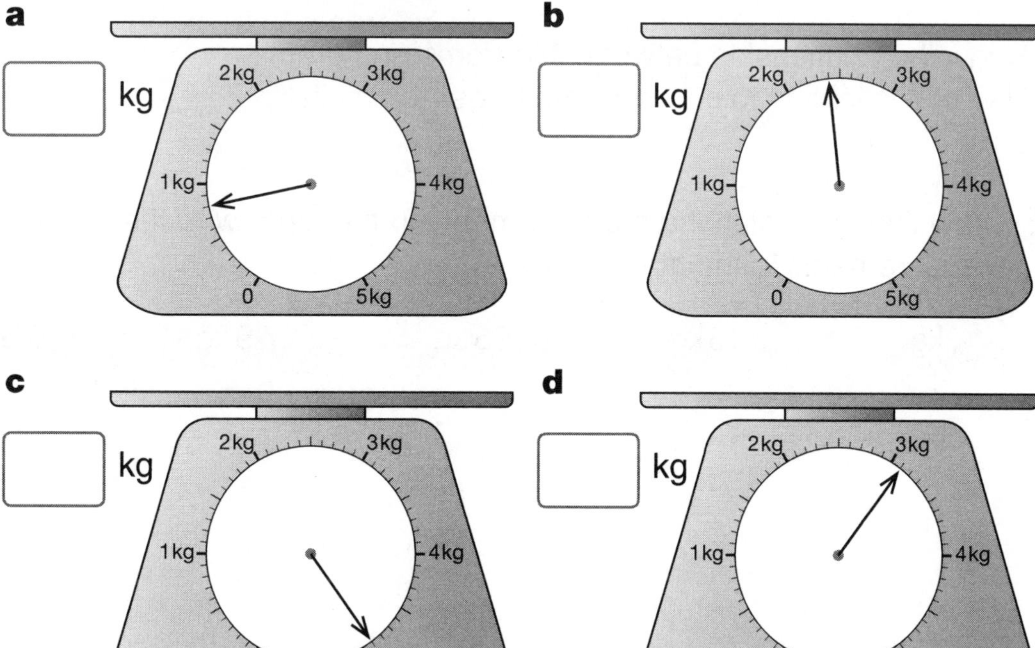

Challenge **3** Draw the scale pointer for each mass measurement.

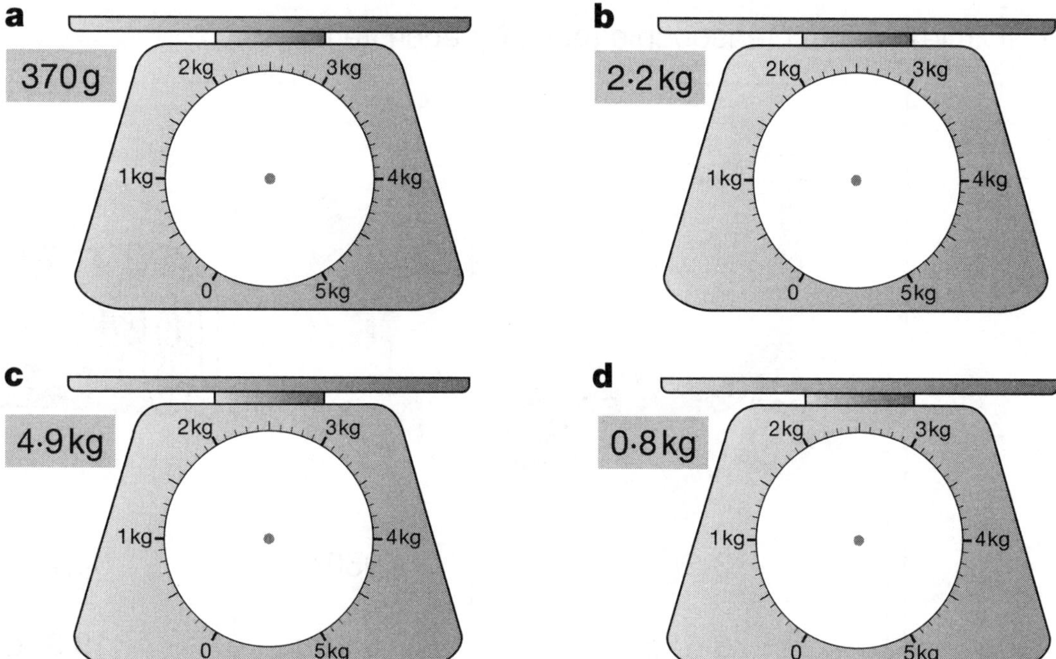

Measure

Lesson 2: Converting units

- Know the relationship between kilograms and grams
- Use multiplication to convert from larger to smaller units of mass

Challenge 1

Draw lines to match the measurements in the top row to their equivalent measurements in the bottom row.

4 kg	16 kg	55 kg	7·9 kg	5·5 kg
7900 g	16 000 g	5500 g	4000 g	55 000 g

Challenge 2

1 Circle the most reasonable mass for each item.

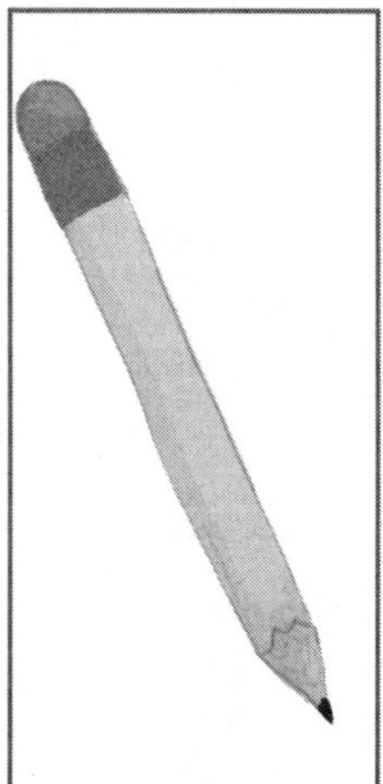			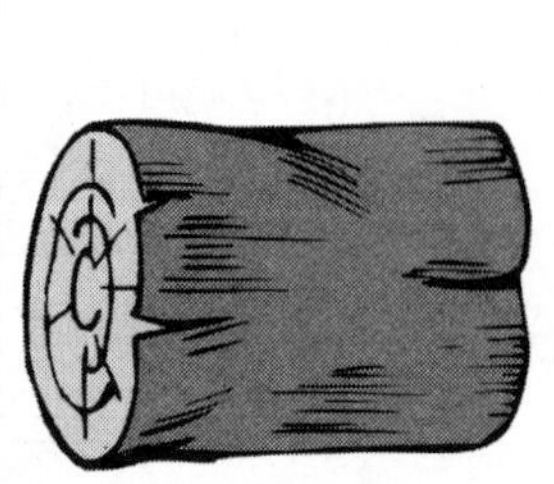
2·1 kg	3·5 g	950 g	0·8 kg
210 g	3·5 kg	0·9 kg	18·9 kg
21 g	35 kg	90 g	1800 g
2·1 g	350 g	9 g	1800 kg

2 Convert between kilograms and grams.

a 2 kg = ______ g

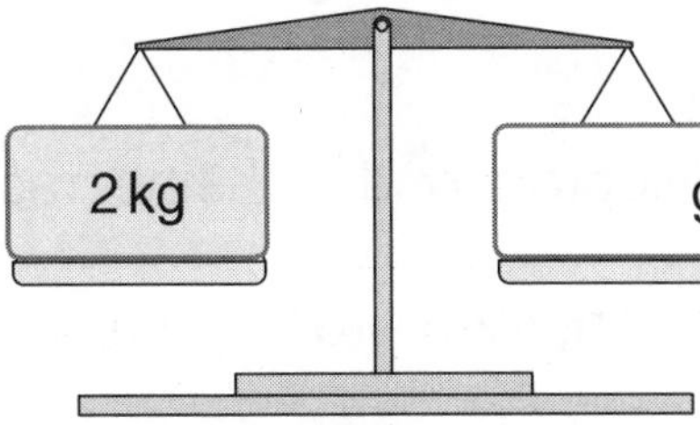

b 7 kg = ______ g

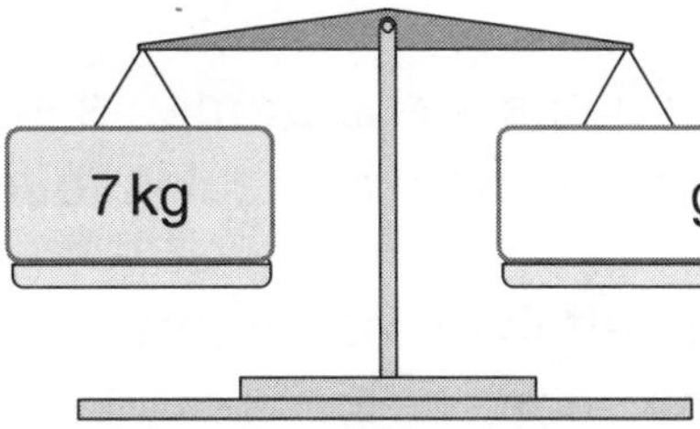

c 10 kg = ______ g

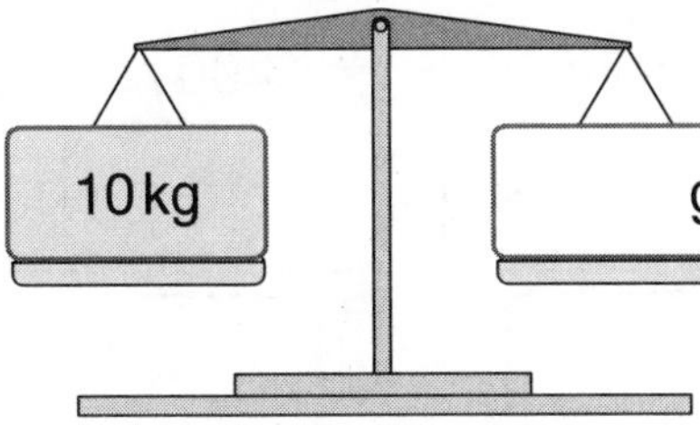

d 31 kg = ______ g

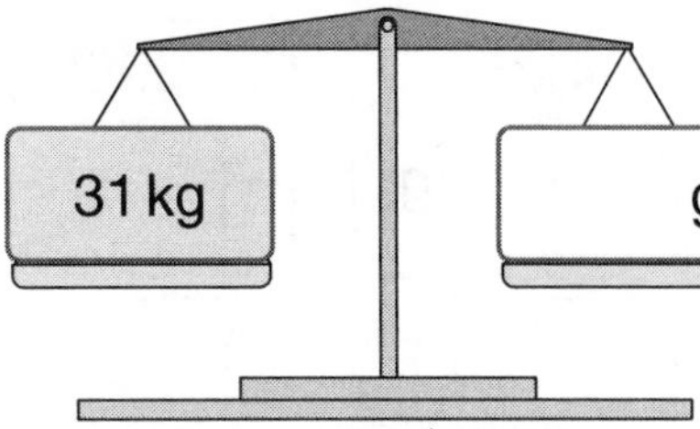

e 3·1 kg = ______ g

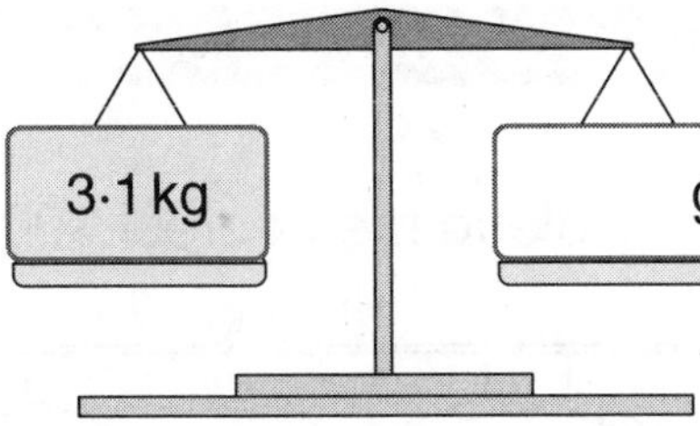

f 4·3 kg = ______ g

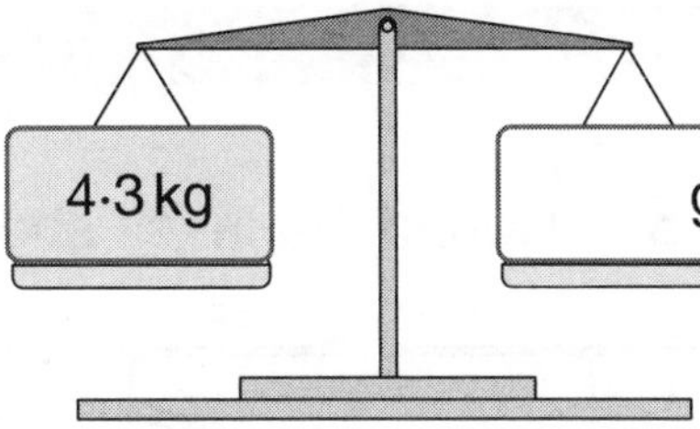

g 43·3 kg = ______ g

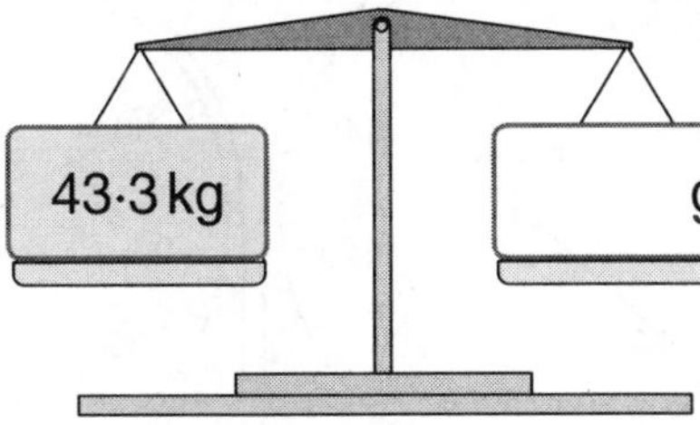

h 99·9 kg = ______ g

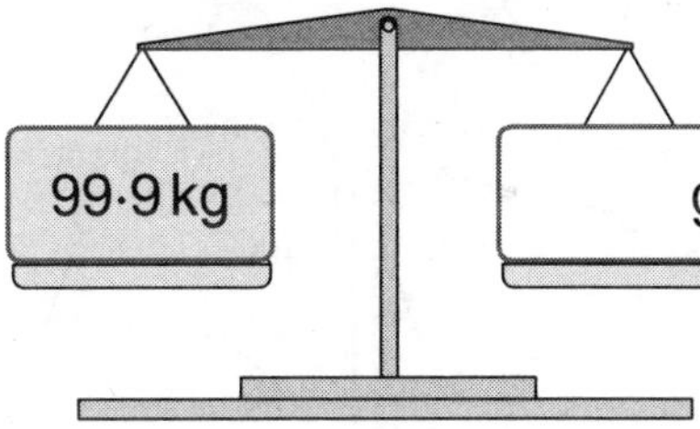

Challenge 3 Calculate the mass of parcels A, B and C in grams.

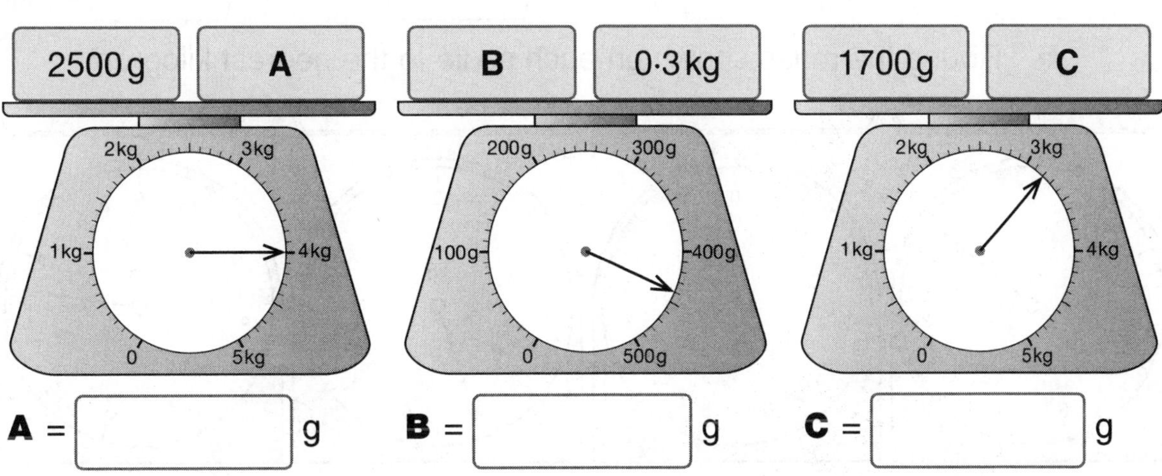

Measure

Lesson 3: **Ordering and rounding mass**

- Order mass measurements in mixed units
- Round numbers on scales to the nearest kilogram and to the nearest 100 g

Challenge 1

Convert the measurements to the unit given, then order them from lightest to heaviest.

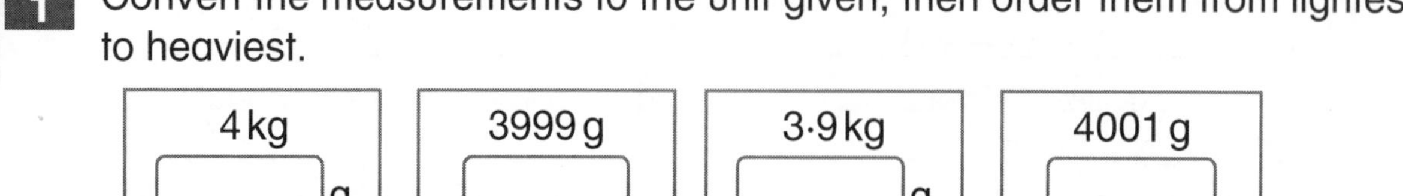

lightest heaviest

Challenge 2

1 a Round the mass shown on each scale to the nearest 100 g.

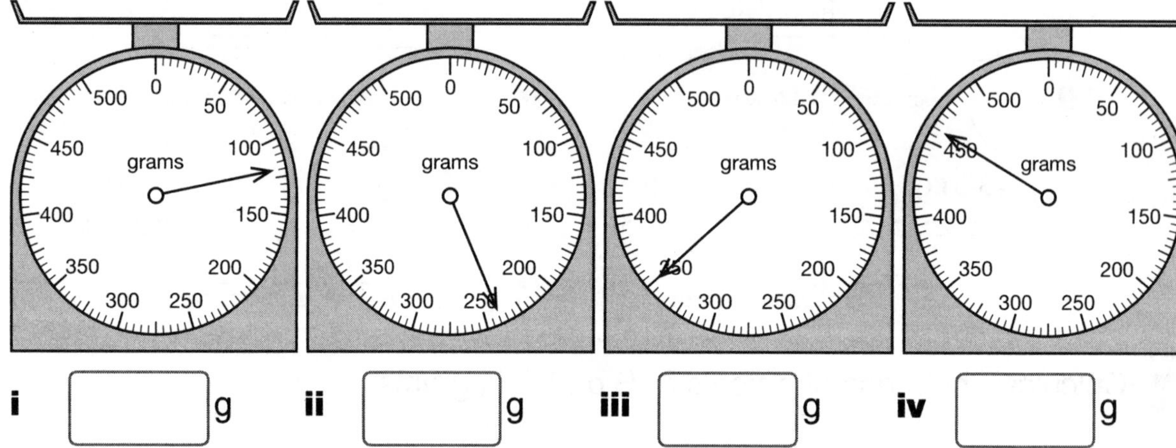

i ☐ g **ii** ☐ g **iii** ☐ g **iv** ☐ g

b Round the mass shown on each scale to the nearest kilogram.

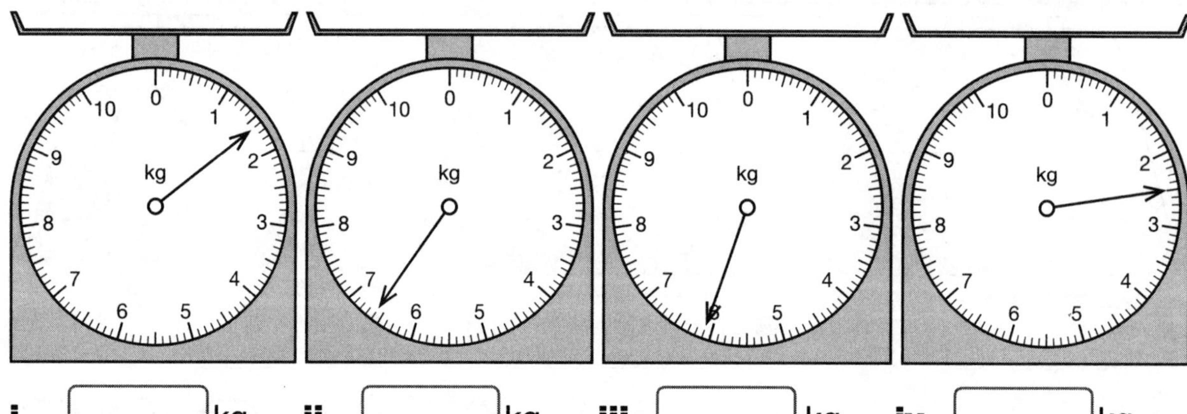

i ☐ kg **ii** ☐ kg **iii** ☐ kg **iv** ☐ kg

2 Order the boxes by their mass, from lightest to heaviest. Write the letters in the correct order.

a Order: ☐ ☐ ☐ ☐ ☐

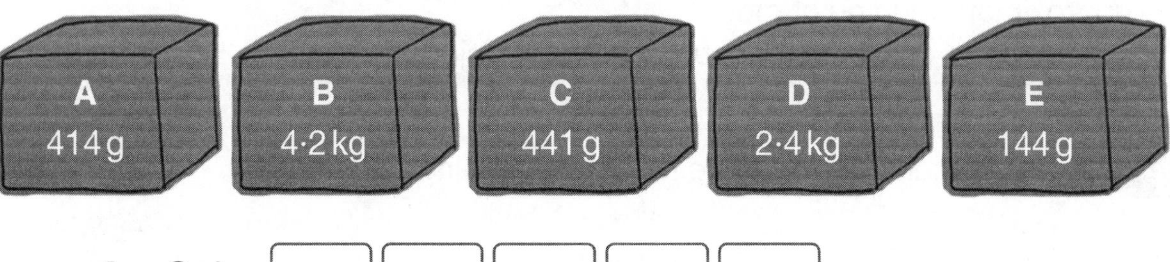

b Order: ☐ ☐ ☐ ☐ ☐

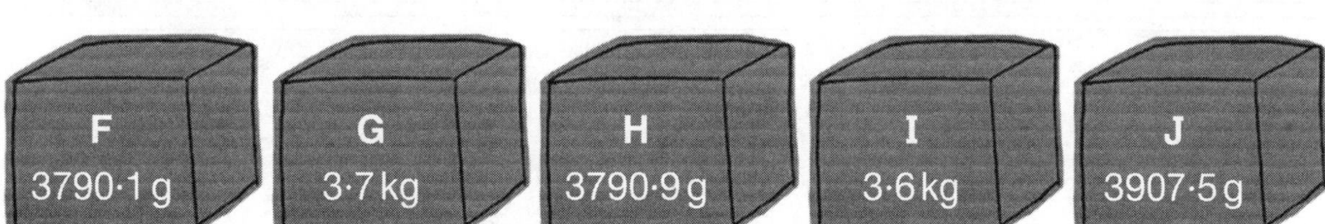

Challenge **3** Round the mass of the children to the nearest tenth (1 decimal place). Then write the letters a to d in ascending order of rounded mass.

a

Becky 31·97 kg

Rounded: ☐ kg

b

Gopal 31·76 kg

Rounded: ☐ kg

c

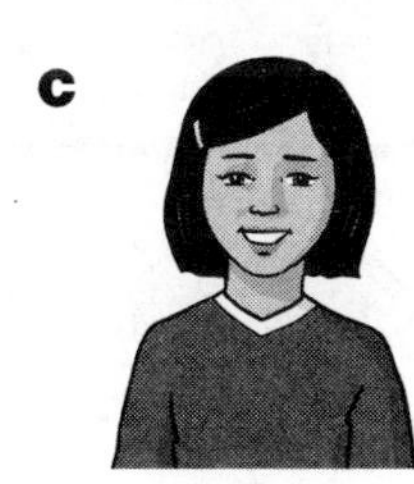

Lucy 31·65 kg

Rounded: ☐ kg

d

Jackson 37·94 kg

Rounded: ☐ kg

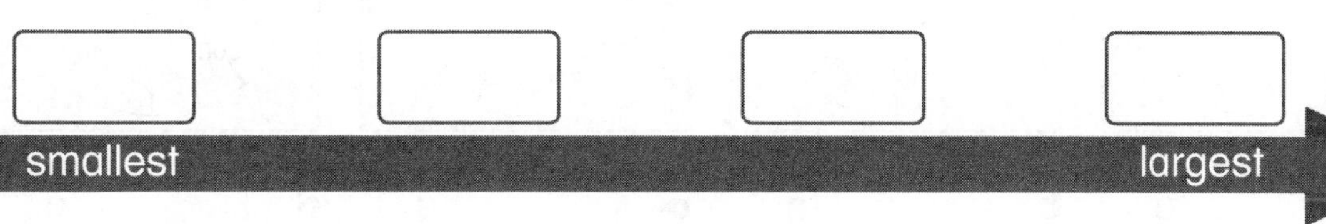

Lesson 4: **Reading weighing scales**

- Know the equivalent of $\frac{1}{2}$, $\frac{1}{4}$, and $\frac{1}{10}$ of a kilogram in grams
- Find the value of each interval on a scale to give an approximate reading of mass
- Use different scales to measure the same object.

Challenge 1 Read the scale and write the measurement in the unit given.

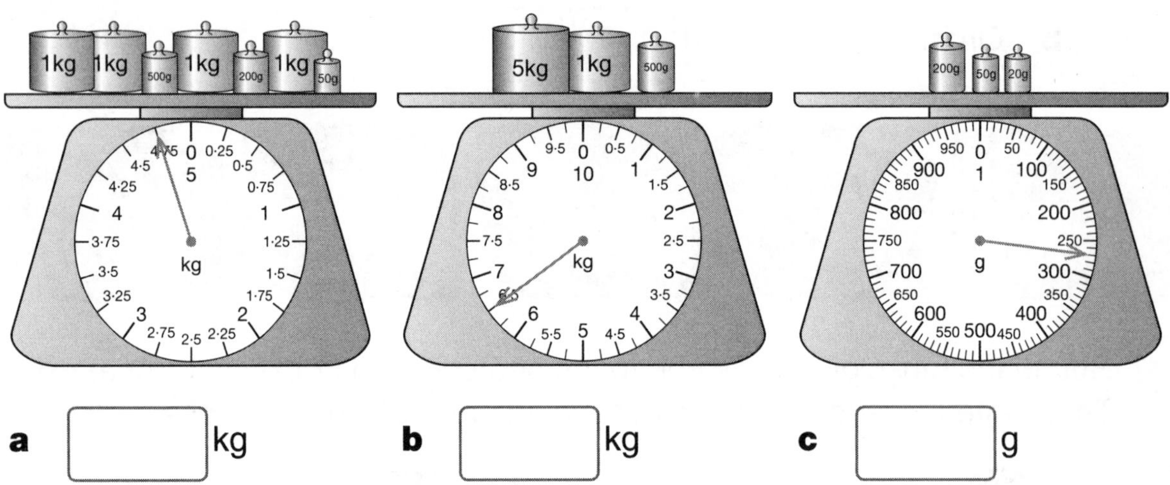

a ☐ kg **b** ☐ kg **c** ☐ g

Challenge 2 **1** Read the scale and write the measurement in grams.

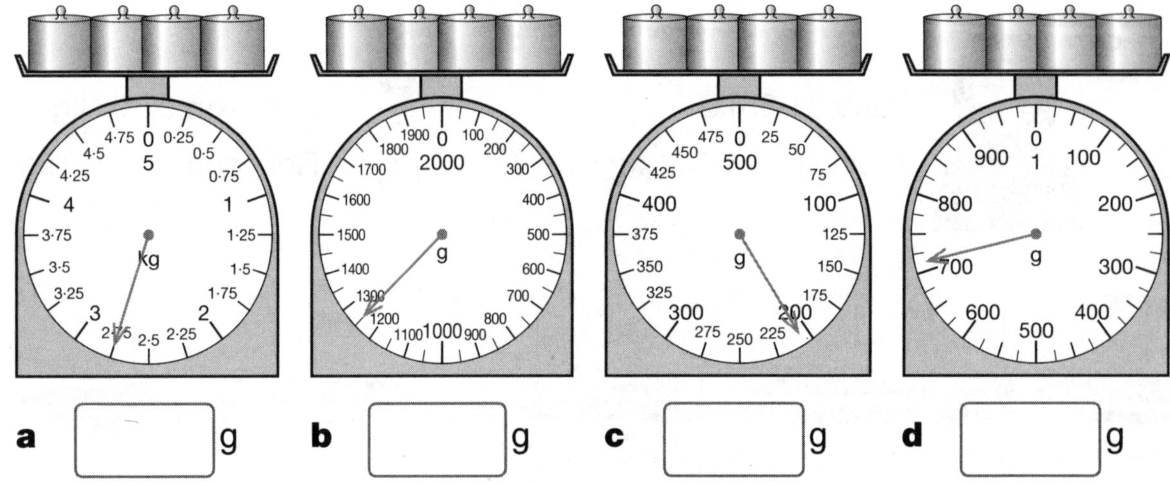

a ☐ g **b** ☐ g **c** ☐ g **d** ☐ g

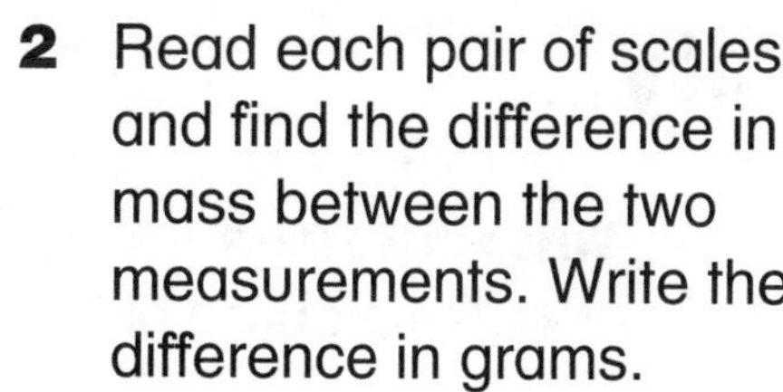

2 Read each pair of scales and find the difference in mass between the two measurements. Write the difference in grams.

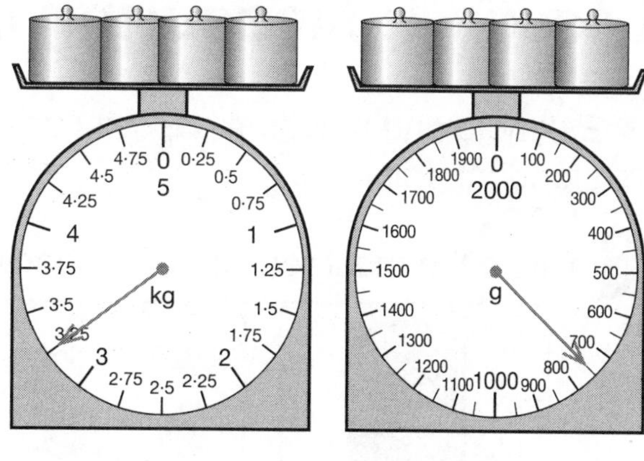

a g

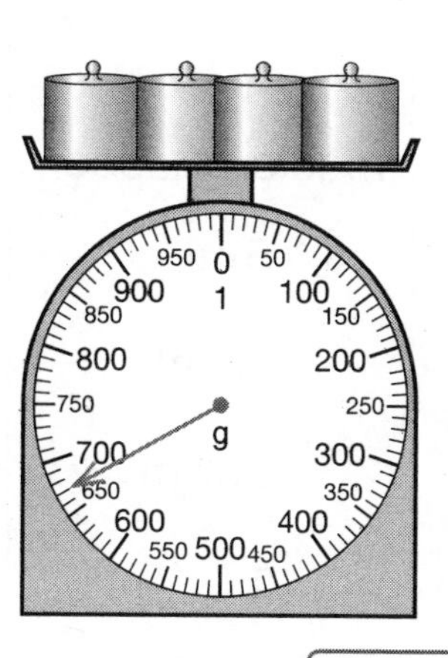

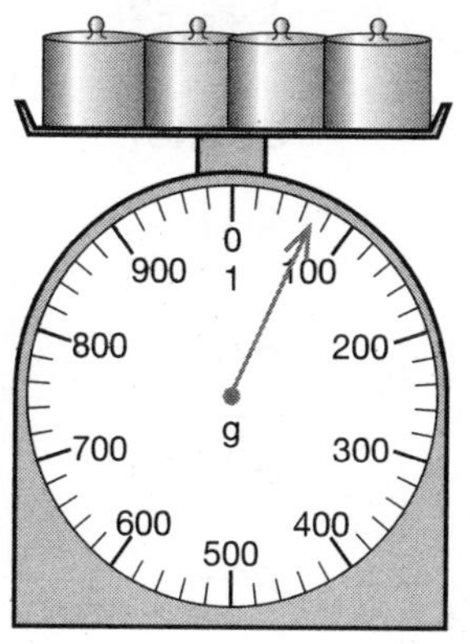

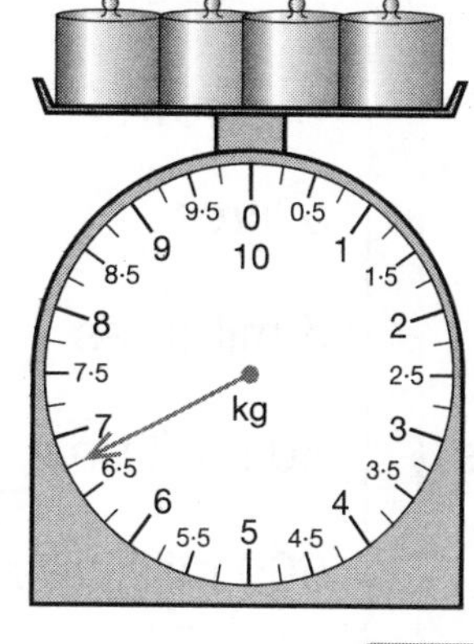

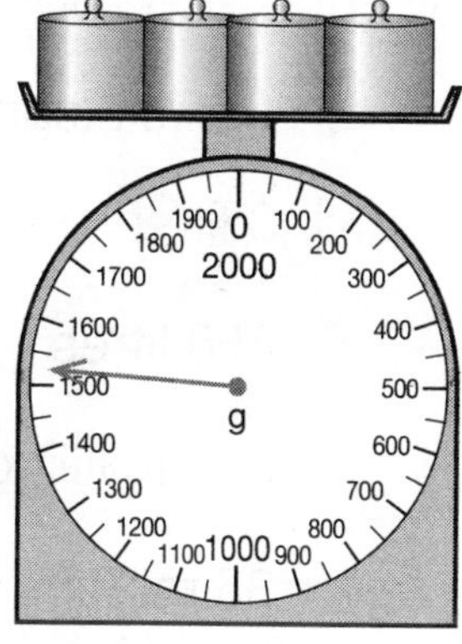

b g

c g

Challenge 3 Calculate the missing measurements. Write the measurement in the box and draw a pointer on the scales to show the reading.

a

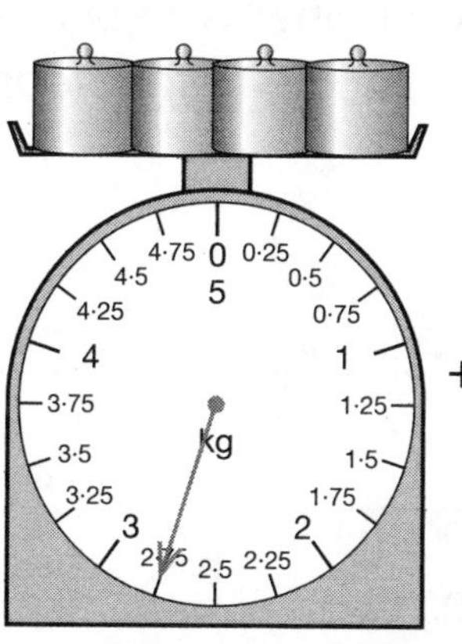

+

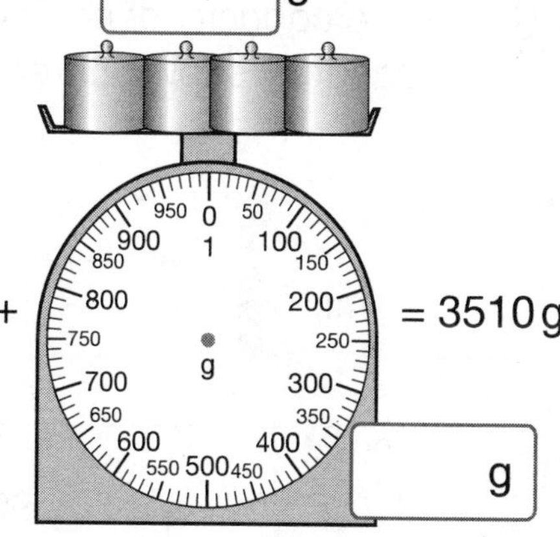

b

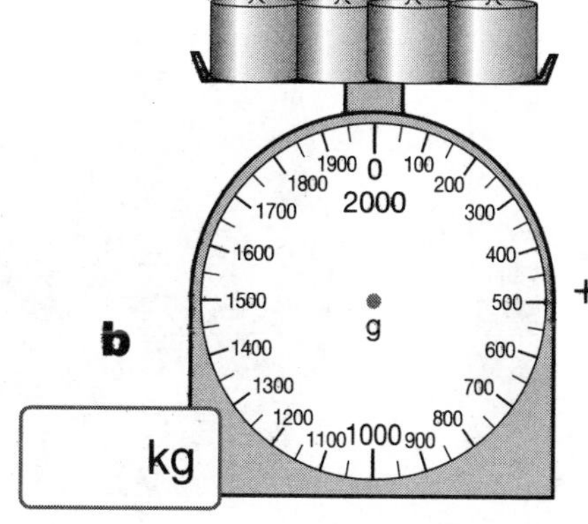

+

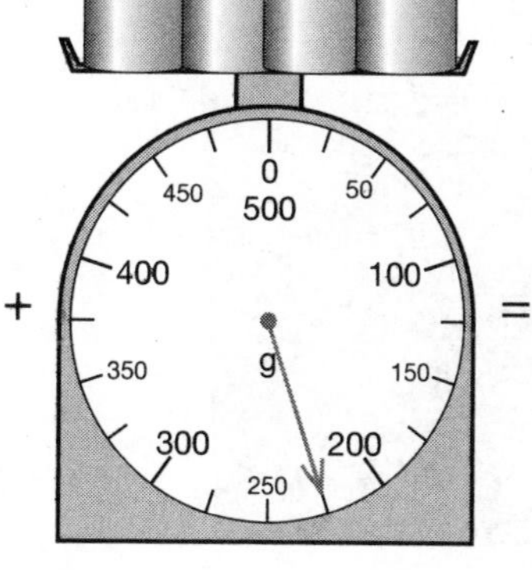

= 2025 g

Measure

Lesson 1: Measuring capacity

- Estimate and measure capacity using standard units (ml, *l*)

You will need
- blue coloured pencil

Circle the most reasonable capacity for each container.

			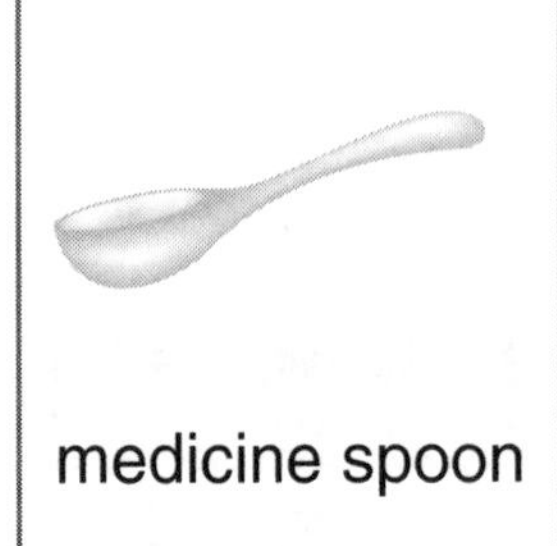
drinks can	bowl	bucket	medicine spoon
3 litres	5 litres	80 *l*	5 ml
350 litres	5 millilitres	8 *l*	50 ml
350 millilitres	50 millilitres	800 ml	500 ml
35 millilitres	500 millilitres	80 ml	1 *l*

1 The capacity of each container A to D has been measured. Write the capacity shown on each scale to the nearest 50 ml.

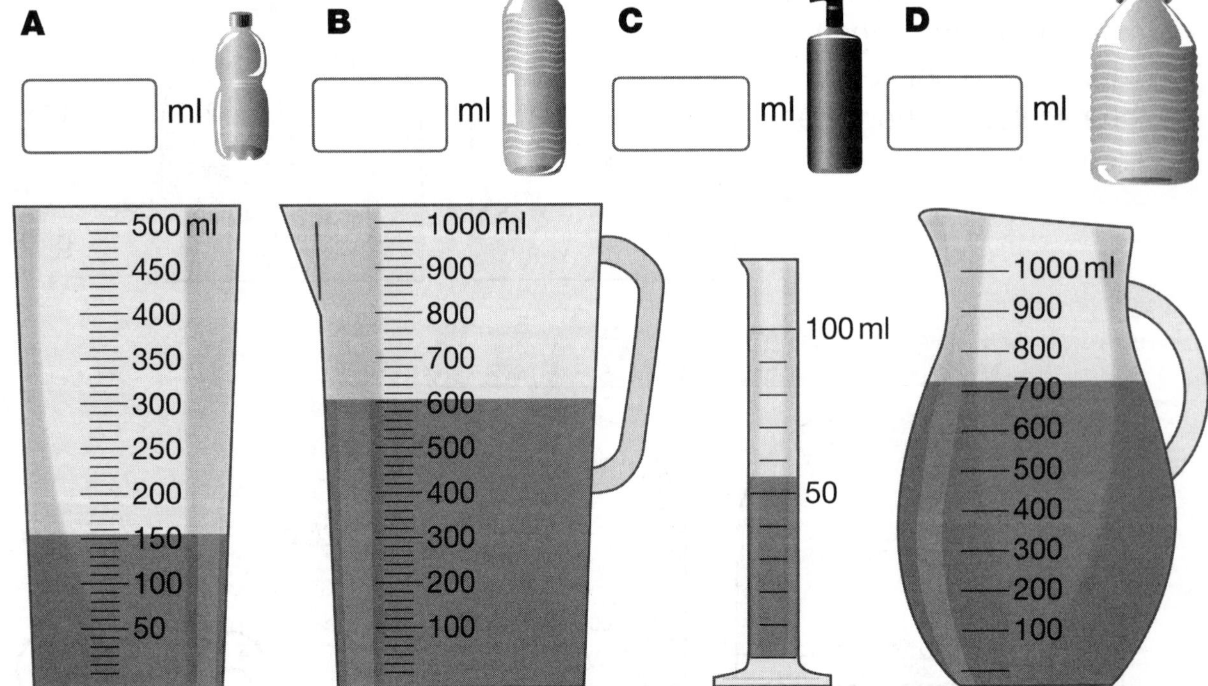

2 Fill each measuring jug with the water from the container above it. Mark the water level on the scale.

a 750 ml

b 400 ml

c 150 ml

d 7·5 l

2000 ml, 1900, 1800, 1700, 1600, 1500, 1400, 1300, 1200, 1100, 1000, 900, 800, 700, 600, 500, 400, 300, 200, 100

1000 ml, 900, 800, 700, 600, 500, 400, 300, 200, 100

500 ml, 450, 400, 350, 300, 250, 200, 150, 100, 50

10 litres, 9·5, 9, 8·5, 8, 7·5, 7, 6·5, 6, 5·5, 5, 4·5, 4, 3·5, 3, 2·5, 2, 1·5, 1, 0·5

Challenge 3 Fill each measuring jug with the water from the two containers next to it. Mark the water level on the scale.

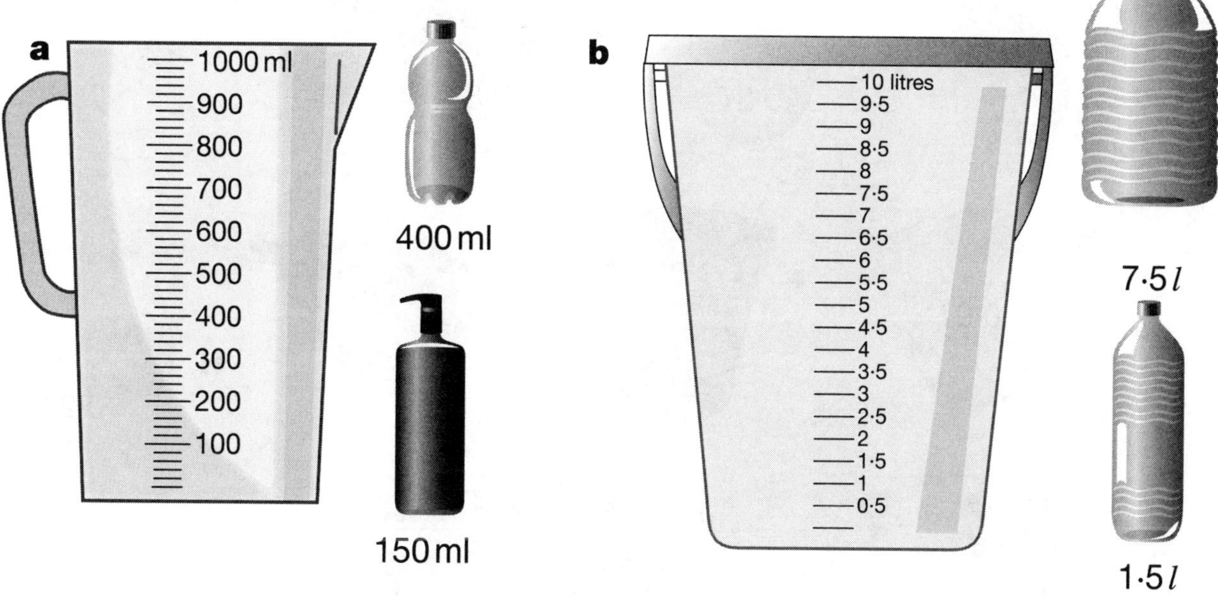

Lesson 2: Converting units

- Know the relationship between litres and millilitres
- Use multiplication to convert from larger to smaller units of capacity

You will need
- blue coloured pencil

Challenge 1

Draw lines to match the measurements in the top row to their equivalent measurements in the bottom row.

3 *l*	7 *l*	4·3 *l*	19 *l*	43 *l*
43 000 ml	19 000 ml	4300 ml	7000 ml	3000 ml

Challenge 2

1 Write the letter for each container in the correct set for its capacity.

less than 250 ml	between 250 ml and 950 ml	between 950 ml and 8000 ml	between 8000 ml and 15 000 ml

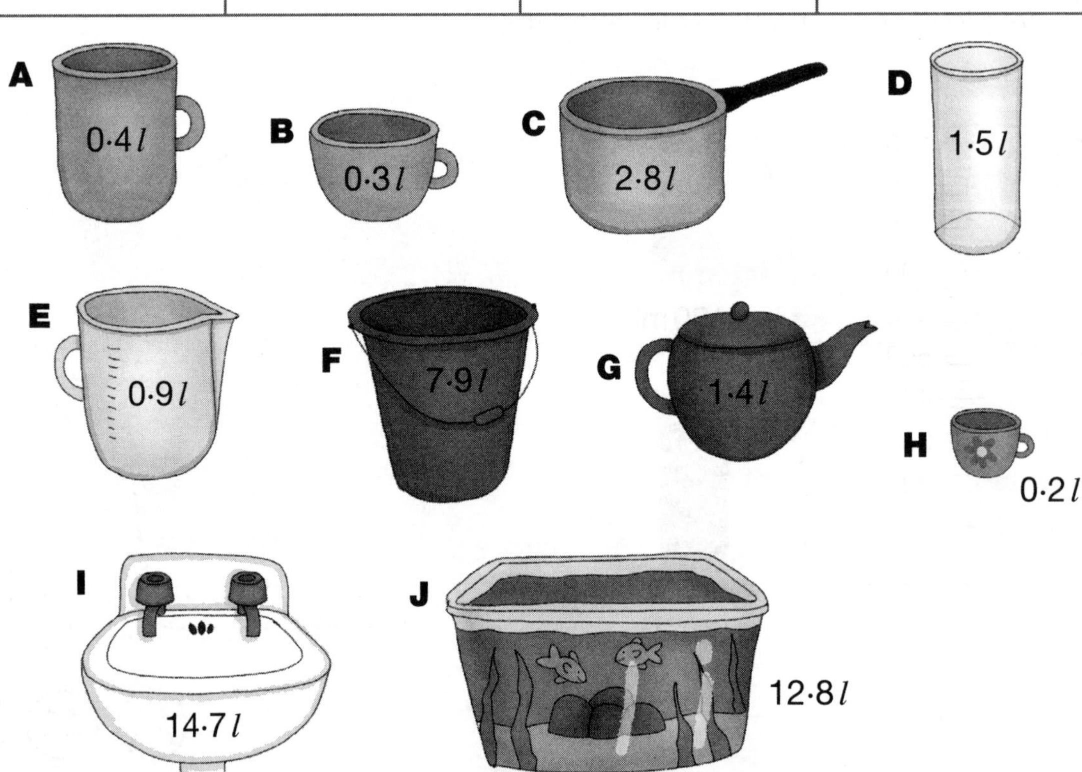

2 The water in each container on the left is poured into the measuring container on the right. Mark the water level in the measuring container.

a 0·7 l

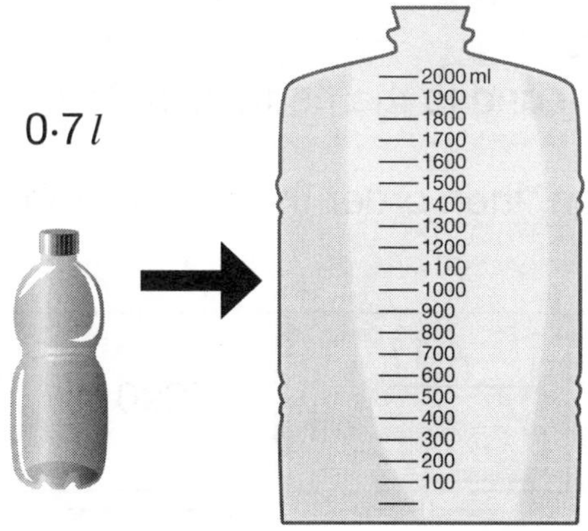

2000 ml
1900
1800
1700
1600
1500
1400
1300
1200
1100
1000
900
800
700
600
500
400
300
200
100

b 1·3 l

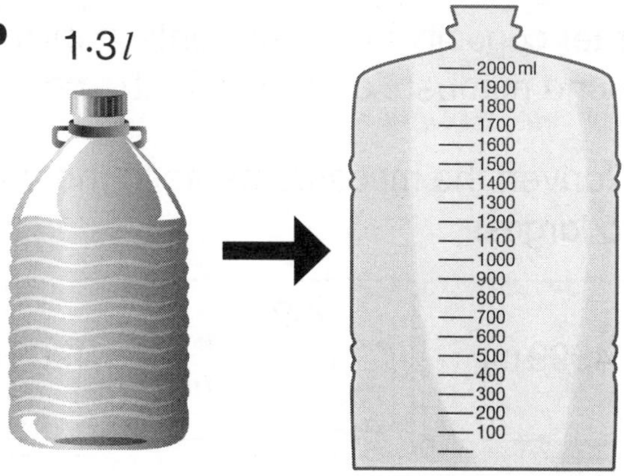

2000 ml
1900
1800
1700
1600
1500
1400
1300
1200
1100
1000
900
800
700
600
500
400
300
200
100

c 5·5 l

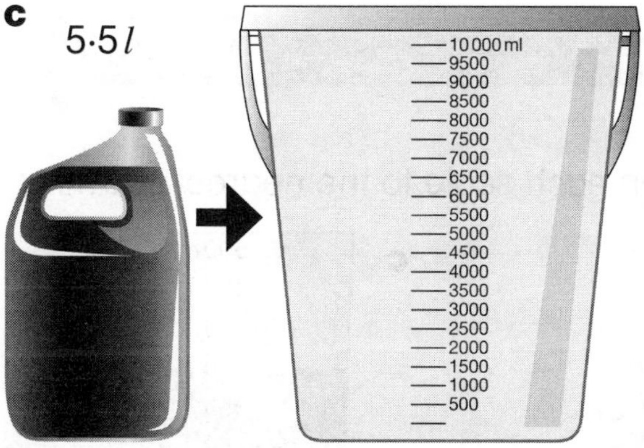

10 000 ml
9500
9000
8500
8000
7500
7000
6500
6000
5500
5000
4500
4000
3500
3000
2500
2000
1500
1000
500

d 35 l

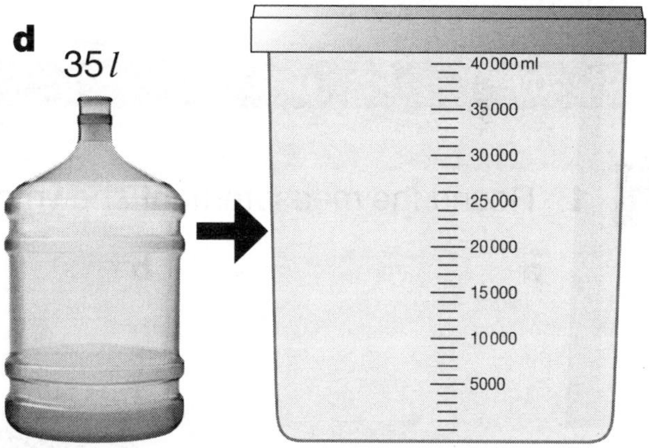

40 000 ml
35 000
30 000
25 000
20 000
15 000
10 000
5000

Challenge 3 Maisie wants to make some blackcurrant squash for a party, but the only water available is in plastic containers. Draw arrows to show the water bottles she should combine to make each amount of squash. She can only use the water in each container once.

50 ml
200 ml
750 ml
250 ml
100 ml
250 ml
150 ml
1250 ml

0·5 l
1 l
1·5 l

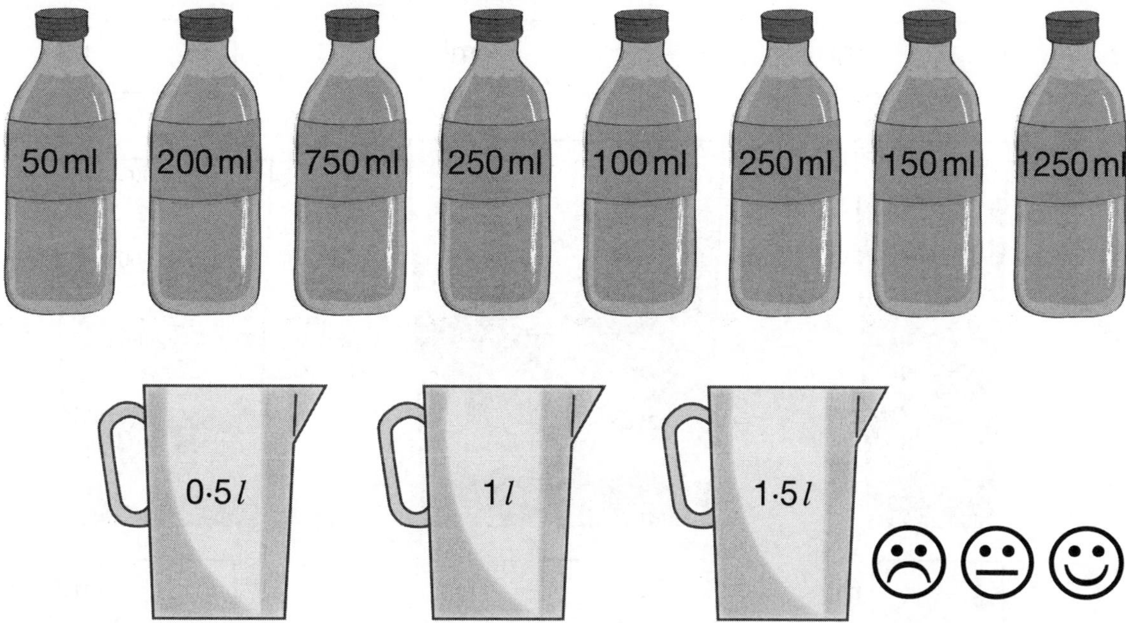

Measure

Lesson 3: **Ordering and rounding capacity**

- Order capacity measurements in mixed units
- Round numbers on scales to the nearest litre and to the nearest 100 ml

Challenge 1 Convert the measurements to the unit given, then order them from smallest to largest.

4999 ml	4·9 *l* ☐ ml	4909 ml	4·1 *l* ☐ ml	4990 ml
☐	☐	☐	☐	☐

smallest → largest

Challenge 2

1 Round the measurement shown on each scale to the nearest 100 ml.

a 100 ml, 50 — ☐ ml

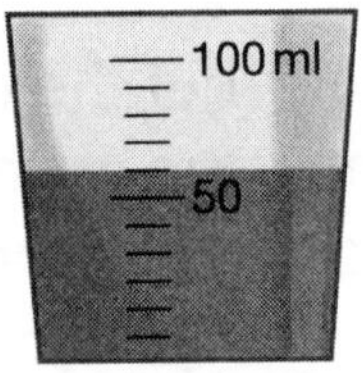

b 350 ml, 300, 250, 200, 150, 100, 50 — ☐ ml

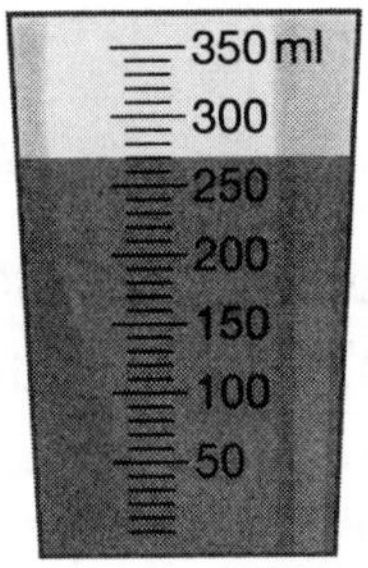

c 500 ml, 450, 400, 350, 300, 250, 200, 150, 100, 50 — ☐ ml

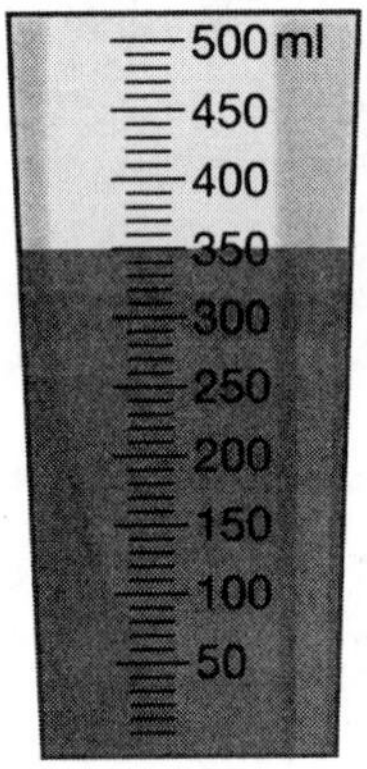

d 1000 ml, 900, 800, 700, 600, 500, 400, 300, 200, 100 — ☐ ml

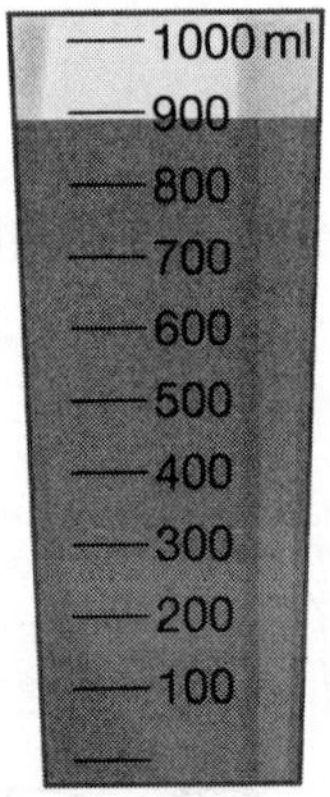

e 5 litres, 4·5, 4, 3·5, 3, 2·5, 2, 1·5, 1, 0·5 — ☐ ml

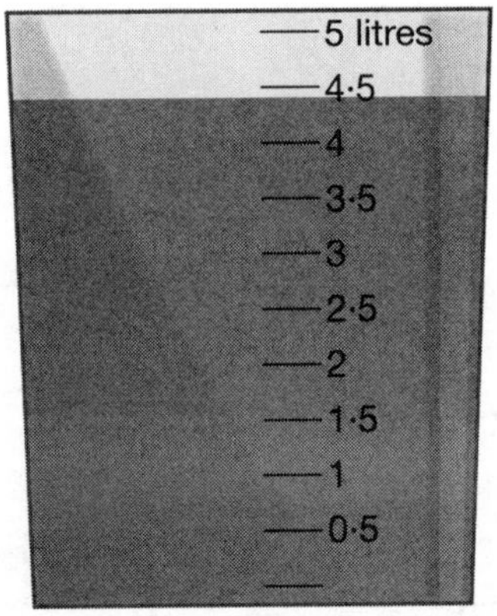

f 2 litres, 1500, 2 litres, 500 — ☐ ml

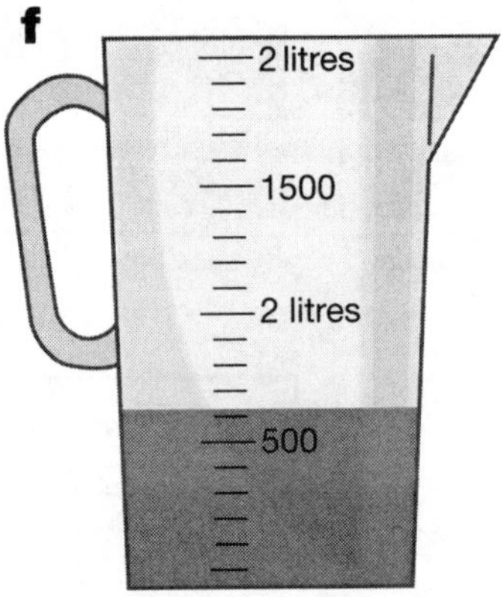

2 Order the jugs and the buckets by capacity, from smallest to largest. Write the letters in the correct order.

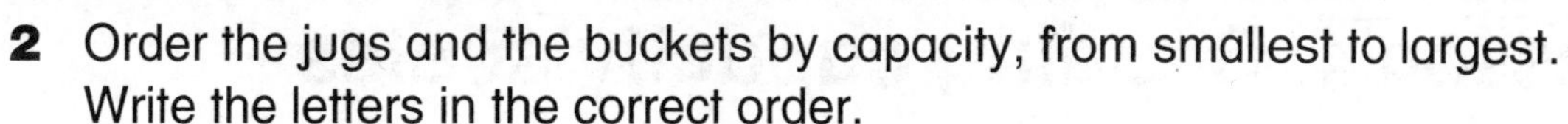

a Order: ☐ ☐ ☐ ☐ ☐

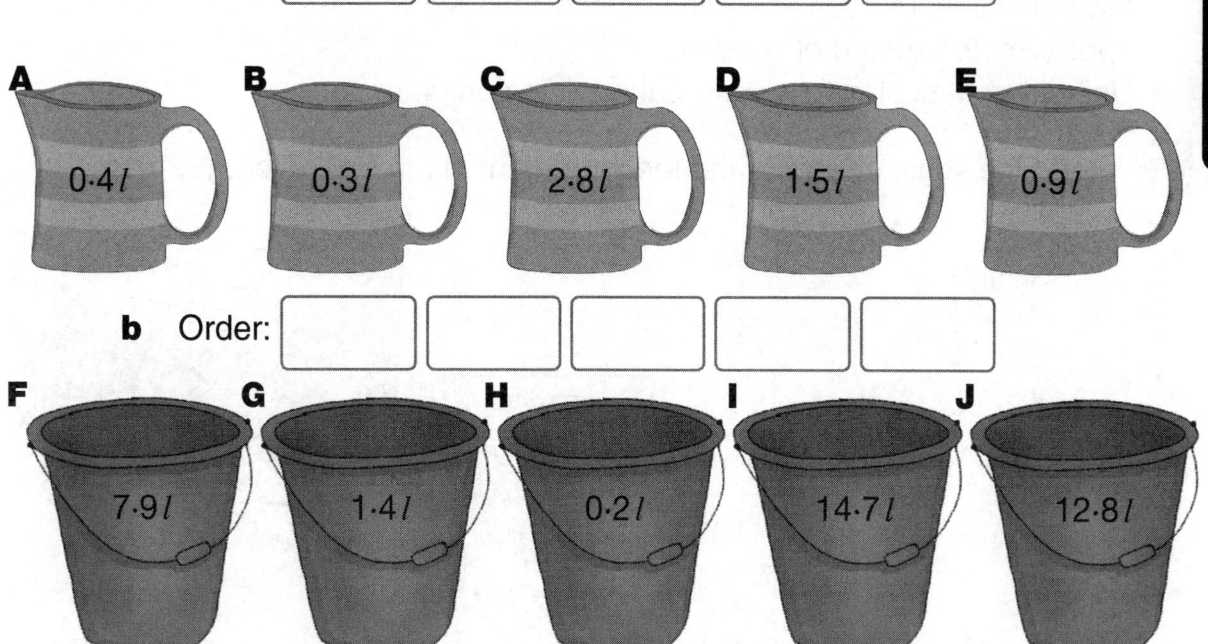

b Order: ☐ ☐ ☐ ☐ ☐

Challenge **3**

1 The table shows the capacity of three sizes of fish tank. Complete the table.

Capacity	Round to the nearest			
	10 ml	50 ml	100 ml	1 litre
12 425 ml				
16 951 ml				
18 078 ml				

2 Order the jugs by capacity, from smallest to largest.

Order: ☐ ☐ ☐ ☐ ☐

Measure

Lesson 4: **Reading capacity scales**

- Know the equivalent of $\frac{1}{2}$, $\frac{1}{4}$, and $\frac{1}{10}$ of a litre in millilitres
- Find the value of each interval on a scale to give an approximate reading of capacity
- Use different scales to measure the same container

Challenge 1 Read the scale and write the measurement in the unit given.

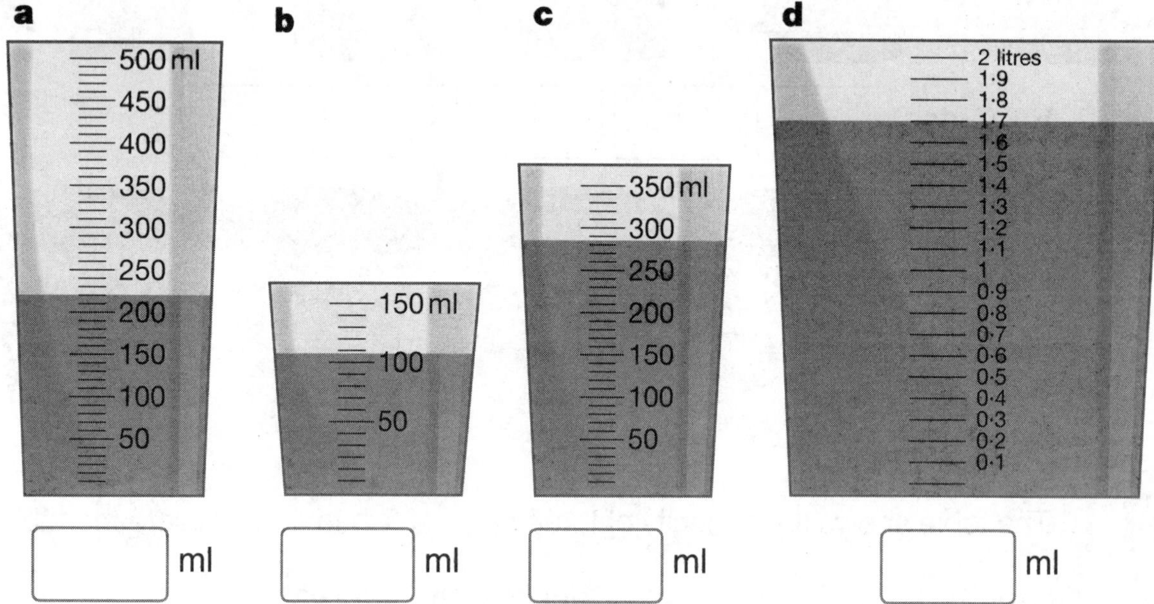

Challenge 2 Read the scale and write the measurement in the unit given.

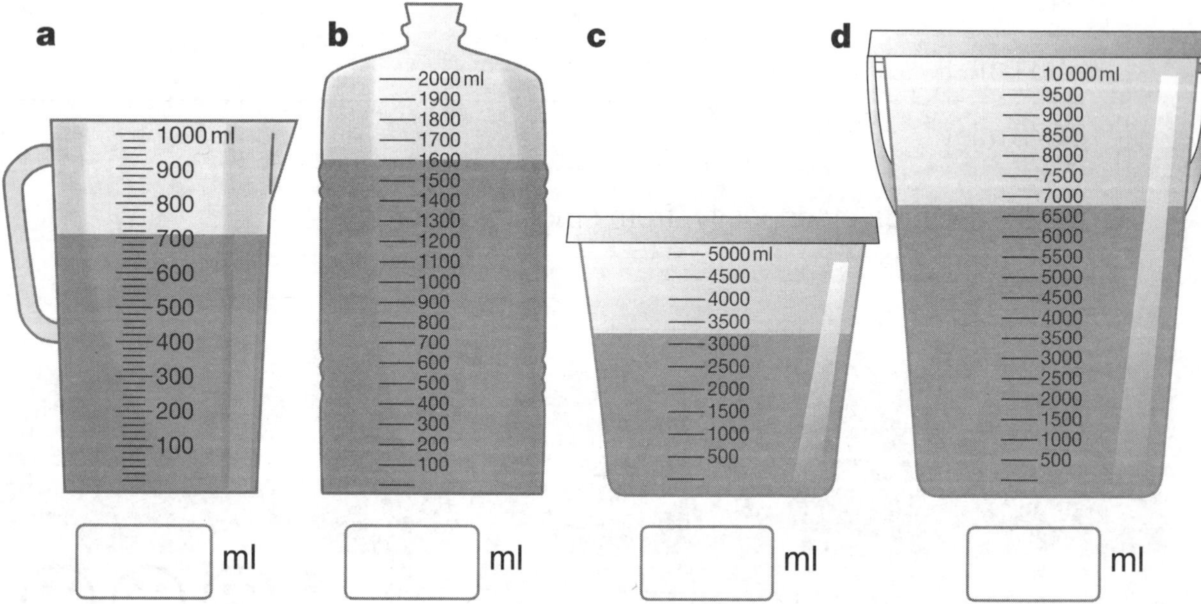

Challenge 3

Five learners each fill a container and then pour the contents into a measuring jar. Look at the table of clues and work out which container belongs to which learner. Write the letter of the container next to the learner's name.

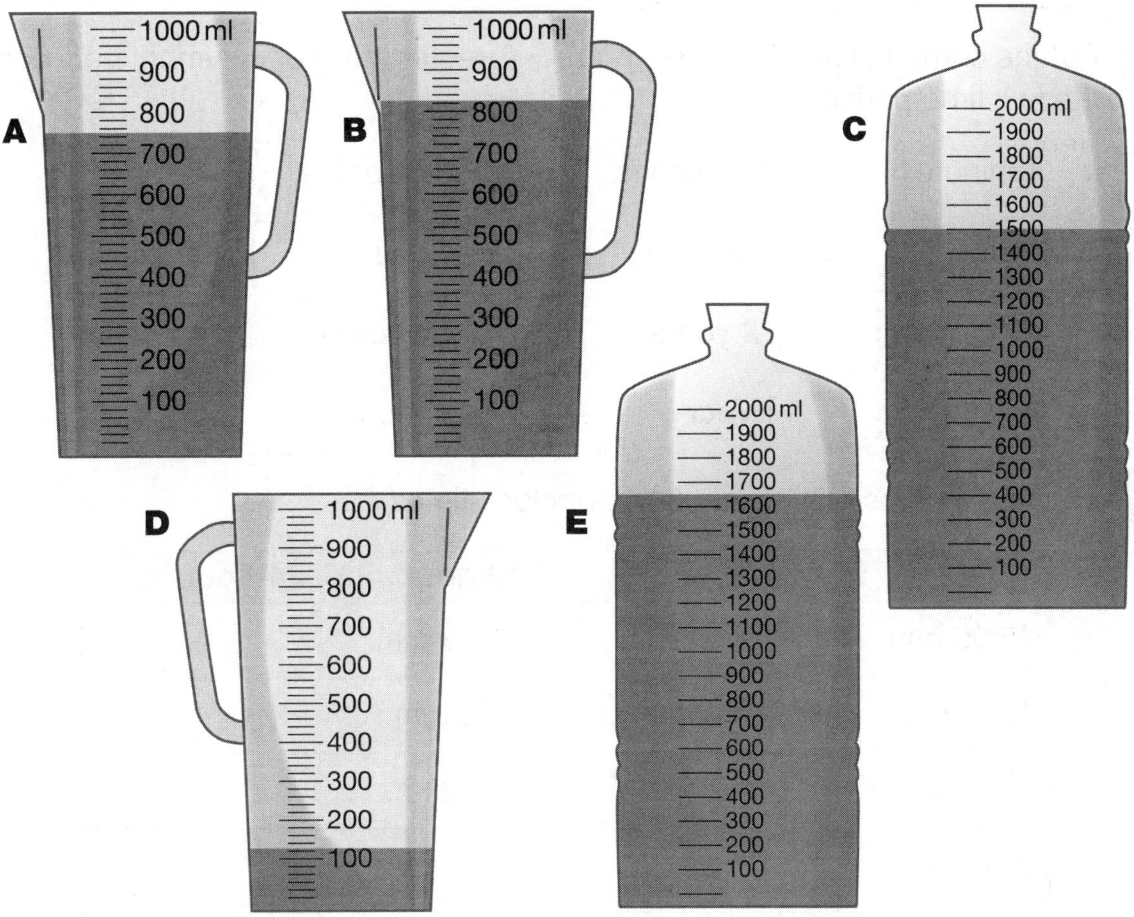

A
1000 ml
900
800
700
600
500
400
300
200
100

B
1000 ml
900
800
700
600
500
400
300
200
100

C
2000 ml
1900
1800
1700
1600
1500
1400
1300
1200
1100
1000
900
800
700
600
500
400
300
200
100

D
1000 ml
900
800
700
600
500
400
300
200
100

E
2000 ml
1900
1800
1700
1600
1500
1400
1300
1200
1100
1000
900
800
700
600
500
400
300
200
100

Learner	Clue	Container
Anwar	The capacity of my container was twice as much as Ella's.	
Samina	My container had 1525 ml less capacity than Rajesh's container.	
Harry	My container is half that of Rajesh's.	
Ella	The capacity of my container was 625 ml larger than Samina's.	
Rajesh	The capacity of my container is twice that of Harry's.	

Measure

Lesson 1: Telling the time

- Tell and compare the time between analogue and digital 24-hour clocks

Challenge 1

Put the correct symbol: < (less than), > (greater than) or = symbol between the two time periods.

a 1 minute ☐ 30 seconds

b 13 months ☐ 1 year

c 1 day ☐ 22 hours

d 1 hour ☐ 100 minutes

e 26 months ☐ 2 years

f 2 weeks ☐ 14 days

g 360 days ☐ 1 year

h 2 years ☐ 750 days

Challenge 2

1 Convert these times into 24-hour clock times.

12-hour	24-hour
12:05 a.m.	
1:37 a.m.	
4:35 a.m.	
6:10 a.m.	
9:15 a.m.	
11:22 a.m.	

12-hour	24-hour
12:19 p.m.	
2:58 p.m.	
5:04 p.m.	
8:31 p.m.	
10:23 p.m.	
11:46 p.m.	

2 Convert these 24-hour clock times into 12-hour clock times.

24-hour	12-hour
02:33	
11:54	
12:07	

24-hour	12-hour
14:41	
17:26	
23:16	

3 Convert the times on the clock faces into 24-hour clock times.

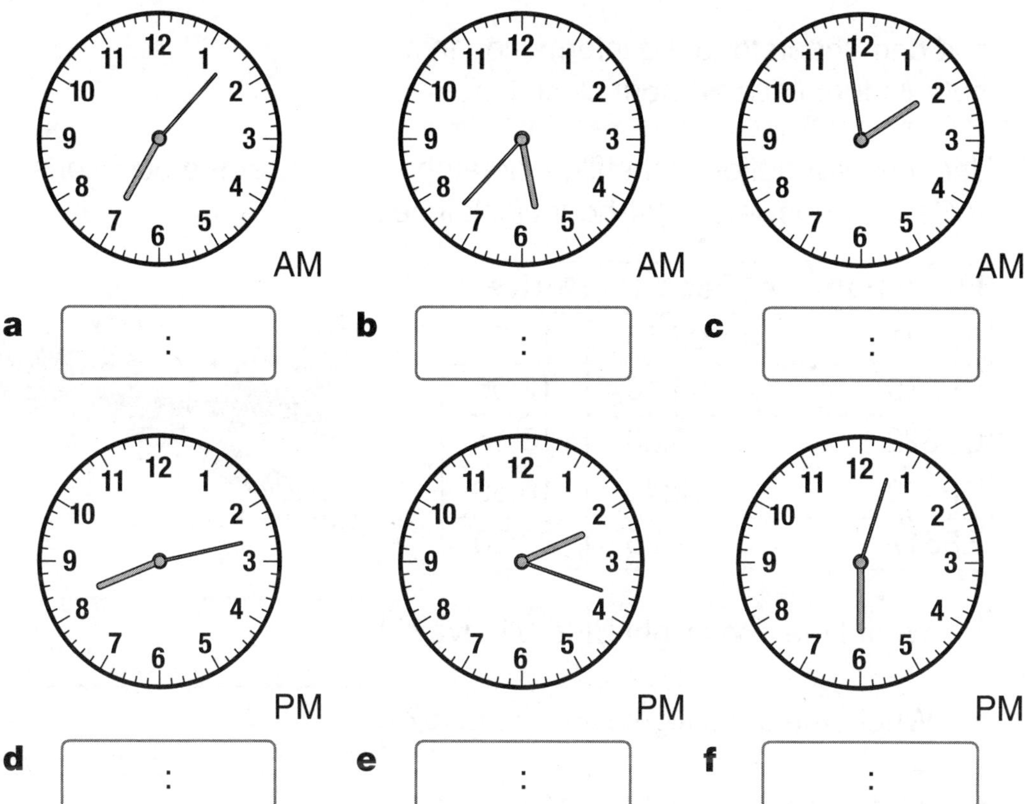

Challenge 3

Every 20 minutes a bus leaves a bus station. The first bus after 11:00 a.m. leaves at 9 minutes past 11. Write the times of all the buses between 11:00 a.m. and 2:49 p.m. in 12- and 24-hour clock times.

12-hour	24-hour
11:09 a.m.	
12:29 p.m.	

12-hour	24-hour
1:29 p.m.	
2:49 p.m.	

Lesson 2: **Reading timetables**

- Read and understand the information in a timetable that uses 24-hour clock times

Use the information in the flight timetable to answer the questions. Write your answers in 24-hour clock times.

Flight number	Depart	Arrive
AF121	05:55	10:35
BF275	08:10	12:05
CF322	10:30	13:15
DF409	12:45	16:50
EF517	19:25	23:20

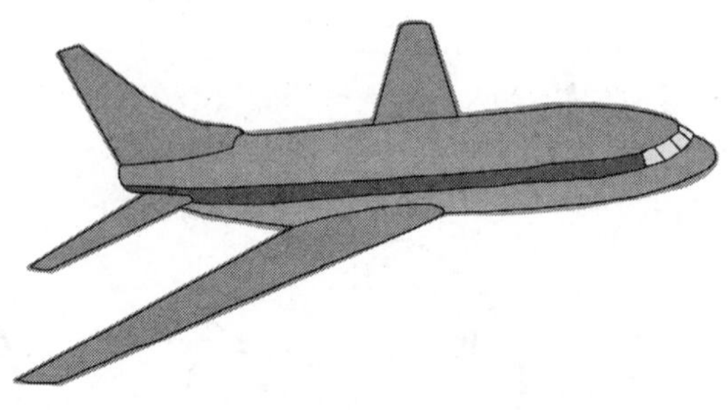

a What time does flight BF275 leave?

b What time does flight DF409 arrive?

c What time does flight AF121 leave?

d What time does flight CF322 arrive?

1 Complete the school timetable by converting 24-hour clock time to 12-hour clock time using a.m. and p.m.

Lesson	Monday (24-hour clock)	Monday (12-hour clock)
Mathematics	09:35	
English	12:05	
Science	13:10	
Geography	14:15	
Art	15:00	

2 Three buses leave the city bus station and travel to these places. The journey time between each place is 15 minutes. Use this information to complete the table.

Station	Arrival time		
	Bus 1	Bus 2	Bus 3
Central Station	07:15		
Market Square	07:30		15:10
Church Lane		11:15	
The Bank	08:00		15:40
High Street		11:45	

Challenge **3** The table shows some of the bus times between two places in a city, City Square to The Cathedral. Assume the arrival and departure times are the same.

Bus station	Arrival time				
City Square	19:32	19:59	20:28	21:01	21:37
The Cathedral	20:11	20:37	21:08	21:43	22:16

a What is the latest bus someone could catch from City Square that would get them to The Cathedral by 9:45 p.m.?

b How long does the 19:59 bus take to travel from City Square to The Cathedral?

c Which bus takes exactly 40 minutes to travel from City Square to The Cathedral?

d Which bus from City Square has the longest journey time?

Measure

Lesson 3: **Time intervals**

- Convert between analogue and digital 24-hour clocks to calculate intervals of time
- Use mental strategies to calculate time intervals

Calculate the amount of time each learner has spent completing their homework.

All the clocks show times in the evening.

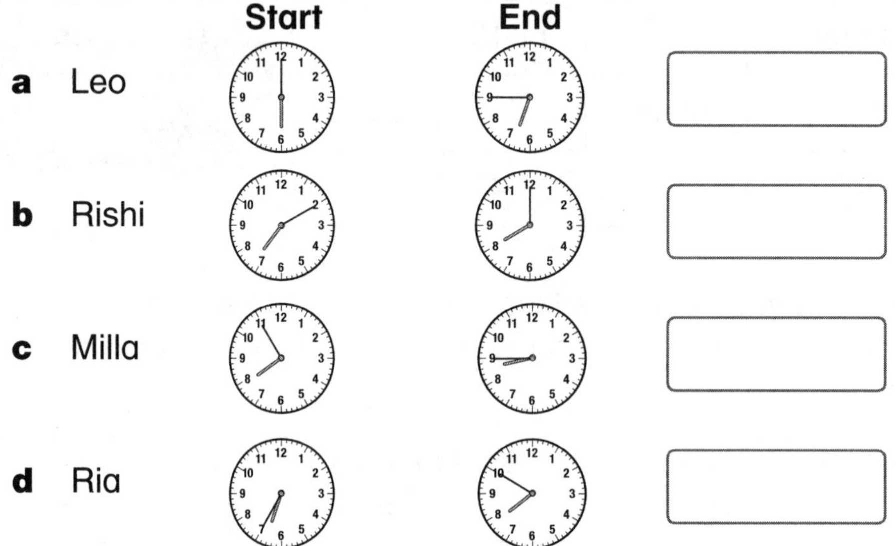

Start **End**

a Leo

b Rishi

c Milla

d Ria

1 Calculate the amount of time each learner has spent completing their homework.

All the clocks show times in the evening.

Start **End**

a Daniel

b Manjeet

c Leo

d Freya

2 Calculate the amount of time each person has spent at work.

Name	Start time	Finish time	Time spent at work (hours, mins)	Time (mins)
Mr Levi	08:15	17:25		
Mrs Taylor	07:35	18:20		
Mr Shah	07:44	18:12		
Mrs Chang	08:23	17:56		

Who spent the longest time at work?

3 Solve these time problems.

a Mrs Davis finished cleaning her house at 17:43. If she began cleaning at 14:02, how long did it take her to clean the whole house?

b Mr Ahmed finished gardening at 19:12. If he began working in his garden at 11:33, how long did the work take him?

c Pavel arrived home after work at 18:57. If he left the house at 07:19 in the morning, how long was he out of the house?

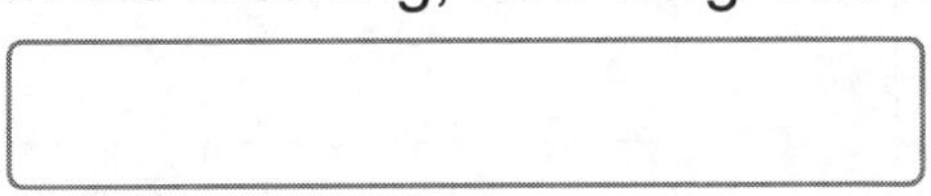

Challenge 3 The table shows the time it took people to walk a long distance route. Complete the start times, using the 24-hour clock.

Name	Start time	Finish time	Time taken
Clara		12:25	3 hours 13 minutes
Freddy		13:17	4 hours 26 minutes
Jay		13:49	5 hours 57 minutes
Antonio		12:09	4 hours 33 minutes

Lesson 4: **Calendars**

- Use a calendar to calculate time intervals

Challenge 1

Calculate the time interval in days between the dates indicated (do not include the first date).

JUNE						
Sunday	Monday	Tuesday	Wednesday	Thursday	Friday	Saturday
			1	2	3	4
5	6	7	8	9	10	11
12	13	14	15	16	17	18
19	20	21	22	23	24	25
26	27	28	29	30		

AUGUST						
Sunday	Monday	Tuesday	Wednesday	Thursday	Friday	Saturday
	1	2	3	4	5	6
7	8	9	10	11	12	13
14	15	16	17	18	19	20
21	22	23	24	25	26	27
28	29	30	31			

a ☐ days **b** ☐ days

Challenge 2

1 Use the calendar pages to calculate time intervals in the units given. (Do not include the first date.)

MAY						
Sunday	Monday	Tuesday	Wednesday	Thursday	Friday	Saturday
1	2	3	4	5	6	7
8	9	10	11	12	13	14
15	16	17	18	19	20	21
22	23	24	25	26	27	28
29	30	31				

JUNE						
Sunday	Monday	Tuesday	Wednesday	Thursday	Friday	Saturday
			1	2	3	4
5	6	7	8	9	10	11
12	13	14	15	16	17	18
19	20	21	22	23	24	25
26	27	28	29	30		

JULY						
Sunday	Monday	Tuesday	Wednesday	Thursday	Friday	Saturday
					1	2
3	4	5	6	7	8	9
10	11	12	13	14	15	16
17	18	19	20	21	22	23
24	25	26	27	28	29	30

From	To	Days	Weeks, days
May 4th	June 17th		
May 22nd	June 30th		
June 4th	July 18th		
May 24th	July 25th		

2 Use the calendar pages to solve the time problems.

a A sports competition began on September 7th and ended on October 5th. Over how many days was the competition held?

b A building project began on September 3rd and was completed on October 27th. How many weeks and days did the project take?

SEPTEMBER						
Sunday	Monday	Tuesday	Wednesday	Thursday	Friday	Saturday
				1	2	3
4	5	6	7	8	9	10
11	12	13	14	15	16	17
18	19	20	21	22	23	24
25	26	27	28	29	30	

OCTOBER						
Sunday	Monday	Tuesday	Wednesday	Thursday	Friday	Saturday
						1
2	3	4	5	6	7	8
9	10	11	12	13	14	15
16	17	18	19	20	21	22
23	24	25	26	27	28	29
30	31					

Challenge **3** A children's playground needs to be built in a period no longer than 18 weeks. Using this year's calendar, work out which of the construction proposals in the table will complete the playground on time.

Proposal	Start date	Finish date	Time taken	Will the project complete on time (yes/no)?
A	Feb 12th	June 14th		
B	April 19th	Aug 27th		
C	July 6th	Nov 13th		
D	Aug 16th	Dec 18th		

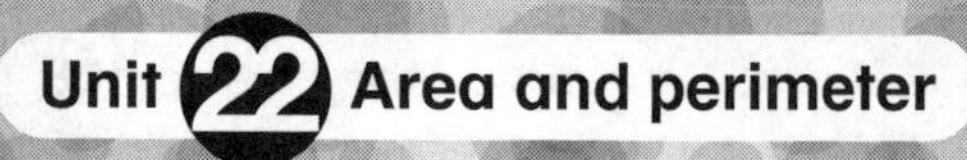

Measure

Lesson 1: **Perimeter of regular polygons**

- Measure and calculate the perimeter of regular polygons

Challenge 1

Find the perimeter of the square patches of grass and large fields.

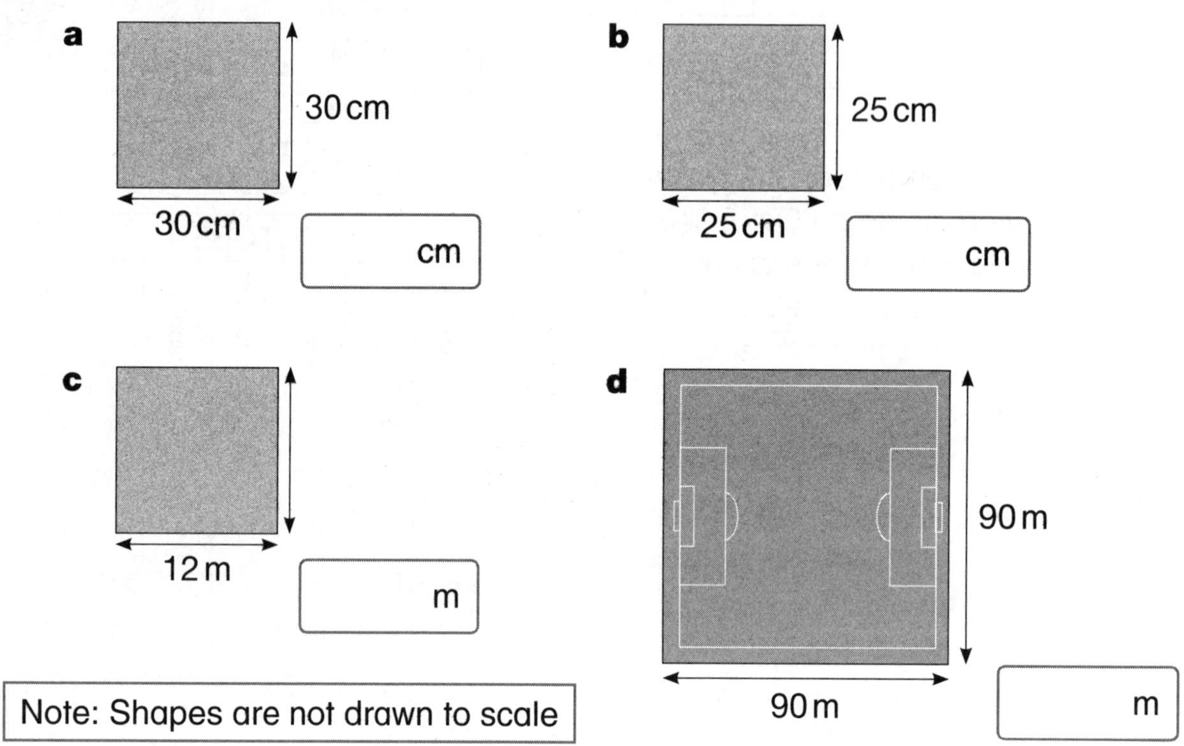

Note: Shapes are not drawn to scale

Challenge 2

Find the perimeter of each regular polygon.

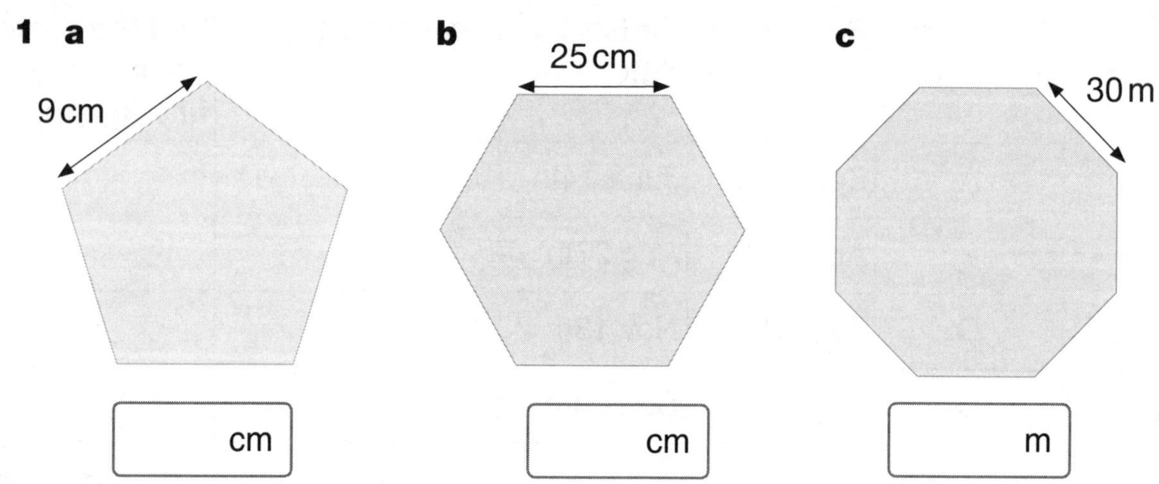

2 Your teacher will give you some large 2D shapes. Measure the perimeter of the shapes and record them here.

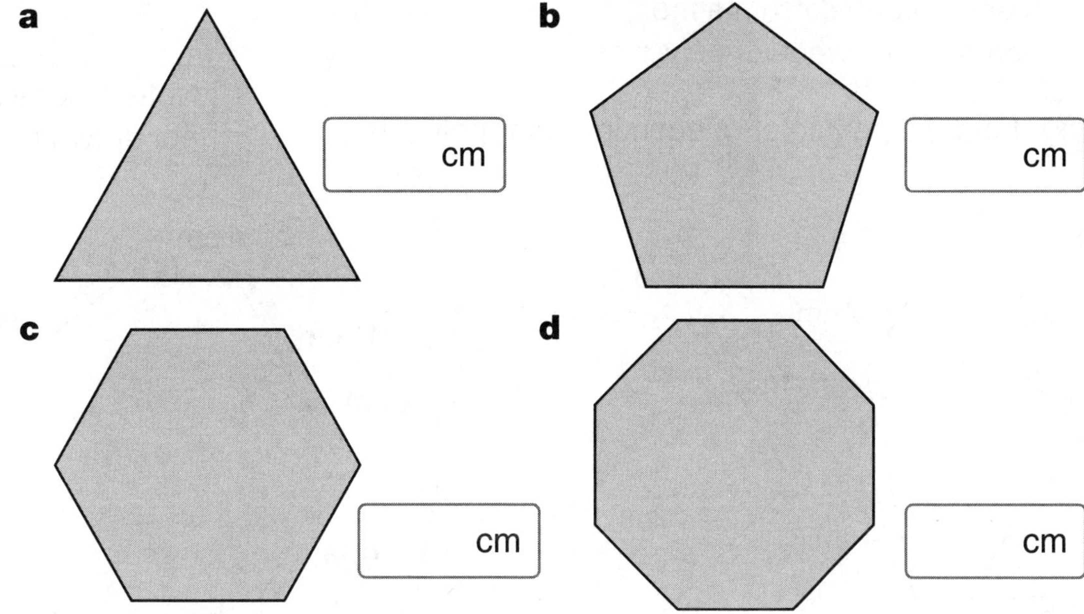

Challenge 3 Calculate the perimeter of each compound shape. Each shape is made from regular polygons.

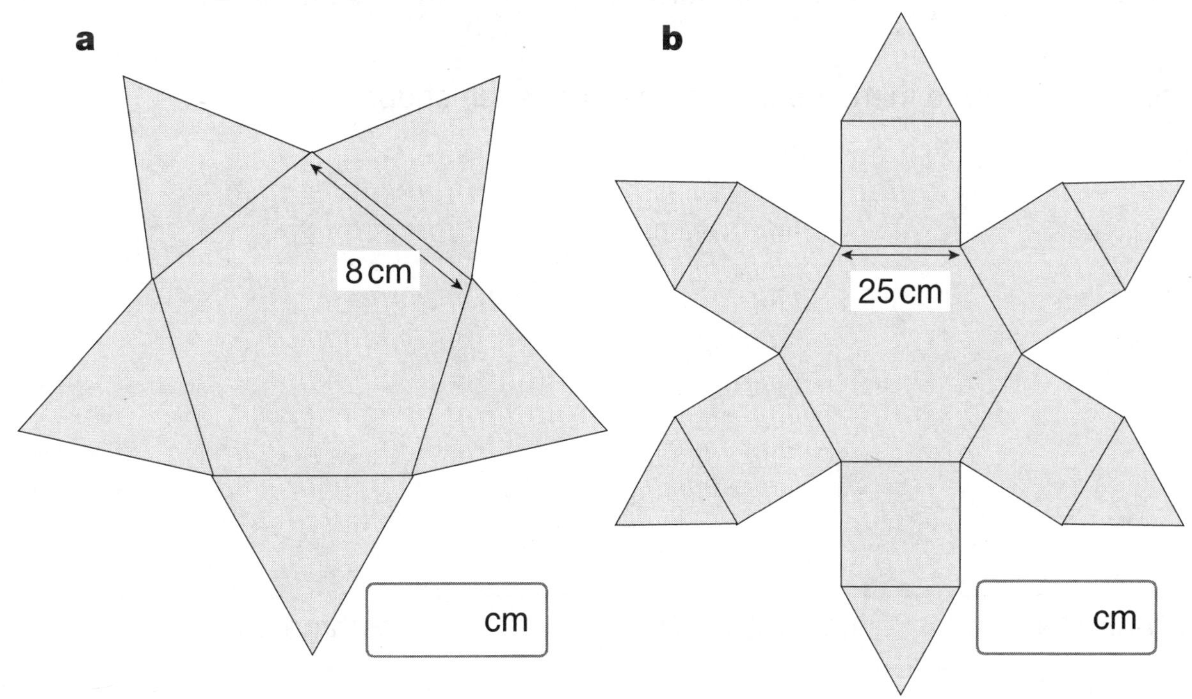

Measure

Lesson 2: **Perimeter of irregular polygons**

- Measure and calculate the perimeter of irregular polygons

Note: Shapes are not drawn to scale

Find the perimeter of each irregular polygon.

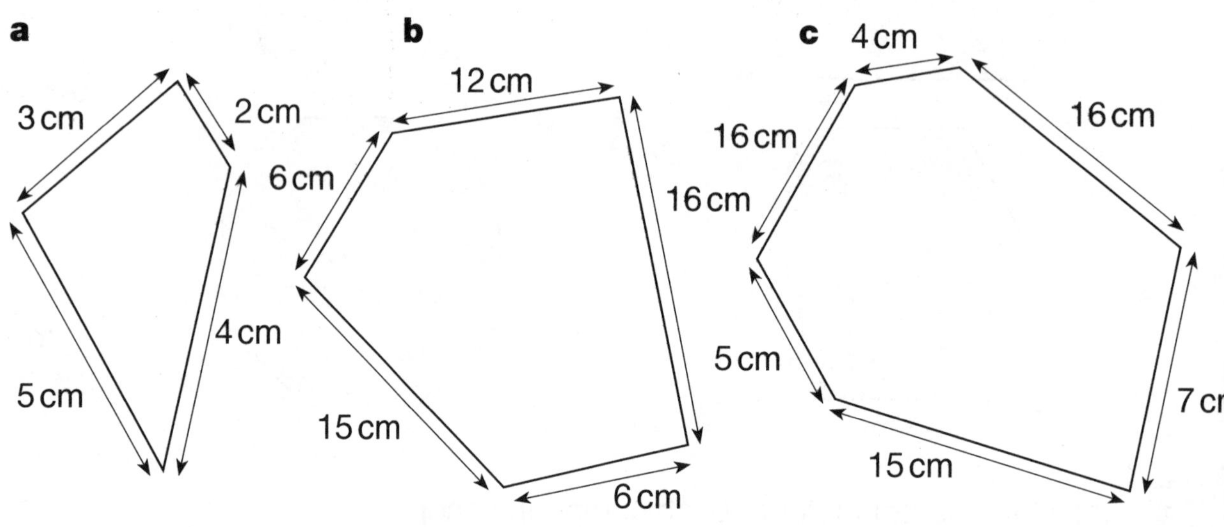

a Perimeter = ☐ cm **b** Perimeter = ☐ cm **c** Perimeter = ☐ cm

Challenge 2 Use a ruler to measure the perimeter of each shape.

a

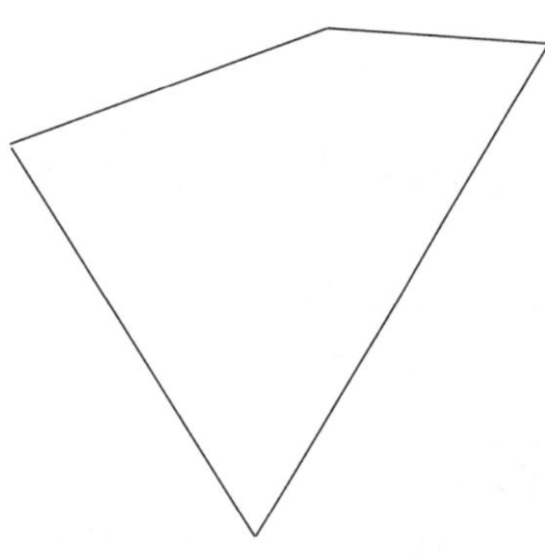

b

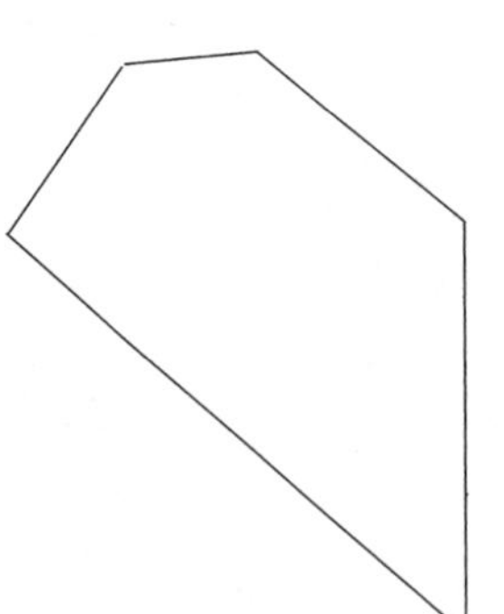

c

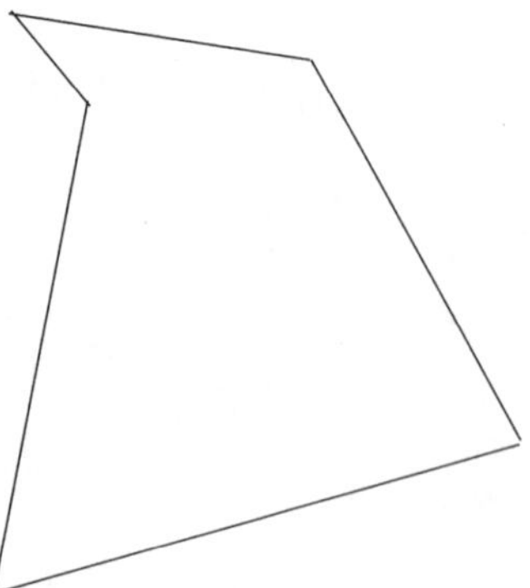

a Perimeter = ☐ cm **b** Perimeter = ☐ cm **c** Perimeter = ☐ cm

d

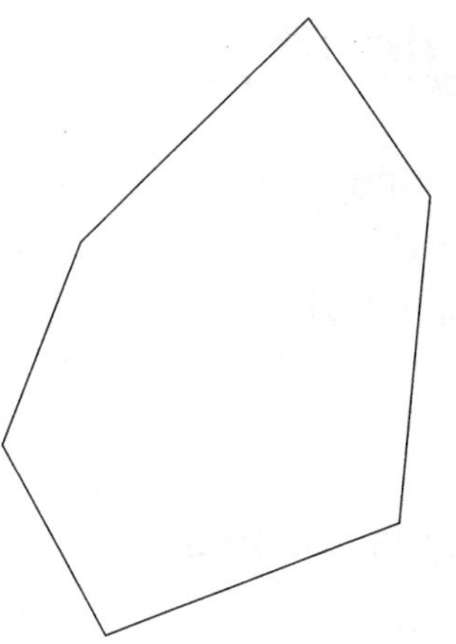

Perimeter = [ ] cm

e

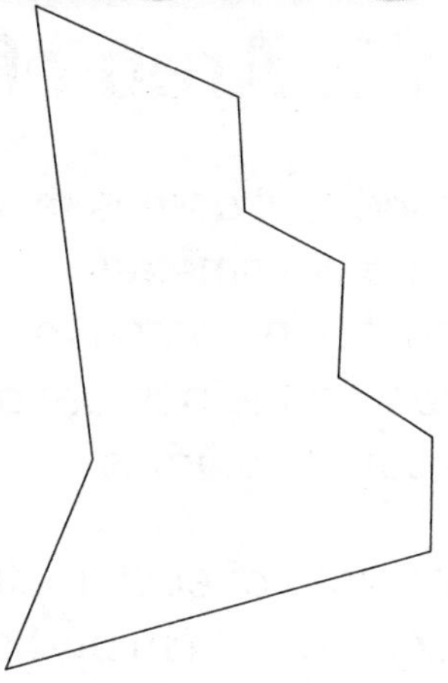

Perimeter = [ ] cm

f

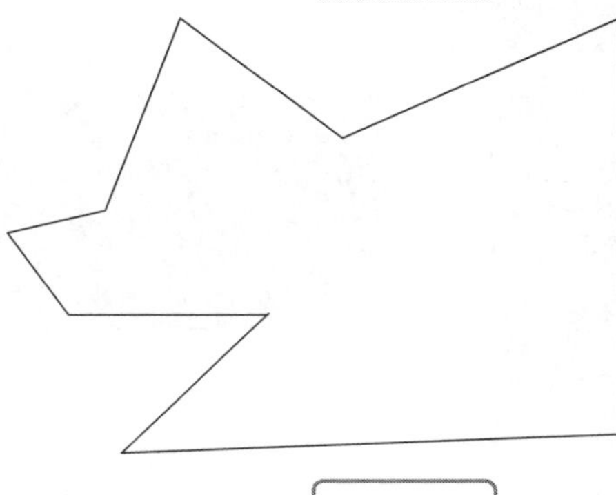

Perimeter = [ ] cm

Challenge 3 You have been given the perimeter. Calculate the missing length for each shape.

a **b** **c**

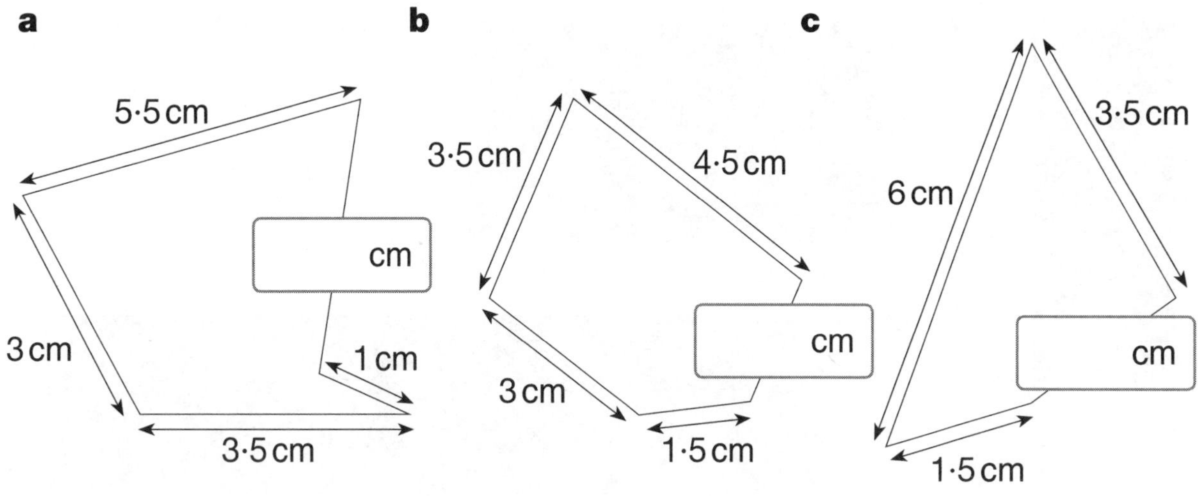

Perimeter = 16·5 cm

Perimeter = 14 cm

Perimeter = 13·5 cm

Measure

Lesson 3: **Area of a rectangle (1)**

- Understand that area is measured in square units, e.g. square centimetres
- Know that the area of a rectangle can be calculated by multiplying the number of squares in a row by the number of columns

Challenge 1 Find the area of each rectangle by counting the squares. Each square is 1 cm by 1 cm.

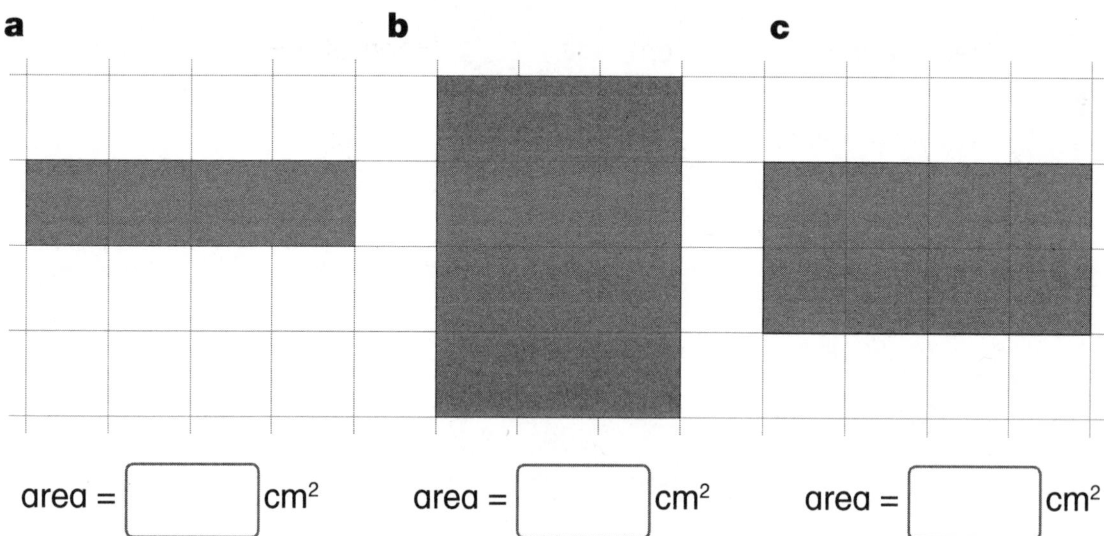

area = ☐ cm^2　　area = ☐ cm^2　　area = ☐ cm^2

Challenge 2 **1** Calculate the area of each rectangle. Each grid square is 1 cm by 1 cm.

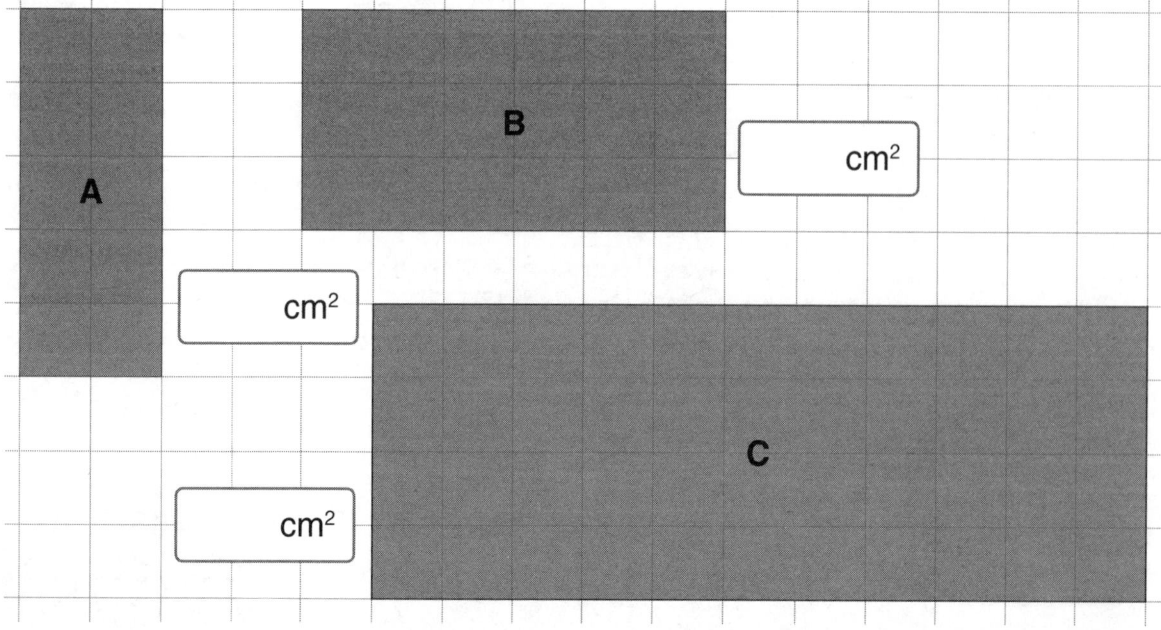

2 Calculate the area of each shape below and write the answer in square centimetres. Write the shapes in order of area, smallest to largest.

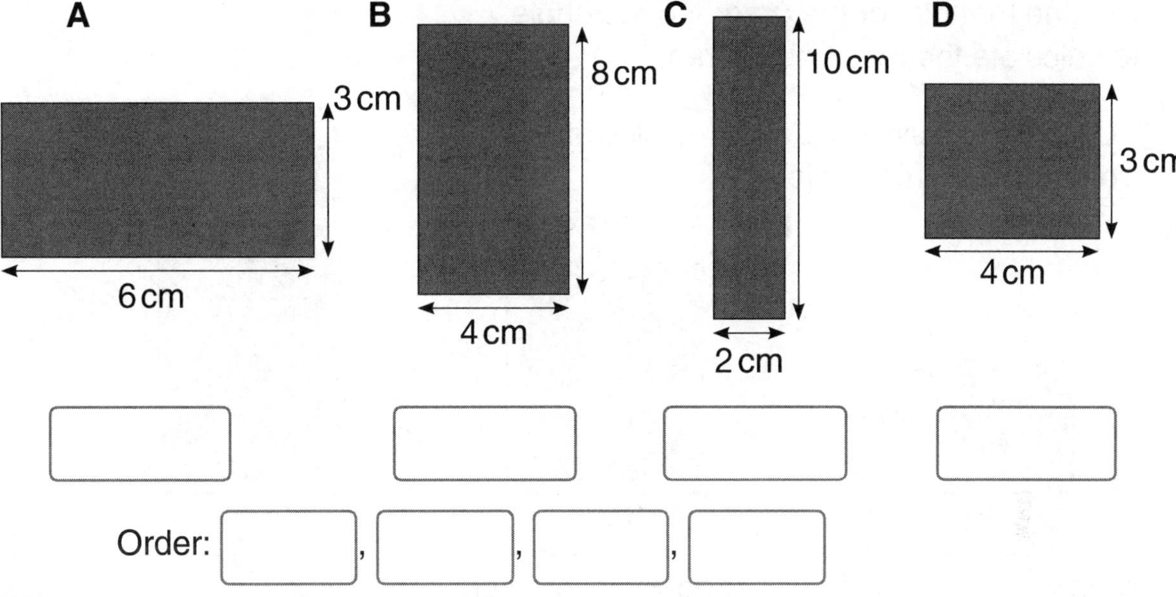

Order: ______, ______, ______, ______

Challenge **3** Calculate the area of each wall. Given the amount of paint available, circle the walls that can be painted.

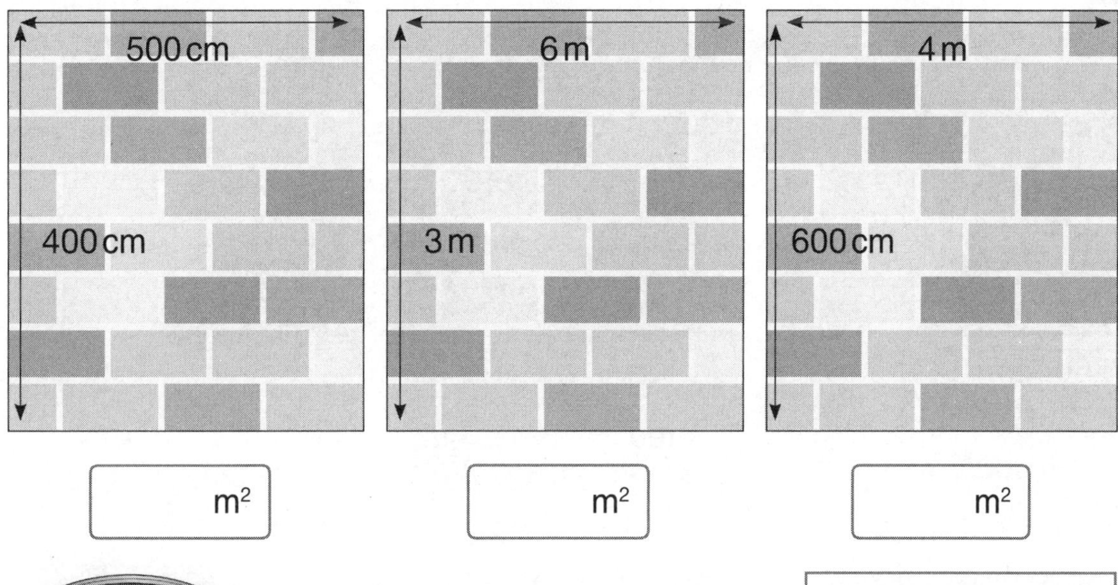

______ m^2 ______ m^2 ______ m^2

Note: Shapes are not drawn to scale

To cover maximum area of 20 m^2

Lesson 4: **Area of a rectangle (2)**

- Use the formula for the area of a rectangle to calculate the rectangle's area

Challenge 1

Use the formula A = L × W to calculate the area of each rectangle.

a

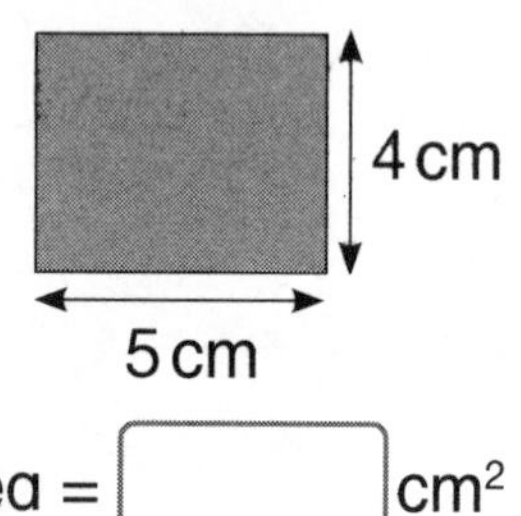

area = ☐ cm²

b

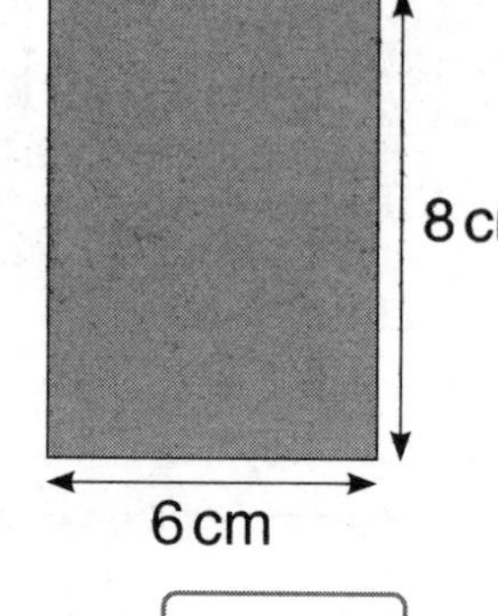

area = ☐ cm²

c

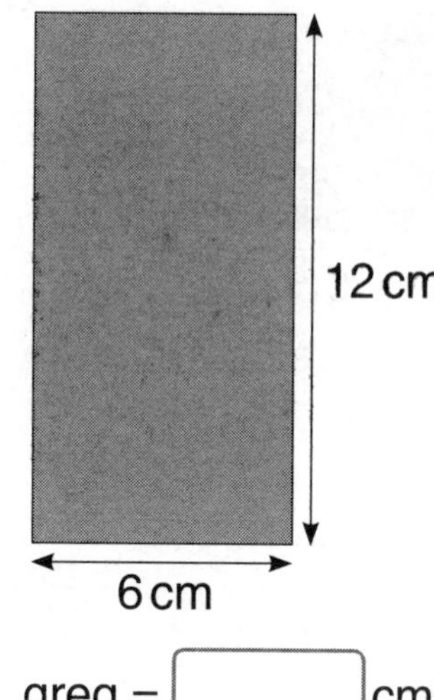

area = ☐ cm²

Challenge 2

1 Calculate the area of each brick wall in square metres using the formula.

a

7 m

600 cm

area = ☐ m²

b

area = ☐ m²

c

800 cm

area = ☐ m²

Note: Shapes are not drawn to scale

2 Find the area of each object, giving your answer in the unit given.

a

50 cm
40 cm

☐ cm²

b

20 cm
30 cm

☐ cm²

c

3 m
20 cm

☐ cm²

d

55 m
100 m

☐ m²

e

20·5 m
3 m

☐ m²

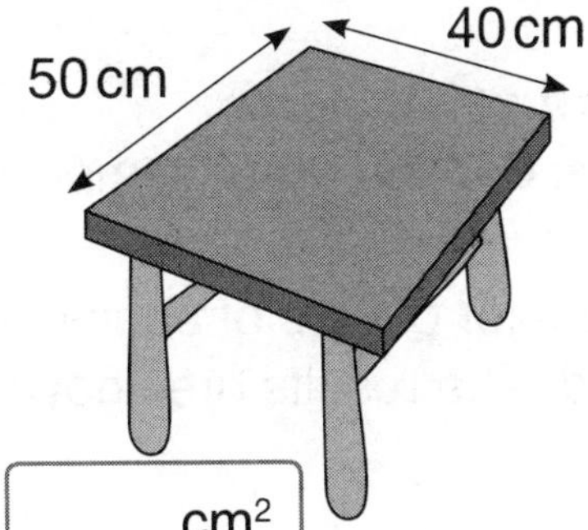

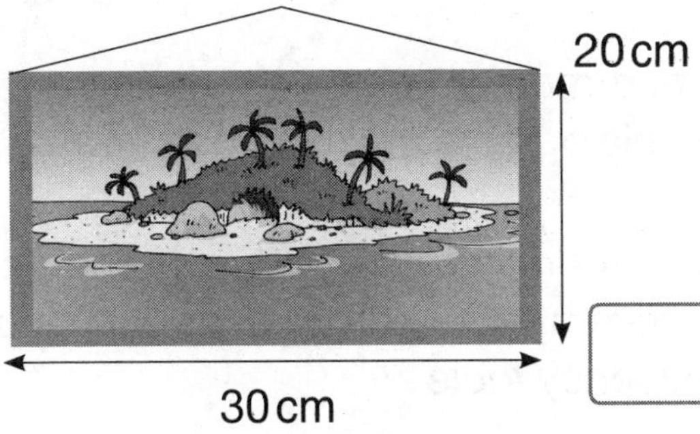

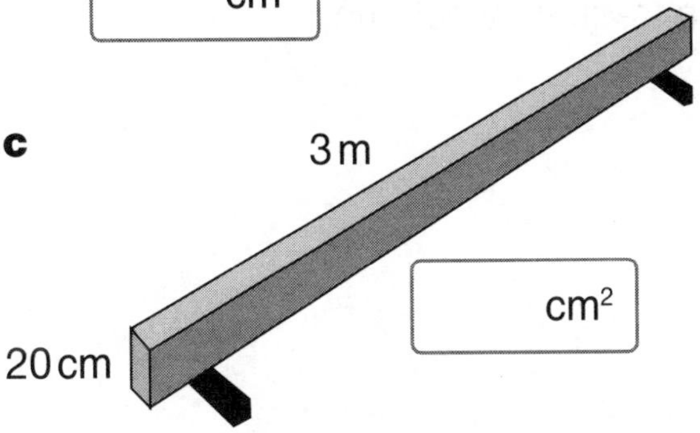

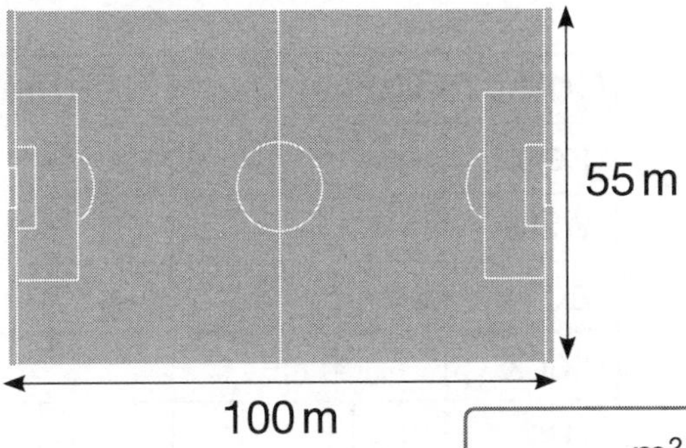

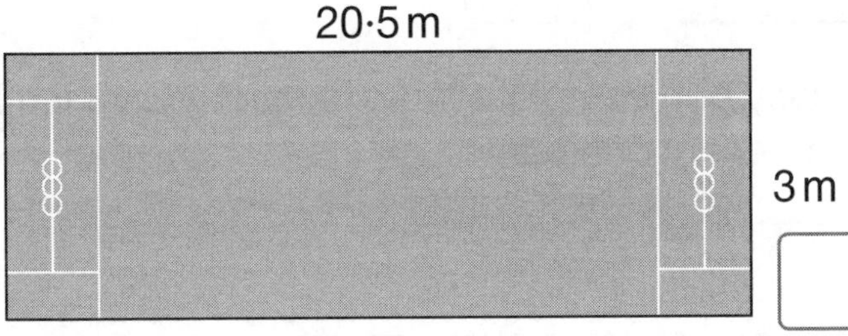

Challenge 3 Write down the missing length for each rectangle in the unit given.

a

8 m
A = 72 m²

☐ m

b

12 m
A = 156 m²

☐ m

c

25 m
A = 775 m²

☐ m

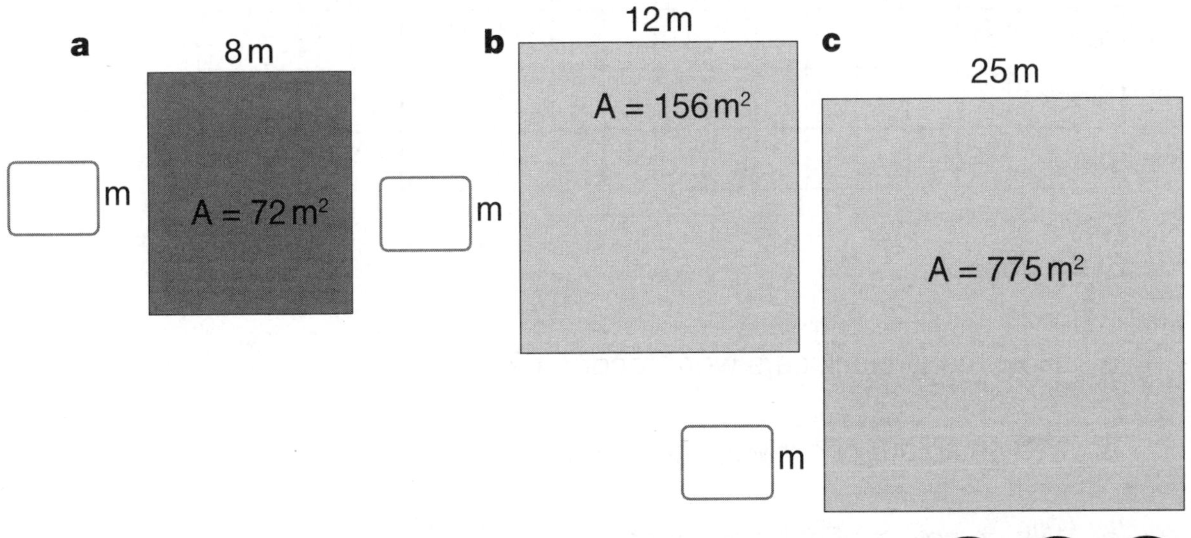

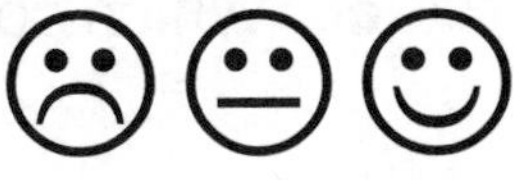

Lesson 1: **Interpreting graphs and tables**

- Draw and read data from frequency tables, pictograms and bar line charts

You will need

- Bar line graph template

The learners in Class 5A have recorded the number of cars of each colour that drive by their school over a 5 minute period. The results are shown in a frequency table.

Count the tally marks and complete the frequency column.

Colour	Tally	Frequency
green	𝍸 𝍸 𝍸 |	
white	𝍸 𝍸 ||||	
red	𝍸 𝍸	
black	𝍸 𝍸 ||	
blue	𝍸 |||	

Using the table, copy and complete the pictogram. Give it a heading and draw a circle to represent one car.

green																
white																
red																
black																
blue																

Key
○ = 1 car

a How many black cars were recorded?

b Which colour of car was most common?

c Which colour of car was least common?

Challenge 2

1 Year 5 voted for their favourite non-fiction book subject. The tally chart shows the results. Complete the frequency column. Then complete the bar line chart using the data in the table.

Subject	Votes	Frequency
history	卌 |	
space	卌 卌 ||	
sport	||||	
art	卌 卌 ||||	
nature	卌 卌 卌 |	

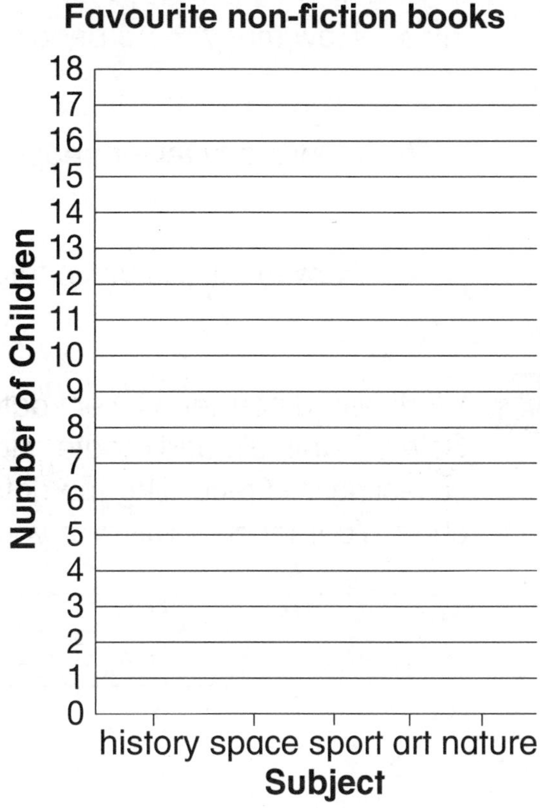

a Which subject was the most popular?

b Which subject was the least popular?

c How many more learners voted for nature than history?

d How many learners voted in the survey?

2 The owner of an ice cream shop made a pictogram of the different ice cream flavours that sold over a short period. Use the data in the pictogram to complete a bar line chart. Your teacher will give you a template for this. Remember to number and label the axes.

Number of ice creams sold	
vanilla	
mint	
chocolate	
bubblegum	

= 4 ice creams = 2 ice creams

a How many more people liked bubblegum flavour than mint? [ ]

b How many fewer people liked vanilla than chocolate? [ ]

c How many people in total bought ice creams? [ ]

Challenge 3

Work with a partner. Collect data for a survey, 'Favourite animals'. Select 5 animals and create a tally chart and frequency table for collecting and recording the data. Represent the data in a bar line chart. Your teacher will give you a bar line chart template.

Use the graph to make four statements about what the data shows.

____

____

____

____

Lesson 2: **Changing the scale**

- Read and interpret data for tables and graphs where the vertical axis is labelled in intervals greater than 1

The pictogram represents the data collected from a survey that asked the question, 'How many hours of television do you watch each week?' Use the data to construct a bar line graph.

Hours of TV watched per week

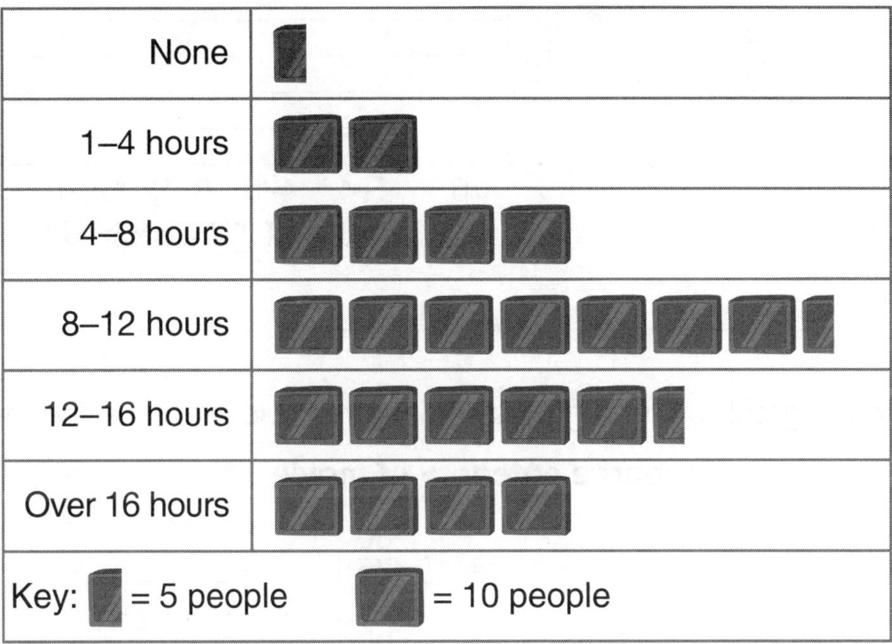

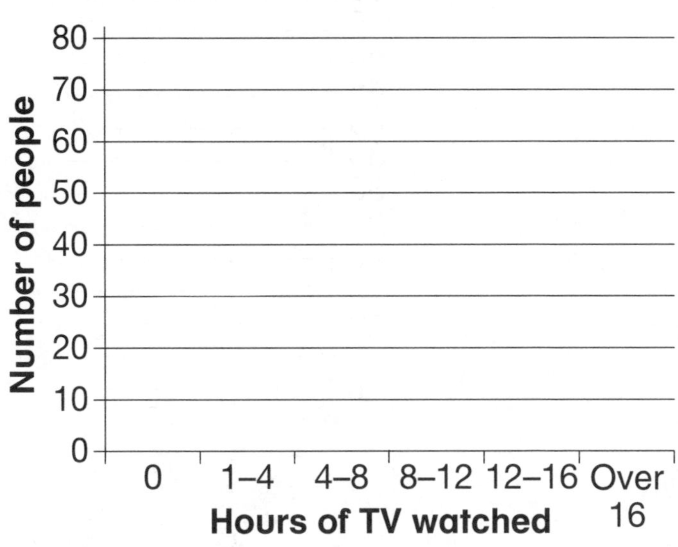

Challenge 2

Handling data

1 Complete the graph here using data from the graph in Challenge 1. What effect does the change in scale have on the graph?

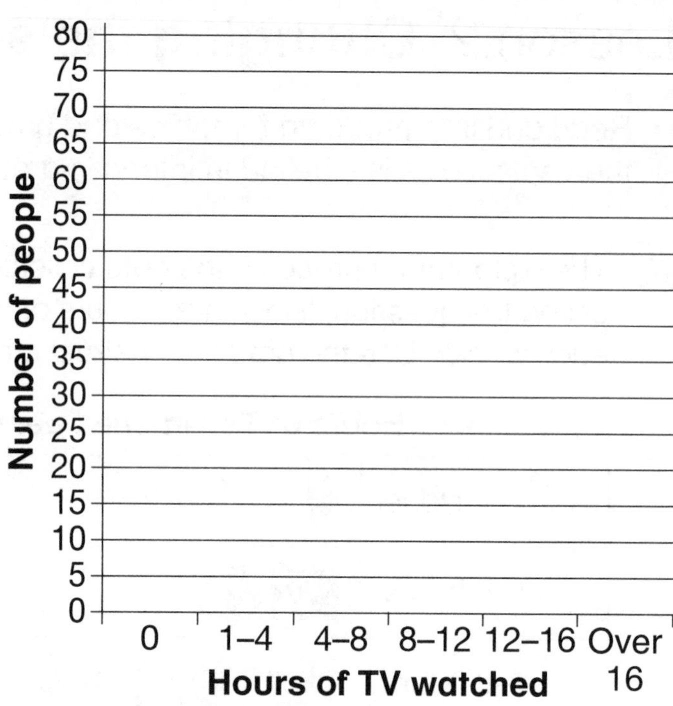

---

2 Complete the graph on the right using data from the graph on the left.

Favourite category of movie

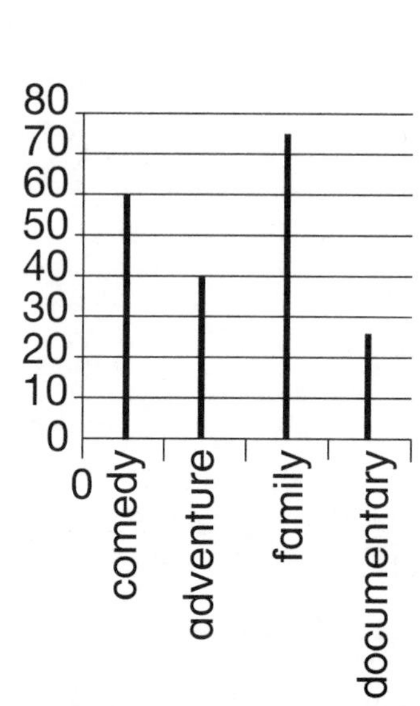

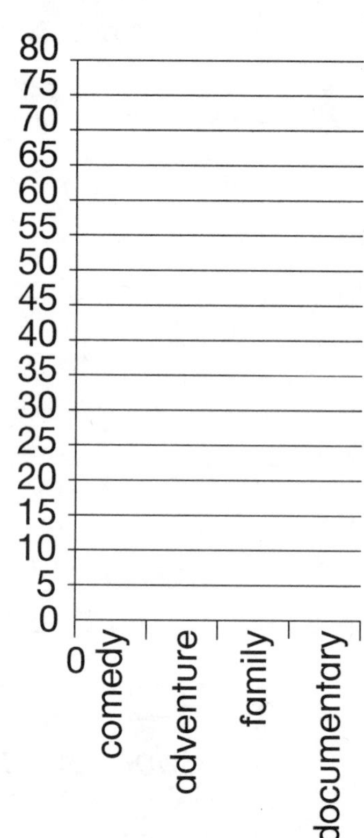

What effect does the change in scale have on the graph?

___

___

The pictogram shows the different ways learners travel to school every day. Complete both graphs using the data in the pictogram.

How learners travel to school

Walk	
Bike	
Car	
Bus	

KEY

= 10 pupils = 20 pupils

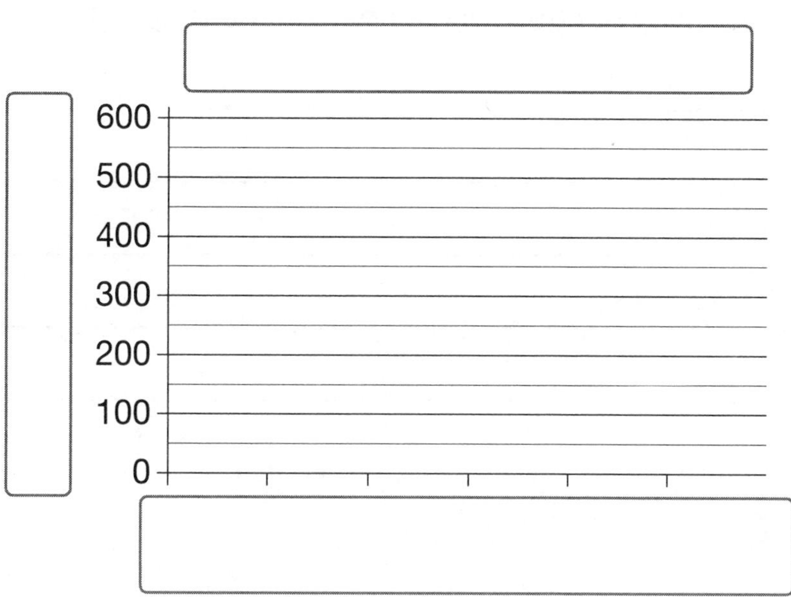

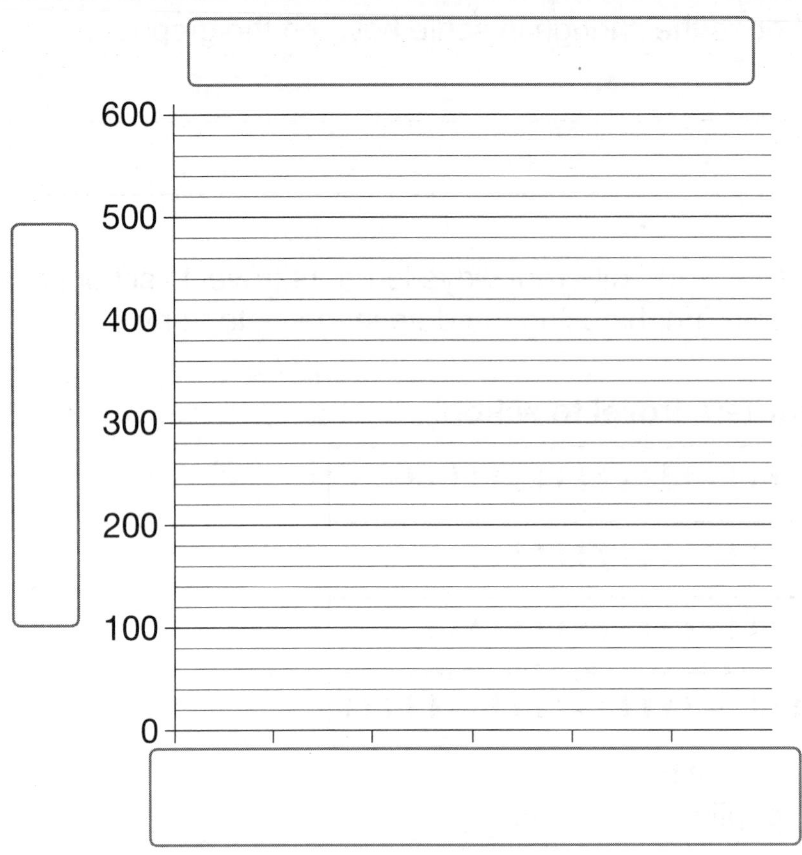

a What effect does the change in scale have on the graph?

____

____

____

____

____

____

Lesson 3: **Line graphs**

- Construct and interpret a simple line graph

You will need
- squared paper

The table shows the scores (out of 20) achieved by Katie in her weekly spelling test. Complete the time graph. Mark each point on the graph using a cross. Join the crosses using straight lines to make your line graph. Then answer the questions.

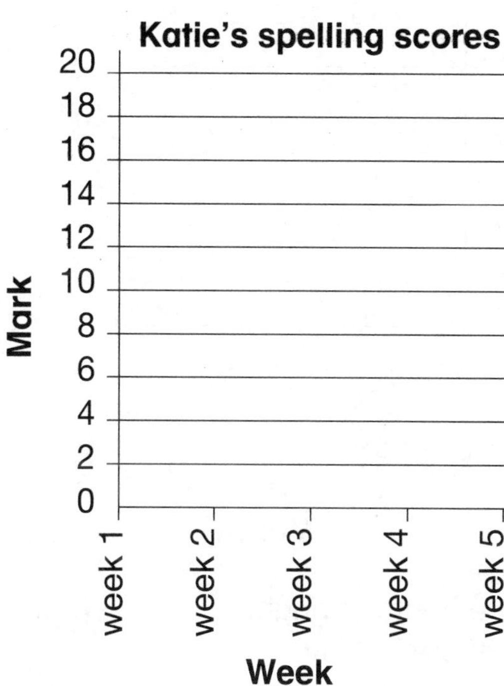

a In which weeks were Katie's scores the same?

b In which week did Katie achieve her highest score?

Week	Score
1	10
2	12
3	10
4	15
5	18

Challenge 2

1 The table shows the average number of hours of bright sunshine per day over a period of five months. Complete the time graph. Mark each point on the graph using a cross. Join the crosses using straight lines to make your line graph. Then answer the questions.

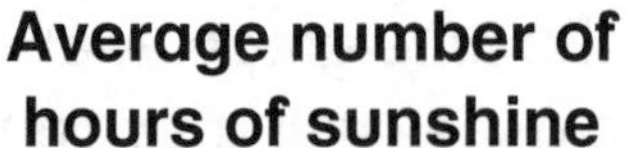

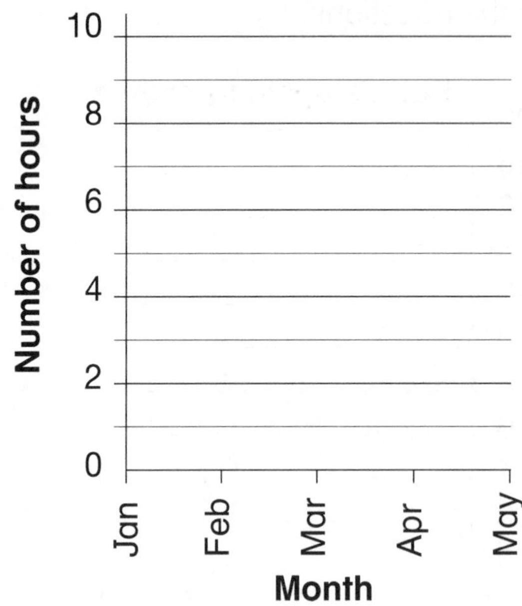

Month	Hours
January	1
February	2
March	4
April	5
May	8

a How many more hours of bright sunshine were there in May, compared to February?

b How did the number of hours of sunshine change over time?

c Why do you think this happened?

2 Plot the data from Challenge 1 as a line graph with a different scale.

How does changing the scale change the look of the graph?

___

___

___

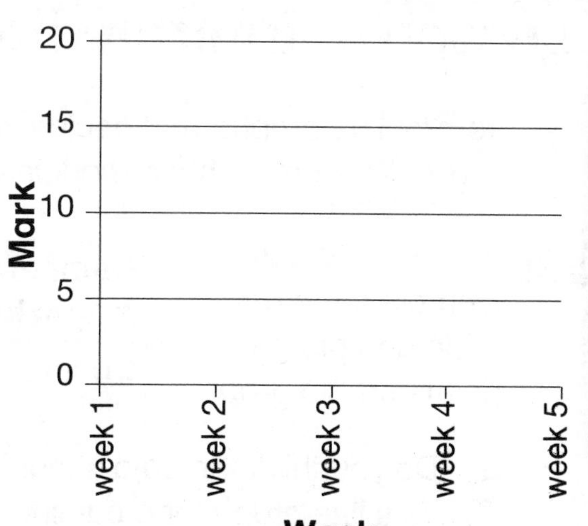

The table shows the height of a bean plant over time. Draw a line graph and plot the data. Your teacher will give you some squared paper.

Plant growth over time

Time (days)	Plant height (cm)
0	1·43
7	2·16
14	2·67
21	3·25
28	4·04
35	4·67

a Describe how the height of the plant changed over the 35 day period.

b Between which period of days did the plant show the greatest growth?

c Between which period of days did the plant show the slowest growth?

Lesson 4: Intermediate points

- Interpret line graphs and decide whether intermediate points have meaning

You will need
- ruler

Challenge 1

A magazine costs $5. Complete the data table and plot the points on the graph.

Number of magazines	1	2	3	4	5	6	7	8
Cost ($)	5	10						

a Do you think the data should be plotted as a line graph, or a bar line chart?

______

b Explain why. ______

______

______

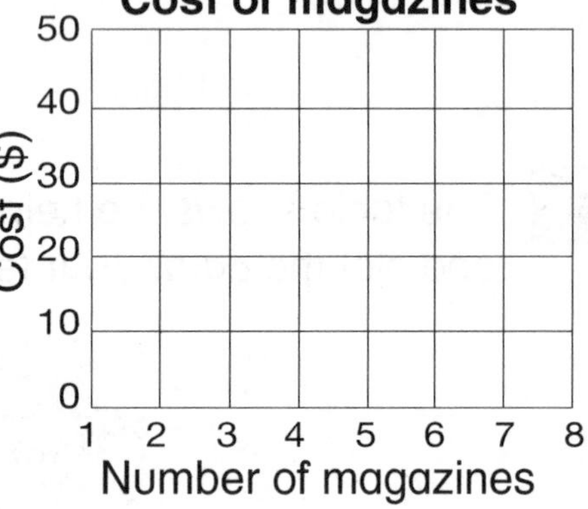

Challenge 2

1 The table shows Lisa's height to the nearest centimetre from age 6 to age 13. Plot the data on the graph.

Age	6	7	8	9	10	11	12	13
Height (cm)	116	122	128	134	140	147	152	156

a Do you think the data should be plotted as a line graph, or a bar line chart? ______

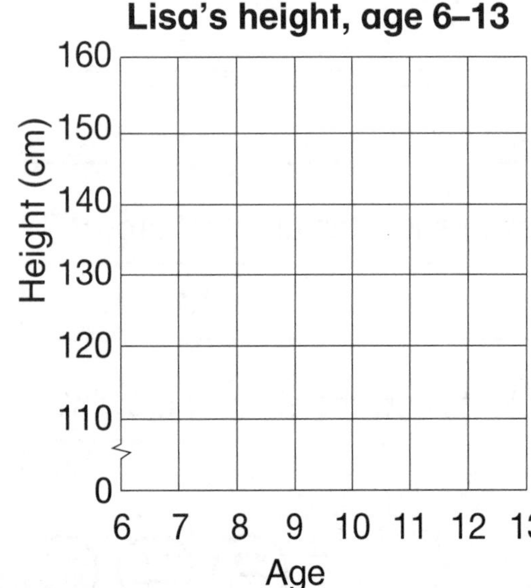

b Do the intermediate points between the plotted points have any meaning? (Yes/No)

______

c Explain why. ______

______

d What would you expect Lisa's height to be at age 7 years, 6 months?

______

e At age 11 years, 6 months?

______

The graph shows the speed of a car over a period of 60 seconds.

a Do the intermediate points between the plotted points have any meaning? (Yes/No) ______________________

b Explain why. ______________________

____

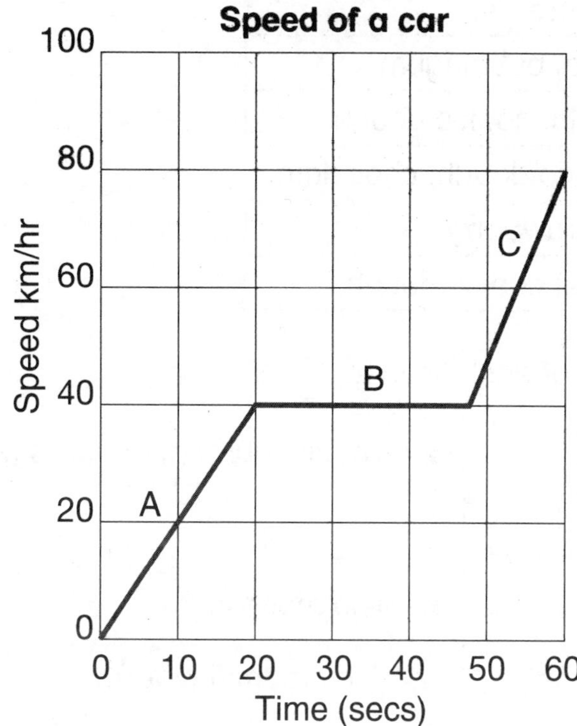

c Complete the table to show the expected speed of the car at the times given.

Time (s)	10	30	40	55	60
Speed					

d Describe what is happening to the car during the following sections of the graph:

Section A ______________________

Section B ______________________

Section C ______________________

Lesson 5: Mode

- Find and interpret the mode of a set of data

Challenge 1

Tom did a survey of his friends' favourite ice cream flavours. He put the results in a table.

Friend	Favourite flavours
Amir	chocolate, vanilla, bubblegum
Florence	strawberry, vanilla, cookie dough
Jack	bubblegum, cookie dough, chocolate
Ashia	cookie dough, strawberry
Ethan	vanilla, chocolate, cookie dough

Count how many there are of each flavour.

chocolate	
vanilla	
bubblegum	
cookie dough	
strawberry	

a The flavour that appears most is ______.

b The mode is ______ (ice cream flavour).

Challenge 2

1 Find the mode of each data set.

a 3, 13, 16, 3, 12, 8, 22, 16, 8, 6, 3 Mode: ______

b 17, 7, 3, 12, 3, 5, 5, 12, 10, 24, 12 Mode: ______

c apple, banana, apple, pear, peach, banana, peach, apple Mode: ______

d red, blue, green, pink, pink, green, red, blue, pink, green, pink, red, pink Mode: ______

e B, X, P, R, C, C, R, P, R, B, X, R, C, X, R Mode: ______

f 13 cm, 5 cm, 9 cm, 3 cm, 11 cm, 13 cm, 9 cm, 3 cm, 9 cm, 9 cm, 5 cm, 13 cm Mode: ______

Handling data

2 Here is a music score, which shows the notes and chords that are played in a piece of music. The chords are the letters and numbers above the lines of music, e.g. C and D7. Construct a frequency table to find the mode chord in this piece of music.

C C C G D7 G G

Chord	Frequency

Mode:

Challenge **3** Look at the table. Write the mode of the high and low temperatures recorded over a period of 12 months.

a What are the modes of these sets of temperatures?

High | Low

b How would the mode change if the first four low temperatures from January to April were: 23, 28, 29 and 28?

____

Month	High	Low
January	50	27
February	54	29
March	61	34
April	71	42
May	79	50
June	86	58
July	61	59
August	87	60
September	83	50
October	73	43
November	61	33
December	52	28

Lesson 6: **Collecting data**

- To test a hypothesis by collecting and organising data from an enquiry

You will need
- dice, or 0–6 spinner
- wooden plank
- toy car
- books

Challenge 1

Work with a partner to test a hypothesis:

Most learners in our class are in bed by 8pm.

a Collect data from the learners in your class and complete the frequency table.

Bed time	Tally	Frequency
Before 8 p.m.		
8 p.m. or later		

b What does the information tell you about bed times for the learners in your class? ______________________

Challenge 2

1 Work with a partner to test a hypothesis:

The girls in my year group are taller than the boys.

a Collect data from equal numbers of boys and girls in your year group and complete the frequency table.

	Boys		Girls	
Height group	**Tally**	**Frequency**	**Tally**	**Frequency**
Shorter than 132 cm				
132–137 cm				
138–143 cm				
Taller than 143 cm				

b What does the data tell you about the differences in height between boys and girls?

____

____

2 Work with a partner to test a hypothesis:

You are more likely to throw a 6 on a 1–6 dice than any other number.

Is this true?

a Draw and complete your own frequency tables in the space below. Collect data from 30 rolls of the dice.

b What do the results tell you about the frequency of dice rolls that result in a 6?

____

____

Work with a partner to test a hypothesis:

The higher the ramp the further a toy car will travel.

a Construct a wooden ramp. Begin at a height of 30 cm and use a ruler to measure the distance travelled by a toy car released at the top of the ramp. Raise the ramp by 10 cm and repeat. Continue increasing the ramp height by 10 cm and measuring the distance travelled. Stop at 80 cm. Draw and complete your own data recording table in the space below.

b Did the results support the hypothesis? Explain how you know.

____

____

c Why is it important to use the same car and release the car from the same position each time?

____

Lesson 7: **Presenting data**

- To test a hypothesis by presenting data from an enquiry and drawing conclusions

You will need
- squared paper

These challenges use the data collected in Lesson 6: Collecting data.

a Complete the bar line chart using the data you collected in Lesson 6 to test the hypothesis:

Most learners in our class are in bed by 8 p.m.

b Does the data support the hypothesis? Explain how you know.

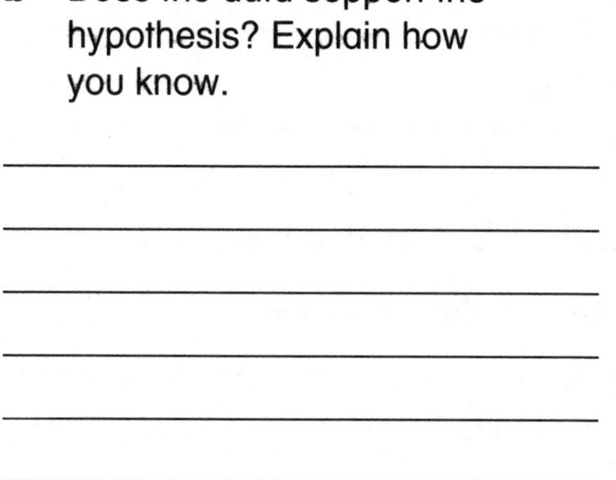

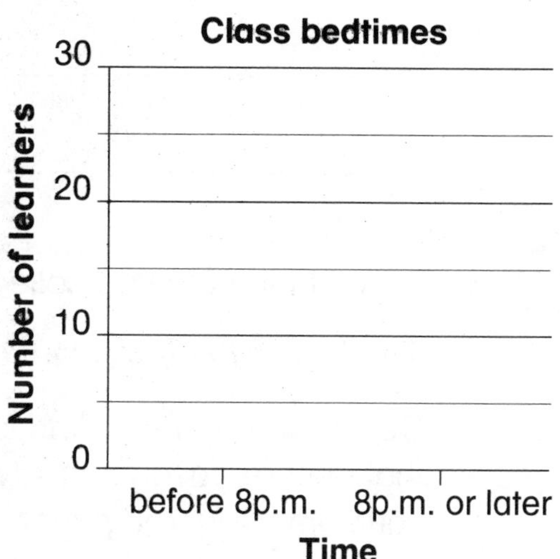

1 a Complete the bar line chart using the data you collected in Lesson 6 to test the hypothesis:

The girls in my year group are taller than the boys.

Draw bar lines next to each other for boys and girls in the same height group.

b Does the data support the hypothesis? Explain how you know.

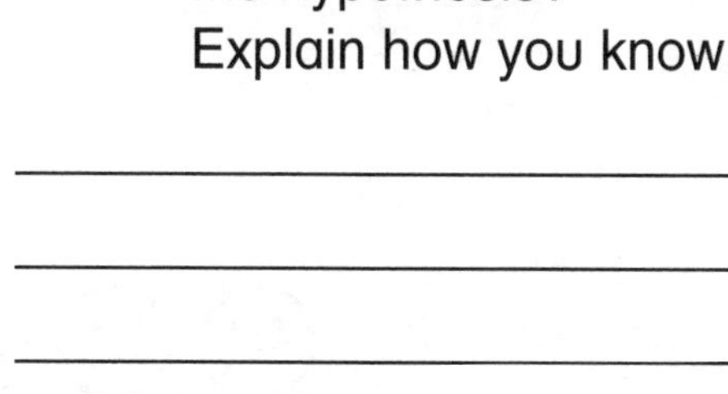

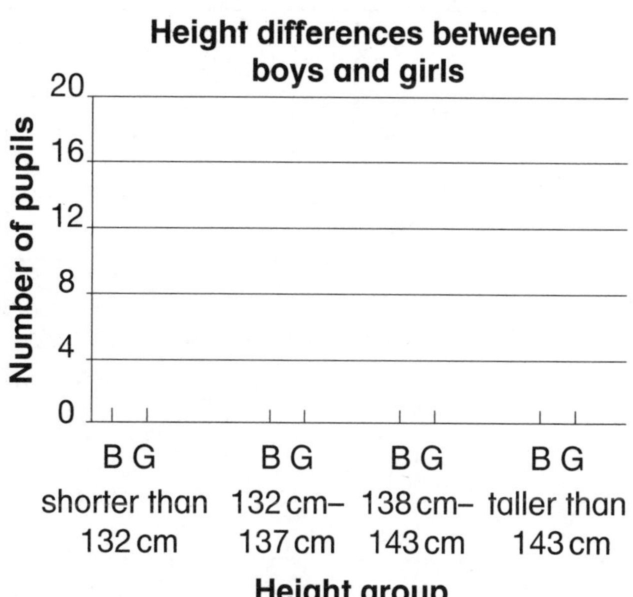

2 **a** Present the data you collected in the Lesson 6 to test the hypothesis:

You are more likely to roll a 6 on a 1–6 dice than any other number.

Decide whether the data is continuous or discrete and choose a graph that best represents this type of data to present it. Your teacher will give you some squared paper.

b Does the data support the hypothesis? Explain how you know.

____

____

____

Challenge **3** **a** Present the data you collected in the Lesson 6 to test the hypothesis:

The higher the ramp the further a toy car will travel.

Decide whether the data is continuous or discrete and choose a graph that best represents this type of data to present. Your teacher will give you some squared paper.

b Does the data support the hypothesis? Explain how you know.

____

____

Lesson 8: **Probability**

- Describe the likelihood of an event happening using the language of chance

For each event, tick the likelihood of it happening.

Event	**Probability**		
	Impossible	**Possible**	**Certain**
pick a blue counter from a bag of red counters			
pick a counter from a bag of counters			
pick a yellow counter from a mixed bag of green and yellow counters			
pick a green counter from a bag of green counters			

1 Look at the letters on the spinner. Then tick the boxes in the table that apply.

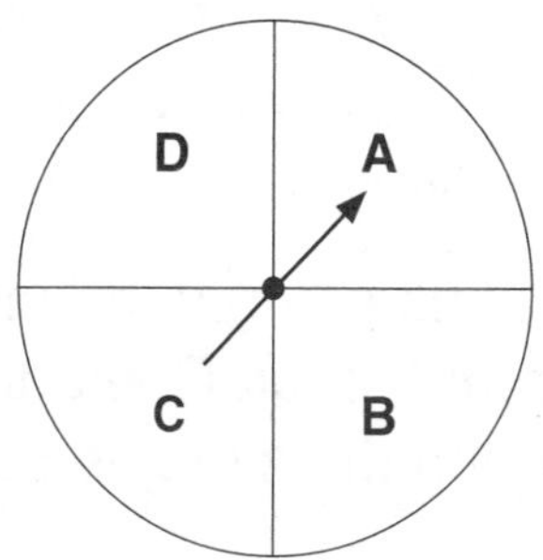

Event	**Probability**		
	impossible	**possible**	**certain**
the probability of spinning **B**		✓	
the probability of spinning **C**		✓	
the probability of spinning **E**	✓		
the probability of spinning a letter			✓

2 Label the spinners with numbers 1, 2, 3 or 4 to satisfy the probability rules given.

a

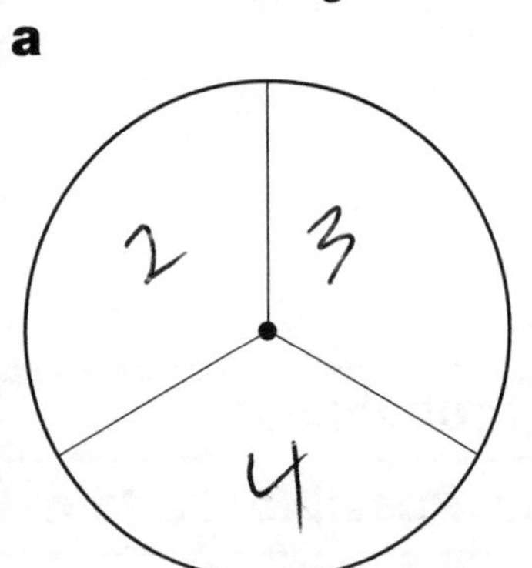

It is **possible** to spin 2, 3 or 4. It is **impossible** to spin 1.

b

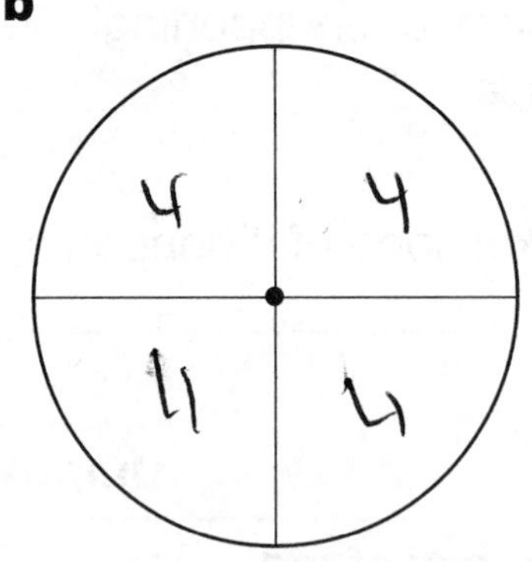

It is **certain** to spin 4.

c

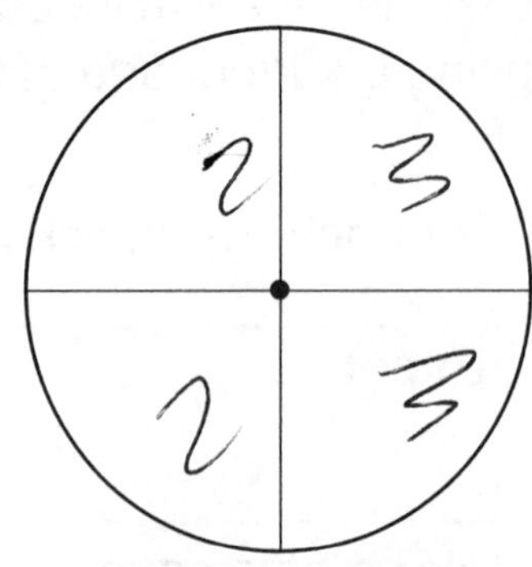

There is an **even chance** of spinning 2 or 3.

1 Draw an arrow from each event to where you think it should be placed on the probability scale.

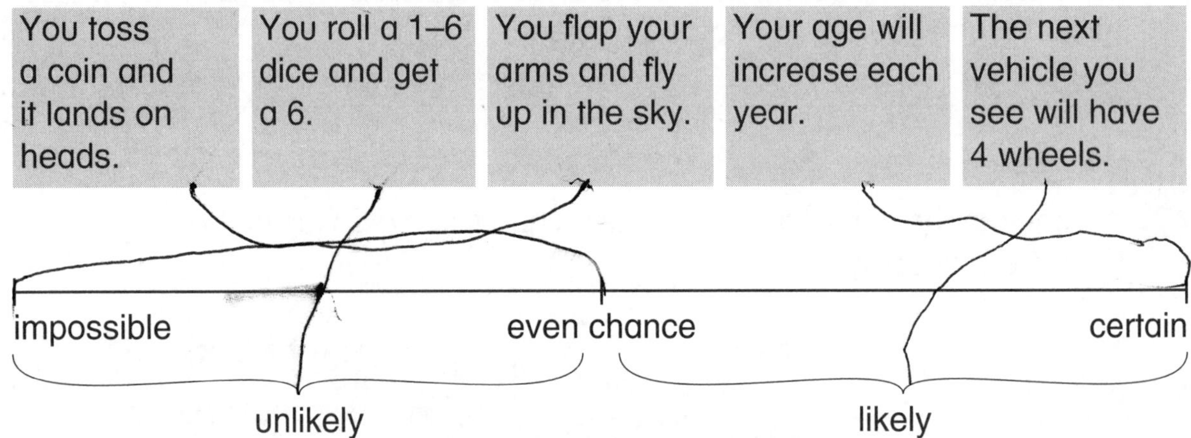

2 A jar contains 4 red counters, 7 green counters, 3 blue counters and 4 yellow counters. A counter is taken at random from the jar. Compare the probabilities by writing the symbol >, < or = between the statements.

probability of taking a green counter [>] probability of taking a red counter

probability of taking a blue counter [<] probability of taking a red counter

probability of taking a green counter [>] probability of taking a blue counter

probability of taking a red counter [=] probability of taking a yellow counter

Notes

Notes

Notes

Notes